WHO OWNS CANADA NOW

WHO OWNS CANADA NOW

OLD MONEY, NEW MONEY
AND THE FUTURE OF
CANADIAN BUSINESS

DIANE FRANCIS

HarperCollins*PublishersLtd*

Published by HarperCollins Publishers Ltd.

First edition

HarperCollins Publishers Ltd
2 Bloor Street East, 20th Floor
Toronto, Ontario, Canada
M4W 1A8

www.harpercollins.ca

Library and Archives Canada Cataloguing in Publication

Francis, Diane
Who owns Canada now : old money, new money and the
future of Canadian business / Diane Francis.

ISBN 978-0-00-200705-4 (bound)

1. Business enterprises—Canada. 2. Entrepreneurship—Canada.
3. Canada—Economic conditions—1991–. 4. Capitalists and
financiers—Canada—Biography. 5. Businesspeople—Canada—
Biography. I. Title.

HD2809.F736 2008   338.7'6092271   C2007-907032-9

RRD 9 8 7 6 5 4 3 2 1

Printed and bound in the United States

To all my loved ones

CONTENTS

AUTHOR'S NOTE

This book is based on my experiences, relationships, interviews and observations since 1981 as a full-time business writer and editor. Quotations are taken from interviews by me or have been attributed to periodicals or other sources. The financial and operational information published here about publicly listed companies is based on the *Financial Post* FP500 magazine published in summer 2007 or is drawn from websites and annual reports of the companies involved. Figures concerning privately owned companies are either from owners or gathered from other sources as noted. All dollar figures are in Canadian dollars unless otherwise noted.

PART ONE

THE LAST GENERATION

I t is hard to imagine how parochial, protectionist and elitist Canada was just one generation ago. It is also hard to remember life without the Cold War, automatic teller machines, personal computers, wireless appliances, cellphones, the BlackBerry, e-mail, blogs, Google, the Internet, cable television with hundreds of channels, just-in-time manufacturing, eBay, 24-hour trading, al Qaeda, the euro or the North American Free Trade Agreement. Back in 1986, when I published my book *Controlling Interest: Who Owns Canada?*, there was no ubiquitous Bloomberg financial wire service, Eliot Spitzer or Sarbanes-Oxley; there were few vigilant business journalists and crusading bloggers, Canadian antitrust laws or activist shareholders, and no class action lawsuits.

Two decades ago, the level of concentration of economic power in Canada was high compared to the United States. Five conglomerates and 32 families had a stranglehold on business, banking and politics. In researching *Controlling Interest*, I found that these Canadian conglomerates and families collectively controlled 40% of Canada's 500 largest public corporations and that families alone owned 31%. The influence of this group, politically and financially, was greater than that of foreign investors, who owned a combined total of 25% of Canada's largest 500 public corporations. The biggest foreign entries were large in the Canadian context but were really just branch plants owned by Exxon, Royal Dutch Shell, General Electric, Westinghouse, Detroit automakers and Japanese trading companies. Nonetheless, their relative size—and occasional abuses—created a populist and political backlash against foreign ownership, which gained steam in the 1970s.

Such economic nationalism led to the creation of Ottawa's Foreign Investment Review Agency, the National Energy Program (which taxed foreigners and gave grants to domestic companies) and Crown corporations like Petro-Canada, designed to compete against foreigners. Crowns performed other state-engineering tasks: filling vacuums, undertaking job creation or regional development projects, bailing out companies or financing Canadian enterprises that the banks and big stockbrokers would not support. The provinces also had their own state instruments, such as hydro utilities, the Potash Corporation of Saskatchewan, Alberta's treasury branches, Ontario's Suncor and a number of entities controlled by the Quebec government. By 1986, government-owned corporations like these represented 22% of the biggest 500 companies. Such government activism meant that ownership of the country was divided among three large camps: the powerful families and conglomerates; foreign subsidiaries; and a clutch of public-sector corporations.

Canada's business climate was also different, more like Europe's. Most of the 32 dominant families had inherited empires or had built them from inherited wealth. Most were ranking members of the "Canadian Establishment" that Peter C. Newman exposed, then chronicled, in his books. For decades, or in some cases generations, old-money families had prospered without many private-sector rivals, Canadian or foreign. They dominated a big country with a small economy, by doing business together, intermarrying and socializing with one another.

The tax system favoured conglomerations, and they gobbled up companies into giant entities such as the Argus Corporation and

Power Corporation. Their leaders gathered in rarefied places like the Toronto Club or York Club, Winston's, the Vancouver Club or Montreal's Ritz-Carlton Hotel. Such concentration of economic power also bred an unhealthy coziness between businessmen and politicians, fostered by large campaign contributions, which are now no longer allowed. Jean de Grandpré, former chairman of Bell Canada, who held the record for political access, once told me he landed meetings with eight federal cabinet ministers—and the prime minister—all within 24 hours' notice.

Shareholder rights was an oxymoron. Securities laws were poorly enforced—or non-existent—on issues such as insider trading or tipping. Stock exchanges were self-regulated by an old boys' network of brokers. Annual meetings of public corporations were extravaganzas staged in hotels with lavish buffet lunches to treat the minions, or were grudgingly held in small conference rooms. Shareholder activism slowly began growing in the 1990s as a result of the growth of personal investment interest and gigantic pension and mutual funds with occasionally feisty money managers.

But back in the 1980s, when I covered business for the *Toronto Star*, Conrad Black and Hal Jackman, for instance, had a standing bet on who could hold the shortest public company annual meeting. Black won with a meeting that dispatched the year's business on behalf of one of his many public corporate entities in a mere five minutes. Today, Hal Jackman prides himself on corporate morality and hands out a business card that chastises executive compensation excesses. "Those days were a very different time, with very different people. It was an era of entitlement that some of us recanted. It was pretty bad, I must say," said Jackman in an interview with me over lunch in 2007.

Canada's business press ignored such high-handed business behaviour. Publications were timid, fawning or captive to the captains of industry and finance. We had our place and were reminded constantly of that reality. Getting an interview with a bank chairman required weeks of careful letter-writing aimed at convincing layers of banking centurions. Once granted an audience, one would be escorted into an elegantly appointed office, as large as a bungalow, with adjoining sitting, board- and dining rooms. These executive suites, which still exist at the tops of Toronto's bank towers, were ringed with phalanxes of female secretaries equipped with typewriters and noisy telephones and wearing smart suits, high heels and scowls.

I remember being shown the boardroom of the Canadian Imperial Bank of Commerce in the 1980s, where its 48 or so directors and officers sat in judgment over every credit and creditor. Bank boards were as big as the parliaments of small countries and were riddled with conflicts of interest, because directors were also customers. At each director's seat was a button that turned on a red light to signal a director's conflict. Once it was pushed, proceedings would stop until the director could recuse himself. The chairman also had a button, which turned on a green light to signal to a departed director, sitting in an anteroom, that he could return because the item had been completed. There was a handful of women and members of visible minorities on bank boards in 1986, but they were unable to join business watering holes such as the Petroleum Club, the Toronto Club or the York Club.

"The banks' directors were up and down like yo-yos all the time," said a former CIBC director and later oil promoter, Dome Petroleum chairman Jack Gallagher, in an interview with me in 1979. "Directors were customers of the bank and all had conflicts from time to time. When our loans came up, we had to leave. One of the bank's directors was on 20 different companies so he was up and down constantly."

Those holding multiple directorships extended cronyism to the furthest reaches of the economy. Such a workload today would be untenable because of increased regulation, but back then most professional directors just showed up and voted along with the wishes of officers or owners. These directors, notably those on bank boards, functioned in the Canadian business world like economic aristocrats, without checks and balances. Banks readily loaned money to them, or to the companies whose directorships they held, while start-ups or outsiders, such as Calgary oil companies and small firms, were shut out. This nepotism and cronyism undermined the country's business climate because it led to inappropriate loans for inappropriate people while worthier entrepreneurs or endeavours were ignored.

Business practices were also oppressive. Eaton's of Canada used to dictate terms to suppliers, pay some bills six months late and refuse to deal with any supplier who also sold goods or services to competitors like Simpsons or the Bay. Conrad Black once tried to get me in trouble with the *Toronto Star* when I was a columnist for quoting the chairman of the Ontario Securities Commission, Henry Knowles, about alleged securities violations by Black involving Cleveland-based Hanna Mining. (Black subsequently pleaded "no contest" without admission of any wrongdoing concerning that matter with the U.S. Securities and Exchange Commission.)

Fortunately for me, the *Star*'s publisher, and one of its founding shareholders, the late Beland Honderich, took Mr. Black's phone call early one morning and politely but routinely referred him to the paper's ombudsman. Honderich's handling of the matter was impressive. At the time, Black controlled Dominion Stores and had Fred Eaton on his board. Their companies were the *Star*'s two largest advertisers. Eventually, Black and I became friendly, after I was made director of the *Financial Post* in 1987 and its editor in 1991. At that time, he owned a minority interest in the investment newspaper.

Canada's powerful were, like Black, mostly Anglo-Saxon anglophiles. They admired, and sought, peerages or knighthoods in Britain. They wore pinstripes and lived muted existences. They operated at the top in a different era. In the workplace, bosses were addressed by surnames, and casual Friday was non-existent. Extravagance and conspicuous lifestyles were sneered at and relegated to the blue-eyed sheikhs in Calgary, to Americans or to flamboyant men like mining financier Peter Brown or stock promoter Murray Pezim in Vancouver. Toronto was run by old money. So were Montreal and Vancouver. Even those immigrants who had made it to the top by 1986 were not self-made individuals from humble backgrounds. Most were transplanted industrialists or financiers from war-torn Europe who knew how to work and join any establishment.

In those days, personal safety was not a concern, and there had been only two kidnappings involving wealthy persons—Hyman Belzberg in Calgary and an Eaton heiress. Canada's richest man, Paul Reichmann, used to freely and safely walk, relatively unnoticed, along Bay Street's canyons in his dark suit, beard and yarmulke. He and his billionaire brothers lived near one another in large homes but in a relatively modest Toronto neighbourhood. They walked, unguarded, to their respective synagogues. Today, tycoons have bodyguards and security consultants because there are at least half a dozen kidnappings, or attempts, a year across Canada that go unreported to the police or the press, according to investigators and security consultants. Several billionaires declined interviews for this book because of concerns about crime. Others asked that certain information be left out of the book, such as the location of residences or the names of their children and grandchildren.

"I don't give interviews to the press because it does me no good whatsoever. I don't need it for my business or my ego, and it may end up getting my grandchildren kidnapped," said Dundee-Wealth founder and billionaire Ned Goodman, a friend of mine, in an interview for this book in 2007.

Back in 1986, Canada's economic landscape was also different. Toronto had benefited from the exodus of financiers out of Montreal, from the Auto Pact with Detroit and from immigration. Vancouver grew as it became a prime destination for retirees and for an influx of wealthy Hong Kong business people who wanted to establish a safe haven before the handover of the city in 1997 to China. Calgary was licking its wounds, flattened following the catastrophic National Energy Program and the collapse of oil prices in 1986 from US$36 to US$18 a barrel. Likewise, mining was also in a funk, due to a depression in metals and minerals prices that did not end until 2003. Quebec limped along, the businesses that remained bolstered by help from the province and favoured by institutions such as the Caisse de dépôt et placement du Québec, National Bank, the Desjardins Group, the Montreal Stock Exchange and various provincial Crown corporations.

In fast-growing southern Ontario and BC, real estate was riding high, but values were eventually devastated, beginning in 1989 as a worldwide property recession swept many big cities. Canada's biggest property empires changed hands or were carved up by banks. Bad loans and foreclosures, however, did not sink Canada's banking oligopoly. Bankers weathered storms, from bad loans in Mexico in the early 1980s to Dome Petroleum in the mid-1980s and the collapse in real estate prices in the late 1980s, through a combination of special banking write-off privileges granted by Ottawa. They were also protected from foreign competition and, in the late 1980s, were given permission to acquire the country's profitable investment banks and mutual fund companies. Now they dominate both industries.

"In 1976, Toronto was an old boys' club," said Jack Cockwell, an accountant from South Africa who helped mastermind Edper, the empire of the late Peter and Edward Bronfman, and its successor holding company, Brookfield Asset Management. "Jews and women were not allowed into clubs. All that changed in 30 years. There was no insider reporting. No securities laws. Underwriting was done on the basis that the bankers were put on the preferred buyer list [for their personal benefit]. But the biggest change is access to capital. The bankers in Canada used to phone each other up and say whether somebody should get a loan or not. Now the U.S. guys are here with their suitcases. You can raise bond money or equity. They opened it right up for everyone. With one phone call."

A NEW CANADA

I n the last 20 years, Canada has been transformed by both external and internal events. The end of the Cold War, marked by the dismantling of the Berlin Wall in fall 1989, liberated billions from the communist system and turned them into entrepreneurs, customers, traders, rivals and investors. That, plus lower inflation, contributed to the greatest uninterrupted economic expansion in world history. At the same time, technology, trade and immigration brought about a truly global village, connecting people and markets.

Politicians in Europe and North America integrated their economies and created gigantic trading blocs. Prosperity led to the creation of huge pools of savings in the form of pension funds, mutual funds and investment portfolios. This capital was made available to, and invested in, thousands of companies and innovations. Besides leading to equity infusions, low inflation made borrowing cheap, and a generation of aggressive consolidators—or takeover artists—borrowed money to buy assets that ended up appreciating faster than did their debt payments. A new set of players gobbled up real estate, retail, oil, mining, finance, telecommunications and cable assets, becoming billionaires along the way.

The growing economy, coupled with greater access to higher education, yielded more opportunities. Go-getters, with or without connections, harnessed these tools for success and benefited from the fact that the information revolution and the globalization of capital markets allowed them to bypass Canadian bankers and brokers in order to find the best and most profitable means of raising money to get ahead.

The happy confluence of events was that Canada's internal transformation was mostly in sync with global changes. The negotiation of the Canada-U.S. Free Trade Agreement, and its affirmation in the 1988 election, happened just as more middle-class Canadians, Quebeckers, women, visible minorities and immigrants were able to reach for the brass ring. This led to a change-up in players. The world was becoming more competitive, and 16 of 1986's 32 richest families fell by the wayside. Philip Reichmann is a member of the storied family that had been Canada's richest until the early 1990s but that then lost everything and has since partially recovered. His explanation as to the reasons behind such family vicissitudes is that great self-made fortunes have as much to do with luck as with effort.

"We always believed in hard work," he said in an interview with me in 2007. "But we also believed that our success in the past was a matter of good fortune. Then we had bad fortune," he continued. "For our [younger] generation, it has meant we have a lot less money than we would have had if 1992 [Olympia & York's crash] hadn't happened, but it has been a great opportunity to do our own thing and make our own money. And doing things for yourself makes a big difference."

While the Reichmanns rebuilt, rejoining the ranks of the country's most successful, others, such as the two branches of the Bronfman family, have not been so lucky. Edgar Bronfman Jr. managed to lose the family distillery and chemical fortune by investing poorly in a French conglomerate. In a *Globe and Mail* article on August 30, 2002, his father, Edgar Bronfman Sr., was quoted as saying, "Not to pooh-pooh the money, but that's not the real disaster. The real disaster is bad judgment. [We] took something my father had built and my son converted into something which was really dynamic . . . And suddenly it blew up in our faces."

A NEW SLATE

B y 2007, Canada was more of a meritocracy than ever before in its history. For instance, in 1986, only 11 of the country's 32 richest family fortunes were self-made from nothing. The rest were inheritors. Only 5 of the 32 richest people were immigrants, and none was female. Little more than 20 years later, at the top are 75 Canadian billionaires, or clusters, who control or have created enterprises worth tens of billions. Of these, 56 fortunes were self-made and 28 belong to immigrants. Women have also gained entry, albeit a toehold. One empire is run by a woman and another 6 involve women in key ownership and managerial roles. Another distinguishing characteristic of today's successful is their relatively young ages. Nine of these 75 were in high school or university in 1986.

"I don't recognize any of the names of really successful people these days, which tells you something," said Hal Jackman, whose family was one of Canada's 32 most successful back in 1986 and is one of the 75 richest today. "It's an open marketplace now. In the past, I would have gone to school with most of the top people. Back then, in the financial business, everyone was what we called a 'legacy' . . . that is, they were the son of a prime minister or the son of a bank chairman. Today, people in trading must be bright and sophisticated. But when I started, almost any chump could trade."

Canada's new business leadership style is different too. Gone are the suits and two-martini lunches at Winston's or the Ritz. Most of these CEOs and entrepreneurs, like all bosses, are addressed by their given names, do their own typing, place their own phone calls and wear open-necked shirts or even jeans on Friday. They are down-to-earth people who are more likely to be found at the gym than in a watering-hole at lunchtime, and are more likely to communicate directly via cellphone, BlackBerry or e-mail. Mining billionaire Robert Friedland, for example, is from a modest background, works constantly, lives simply and has a gym in his corporate jet. Research In Motion founder Jim Balsillie plays pickup hockey with school chums every week. Oil billionaire Clay Riddell can be seen many days lining up with employees to buy coffee at a downtown mall in Calgary.

Today's business proprietors are also comfortable internationally and network as much outside Canada's borders as within them. They are sought out—and pursued—by brokers and investors from around the world. Their companies and markets are prey to foreign competitors or acquisitors. Their assets are located everywhere, as are their customers, and their stocks are listed on foreign exchanges. They think globally, not just locally.

Few are building dynasties, and most are busily distributing their wealth to charities or to institutions that will make a difference. Like Bill Gates and Warren Buffett, they are philanthropists who aren't inclined to hand over huge fortunes or empires to their children. This is part of the modern-day meritocrat's creed. As Buffett said, when interviewed after giving away his entire fortune in 2006 to the Bill & Melinda Gates Foundation, "Handing down inheritances is like putting on the Olympic team the children of all the former gold medallists. It makes no sense."

A NEW WORLD

"The World Trade Organization, low interest rates and the PC [personal computer] created the world's wealth in the last generation," said Claude Lamoureux, former CEO of the Ontario Teachers' Pension Plan. He helped build the plan into Canada's second-largest pension fund, with $106 billion in assets as of June 2007.

"Take the PC. In my first job, as an actuary, it took hours for me to figure out bond price yields, but now everyone with a PC can design instruments and model financial outcomes," he said. "This has changed the nature of investing. If interest rates go up by 1%, we can model it. This mitigates risk and accelerates wealth creation."

The PC has created smarter investors, which means that smarter businesses have been backed for better reasons. That, combined with lower inflation, has helped people accumulate wealth. "The end of high inflation created low interest rates for the baby boomers, who created a stock market boom, a mutual fund boom, a real estate boom, a private equity boom and a pension fund [including RRSPs] boom," said Lamoureux.

In 1988, there were $150 billion in pension funds, and by

2006 there were $1.065 trillion, a sevenfold increase, according to Canada Benefits. In 1986, there were $17.5 billion in mutual funds, and by 2006, $679.98 billion—a 38-fold increase—according to the Investment Funds Institute of Canada. In 1990, there were $137.6 billion in RRSPs, and by 2006 there were $500 billion.

These pools of capital have taken major stakes in public corporations, in government privatizations and in partnerships with Canadian entrepreneurs. Commercial real estate is a case in point. By 2007, pension funds and REITs (real estate investment trusts) owned most of Canada's skylines, bank towers and major shopping centres. Back in 1986, these assets were mostly owned by banks, families or conglomerates.

A vast democratization of ownership has taken place in Canada in just two decades. To compare, in 1986 there were 32 families and five conglomerates who controlled 40% of the 500 biggest companies; foreigners controlled 25%, governments 22%, and the remaining 22% were widely held companies. By 2007, the pie was divided differently. Only 21% of the biggest 500 in terms of revenue were family-controlled, by the 75 profiled here plus dozens more; 30% of the country's biggest 500 were foreign-owned, 8.5% government-owned and 38% widely held, with another 3.2% owned by franchisees or partners. This change in ownership reflects the enormous participation by pools of capital, by individuals and by foreigners in a variety of Canadian companies. It also reflects the decline in government ownership—from 22% to 8.5%—due to privatizations.

The increase in foreign ownership from 25% to 30% is not unique to Canada and matches increases experienced by other developed countries with open economies. And foreign stakes are more fragmented. The Americans no longer have a stranglehold. Of Canada's current 50 biggest corporations (which are as large, taken together, as the next 450 biggest companies), 37 are Canadian-owned. In 1986, the biggest 50 were dominated by American, Japanese and European subsidiaries.

Besides having diversified ownership, the top 50 companies in 2007 were diversified geographically and sectorally, involved in energy, mining, high-tech, manufacturing, banking, insurance, tele-communications and retail. Some, such as Brookfield Asset Management, Onex Corp. and Thomson Corp., were truly global, with headquarters in Canada but with the majority of their assets and employees beyond Canadian borders.

CHANGE

Canada's economy has proven resilient and has overcome recessions in several industries, as well as business downturns, high taxes, periods of high interest rates, the 1995 Quebec referendum, major bankruptcies, low commodity prices and additional competition resulting from communism's collapse and from freer trade. By 2007, the country had maintained respectable living standards, a good quality of life and a reasonable environment for entrepreneurship.

"Canada looks good. Unemployment is low. We have good, honest government. Corporate taxes are coming down. The dollar is up," said Peter Munk in an interview in 2007. "Sure there are problems, but just look at Magna International [auto parts] and Detroit's Delphi Corp. Delphi goes bust and Magna keeps making money. It's about the people, the entrepreneurs. Bad people fail in good conditions and good people succeed in bad conditions."

Munk is a serial entrepreneur who was born in Hungary and is founder and chair of the world's biggest gold company, Barrick Corporation. He has also built large manufacturing, hotel and real estate businesses. His pride in Canada, his confidence and his optimism are not unusual. Many of these successful people agree, and their stories will inspire and tell us where we have been for the past 20 years, what needs repair and where we are heading.

PART TWO

CANADA'S 75

The new players belong to many ethnic groups, have made fortunes in high-tech and low-tech sectors and have succeeded in both depressed and prosperous regions. Some control public companies, some private. Some are globally oriented, some not. Some compete around the world while others stick to Canada. Some are free-wheeling in wildly competitive markets and others are cosseted as government-granted monopolies, as regulated industries or by virtue of special financial assistance.

Their experiences and backgrounds are as varied as their business models. One billionaire lived in a cave in India for months. Another slept on park benches while busking in Europe for a living. Among them are high school dropouts, a teacher, two pharmacists, a scientist, a tool and die maker, a police officer, a sailor, several lawyers, geologists, engineers, a plumber, a drywall plasterer, physicists, accountants, a disc jockey and magician, a Class A mechanic, a used car salesman, money managers, brokers, three architects, a jazz pianist, a truck driver, a Hindu mendicant, a tanner and a fire-eater.

They share character traits such as ambition, optimism, energy, street smarts, discipline and a love for the game itself. Money, for the most part, is merely a by-product, however enjoyably most of them spend it. Unless otherwise noted, all were interviewed by me. Some are social friends. Others I have only observed from afar. Most are gun-shy, many are unknown to most Canadians and three dozen had never been interviewed by a journalist before this book. Some can be ruthless and push others aside; a few have been or may be accused of running afoul of the rules or other people.

The list is mine, as are the criteria, and is based on publicly disclosed corporate information combined with my experiences and contacts in business and in charitable fundraising. This book does not rank their wealth, because figures, particularly for private fortunes, are unreliable and volatile. But all the individuals and families in this book rank among the world's wealthiest, are likely worth at least $1 billion and often have created or control tens of billions in assets. One caveat, however, is that by the time this book is read, some of these fortunes may have ebbed. This is due to the nature of the business today, as it operates in a ruthlessly volatile global context. "Here today and gone tomorrow" is not just a cliché.

The list is not definitive. Absent is André Chagnon, a Quebec electrician who sold Groupe Vidéotron for $1.3 billion. The net proceeds were donated to his foundation, which is Canada's largest, and today his time is spent doing philanthropy. His wealth is deployed no longer to create more wealth but to be shared.

THE 16 FROM 1986 WHO DIDN'T MAKE THE CUT

H alf of the 32 families I profiled in 1986 in my first book—*Controlling Interest: Who Owns Canada?*—are not among the wealthiest people in Canada today. Some have gone out of business as a result of selling or folding. Some were blindsided by unforeseen events. The real estate recession of 1989 clobbered 6 of the 32—Peter and Edward Bronfman, who owned chunks of Bramalea and Trizec; Robert Campeau; Don Love and his Oxford Properties; the Belzbergs and Singers in western Canada; and the Reichmanns. Notably, however, Don Love's son, Jon Love of King-Street Capital Partners, may not be in the top 75 list but has become a significant player, as have the two branches of the Belzberg family, run separately by Sam and Brent Belzberg. And the Reichmanns have staged an impressive comeback and are listed in this book.

Retail giants in 1986, such as the Eatons and the Posluns (with fashion retailer Dylex), disappeared. So did two grocery fortunes, owned by the Steinberg and Wolfe families. Both chains, called Steinberg's and IDA respectively, were sold to rivals because of family squabbles. Similar dissension has also divided the Molson family. Their brewery was merged with U.S. brewery Coors and their control diluted.

Montreal steelmaker Paul Ivanier limped along for years until he sold out in 2003; and Peter Bentley, patriarch of the Bentley-Prentice forestry clan, grew Canfor Corp. into a world-beater, but family control was diluted to 4% as the 10 members of the next generation mostly cashed out. Jimmy Pattison now owns 25% of Canfor and two pension funds own another 40%.

Similarly, businesses run by the Websters, George Mann and Stephen Roman flagged, were sold or simply did not keep pace. Most surprisingly, the Bronfman family, of distillery fame, lost it all through a series of mistakes made by a member of its third generation. The exception was Charles Bronfman, whose investments in Israel have paid off hugely and allowed him to retain his place among Canada's most successful. Finally last, but far from least, has been the tragic downfall of Conrad Black—my nemesis, then colleague and the proprietor of the *National Post*. The media tycoon was convicted in Chicago in the summer of 2007 of fraud and obstruction of justice and has appealed his conviction.

Here is a list of the 16 who did not make the cut, in alphabetical order:

The Belzbergs	The Manns
The Bentleys	The Molsons
Conrad Black	The Posluns
Edward and Peter Bronfman	The Romans
Robert Campeau	The Singers
The Eatons	The Steinbergs
The Ivaniers	The Websters
Don Love	The Wolfes

CANADA'S DIASPORA

I have included some who have moved offshore for tax purposes, such as Michael DeGroote, Frank Stronach, Eugene Melnyk, Calvin Ayre, the Bata family and John MacBain. They are included because they built sizable Canadian enterprises, still live here part-time or have companies headquartered in Canada. On the other hand, I have excluded Canadians who have always been expatriates and who built fortunes totally outside the country. These include New York publishing/real estate magnate Mort Zuckerman; Australia's fast food giant Jack Cowin; Robert (Bobby) Julien and his aunt Delia Moog, who are now developers in Florida; eBay founder Jeff Skoll in California; Fiji water tycoon and Barrick Corp. co-founder David Gilmour; Li Ka-shing's sons Victor and Richard Li, who live in Hong Kong; and Chinese-Canadian tobacco heir David Ho, who briefly operated Harmony Airways out of Vancouver. These people may have Canadian passports, but they also have other passports and do not live here, nor have they built business lives here.

What's been interesting in researching this book is that Canadians appear to be disproportionately entrepreneurial. In 2006, *Forbes*

Magazine proclaimed that there were 415 billionaires in the U.S., 242 in Europe and only 23 in Canada. My estimate is that most of these 75 profiled in the book are net billionaires. Besides that, thousands more Canadians have amassed tens of millions in assets, or even hundreds of millions, building enterprises, investing, inventing software, designing auto parts, finding oil fields and metals and minerals, devising unique financial products, doing investment deals, creating pharmaceuticals, discovering industrial enzymes or developing real estate.

Another three dozen are nearly in the billionaire league: in Montreal, the Péladeaus, Serge Godin, Jan Peeters, Richard Renaud, Herbert Black, Joseph Kruger, the de Gaspé Beaubiens, Aldo Bensadoun, Jeremy Reitman, the Lemaire brothers, Alain Bouchard, Rémi Marcoux and Robert Beamish; BC's Hassan Khosrowshahi, Joe Houssian, Joe Segal, Ron Stern, Stuart Belkin, David Black, Frank Giustra, the Gagliardis, the Chans and Peter Brown; Winnipeg's Peter Nygård; Ottawa's Michael Potter; Toronto's Joseph Rotman, the Goldhar brothers, Pierre Lassonde, the Appels, the Phelans, Eugene McBurney, Eric Sprott, Lawrence Bloomberg, Albert Latner, Prem Watsa, Ian and Kiki Delaney, Robert Schad, Peter Gilgan, Vic De Zen and Saul Feldberg; Kitchener's Hasenfratz family and, from Research In Motion, Doug Fregin; Newfoundland's Dobbin family; and Calgary's Rob Peters, Jim Kinnear, Ron Mathison, Jim Grenon, Doc Seaman and Harley Hotchkiss—to name just a few.

No matter the methodology, the number of hugely wealthy Canadians in an economy with widespread ownership overall is impressive, and an indication that the country has become an incubator for entrepreneurship. Naturally, there are challenges in the future, which are outlined in the final part of this book, but nothing that cannot be surmounted. Canada has transformed itself and has made necessary adjustments. Still, the velocity of change will increase and will require the country to keep replenishing its pool of business talent. In fact, dramatic events that have impacted the members of my list of 75, a list completed in fall 2007, may have already greatly reduced their fortunes. In two cases, there have been unsubstantiated rumours of financial problems. This only underscores that in another generation most of these 75 leaders—and their businesses—will not be around, nor will their heirs make Canada's top list. That's just the Darwinian nature of business today.

What is most striking about this 75, but slightly misleading, is that women remain underrepresented. However, it is safe to speculate that there are more wealthy females in Canada than ever before, thanks to a combination of women's liberation and family property law reforms enacted in all provinces by 1980.

In practice these days, daughters as well as sons receive equal inheritances whether or not they participate directly in the family business. Traditionally, and in other cultures, male offspring have inherited empires and their sisters dowries with which to attract well-heeled husbands. No longer is that the case.

In developed countries, laws also stipulate that upon divorce, half of the assets accumulated during marriage belong to wives, common-law spouses or even gay life-partners. This entitlement excludes inheritances and can be signed away, but it has made thousands of ex-wives and others extremely wealthy.

"Mrs. Anderson was very well looked after, that's for darned sure," said rich oil man J.C. Anderson in an interview with me in 2006 at his Alberta ranch. Likewise, rumours are that Louise Blouin MacBain got nearly $1 billion upon divorcing advertising king John MacBain a few years ago.

Wealthy stockbroker Frank Giustra of Vancouver has probably made more than $1 billion in his career but has sustained expensive divorces over the years, thus substantially reducing his personal net worth to "mere" hundreds of millions.

I have broken down the list into various business sectors, beginning with real estate and ending with a few jacks of all trades.

REAL ESTATE

Throughout history, land has been the basis of fortunes, the cause of wars and the world's most prized commodity. They are simply not making any more of it, as the aphorism goes. The result is that prices have escalated, most dramatically in Toronto and Vancouver, where some of the country's greatest real estate fortunes have been made. Both cities have maintained strict land-use restrictions at the same time as their populations have exploded. But great property fortunes have also been made in parts of Canada where a supply-demand squeeze has not existed, such as in Quebec and in sprawling cities like Calgary and Edmonton.

It's ironic that in a country with a land mass as huge as Canada's there should be such a disproportionate number of property empires. But 90% of Canadians are huddled in a handful of cities, and the income-tax system encourages real estate investing. In Canada, properties can be depreciated faster (sheltering more profits) at 4% a year, over 25 years, compared to 40 years at 2.5% per year in the United States. Another benefit is that capital gains apply only when properties are sold, so smart owners never sell: they simply remortgage their portfolios as they appreciate in order to buy even more real estate.

Canada's biggest property portfolios have been amassed disproportionately by immigrants. This is partly traditional: owning a piece of the rock has always been every newcomer's dream. In the 19th century it was homesteading or buying a small farm. In the 20th century it was buying a home, a small apartment building or a store in a new city. Besides having a proclivity to own, immigrants have gravitated toward the business because there are few barriers to entry. Education and pedigree always help in life, but these traits are not necessary calling cards in the property game: shrewdness and steeliness are. Eleven of the 12 real estate fortunes profiled here have been built by people born outside Canada.

To do this, these developers have had to become cunning negotiators, able to deal with casts of difficult characters and conditions, from sleazy politicians to difficult trade labour unions, tough landlord restrictions, cranky and uncreditworthy tenants or buyers, powerful banks, fickle zonings and fluctuating interest rates. All have built vertically integrated enterprises that include land banking, property management, leasing, construction, finance, acquisition, design and marketing expertise. These are not passive landlords. They have been aggressive and also very lucky.

"In 60 years of real estate, there has always been a recession or crash every 10 years at the top of the decade, in 1960, 1970, 1980, 1990," explained Toronto lawyer and property baron Rudy Bratty. "But since 1995 we have had 12 years of prosperity because governments are running surpluses, inflation is low, interest rates stayed down, immigration and job creation have stayed strong, and there's nothing better for real estate than those conditions."

MARCEL ADAMS

In the early 1950s, Romanian immigrant Marcel Abramovich scoured the Quebec countryside for cowhides to export to Europe, and to make things easier he changed his last name to Adams.

"I would make appointments to see farmers or butchers or slaughterhouses and have to spell my name out," he said in an interview in Montreal. "My boss said, 'You are very efficient, you work seven days a week, but your phone bill is $50 extra a month, or $1.75 a minute. Tomorrow you will shorten your name. You will be Adams.'"

Simultaneously, his wife, Annie, was giving birth to their second child. "So she entered the hospital Abramovich and came out as Adams," he said.

His given name is also a story: he was named Marcel after a French soldier who helped his father escape a prisoner-of-war camp run by the Germans in the First World War.

I met Marcel Adams in May 2007 in his cluttered, no-frills office building away from Montreal's downtown. Adams is a small man with a ready smile and impish appearance. His offices are rented, he kids, and not in one of his own buildings. "I would charge myself too much rent," he joked.

He had never been interviewed before, and our conversation lasted for nearly two hours. At the end he said, "You undressed me with all your questions."

Marcel Adams, born in 1920, is a charmer whose wit undoubtedly helped him become one of Canada's most successful real estate developers. His Iberville Developments Ltd. is privately owned by Adams and his four grown children. His son Sylvan, an MBA, runs operations "and tells me how to behave," he said.

The extent of Iberville's real estate portfolio is unknown, but it is huge. In 2005, Iberville sold malls in Sherbrooke and Quebec City to pension funds for $800 million. In 2007, Iberville was building two gigantic shopping-mall and mixed-use projects, 1 million square feet each, on the outskirts of Montreal.

"My son does not want to travel all over the place and is not prepared to put in 84 hours a week like I was, so he's building in Montreal," Adams said. "We are building because money is very cheap and selling because there are more buyers than good properties to buy."

Adams works every day and enjoys evenings out going to dinner with friends or to the opera or theatre. He does not own a cellphone or computer and writes down his upcoming appointments on pieces of paper, using both sides.

Like fellow developers David Azrieli and John Daniels and pharmaceutical tycoon Leslie Dan, Adams has overcome wartime tragedy. He has also weathered Quebec's politics and economic deterioration, and has never considered leaving.

"I was not politically oriented, and I said to myself, people are fair and will deliver what they sell," he said.

Adams, who speaks French, like many Romanians, was born in a scenic town in Romania's Carpathian Mountains. The Nazis "took over" Romania before the Second World War officially began, for its oil fields. But a deal was struck: Romania would provide oil and soldiers for the German army, but the Germans would stay out of Romania's internal affairs. The result was that Romania protected its Jews, Gypsies, dissidents and others from death in concentration camps.

"I did not lose anyone in the war," he said. "Romania looked after us. But when I was in high school in 1939, the Jewish guys like me went into forced labour camps and the other Romanian guys went into the German army. I was upset I couldn't go into the army."

He eventually escaped with pals to Palestine, now Israel, via Turkey and Syria, and paid many bribes. He was drafted into Israel's War of Independence, then left for France, where he spoke the language, and worked as a tanner.

His five sisters and parents were stranded in Romania until 1962, when Israel began buying freedom for Eastern European Jews. By that time, Adams had already immigrated to Quebec City, in 1951.

"I got to Quebec City when I was 19 years old. I was single and lived in a rooming house, but I didn't mind the cold weather or the lousy place I lived. I counted my blessings," he said. "I also was very careful and thrifty, after living in the labour camps and working in France. I came with some money, about $30,000. That was my insurance policy."

He hoped to start his own business with this nest egg.

"I wanted my own tannery, like my father had in Romania, so I was looking for opportunities. My $30,000 had grown, and I met a contractor who said, 'If you buy the land, I can build 72 apartments, 9 towers of 8 each. If you give me the land as a guarantee, I can get a mortgage.' That was my first venture," he said.

He quit his job to become a landlord. But he soon tired of chasing rents from the low-income tenants who occupied his buildings, so he developed residential properties in better districts.

"Then I went from residential real estate to mixed to shopping centres in 1960," he said. "I went from strip plazas to malls, or community centres. Our reputation was good because we delivered on time and on budget, and the tenants got to know us, which made it easier to get into major shopping centres."

Adams was apolitical but friendly with politicians from both sides of the aisle, notably Gilles Lamontagne, a cabinet minister and eventually Quebec's lieutenant-governor, who became a friend.

During the 1960s and 1970s, Marcel grew his business slowly and carefully.

"If you have the majors [tenants] and have tied them up, pre-development, you got the permits and the mortgages so you could go to the end. I never had a failure and I wasn't greedy," he said. "The brokers would call me and say, 'Mr. Careful, I have land for you.'"

Was luck involved?

"What is luck? We have to make our own luck," he said.

In 1970, Adams left Quebec City for Montreal because the English-language schools in Quebec City were so small that teachers had to double up on the subjects they taught. He was also spending more time in Montreal doing business.

In Montreal he had become friends with grocery king Sam Steinberg.

"In 1965, he said to me, 'I'm opening 11 stores next year, and how many do you want to build for me?' I said I would take one, but he said, 'Take 5.' We did that deal without lawyers. I ended up developing 12 shopping centres for him."

At its peak, Iberville employed 200 engineers, planners, accountants and other professionals in its head office, and 30 were key employees. At any given time, thousands would be working on-site as tradesmen for Iberville's developments.

"I give my team work conditions so they cannot leave," he said. "I get involved in their personal life and problems. Give them money, help or special vacations. I give them what I would've expected my tanner boss to give me, but didn't. So they stay," he said.

Adams also has a good relationship with his 4 children and 11 grandchildren. His son Julian earned a PhD in chemistry from the Massachusetts Institute of Technology and is a pre-eminent medical researcher in Boston who has been featured twice on the cover of *Forbes* for cancer breakthroughs. One daughter is a nurse in California and another a lawyer in Montreal. Sylvan runs Iberville.

Marcel believes that success has a lot to do with attitude.

"I get up in the morning, look in the mirror and take inventory every day," he said. "I realize that anything else was better than what I lived through. I have always had a positive attitude, even during the lousy weather and even when I was living in my lousy rooming house. I'm a born optimist. Optimism, or pessimism, both are wrong historically, but if you are an optimist you feel better."

Although money has flowed from his efforts, it was never the motivation.

"Money? I will die a pauper. The money will go to all my children and to good causes."

DAVID AZRIELI

David Azrieli lost his family in the Holocaust, fought in Israel's War of Independence, built a business empire, then decided in 1995 to go back to school—at 73 years of age. He obtained a master's degree at Carleton University in Ottawa.

"I studied architecture in Israel and thought of myself as an architect," he said in an interview in the elegant Dorchester Square offices of his Canpro Investments Ltd. in Montreal. "Getting a master's was a luxury I could afford."

For two years, he commuted and stayed overnight to attend classes, hear lectures, write papers and do assignments with fellow students younger than his own children.

When asked for an interview, he not only agreed, but invited me to his 85th birthday party in Montreal that weekend and to stay in his classy Sofitel Hotel on Sherbrooke Street. "You will come to my party. I have 600 coming," he said.

The evening was dazzling. It involved two hours of "high cocktails" (Montreal terminology for drinks and tons of food) followed by a concert by world-class musicians, including Azrieli's daughter, who is an esteemed opera singer. It was also a fundraiser for Israel's Technion in Tel Aviv, the university where he studied to be an architect after a harrowing escape from Europe.

"Technion was not only a place for a lonely boy to study and see things differently . . . it was a home—a place where I could forget the war, the running. It was to me more than just a university," he told party guests.

Azrieli not only survived his ordeals, but has triumphed in the world of business. His Canpro Investments is the largest private developer in Israel and owns billions of dollars worth of properties in North America.

"I have survived because I'm an optimist," he said. "And I did not know what happened to my family until 1946. It affected me very badly, and my studies. I became quite sick. But I was young and recouped and recognized that there were many things to look forward to."

Azrieli and his younger brother fled in 1939 from their small village in Poland. Their father designed special knapsacks with hidden pockets in the lining, where they concealed money and valuables. They escaped to Russia, then to Central Asia, but Azrieli lost his brother in a crowd and never heard from him again. In 1942, he reached Palestine alone.

He survived by using his wits to make money, and by being able to engage helpful friendships. Tragically, his parents and a younger sister never escaped and were murdered in Auschwitz.

In 1948 the War of Independence broke out and he joined the Israel Defense Forces. In the 1950s he travelled to South Africa, England, Western Europe, the United States and Canada. In 1954 he decided to immigrate to Montreal, where he met his wife-to-be, Stephanie, on a blind date. Four months later, they were married, and have been now for 50 years.

He arrived to a job as an architectural draftsman with $100 in his pocket. In 1957, he launched his own business, which was a turning point.

"I'll never forget the first day. It was 5 a.m. in Montreal. I was in a field which was covered in snow, waiting for the crew to arrive to dig the foundation for my first little building," he said. "When the shovel came out with the first scoop for my building, the earth was steaming. I nearly dropped to my knees. It was a sense of reverie, and I said to myself, 'I'm finally building. This is what I want to do.'"

He said, in our interview, that he has never sold a property since, except marginally profitable ones, because deferring capital gains taxes creates more working capital with which to buy more property. This is the virtuous cycle that has created some of Canada's greatest fortunes.

Azrieli also never rested. In 1982—at 60, when others as rich as he were retiring—he started another property empire, thousands of miles away in Israel. By 2007, 60% of his billions in holdings were in Israel and 40% in North America. He also diversified out of real estate for the first time at the age of 75, and paid $200 million in 1996 to buy Israel's third-largest energy distribution company.

But his real passions are architecture and music. Azrieli inherited his talent for drawing, perspective and design from his father, who was a fashion designer. Property development let him combine his love of architecture with his natural aptitude for finance and his caution.

"I was very conservative and never undertook anything unless I could bring it to fruition by tying up tenants ahead of time and designing it to succeed," he said, "so the ups and downs never affected me."

In fact, during the recession in the early 1990s, Azrieli was an acquirer of commercial buildings across North America because he was flush with cash. He picked up assets in Colorado, California, Texas, Massachusetts and Florida. This also helped him steer through the economic shoals of Quebec's separatist movement, events that led some family members to head for Toronto.

"In the early '70s, when the Parti Québécois became strong and when the bombs were exploding in mailboxes, I was building two large centres in Ontario and also building a house for my family in Westmount," he said. "My decision was clear. I love this city, and this is where I'll stay. I had lived in Montreal longer than I had lived anywhere else."

Then, in 1982, he turned his business talents to Israel, after attending an architectural conference there. The mayor of a Tel Aviv suburb took Azrieli to a location that was not inspiring.

"He said, 'I want you to do a shopping centre.' I stood on the pile of garbage and saw lots of traffic. I found out that suburbs nearby had families with two cars, even then. It was also beside the national stadium, so I began to see the potential," he said.

He bought the site and hired a former classmate from Haifa's Technion Institute of Technology. It was a huge challenge, because

Israel's retail sector consisted of dusty little shops owned by independent shopkeepers.

So Azrieli reinvented the country's retail by building shopping centres with leases based on sales percentages. He also introduced enclosed malls with air conditioning and coined a new word in Hebrew for "shopping centre," *canyion,* because none existed. The word combines "shopping" with "parking."

"Almost from day one, when I left Israel to see the world and visit relatives, my desire was to go back and do things in Israel," he said. "I also undertook projects that, if I lost, were not big enough to hurt me badly elsewhere."

Ever since those first projects, he has never taken a penny of dividends out of Israel but has reinvested it all in more developments there.

"I don't need money," he said.

Azrieli is Israel's largest private developer and owns Tel Aviv's prestigious Azrieli Centre, with its distinctive office towers and vast shopping mall twice the size of Toronto's Eaton Centre. He owns another giant shopping mall in Jerusalem, the largest in the Middle East, with a synagogue in the basement and the world's first kosher Burger King.

Canpro Investments has no mortgages on any properties in North America. In 2007, the company obtained a preferred bond rating and was easily able to raise hundreds of millions of dollars for future expansion at rates below current mortgage levels.

Azrieli keeps up an astonishing pace for his age. He commutes between Montreal and his gorgeous 8,000-square-foot home in Tel Aviv. He and his wife have four children and seven grandchildren. Daughter Naomi is president of the charitable Azrieli Foundation, daughter Danna is a lawyer in Israel who works in the family business, and daughter Sharon, the talented opera singer, has performed all over the world. A son, Rafi, has health problems.

The family enjoys quiet times on its beautiful compound in the Laurentians. Azrieli's hobbies include music and collecting Canadian art and Judaica, 19th-century Russian bronzes and, lately, Israeli art.

"I love Canada even though I have a close association with Israel. Canada has a great future and is a wonderful place to live and work," he said.

Azrieli also maintains the Jewish tradition of *tzedakah*, or charity. His foundation totalled $200 million in 2006. He has given millions to Technion, Tel Aviv University, Yeshiva University in New York, Concordia University and Carleton University.

"This is a privilege and I am lucky to be around to do all these things," he said. "I have energy because I do exactly what I love to do. Retire? I've been retired for the last 40 years."

RUDY BRATTY

Rudy Bratty grew up fetching tools and water for his Italian immigrant father's workmates, then graduated to hodding bricks and banging nails. By 14, he was a full-fledged carpenter, and by 17, in 1950, he had begun to build half a dozen houses a year with a buddy and a cousin. Within a handful of years, and while still in school, Rudy and his partners were building 20 or 30 houses a year.

"I borrowed $3,000 from my mother. When I worked as a newspaper delivery boy or mailman or helping my dad, I always gave all my money to my mom—that's an Italian thing," he said.

The three teenagers bought six lots, then built and sold their first six houses, netting a profit of $12,000.

"Our parents thought we were going nuts, because they were more conservative with their money, but I have never felt as rich as I did when we finished the first six homes," said Bratty in an interview on a sunny Saturday afternoon in the law offices of Bratty and Partners.

Bratty is a legendary workhorse, and at 75 years of age still puts in 12-hour days. He's tall, good-looking and jovial, and has, with many partners along the way, carved out a great law firm and one of Toronto's biggest private-property fortunes.

He is one of four Italian billionaires in southern Ontario who were part of the wave of 600,000 Italian immigrants who settled in and around Toronto. They worked as labourers, then many got into development, building a city that would grow faster than any part of Canada, thanks to immigration, to in-country migration from the Maritimes and Quebec, and to economic growth due to proximity to U.S. markets.

Bratty wanted to stop his education at high school to build houses, but his father insisted that he become an engineer, lawyer or architect.

"I reluctantly attended law school and did four grudging years, but it was great training because it helped me so much in real estate negotiations," he said. "It helps me anticipate both sides of the negotiation. My uneducated father was totally right to insist that I finish my education."

Bratty and a law school pal, Emilio Gambin, opened a firm, and the plan was that Bratty would bring in clients and Emilio would practise law.

"There were 11 Italian lawyers in Toronto, and we thought we were too late to crack the market, but in 2 years we were the largest Italian firm in the city," Bratty said. "We had so much business that Emilio was going crazy and I had to practise law too. So I did."

By 1997, Bratty and Partners had 22 lawyers and another 80 employees as well as the family's real estate companies, which employ about 100 employees directly and thousands more depending on what they are constructing.

Bratty got into big-time real estate because he attracted so many successful Italians to his firm. Some clients became partners, notably Fred DeGasperis and the late Marco Muzzo.

"Fred is a great partner, very creative, and he knows servicing, which forms a large part of land development," Bratty said. "He knew where the pipes were going or could go, the watersheds and all of that information which anyone can get now through government agencies."

This expertise came in handy when Bratty took his first huge gamble in 1973: an 800-acre farm owned by Massey-Ferguson on the other side of the city limits, bought with another partner.

"It was $10 million and a huge gamble for us because it was just unzoned farmland, but it became [part of the Town of] Markham's development area. We added 3,000 more acres and are still not finished developing it," he said.

In 1982, the threesome (Muzzo, DeGasperis and Bratty) hit another jackpot when they pulled off one of the biggest real estate deals ever. They bought half of a western suburb of Toronto called Erin Mills, in Mississauga, for $95 million. The Seagram distillery–owning branch of the Bronfman family was divesting its real estate portfolio, except for offices, through their real estate arm, Cadillac Fairview Corp. The three Italians and two other partners took the 4,600 zoned acres off Cadillac's hands and made hundreds of millions of dollars.

Bratty and his family now own "millions of square feet" of property through their private companies, and his four sons divide duties so that there's little overlap except in terms of big decisions and strategy.

"I really don't know how many square feet we own," he said, "but I'm very lucky. My four sons love the business and work very well together."

Bratty works six days a week and takes two weeks' holiday a year. Our interview took place on a beautiful day in May 2007 just before a long weekend, when he could have been found on a golf course beside his home or at his cottage on Georgian Bay.

"People think I'm a workaholic. Like today, I'm the only guy in here and the only guy who shouldn't be because I'm the oldest and I'm the boss," he said. "But I love what I do. It's not work, it's a hobby."

Bratty loves to laugh and thoroughly enjoys everything in life. His sons live well—the oldest has a "ranch" north of Toronto with an indoor hockey arena, complete with seating, locker rooms and a Zamboni.

"I'm pretty frugal compared to my kids. I was poor, and you never feel rich once poverty has touched you," he said. "But I enjoy my life. I believe the cheapest medicine in the world is laughter."

Bratty's routine has been the same for 60 years. In the mornings, he works at his law firm, which is the largest Italian firm in the city, mentoring and helping with deals or disputes. In the afternoon, he goes down to the first floor of his office tower, "where the money is made," and does real estate with his four sons, who are involved in home building, condos, office towers, income properties, land deals, high rises, and industrial and retail development in Ontario.

Bratty's dad came to Canada from Italy in 1921 with a couple of siblings. They anglicized the spelling of their name from Bratti to Bratty because they married Anglo women. When war broke out, he and other Italian immigrants were required to register with local police because Italy was on Germany's side.

"I never hide my Italian background, but I'm fiercely Canadian. I have a bit of resentment about that and I remember having some problems when I delivered newspapers to some people who didn't like Italians," Bratty said. "I probably have a chip on my shoulder which probably drives me."

He and his wife, Cathy, have five children and five grandchildren. They socialize constantly and enjoy holidays together in Florida and at the cottage up north.

"My kids know how to enjoy life more than I do. I'm frugal. My wife's quite the contrary," he said.

But his immigrant father's frugality and cautiousness paid off for Bratty even though he was a risk-taker.

"I was aggressive and have been in oil and other things. I'm a deal junkie," he said. "I'm probably more leveraged than Fred or Marco, but not crazy. And I always had income from my law firm and I never touched my father's estate at all, so I always had those things to fall back on. So I could be more aggressive."

JOHN DANIELS

John "Jack" Daniels was 12 when his family fled Poland for Toronto in 1939, and he left behind his boyhood woodworking tools and paintbrushes. He became an architect, and Canada's master builder, and has created some of the most enduring buildings and developments in North America.

At 80, he owns the Daniels Corporation in Toronto, a development giant that builds 2,000 condos and 500 houses annually. It also owns 800 rental units, specializes in subsidized housing in partnership with governments and has a significant land spread in the Toronto region.

"I flunked retirement when I was 55 years old," said Daniels in an interview in his Toronto office in 2007. "I quit, but could only stand it for three months. I always say my hobby is pouring concrete."

Daniels also provided seed capital for the Toronto International Film Festival and Cineplex multi-screen movie theatres, as well as the Toronto Sun Publishing Corporation, a profitable newspaper chain now owned by Montreal-based Quebecor Inc.

He has always shunned publicity, even when he was chair of a public company, and had never granted an interview about his life and career until this book. He is a handsome, well-groomed gentleman.

He is also a legend in the real estate business. He parlayed a grubstake from an uncle into ownership in Cadillac Fairview Corporation, which was North America's largest developer until the early 1980s, and now the Daniels Corporation.

He was Cadillac's driving force in many gigantic deals in Toronto, California, and Colorado, and with Texas Eastern, which involved developing 32 square blocks of downtown Houston. In Toronto, he was instrumental in shaping Toronto's skyline with construction of the Eaton Centre and the Toronto-Dominion Centre.

"I stepped down in 1982 because we had merged our company, Cadillac, with the Bronfmans' Fairview [Seagram Distillery] and it wasn't working. We had lost control of our company. It was the biggest mistake we ever made," he said. "It was affecting me physically."

Cadillac's board was too cautious and refused deals that Daniels brought to them, which upset him.

"I had a deal to buy the Irvine Ranch in California—80,000 acres in Orange County—but the board turned it down. They left $50 billion on the table," he said. "I had also done a deal with Li Ka-shing in Hong Kong they didn't want to do. It was embarrassing."

Daniels said he hit rock bottom because of the sell-off. Then the board panicked during the early 1980s recession and decided to dump all its vast residential property holdings onto the market, thus depressing prices even further.

"We sold off 20,000 apartments, and gave away billions. It was heartbreaking to me. A building is like a child to an architect," he said.

Daniels licked his wounds in "retirement" for three months, then started the Daniels Corporation. He decided to buy assets that Cadillac hadn't already sold, such as 4,700 acres of land in Mississauga. He bought one-third and the rest was divided among Fred DeGasperis, Marco Muzzo, Rudy Bratty and Elly Reisman. The five men together paid $95 million.

"No Canadian bank wanted to touch it because it was raw land. Not a dime. So I went to a Florida bank, which said, great, but suggested that all we needed from them was a guarantee. So we got that and then the Canadian bank financed it because it was guaranteed by an American bank," he said. "It was a home run."

Daniels has always had a knack for the business side of real estate. This, along with his creativity as an architect, vaulted his career. In fact, his moxie came through before he had even graduated from the University of Toronto in architecture.

"Me and two friends built six homes in Toronto one summer and did all the plumbing, carpentry, bricklaying, everything," he said. "Two of these houses are still standing, I think. Back then, they were radical—flat roofs, radiant heating, things that young architects would build."

After he graduated in 1949, an uncle gave him $40,000 to start his own practice. Within two years, he was too busy to keep up with the volume of business that came to his start-up. His developer clients appreciated his business smarts and began to rely on him to help negotiate their deals with banks and mortgage companies.

"I was doing more than just architecture. I was doing the deals and I loved it, so I became a developer," he said.

He began with small apartment buildings in Toronto, never selling, and ended up with a portfolio of 1,000 rental units in 1961, when he joined forces with Ephraim Diamond and Joe Berman in Cadillac Corp. Each owned one-third and the others ran operations while Daniels scoured the city and the rest of the continent for opportunities.

In 1968, they went public and shortly after teamed up with Fairview Corp., owned by Cemp, the holding company for the Montreal-based Bronfman family.

"It was our biggest mistake because we lost control," Daniels said. "That's why today this company is 100% owned by me. Control is what it's all about."

The Daniels Corporation now occupies most of the 30th floor in one of the towers that book-end the Eaton Centre. The cavernous shopping mall is more than 30 years old but remains a successful, and stunning, space that is still Toronto's top tourist attraction.

Daniels' corner office enjoys a sweeping view of the skyline and the bank towers that he helped build and of Lake Ontario's shoreline. He had been away for some time prior to our interview and on his desk were piles of documents and files for his attention. Some were deals, but most were charitable requests.

"I now spend half of my time on charitable matters and give away a fortune every year," he said. "To me success isn't about money. Money is great because what it can do for you is give you the ability to do good things for humanity and society, and that is satisfying."

Daniels contributes to causes in Toronto, New York and Israel in the health care, arts and educational fields. He mostly gives away money anonymously. But among his known causes are Habitat for Humanity, Second Harvest and, with $10 million earmarked for a permanent headquarters he is building on King Street West along with a condo development, the Toronto International Film Festival.

In his company, Daniels has also devised home-ownership opportunities for lower-income people in 4 projects involving 150 townhomes each. Daniels builds 150 units at a time, complete with landscaping, in an assembly-line fashion, then passes along to buyers the cost savings on a first-come, first-served basis. These homes sell for between $160,000 and $220,000 apiece.

"This gives me more pleasure than anything because we are providing homes for people who never dreamed they'd be able to afford their own home," he said. "They are sold on a Saturday morning and the sales tent goes up on Wednesday. People line up for three days and three nights to buy. It's incredible. We serve them pizza and water and they police the lineup themselves."

Daniels and his American wife, Myrna, live in Toronto but also have an apartment in New York City's Pierre Hotel. Daniels' five sons live in Canada but are not shareholders or executives in the Daniels Corporation.

"None are with me, and they are well off on their own," he said. "They don't own this and will get nothing when I'm gone. But they have been looked after."

Such unimagined success has also been accompanied by setbacks—Daniels has had a few.

"I had my tough times, like when I started and the bank reneged on financing something I was doing," he said. "But you have to work your way around these setbacks. You deal with it. Look on the bright side of things, and that's how you can handle problems."

Another constant annoyance to Daniels is what a lot of people call the "NIMBY" phenomenon: the not-in-my-backyard resistance to new development. This afflicts all developers.

"NIMBY wastes time and money, and the politicians side with these people," he said. "The problem is we generally have weak leaders and politicians who aren't very intelligent and don't understand business."

If he were starting his career today, he said, he'd head off to Alberta, where demand and attitudes are better.

"It's just incredible what's happening in places like Calgary and Fort McMurray. That's the future," he said. "But Toronto will continue to get most immigrants, and this has been the benefit of being here over the years. Within two or three years, the immigrants save up enough money for a down payment."

He also believes that his success is due to the fact that he did for a living what he was best at doing.

"If asked for advice, I would say find something you're good at that's useful for society and humanity, not running a hedge fund to make a lot of money," he said. "Then pursue that interest strongly."

FRED DeGASPERIS

Fred DeGasperis stomped on grapes in Italy as a boy for his vintner grandfather and also negotiated cattle purchases for his father.

He applied both a strong work ethic and business smarts as an adult when he immigrated to Canada in 1952 with his brothers. By 2007, the three had built the Con-Drain Group of Companies in Toronto, one of Canada's largest contractors, landlords and real estate developers.

DeGasperis, a handsome and fit man who fixes you with intense black eyes, started off as a labourer and, two years later, wagered his $4,000 in savings to launch a business.

"I was driving a truck for a lumberyard and knew that I didn't want to do that for the rest of my life, so I bought my own truck with my brother and started doing small jobs," he said.

A replica of the original green truck is parked in the front of Con-Drain's grounds in Concord, Ontario, north of Toronto. It was a fitting gift from the second generation.

DeGasperis is 73, looks 60 and is the family patriarch. He is also owner of Vineland Estates Winery in Ontario's Niagara Peninsula. It is a thriving winery that sells 50,000 cases per year of red and white wines.

"We have won awards. Our white is better than Italian white wines. Our reds are going to get better and we're going to keep them 18 months in a barrel," he said.

Vineland's gently rolling 200 acres includes production facilities hidden behind a 19th-century Amish bell tower, complete with gourmet restaurant, tasteful gift and wine shop, conference centre and bed-and-breakfast inn. His wines have won many prestigious awards and he averages one day per week there.

DeGasperis is a Greek surname, but the family lived for generations in Italy and Fred DeGasperis is a ranking member of Toronto's successful Italian families, along with project partners Rudy Bratty, Marco Muzzo and Carlo Fidani.

All four businessmen have remained under the radar for years. So has the DeGasperis family.

"We are not public and will never be," he said in an interview. "We [the family members] meet for lunch every Saturday at 1:30 p.m. We have no outside directors. We have no time for that."

The Con-Drain team has included Fred and his brothers Tony and Angelo. Since 2005, Fred and Tony—along with their sons Fred Jr. and Jim and nephews Robert, Andrew and Romeo—have also owned and operated Aspen Ridge Homes and Metrus Properties in Toronto. Angelo was bought out a couple of years ago.

"We keep a low profile," said DeGasperis. "Not like that guy Donald Trump. And we are also different than him because we have never walked away from any debts or any obligations. Our name is more important to us than money. We have enough money."

In 1952, DeGasperis met a lifelong partner, the late Marco Muzzo, who died in 2006. The two did most deals together and complemented one another's skills.

"He was doing the drywall, and I was doing concrete and drain. We hit it off and started to do things together. I still do lots of business with the Muzzos now, his son Marco and nephew Alex, and will do more with them," he said.

In 1961, DeGasperis and his brothers graduated from building sidewalks and digging drains to doing sewer, or infrastructure, work. That led to contracts for laying pipe beneath vast tracts of land being developed by huge and growing companies like Revenue Properties and Cadillac Fairview.

"Then I bought land—50 acres of land in Grimsby for $3,000 an acre—and it was soon worth $10,000 an acre. I also began to learn where to buy land, because when you do the service [sewers], you know what's going to be developed next," he said. "It was also easier for me to buy land because I knew how to service it."

In the early 1980s, DeGasperis and Muzzo hit it big when they participated in a consortium to buy suburban property assets from the Montreal branch of the Bronfman family, which owned Seagram Distillery.

"Marco, Rudy Bratty, me, Jack Daniels and Elly Reisman bought Erin Mills," he said. "We had to go to the States to borrow the money. Banks were holding the bag for other big developers in Canada and didn't want to lend us any money."

Eventually, retail and housing for 270,000 people was built, which catapulted all the players into the moneyed big leagues. DeGasperis's next big deal was Genstar Corp., with Muzzo and Carlo Fidani, which involved valuable holdings in Ontario and Alberta.

"Genstar has been my greatest-ever deal," he said. "It's quite unbelievable."

Being in the right place at the right time has helped, but so have certain unorthodox business practices, he added.

"Some developers use agents, then go behind their backs to save 10% and end up blowing millions. I know what I can do, and I know what they can do, and I pay them to do it," he said.

"I also didn't gamble but paid cash for my land," he told me. "My industrial buildings were without mortgages when both the recessions hit. My philosophy is that when you make a car, you have shock absorbers. Well, not having debt is a shock absorber."

This avoided other issues.

"If you don't leverage, you don't grow too fast," he said. "If you grow too fast, you have a problem getting the right people. So grow slowly and also stay with what you know and don't get distracted."

For instance, his company was approached, because of its expertise in construction and pipe-laying, to participate in a gigantic arctic pipeline consortium.

"An arctic pipeline? I said to myself, 'What am I thinking? We don't know anything about this. This is crazy.' The thing is you just have to learn to say no in business, even if it's intriguing," he said.

Con-Drain does business mostly in Ontario and by 2017 will have finished a 2,000-acre development called Springdale, near Toronto's airport. It will house 85,000.

Toronto's land price increases have created some of Canada's biggest real estate fortunes, including this one. Values have gone from $3,000 an acre in 1952 to more than $400,000 an acre for developable land, DeGasperis said. But that run is over.

"If I was 35, I would sell everything and move to Florida. That state will be twice the population it is now in 15 years, and developing there is much easier," he said. "And our country is too socialist. Too much to the left."

Interestingly, none of DeGasperis's kids has bolted for a sunnier clime, but in 2007 Fred bought 2,000 acres outside Orlando to develop a community. Meanwhile, the DeGasperis tradition of hard work continues.

"If the father isn't spoiled, then the kids won't be," he said. "My son Jimmy has three or four Ferraris, but he can afford them. None of my kids gamble, they have raised good kids and given them good educations and are setting a good example for their kids."

CARLO FIDANI

The largest private developer and richest Italian in North America is a modest, publicity-shy, middle-aged Etobicoke resident, Carlo Fidani.

"He's a billionaire with a capital *s* [meaning billions], and is bigger than most of us combined," said lawyer and developer Rudy Bratty in an interview in 2007. "He's the richest Italian in North America by far."

Fidani became chair of Orlando Corporation in 2000 after the death of his father, Orlando "Orey" Fidani, who built the company over four decades. Carlo Fidani's first act, after taking control, was to donate $6 million to Mississauga's Credit Valley Hospital to help build the Carlo Fidani Peel Regional Cancer Centre. (His father, an ex-smoker who died of lung cancer, had been known to offer employees $1,000 to kick the habit.)

The gift was in recognition of "the hospital's extraordinary health care excellence," said Carlo in a rare public appearance in 2001. He declined an interview for this book for personal reasons.

His father, Orey, was equally reclusive even though he was a larger-than-life figure who was dubbed by fellow land developers as "the King." He was aggressive and prescient and had jumped into the construction and land business as a teenager. His goal was to eventually make $100,000—but he did that in his first year as a house builder.

Throughout the 1960s, Orey Fidani specialized in acquiring tracts of land in southern Ontario and turning them into business parks. This speciality, and the huge growth of Toronto, led to the creation of Canada's largest property portfolio by far—an estimated 35 million square feet of real estate holdings. This total is divided into industrial buildings, business parks, industrial parks, and retail and office developments.

Such industrial and commercial real estate is more lucrative and sustainable than residential or retail property. Housing and malls involve dealing with the public, which is sometimes fickle. But Orlando's tenants are corporations that sign leases that can be borrowed against at banks and that are long-term, 10 to 25 years.

The fact that these leases are "bankable," or creditworthy at the bank, allows landlords to mortgage the properties to buy or develop even more properties. These long-term leases are also called "triple net," which means tenants pay rent but also pay for all the other expenses involved, such as taxes, improvements, maintenance and interior fixtures.

This in turn means that the landlords sit back and collect rents without much risk for years: they can borrow to buy more against the value of the leases, and they can also raise rents based on an inflation escalation formula. Best of all, as rents pay down debts, the land appreciates in value and the tenants pay all the costs of carrying the property.

But what's made Orlando the biggest property developer in the country has been the exponential increases in land prices around Toronto. This has been due in the past 20 years to the departure of businesses from Quebec as well as to the influx of U.S. and other foreign subsidiaries establishing head office operations in the western suburbs of Toronto.

The Fidanis have also been innovative. Orey pioneered what's known as "design/build," which meant that he would customize facilities for corporate tenants in return for longer-term leases.

Orlando is not merely a landlord. Its construction division is still enormous, and other profit centres include site search, leasing search, property management services and leasing services on behalf of independent clients.

"Carlo 'owns' Mississauga," said Fred DeGasperis, who has been a partner of Bratty, Marco Muzzo and the Fidani family for years.

Now a city of 700,000, Mississauga amalgamated 30 years ago into a city from a collection of rural villages and towns. Its rapid growth was mostly a result of spillover from Toronto's population increase from about 1.5 million to 5 million in two generations.

Mississauga also benefited from being able to offer land and tax advantages to industries new to Canada or wanting to relocate from more expensive, congested or antiquated facilities in downtown Toronto. The result is that the region is home to the largest cluster of U.S. subsidiary head offices in Canada.

Orlando Corporation's Heartland Business Community has provided custom-built industrial and office facilities to hundreds of these companies. It encompasses 1,250 acres and is the largest undertaking of its kind in Canada. When fully developed, it will accommodate another 35 million square feet of office, industrial and retail space. This is on top of Orlando's existing 35-million-square-foot portfolio.

Like the other Italian developers—DeGasperis, Bratty and Marco Muzzo—Carlo Fidani and his father avoided bankruptcy during the severe real estate recession of the early 1990s. None were over-leveraged, and they financed their expansions conservatively. That allowed them after the recession to take advantage of those who had not by snapping up their properties.

Carlo has two young sons and a brother who is not involved directly in the business. He keeps a low profile and operates quietly out of his suburban headquarters. His personal life is as private as his business existence, but friends say he has a beautiful home in Toronto and commutes to his cottage and to fly-fishing destinations by helicopter. He is both a passionate fisherman and a licensed helicopter pilot.

Orlando now employs thousands of people, and the Fidanis have been able to build—and keep—a loyal team of executives over the years. Their contacts and financial heft have allowed the company to spread farther afield.

They now have developments in the United States and, through a partnership with DeGasperis and the Sobey grocery family, reaped a windfall from a portfolio of properties they bought in the 1990s from Genstar Corp. The lands acquired were in prime areas of the two fastest-growing parts of the country, Ontario and Alberta.

"This is a really nice guy," said Bratty. "Orlando is a huge enterprise and we've partnered from time to time. He's very honourable."

THE GHERMEZIANS

Jacob Ghermezian started off life in poverty-stricken Azerbaijan selling rugs, but ended up creating a property empire in faraway Edmonton, Alberta.

Ghermezian first immigrated to Montreal but was drawn to Alberta because of its oil boom in the 1960s. There he founded what is now Triple Five Group, which accumulated large tracts of land around Edmonton.

Then in 1980, the audacious Jacob and his sons opened the world's first megamall, the West Edmonton Mall, with hundreds of stores, multiple theme parks, hotels and theatres, and a parking lot for 30,000 cars. In 1992, another giant centre followed, in Minneapolis, called the Mall of America, which is the equivalent of 78 football fields in size. And in 2007, a third was underway in Las Vegas.

Despite the high-profile nature of these retail assets, the family has protected its privacy, occasionally surfacing as a result of financing issues or litigation; I did not interview the family for this book.

Rumours that they were a front for the shah of Iran's money abounded for years. One of Jacob's sons, Raphael, confirmed they had partners in a 1978 interview in the *Toronto Star*. Their company, Triple Five, was named that because it had 555 partners, including the Ghermezians.

"The others are silent partners who make available to ourselves [*sic*] silent money," Raphael said in an interview with the *Toronto Star*.

This "silence," or need for anonymity, explained Triple Five's strange bylaw that stated in the 1980s that shares in the company could never be sold to the public. At the end of 2007, the company remained privately held, but sources say the family has bought out most of their silent partners over the years.

Triple Five owns a small trust company, called Peoples Trust, in Vancouver (which has a community of 50,000 people from Iran), with $45 million a year in revenues. There is also a U.S. venture capital outfit with a portfolio of US$135 million, called Selby Venture Partners, and Ghermezian-financed Alberta start-ups Global Switchgear and Celonex Inc.

Nobody knows how much the family, with dozens of heirs and heiresses, is worth.

The Ghermezian megamalls are now considered to be dinosaurs and face tough competition from big-box developments consisting of free-standing megastores. Even so, published figures show that their two operating monsters ring up impressive receipts. Both the West Edmonton Mall and the Mall of America enjoyed average sales per square foot of $500, while standard malls averaged $366 in 2004, according to the International Council of Shopping Centers.

Patriarch Jacob died in 2000, but his four reclusive sons—led by Eskander—continue to operate the assets and have begun passing along operations to the next generation. Jacob reportedly had more than two dozen grandchildren.

Naturally, the family's murky background fuelled gossip, as did their private and unusual lifestyle. For starters, the four brothers raised their families on a family compound in Edmonton, similar to the type of living arrangement that they had had in Tehran, where the extended family occupied an entire apartment building.

They also carefully disguised their religion, a habit learned of necessity living in cultures where minorities could be discriminated against. For years, family spokesmen said the four brothers followed different religions, each having adopted his wife's faith. They also made contributions to different religious institutions. One wife was allegedly Roman Catholic, another Jewish; another belonged to a Persian sect, and the fourth was Muslim.

Another rumour was that in 1981, according to an article in *Forbes*, the family matriarch—Miriam, who picked all her sons' four wives based on the fact they were good-looking and tall—mandated that the entire family practise Orthodox Judaism. One of Jacob's grandsons, David, who is one of Eskander's sons, explained the sensitivity about religion. "In many parts of the world, that [being Jewish] spells trouble," he told the *Edmonton Journal* in 2002.

Most of David's cousins have ended up in New York City or Los Angeles. But he said there remains a sense of solidarity and respect: "After being given this springboard, it's important to do something with it. But it's not easy. If it was, everybody would be opening a business," he said.

Another cousin, Mark, opened an advertising firm in New York and Edmonton: FLUSH media inc., specializing in washroom wall advertising.

"Some [of the cousins] will get into the family business, some will do other things," said Don Ghermezian, who runs the West Edmonton Mall. "We help them all out and get them started. Some may leave Edmonton, but I'll never leave the mall."

His brother David also spoke about succession to the *Journal*.

"We have been handed a unique opportunity," said David, who works in Las Vegas. "There is a transition going on in the family, and I think that the first generation is looking to kind of gracefully exit. My dad [Eskander] has mentioned on occasion that he wants to retire."

Eskander was Jacob's oldest son and remains CEO of the family business. His brothers are Nader, Raphael and Bahman. The four were born between 1940 and 1946 and have, for a few decades now, divided tasks and gone out of their way to stay out of the limelight.

But the family's story is fascinating. Jacob was born into a struggling family in 1902 in Azerbaijan. During the Depression, he and his wife headed to Tehran. Obviously a genius at business, he built a rug export-import business that expanded into Europe. But the rug business is about more than selling and buying rugs.

Carpet merchants in many unstable parts of the world have functioned like merchant banks. Rugs, like diamonds, can be easily transported across borders, thus providing a handy way to get around currency and customs restrictions.

For generations, wealthy Iranians, Arabs, Ugandans, Chinese and others have smuggled their money out by acquiring these rugs, then divesting them to traders in other countries.

Jacob was obviously a master. Despite being a foreigner and an infidel, he made a name for himself in Iran. He hobnobbed with politicians and potentates in the country and once told a Canadian reporter that the Tehran Conference—a 1943 summit between Roosevelt, Churchill and Stalin—took place in his hotel-like five-storey "house." There is no way to check this fact, but it seems plausible due to his contacts.

Jacob also allegedly served in the postwar government under the shah, but he left before extremists toppled the regime. He sent three of his sons, in 1959, to study business at McGill University, then opened a rug store in Montreal. In 1963, he was able to sponsor the rest of his family to immigrate to Canada.

The discovery of huge amounts of oil in Alberta enticed him westward in the same way that oil-rich Iran must have appealed to an impoverished Azerbaijani during the Depression.

Through Triple Five, the family purchased thousands of acres. By the time they all moved to Edmonton, en masse, in the mid-1960s, some guessed that they owned 15,000 acres and were drilling for oil. They struck out because they knew little about geology or engineering.

However, they began to sell parcels of property at profits. Rezoning farmland into developable property creates instant value to owners, and the family set about learning the rezoning ropes through local politics. They also scored a huge profit when the province bought thousands of acres of their land to retain as a greenbelt. On top of all that, Jacob was no stranger to real estate and had also been a fairly large-scale landlord in Tehran.

Back in the 1960s and 1970s, city and town governments were not as squeaky clean as they are today, and business practices in the Middle East were different from those in Canada. In 1974, a provincial government report claimed that Raphael had offered $40,000 to bribe an alderman, sparking a judiciary inquiry. Weeks later, a judge concluded that Raphael gave the money to reward the alderman for past service, but that in itself was not illegal.

"It was a legitimate token of appreciation for past services and did not constitute a bribe," wrote the judge.

Another controversy involved the financing of the West Edmonton Mall, which fell on hard times when oil prices collapsed during the 1980s. By 1994, the shopping centre was $500 million in debt and had to be bailed out by the province. This caused a political firestorm at the time because many thought the wealthy family should bail itself out.

But oil prices—and prosperity—returned to the oil patch, and Edmonton has become the gateway to the massive oil sands development. The mall prospers along with the rest of the local economy.

And things will improve. A projected $200 billion worth of construction projects and manufacturing is planned for northern Alberta over the next 20 years if all 26 oil sands projects announced by 2007 are completed. By 2020, the province could be exporting twice as much oil and oil equivalents as the country this family came from, Iran.

So once again, Jacob Ghermezian's patience—and prescience—has paid off.

THE GREENBERGS

The biggest private landlord and developer in Ottawa is Minto Developments Inc. The company was started by four brothers in 1955, but by 1962 two (Lorry and Louis Greenberg) had left to pursue other interests, and the firm was continued by Irving and Gilbert Greenberg. In 2007, Minto was owned by seven of their eight children and had become well entrenched in the real estate big leagues in Ottawa, Toronto and Florida.

"Irving was an absolute genius and Gilbert was a great administrator. It was the perfect partnership," said Roger Greenberg, who is Minto's CEO and Gilbert's third child.

The Greenbergs own 8,500 apartments and manage another 7,000 for other owners. They also own 2.5 million square feet of office and retail space and a hotel in Ottawa. Their Florida housing division has been building 500 to 1,000 units per year, their Ottawa division between 1,000 and 1,200 houses, and the Toronto division 100 to 200 annually. Minto has also specialized in high-end condo and rental developments in the fancy neighbourhoods of downtown Toronto. The firm employs 1,400 people and does not disclose its revenues or assets—but both are substantial.

Roger is an outgoing former lawyer who met me in Minto's modest offices in Ottawa at 7:30 a.m. in summer 2007. He was dressed casually in a golf shirt, and the office was already full of workers. The Greenbergs are notably down-to-earth people who live reasonably modest lifestyles and are very philanthropic. Roger Greenberg agreed to an interview reluctantly. The family avoids publicity.

Minto is owned by siblings Roger, Michael, Kenneth, Marion, Alan and Robert and cousin Phoebe. An eighth family member, cousin Dan, cashed out amicably in 2002. Currently, Roger, Alan and Robert work as executives in the organization.

The Greenbergs have overcome challenges that have forced other family firms to divide or disappear. The second generation took control in 1991 at a time when the economy was in the middle of a wrenching real estate recession. Many real estate family fortunes disappeared, including that of fellow Ottawa developer Robert Campeau. At the same time, the Greenbergs inherited a company from founders who had not left any written succession plans in place.

But the family has always been resourceful in the face of adversity. The climb began with Roger's grandfather, his namesake, who emigrated from Eastern Europe to Canada in 1915. He and his wife, Rose, also from Eastern Europe, struggled to raise their large family by peddling fruit door to door.

But the early version of today's supermarket eventually put him out of business, then the stock market crash of 1929 wiped out his meagre savings. The family struggled throughout the Depression.

"At one point, my grandmother and the children had to move in with her relatives in Montreal because he couldn't support them," said Roger.

During the war there was work, and by 1947 his grandfather had started Sterilized Wiper, Towel Supply and Industrial Bag Co., which recycled jute and potato bags. It grew dramatically in 1950 when the federal government awarded the company a contract to supply millions of sandbags to help protect Winnipeg from a flood.

"My grandmother hated that business because it dealt with disease and filth," said Roger. "In 1955, my uncle Irving and my grandfather built a few houses and made some money. That was the start."

They called their start-up Mercury Homes but three years later could not incorporate under that name, so they came up with Minto, after Lord Minto, who was governor general of Canada from 1898 to 1904.

"My grandfather died, at the age of 59, before those original houses were finished. Longevity doesn't run on the male side of my family," said Roger.

But Irving teamed up with Roger's father, Gilbert, and went from house-building to commercial real estate. They also expanded outside Ottawa, and by the late 1970s Roger's two older brothers, Michael and Kenneth, had started a Florida division.

Again health problems struck the family. In 1980 Gilbert died at 57, leaving his mercurial and hard-driving brother, Irving, to run the show.

Irving Greenberg diversified further, and by 1985 there were two Greenberg sons in Ottawa, two in Toronto and two in Florida. Irving ran the show with an iron fist but was also devoted to social causes. He ran three times unsuccessfully for the New Democrats in Ottawa. Lorry was a popular mayor of Ottawa until health problems sidelined him.

"Irving raised lots of money for Biafra, ran for the NDP and sent his kids to alternative schools. He was a huge contrarian," said Roger. "I was involved in a couple of his campaigns."

At the end of the 1980s, Irving began having health problems, and Roger became president when his uncle died in May 1991.

"I had been designated as the son who would represent Gilbert's family in the business, but Irving and I had one formal board meeting in 11 years. There were no financials provided to the rest of the family. Once in 1985 we had a 12-minute board meeting about something important. He was a very controlling guy. Even when he knew he was close to death he didn't set up succession," said Roger.

But the first order of the day was to survive the recession. Fortunately, Irving had great instincts that saved the day.

"We were conservatively leveraged and Irving had stopped buying land in 1986. He had an instinct about what was going to happen, and that helped us," Roger said. "When he died the real estate industry was on the cusp of disaster and we went into survival mode."

At the same time, the family sorted out ownership matters and learned the intricacies of the business in a hurry. In ownership, Irving and Gilbert had been 50-50 partners, but Irving had only two children and Gilbert six, five of whom were directly involved at one point in running operations.

"We got to work understanding the business more and meeting regularly," said Roger. "By 1999, we realized we had to transition from an accidental partnership [determined by birth] into a planned partnership."

Facilitators were hired to work on the "soft" family issues. There were 8 children and 17 grandchildren.

"In the late 1990s, we all realized we don't have longevity genetically, so we started succession planning," said Roger.

Irving's son, Dan, decided to cash in his 25% ownership, and a shareholders' agreement was negotiated giving each of the other seven Greenberg children an equal share. Meetings continue to be held regularly and votes are carried by thresholds that rise based on the seriousness of the matter. A family council was established for spouses and children over 15 years of age, to deal with family-related issues. And Minto's governance was also restructured, to bring in outside influences.

"An executive committee runs the business," said Roger. "There are eight of us, and three are family members. The family's agreed that the board of directors will have seven members: three non-family independent directors, three family directors and Eric McKinney, who has been our advisor for years."

But some things haven't changed. The family continues to be philanthropic and is a huge contributor to Jewish, health care and hospital causes, primarily in the communities where Minto operates.

"They were a great partnership. Irving was the visionary and Gilbert a detail guy. Irving thought at 200 miles per hour, spoke at 150 miles per hour, and most people only understand at 100 miles per hour. So he would get upset," said Roger.

He was a hard act to follow, but it has been 16 years since the last founder died, and the Greenbergs continue to be very successful. Roger enjoys the business and the charitable work alike.

"I don't need to work, but I like it," said Roger. "My days are varied, and that's the way I like it."

THE LALJIS AND THE MANGALJIS

In 1972, the Aga Khan, the spiritual leader of the world's 15 million Ismaili Muslims, called Prime Minister Pierre Trudeau in the hopes that Canada would accept Ismailis expelled from Uganda by Idi Amin. Canada and Britain took in thousands of refugees, and by 2007 there were an estimated 100,000 Ismailis living in Toronto and Vancouver. Ismailis are of Indian descent and believe that the Aga Khan is a direct descendant of Mohammed's daughter, Fatima. Their branch of Islam emphasizes tolerance and charity in the form of tithing, or giving 8% of income per year to the Aga Khan.

But Ismailis have never had their own nation. This is why hundreds of thousands ended up in Uganda and other parts of East Africa after 1860. The British recruited them to help develop and colonize the continent. Many were merchants and tradesmen. Over the generations, they prospered and leapfrogged the Africans economically. By the end of the Second World War, they had become so successful that, when some African countries were given independence by Britain, they became targets of hateful nationalism and populism propagated by Amin and others.

Most Ismailis got out of Africa and lived to prosper again in North America, Britain, Australia and even back in India. The luckiest had British passports and easily got out. But most did not and had just weeks to leave.

Among those who got into Canada were members of the Lalji and Mangalji families. But they were not refugees as we imagine refugees, except in the political sense. These two sets of cousins were heirs to one of the biggest family fortunes in East Africa. And while they left behind all their homes and fixed assets, they remained very wealthy and had, according to some rumours, possibly $1 billion in Swiss and British banks.

Their ancestors had made fortunes in just about everything they touched and, despite the nasty expulsion, the family tradition continued.

The Laljis and Mangaljis are among the richest Canadians. The Laljis live and operate out of Vancouver, but the Mangaljis have moved to the United States and Britain. The two sets of cousins conduct business separately, but collectively they own billions of dollars worth of real estate. The Laljis control one of Canada's largest real estate empires, and the Mangaljis one of the world's largest. Both refused interviews, but close associates cooperated and public sources were available.

The Lalji patriach was Aminmohamed Lalji. He and his family settled in Vancouver and began buying real estate through their Larco Group of Companies. Originally there were five sons, but one was murdered in Uganda by thugs and another died of a heart attack at an early age in Canada.

The three remaining Lalji brothers—Shiraz, Mansoor and Amin—own thousands of apartments and hotel rooms in Canada, as well as storage facilities, West Vancouver's Park Royal Shopping Centre and Whistler Village Centre at the foot of Blackcomb Mountain, to name a few assets. They own hotels, including the SkyDome Hotel overlooking the Toronto Blue Jays' baseball park, which they flipped for a fortune. They are the biggest developers in BC's Lower

Mainland, say industry sources.

The brothers politely declined an interview, through an executive. But occasional public reports appear that demonstrate their aggressiveness and cool-headedness. For instance, they bought a bankrupt Las Vegas casino hotel right after 9/11. Newspaper reports said that Amin Lalji was working on the deal in an office that was just four blocks away from the World Trade Center the day the terrorists struck. Other bidders were frightened away by the tragedy, and by concerns about its effect on market values, but the Laljis stayed in the game. Days later, the family paid US$80 million for the Regent Las Vegas hotel and casino complex, which had cost US$194 million to build.

The Laljis have diversified into hotel management through their company Larco Hospitality. The company's website says, "Larco Hospitality was formed in 1998 to manage a hotel portfolio owned by Larco Investments Ltd., and two additional hotels owned by other investment groups. The Vancouver Airport Marriott, Larco Hospitality's first Marriott property, opened in 1998 . . . In June 1999, LH opened the first ever franchise hotel in Canada for Hilton Hotels Corporation, the Hilton Vancouver Airport . . . Larco is the largest full-service Franchise Hotel Management Company in Canada for Marriott International."

The Laljis remain private except for occasional charity events attended by Amin or his wife, Nazmeen. Amin is also on the board of the Aga Khan Foundation Canada in Ottawa.

Sometimes the Laljis cannot escape notice, making headlines over a purchase or over controversies such as the cutting down of trees around the Park Royal Shopping Centre, which resulted in negative publicity and public protests.

The oldest Lalji brother, Shiraz, moved to London years ago and runs the family's gigantic storage business out of his posh Park Lane office building. He is a bon vivant who loves to entertain guests in his townhouse and in his private box at the Chelsea Football Club grounds. Meanwhile, Mansoor and Amin operate discreetly on one of the lower floors in West Vancouver's only office tower, which they own.

Their cousins, the Mangaljis, operate a little more openly, but only slightly. They also declined an interview but pointed out to an intermediary that there was plenty of information about them because they own two very public companies.

Their patriarch was Sadru Lalji-Mangalji and the family business is also run by three sons, Fereed, Moez and Majid. Majid Mangalji and Amin Lalji are the same age, roughly in their mid-50s. The two cousins did business together 30 years ago and bought modest motels throughout the U.S. south and west, then split up amicably.

The Mangaljis are also Canadian citizens, say sources, but live in Houston, New York City and London. They operate through Westmont Hospitality Group in London and control publicly listed InnVest Real Estate Investment Trust in Mississauga.

In July 2007, both Mangalji corporate giants, Westmont Hospitality Group and InnVest, joined forces with the Caisse de dépôt et placement du Québec and paid $2.5 billion for Legacy Hotels Real Estate Investment Trust. The Canadian-listed Legacy Trust owns the Fairmont Royal York in Toronto and Quebec City's Château Frontenac, plus 23 other high-end hotels across North America, according to its corporate website in 2007.

Westmont is much bigger than InnVest or the newly acquired Legacy: it is the world's third-largest hotel chain, and the world's largest privately owned, with 80,000 hotel rooms. Majid Mangalji is its president, and Westmont has alliances with InterContinental Hotels, Choice Hotels, Radisson, Cendant and Starwood as well as Hilton. It also owns Japan's Ishin Hotels Group, and Majid's brother, Moez Mangalji, is president and CEO. Ishin is Japan's largest luxury chain and manages the Hilton chain worldwide.

Fereed Mangalji is a director of Westmont. He is a graduate of Harvard University in economics and is responsible for Westmont's North American portfolios and its major transactions. He worked in real estate services at Bankers Trust in New York City for more than a decade.

The InnVest website describes Majid and the empire: "Majid Mangalji is Founder and President of the Westmont Group, which started its hospitality business approximately 30 years ago. Mr. Mangalji has been involved in all aspects of the development of the Westmont Group. During this period it has grown from a single hotel to become one of the largest private hotel owner/operators in the world with a significant presence in North America, Europe, and Asia. As head of this global hotel group, Mr. Mangalji has developed an extensive knowledge of international hospitality markets, investing and operating in these markets and has created strong relationships with major international hotel brands, leading financial institutions, and investment funds. Mr. Mangalji sits on the boards of the principal hospitality companies in which the Westmont Group invests."

Westmont also advertises its management services business, which operates facilities on behalf of other owners or in partnership with them. The company's entry on the Hospitality Sales and Marketing Association International website says, "Over the past 30 years, we have also turned many under-performing properties into financial success stories. Our global partners continue to benefit from our extensive experience within the hospitality industry, hands-on management approach and service-first philosophy."

The company's own website describes its management services in more detail: "Westmont Hospitality Group provides skilled management and an owner's perspective to hotels in which we invest, as well as third-party management services to independent properties. Our success is built on a no-boundaries, performance-driven management philosophy. Our employees are motivated, empowered and trained by experts, and our corporate offices around the world share knowledge, best practices and experiences."

Majid Mangalji is also on the board of InnVest in Mississauga and spends at least one week per month at InnVest and Westmont offices in Mississauga.

InnVest is listed on the Toronto Stock Exchange and is a separate corporate entity from Westmont. It had a market value of $800 million as of September 2007 and owned more than 135 hotels in Canada, with 16,000 rooms, mostly in Ontario and Quebec. InnVest, now part owner of Legacy Hotels REIT, owns hotels that operate under the brands of Comfort Inn, Quality Suites Inns, Holiday Inn, Ramada, Travelodge and Best Western.

Majid holds a business degree, with a double major in accounting and marketing, from the University of Bradford in England. He is also the chairman of the InnVest board of trustees and a member of InnVest's Investment Committee. Fereed is also on InnVest's board of directors.

Clearly, the Laljis and Mangaljis are talented businessmen. The two branches of the family are in so many crossover businesses that it may be possible that theirs is really just one gigantic empire that is fragmented for political, optical or taxation purposes.

But community sources say that is not the case, and the family members are cordial, doing some business together but remaining independent from one another. However, their reticence makes it impossible to fully know the structure and nature of their empire.

What is known, however, is that Ismailis are people without a country. But they still must pay "taxes": these consist of contributions of 8% of their income every year to the Aga Khan and his foundations for community philanthropical work around the world, not just for Ismailis. Their leader lives in luxury in Switzerland and is a talented tycoon in his own right.

The paradox is that, as for other diasporas, the roots of their success lie in failure and hardship. They had to learn to help one another, fend for themselves, deal with being targets of discrimination and survive by staying hidden from view. And this is why, despite their enormous successes in democratic countries, they still heed the lessons of the past. And probably always will.

THE MUZZOS

One of Canada's most successful private businesses is in a modest one-storey building in Concord, Ontario, with a muscular-looking "M" logo sculpture in front.

The cryptic M stands for Marel Contractors and for the Muzzo Group of Companies, and this suburban, shrub-shrouded low rise is its headquarters. But these family-owned enterprises are enormous and among the country's largest.

The Muzzo Group runs a large-scale drywall operation but is also partners in many projects with developers Fred DeGasperis, Rudy Bratty and others.

Marel is an acronym for Marco and Elio, the two Muzzo brothers from Italy who started a small drywall business in the 1950s. The patriarch, and driving force, was the late Marco Muzzo, even though he was 10 years younger than Elio.

Marco and Elio were sponsored as immigrants to Canada by a relative, as were most of the 600,000 Italians who settled in Toronto after the Second World War. Elio came over first, on their uncle's sponsorship, then brought over Marco after he had finished a year of high school.

As was the custom, Marco lived in Elio's basement and helped him pay off his mortgage. They both worked for their uncle. Elio taught young Marco the drywall trade by making him build walls in the basement, then making him do them over again if they weren't up to scratch.

"Elio and my dad decided to go on their own and started off with a crew of four or five," said Marco (Mark) Muzzo Jr. in an interview with me in Marel's headquarters in 2007.

The Muzzos had never been interviewed before but agreed to talk to me because we have mutual friends. Mark and his cousin, Alex, are now running the family enterprises. Alex did not show for the interview, and Mark explained that he was "detained but glad he was." Gun-shy, Mark is an attractive, articulate 30-something who was brought up in the business. Because his brother, Robert, died of cancer at 46 years of age in 2004, Mark took over in late 2005 when his father died. Elio also died of cancer at a young age, years earlier.

Mark and Alex, Elio's son, are in charge but operate without titles. They confer constantly, as did their two fathers.

"I'm the baby of my family and was 13 years younger than my brother, Robert," said Mark. "I have two sisters and Alex has one, but they didn't want to be involved in the business. They have kids and the hours are long. They could become involved, if they wanted to. They are informed of everything we're doing."

The long hours are a reference to the legendary Muzzo work ethic. Marco took only one holiday and was always in the office on weekends and statutory holidays.

"People knew he'd be at work on Christmas and they'd call. He was a micromanager and it was difficult for him to let go. He looked at every piece of paper. He wouldn't delegate," Mark said.

This ethic became part of the family's life. The Muzzos insisted on education for their kids and spoke only English at home in order to help their children assimilate into Canada.

"I started going to work at 12 years of age on Saturdays and would do lots of things—push a broom or go to sites with my dad," Mark recalled. "They didn't want any playboys. We would do anything. I remember the one vacation my father took, 23 years before he died, was during Christmas in Florida. He woke us up at 7 in the morning and said, 'We have to wash the windows.'"

The late Marco and Elio Muzzo built a huge contracting business. But they began a climb into the big leagues when they joined up with DeGasperis and Bratty and got into buying land and developing.

The three, operating as separate family businesses, joined forces to build some of Toronto's biggest subdivisions, condo projects and other massive developments, including Erin Mills in Mississauga, now with 270,000 residents. They operated on a handshake basis and talked constantly throughout the day.

While Fred DeGasperis and Rudy Bratty are still in charge of their businesses, the second-generation Muzzos are now running their show.

Alex is in charge of the family's traditional drywall business, which, at any given time, employs 600 workers in the field. Mark, born in 1971, runs development operations, along with one of Alex's two sons. They share the same roof and interact constantly. But every week, they meet formally to discuss all of their upcoming opportunities and challenges.

"Our weekly meetings go over developments, and involve me, Alex and his son," Mark said. "That's when we make decisions on new opportunities. The point is, we totally trust each other. If a decision or problem is big enough, we run it by each other. Our attitude is all in or nobody's in."

Mark earned a degree in economics at the University of Toronto and went straight into the business. His late brother and his cousin were recruited before they could complete their degrees.

"Alex was in law school and they pulled him out because they needed him. Robert got pulled too. They were needed by my dad and uncle," said Mark. "They [the first-generation Muzzos] were very demanding. From day one, they delegated to us what to do. We run very lean. Alex runs the drywall and so did my brother, Robert. On the development side, we have only 30 people, which is not many considering the size of the operation."

So the Muzzo Group of Companies is part construction firm and part merchant bank specializing in real estate deals. The Muzzos' principal partner remains Fred DeGasperis. But the Muzzos are firmly in the development loop, which allows them to work with other developers in the regions. They take pieces of deals. Sometimes their role is passive, and sometimes they run the project. It's "shared around," says Mark, and their participation is based on whether they have the expertise or time available to join the project.

"We don't do anything solely, but we'll drive some and not others. For instance, we'll use our high-rise division to do projects, but do industrial/commercial development through the subsidiaries we are involved in with Freddy [DeGasperis] and other partners," he said.

The late Marco Muzzo was a natural businessman. He only had one year of high school, but he mastered the worlds of construction and finance. He knew how to handle the tradesmen and bankers alike and impressed people with his prodigious work ethic.

"He could read people," said Mark. "I studied economics in university, which was very dry. If I went back to school today, I would study sociology or psychology. My dad was great at this."

Marco was also able to think several moves ahead and to anticipate, then avoid, problems.

"His mentality was, how am I going to get cheated? For instance, when contracting a road-builder, they would guarantee a certain depth of asphalt but only measure it from the side. He would insist that it be measured in the middle too. This is one reason why he pushed Freddy into building roads: because he knew he could trust Freddy to build the roads properly," he said.

Marco also understood the construction business better than most.

"He knew what the deal was, and how they got there was up to the professionals. I would see, in legal and engineering meetings, how he could think out of the box. He had a knack for construction and was creative," said Mark. "He would come up with things they hadn't thought of."

He was also demanding. Mark remembers one large drywall contract offered by Muzzo and partners that the Muzzos' Marel tendered for.

"My dad turned down the bid from his own drywall company because it was too high. The guys couldn't believe it and they had to drop the price," he said.

Occasionally there was controversy in the press, such as the time when Marco invested some money in a public company that bailed out the family firm of Liberal David Peterson, who was premier of Ontario at the time. This raised eyebrows since the province was in charge of development and land use.

"We didn't get involved in politics or politicians," said Mark. "My dad always said, 'We do what we've got to do and they do the same.'"

Marco was also good at settling family squabbles, a reality that has sunk many other family businesses.

"Years ago my brother, Robert, and cousin Alex used to argue all the time," said Mark. "My father made them sit down. They loved each other but always fought. Dad said, 'We'll fold the company because this is not working. You have this and we'll take that.' He looked at them and asked them if this was what they wanted. They said no. So he said if this is what they wanted, they had to work together and trust one another."

The family prefers privacy, and Mark said that going public would not be an option they would consider.

"My dad owned HCI [forerunner of Consolidated HCI Holdings], a public company [that bailed out Peterson's family firm], and it was his biggest headache. He hated the publicity and also liked to make decisions on the spot," he said.

The future of the firm is secure, and the second generation has its feet firmly under the desk now.

"We have the framework to grow. The trick is not growing but just keeping everything okay," he said. "In 10 years, we hope to be bigger."

But there are challenges to taking over from a founder who micromanaged everything.

"I enjoy the work, but right now the workload is excessive. Dealing with people is the most difficult. My dad used to say before we met with someone, 'Keep your ears open and your mouth shut.' Now I have to use my voice," said Mark.

Mark joined the firm at 22 years of age in 1994 and, like his father, doesn't know how to relax.

"My wife forces me to take vacations, and I'm glad," he said. "Life is short and I have to learn to enjoy it. I'm very conscious of this given our family's health problems."

THE REICHMANNS

A perfect storm in 1992 sank the world's biggest private real estate empire, owned by the Reichmann family of Toronto.

Just a handful of years before, the family's privately owned Olympia & York Properties Corporation controlled more than $25 billion in real estate and other corporate assets. They built and owned London's Canary Wharf and New York's World Financial Center, and they controlled a portfolio of Canadian real estate, including the country's tallest building, First Canadian Place in Toronto, plus control blocks in leading Canadian companies such as Gulf Canada, Abitibi Ltd., Hiram Walker and Trizec Corporation.

The storm was a combination of too much debt at high interest rates and sagging property values in all three financial capitals at once. Many other real estate empires disappeared too.

Not surprisingly, the three Reichmann brothers—Albert, Paul and Ralph—had a falling-out over the catastrophe. But what is interesting is that they have come back more than others. That makes them a rags-to-riches-to-rags-to-riches story.

"We always believed in hard work, but we also believed that our success in the past was a matter of good fortune. Then we had bad fortune," said Albert's oldest son, Philip Reichmann, in an interview with me in June 2007. "For our generation it has meant we have a lot less money than we would have had if 1992 hadn't happened, but it has been a great opportunity to do our own thing and make our own money. And doing things for yourself makes a big difference."

Philip met me in a glitzy boardroom in First Canadian Place, the building his father and two uncles erected in the 1970s with record-breaking speed. He is gentle and jolly, and patiently answered my questions. His father avoided the press, and Paul talked occasionally with me, once giving me a tour of Canary Wharf and brunch. The brothers were cloaked in dark suits and hats and ran their affairs through private companies. At our interview, Philip wore a yarmulke. His shirt was pale blue and open-necked.

"At O&Y Properties we ran a public company for eight years, so disclosure and openness is not an issue nor a problem," said the Canadian-raised Philip.

Philip and his dozens of cousins grew up together as neighbours, cloistered in a north Toronto neighbourhood where their Orthodox parents could walk to services at their synagogue.

Their lives changed little because of the collapse, but the nasty headlines and aftermath were very hard on the three brothers. Their family had been the toast of the world's business community, a banking favourite. Suddenly, they had become pariahs and, worst of all, were unable to support many of their religious, educational and other causes. They had been hugely generous, and hundreds of organizations received Reichmann help annually.

"Nineteen ninety-two was more difficult for them, the first generation, than for the rest of us," said Philip. "It strained the relationship."

The brothers are older now. Paul became ill from an infection he caught in a hospital in early 2007 but continues to aggressively invest in real estate deals. Albert is semi-retired and spends much of the winter in Miami, and Ralph is busy, with his two sons, building Olympia Tile, which is Canada's largest manufacturer, wholesaler and retailer of tile products.

"We are all shareholders in that company. Ralph's routine hasn't changed even though he's only five years younger than Paul," said Philip. "He has lots of energy."

There are now many more Reichmanns too. The 3 brothers had 15 offspring and dozens of grandchildren. Those children's and grandchildren's lives were also permanently altered in 1992, but not necessarily in a damaging way. Instead of growing up as well-heeled trust-fund kids, working for Olympia & York, they have all become well educated and are in a variety of businesses.

"Post-1992, we all went off in our own directions," Philip said.

Ralph has built the tile business, and Paul has created a new real estate conglomerate on a smaller scale. But the second generation has also been busy. So far, the leaders of the pack have been two sets of cousins—one each from Paul's and Albert's families. They have created sizable companies that are doing large-scale business.

Philip joined forces with Frank Hauer, Paul's son-in-law, and the two built a real estate empire out of the ashes of Olympia & York. They are now in private equity investments. And Paul's son Barry and Albert's son-in-law Lawrence (Eli) Koenig are relatively large players in retirement residences.

In 1993, Philip Reichmann and Frank Hauer renamed Olympia & York as O & Y Properties Inc. and immediately approached the banks that had seized the Reichmanns' properties. Their selling point was that the banks did not know how to manage these buildings they now owned, while the Reichmanns did, because they had owned them.

"We ended up managing about 8 or 9 million square feet of office space in Canada. Most were Olympia & York buildings, and we were able to persuade the lenders to allow us to continue to manage the buildings," said Philip. "In 1993, we started managing properties for those who took over from the banks—our properties and others. These included pension funds and young companies like RioCan Real Estate Investment Trust. We managed the buildings for them until they got big enough to manage themselves."

Philip and Frank plowed their profits back into buying more buildings, which were much cheaper after the meltdown. In 1996, they went public in order to buy Camdev Corporation, formerly Campeau Corporation, from lender Citibank and a Chinese investor who did not get along with his partners. They merged the operations into O & Y Properties Corp.

Eventually, they were able to buy back the Reichmanns' trophy, First Canadian Place, then they turned the whole company into an REIT, or real estate investment trust. In 2005, they sold it for $2.1 billion to Brookfield Properties (run by Jack Cockwell and his managers, who had also run the Peter and Edward Bronfman empire, which had been Reichmann partners).

In 2007, Philip and Frank left real estate for a while and opened ReichmannHauer Capital Partners, a private equity company that manages their money and raises money from other wealthy investors. They buy mid-cap companies that make lots of money. Their first purchases included the Allan Candy Company, from Cadbury Adams, and the Minacs call centres in partnership with India's Birla family. More recently, they purchased Black's Photography from Fuji Canada.

"Sorry to be crass, but [making money is] our objective. We are not interested in real estate because we feel it is overvalued right now. The pension funds are happy making 5% or 6% returns and pay more than a private company which cannot compete at that level of return," he said. "If there's another collapse, then perhaps real estate will be a good buy."

Philip's greatest accomplishment is that he now does business, along with other Reichmanns, with banks all over the world, including those that lost money in the 1992 collapse.

"We are proud we were able to restore a high level of relationship," he said. "That's very important to us."

While Philip was rebuilding, so were Barry Reichmann and Lawrence Koenig. They grew the family's nursing-home chain into Canada's largest, and the country's 275th-largest, corporation, called Retirement Residences REIT. In 2006, it had $1 billion in revenues and $2.8 billion in assets, some losses and 24,500 employees. In 2007, the Public Sector Pension Investment Board bought 100% of it for $2.8 billion.

Uncle Paul is also a major shareholder in IPC US REIT, a Canadian-listed real estate trust fund involved in dozens of U.S. office buildings, with a stock market value of nearly $600 million in 2007. It had $208 million in revenues in 2006, $1.5 billion in assets and $62 million in profits.

"Paul may be weakened, but he is still very active and aggressive," said Philip.

What's interesting is that the Reichmanns moved on with the few assets that were not seized by banks, as well as by capitalizing on their reputation, built over decades.

But this is nothing new, in fact. The three brothers and their parents barely escaped the Holocaust, fleeing Europe for Morocco just one step ahead of Hitler's Nazis. They built the world's biggest real estate fortune, lost it and are again rebuilding.

The collapse was ubiquitous and was no one's fault, said Philip.

"I rear-ended a Volvo in Toronto recently with my Jag," he said. "Naturally, it's always your fault when you hit someone from behind, which I did. But the driver in the car came out yelling at me and going on and on. I just said to her, 'I didn't mean to do this and my car's smashed too. So let's just calm down and solve the problem.' That's how you move on," he said.

RAI SAHI

In 1971, Rai Sahi landed in Montreal from the Punjab, and worked for $1.15 an hour unloading railway boxcars.

"My brother, an engineer with Northern Electric, sponsored me in. I didn't want to come to Canada, but he said, 'You work five to seven years, save $100,000 and go home and live well,'" Sahi told me in an interview in 2006.

Sahi was underemployed in Canada initially, then moved to Kingston to sell life insurance. He had earned a degree from India in economics, political science and English, and had been a banker there, but the credentials were not useful initially, so while selling insurance for the next five years, he spent his spare time earning a Certified General Accountant licence.

Then, in 1976, he joined the Bank of Montreal as a loans officer and quickly sped up its ranks, working in Toronto and Calgary. In 1982, he left to be in business for himself.

He is now CEO and owns 48% of Morguard Corp. of Mississauga, which had $387 million in revenues in 2006, $2 billion in assets, profits of $58 million and 1,200 employees, according to the *Financial Post*'s FP500 magazine in 2007. Morguard's portfolio includes billions more in commercial, industrial, office, retail and residential properties, and its affiliated companies and subsidiaries also provide real estate services ranging from acquisition strategies to leasing and day-to-day management to clients such as pensions, individuals, banks and corporations.

Sahi is also CEO and the largest shareholder of Tri-White Corp., which owns various tourist assets, and ClubLink Corp., the largest private owner and operator of golf courses in Canada. In 2006, ClubLink made $33 million net income on revenues of $137.8 million on its three dozen courses, which include Glen Abbey in Oakville, Ontario. Sahi also owns 11 car dealerships in addition to his nest of public property companies.

"Rai is the most successful Indian businessman in Canada," said Toronto consul general of India Satish Mehta, who introduced us. "His holdings are considerable."

Morguard's offices are in the middle of Mississauga's suburban "City Centre," which is a cluster of tall condos, office towers, an arts and conference centre and a gigantic shopping mall with a sea of parking.

Sahi has a booming voice and a fierce demeanour. He has bought and sold businesses, waged proxy battles, made hostile takeovers, thrown out managements and culled assets with the alacrity of a Wall Street raider. He also plays a competitive game of tennis every morning to keep in shape. But his golf game, despite ClubLink, is lousy, and he says so.

"I try to play golf, but I'm not the right personality for it," he said.

He acquired 70% of Tri-White in a hostile takeover. It was a real estate play.

"Two objectives of mine are to work at projects I enjoy and I'm not interested in letting the whole world know who I am. I keep as low-key as possible. There is no upside to bragging. It only attracts the attention of undesirable people," he said.

But Sahi is a master of many trades and has, by most accounts, made money at just about everything he's turned his hand, or head, to. In 1982, he left banking to join a partnership that bought a failing enterprise that needed fixing.

"I went into the manufacturing business. We made toothpaste tubes and aerosol cans, and we changed lots of things, cut costs, raised sales and sold that for a profit," he said.

In 1983, he bought Consolidated Fastfrate Transport.

"Then I bought a trucking business and added to that Kingsway Transport, bought from [future prime minister] Paul Martin, who was a major shareholder at the time. He stayed a partner for two years before he went into politics. I bought it from his company, Canada Steamship," he said.

(The two remained friends, and years later, in 2005, Martin appointed Sahi to the Canadian Broadcasting Corporation board of directors, which raised eyebrows because Morguard was the CBC's Ottawa landlord.)

Sahi turned around Martin's trucking business and then became the industry consolidator, buying up companies for the next five years. By 1988, Kingsway Transport had become Canada's third-largest trucking company, and he sold it to Federal Industries. During that deal, he met another big player who became helpful.

"Federal Industries transportation group bought the trucking business in 1989 for $70 million. Gordon Capital was involved, run by Jimmy Connacher. We hit it off and he came onto Morguard's board and stayed on it as a director until the end of 2006, when he turned 70 years of age," he said.

Jimmy Connacher became a mentor. He is the legendary dealmaker who helped the Peter and Edward Bronfman empire become a giant, then rebuild under new management and become the Brookfield Asset Management monolith. Connacher had the moxie and connections on Bay Street that would be helpful to Sahi.

In 1990, Sahi bought 23% of Acklands Limited, a struggling auto-parts maker, then turfed out the management.

"In 1991, I became Acklands' chairman and CEO. It was losing $12 million to $14 million a year with $300 million revenues. We built it up over four or five years to $1 billion in sales, then bought 35 more companies and integrated them. We then sold Acklands to

Grainger [W. W. Grainger Inc.] in December 1996 for $400 million and it operated as Acklands-Grainger," he said.

He then turned to real estate because it was a "capital play" and less people- or technology-oriented. He understood the nuances of financing, valuations and leasing, and his last job at the bank had been in that sector.

"Manufacturing is very tough now. You have to compete with the Far East or you can't survive," he said. "The trucking business is also tough. It involved working with 7,000 Teamsters. It was a great experience, I must say."

"In India, I met a fellow who owns a computer-assembly business that he was phasing out because he said his labour is now $2.80 an hour and China's is 80 cents an hour. I can't compete with China. If he can't compete, we have no hope," he added.

He acquired pieces of real estate outfits through initial public offerings or listed entities. Then he took on managements who, he believed, weren't doing their jobs.

"Some people call these hostile takeovers, but that's too negative," he said. "I am not hostile to shareholders, but helpful. I'm opposed to incompetent management.

"I bought companies—a London Life company with shopping centres, Revenue Properties. Morguard Corporation, from MetLife. It all gave us the platform we needed," he said. "We manage, through subsidiaries, $8 billion in real estate, for 30 pension funds and for ourselves. We own more than $3 billion in real estate through Morguard. We also bought Goldlist Properties and turned it into Morguard Residential."

He said his success is due to the fact that he has always invested in "simple businesses" and stayed away from those that are technologically complex or cyclical.

"Resource businesses are so cyclical. You own an oil field, get rich, then there's the inventory to replace. It requires different skills that I do not have," he said.

Sahi's work ethic is another factor. His parents owned a farm, and he was the youngest of four brothers who got up every morning at 4 a.m. to do their chores. But there are signs of a slight slowdown.

"I used to get involved in everything and now only in major issues. I have a team of competent people. Real estate is a slow, boring business. It takes five years to build a building, and you need a lot of patience," he said. "In Canada we're in every major city. We are the largest landlord in Ottawa, including the CBC head office. My view is that there will be more selling than buying. Prices are pretty high."

Sahi and his wife have two children, both of whom live in New York City. Their son, Neal, is studying at NYU, and their daughter, Angela, is a Certified Public Accountant with Ernst & Young there and "loves it," he said.

"What is work? It's not laying bricks for a few hours. Every successful person works most of his working hours. It's an ongoing thinking process. I enjoy it. I also enjoy a little golf and play tennis every morning," Sahi said. "I don't go out to entertainment venues often. I get enough entertainment at work. My view of retirement is you just wait to die. I enjoy what I do. Why wouldn't I want to do this until I can't?"

And like other successful people, it has never been about the money.

"I had no aspiration or desire to get rich, just to have a decent job and live a decent life."

AGRIBUSINESS

The Industrial Revolution and then the information revolution have relegated farming to a small percentage of the economy, and very few family farms exist anymore. But there is still money in food: growing it, transporting it, raising it or processing it. And Canada remains one of the world's great breadbaskets, blessed with acreage the size of several European countries for growing and grazing.

The result is that there have been fortunes made from farming and food processing, and food's future is rosy indeed. The world economic boom has generated huge demand for food and for crops to make ethanol. The result is that farmland and commodities such as corn or wheat have begun escalating in price along with minerals, metals and energy. The price of corn, for instance, has shot up fourfold over two years due to huge subsidies offered by Washington, Ontario and other governments to produce ethanol from corn. This policy initiative is designed to reduce dependence upon foreigners for energy, but it has also contributed to the agricultural sector's future prospects.

Today's successful "men of the soil" make their fortunes wearing suits in fancy offices in big cities. Agricultural entrepreneurs invest millions in high-tech equipment and in leading-edge research into biotechnologies that may create test-tube nutrition or emissions-free fuels made from vegetation as well as from agricultural waste products. All four profiled here have carved out niches in a difficult sector.

Entrepreneur Ken Field buys most of the corn grown in Ontario and Quebec to make ethanol, as well as commercial alcohol used in fragrances or as ingredients. The Richardson family has owned one of the country's biggest agribusinesses for generations, along with financial assets, and continues to expand. Montreal's Saputo family is Canada's biggest milk buyer and has carved out big pieces of the cheese and yogurt markets in North America, Argentina and Europe. And the legendary McCains of New Brunswick buy more potatoes and sell more french fries, along with other frozen products, than any other food business in the world.

KEN FIELD

Ken Field didn't realize his dream to become a comedy writer, but his consolation prize was better than most people dream of: he's one of Canada's most successful entrepreneurs.

"My friends all went to California to become comedy writers. I wanted to go too. But when I told my father, he said, 'First of all, you've never been to California and you don't know anything about it. Two, you'll come back and be bums. And three, you're not so funny,'" he recalled.

His pal Lorne Lipowitz changed his name to Lorne Michaels and went on to a great career as the creator of *Saturday Night Live*. Another friend became a Hollywood writer. Field ended up in law school in Toronto.

"I never wanted to be a lawyer, but I went because it was a good place to keep warm for three years," he said.

The story illustrates all you need to know about Ken Field. He is a sunny man who has been able to turn adversities into advantages. In business, he has made fortunes in real estate, oil exploration, industrial alcohol and now ethanol. His company, Commercial Alcohols Inc., based in Toronto, is Canada's biggest bottler, packager and distributor of industrial alcohol for use in health care, perfumes and manufacturing. Field began by investing $100,000 in converting the Jerusalem artichoke into industrial alcohol as a tax-shelter play in 1989.

But by 2007, Field's company had become the country's biggest single buyer of corn and its biggest producer of ethanol. It now produces one million litres of ethanol daily and will double production every two years.

"I'm in the oil business again," he quipped over lunch.

Ethanol is a hot commodity south of the border and in parts of Canada because it reduces emissions and provides a lucrative cash crop for farmers. And Field was, as usual, ahead of the curve.

"Our plant was only kept afloat thanks to a marginally profitable contract from Union Carbide. Six months later, the Gulf War started and the price of oil went through the roof. The Americans could not compete with us because they were making industrial alcohol out of crude oil, and we were making it out of corn, which was cheaper. So I bought Union Carbide's alcohol company for $50,000, and with it came 1,500 customers," he said.

Field then realized that there was no difference between industrial alcohol, vodka and ethanol. So he began selling output as vodka and also as ethanol. He landed a large contract with Sunoco in Ontario, the only Canadian gasoline chain that had "greened" its fuel by lacing it with 10% ethanol.

Field is also investing millions in search of the Holy Grail of energy production: the conversion into ethanol of plentiful cellulose, wood or grass. What is needed are enzymes that can efficiently break down these substances.

"The economy is going to become a biotech economy and replace oil as a feedstock to make synthetics, plastics and transportation fuels," he said.

Such a breakthrough not only will reduce environmental degradation but will also have beneficial geopolitical implications, by making the world less dependent upon the troublesome Middle East and Russia, he said.

And if anybody can pull this off, it will be Ken Field, who has made more money at more things than most, and has also overcome obstacles that sideline most.

In 1992, he had a skiing accident, slamming into a tree, severing all the nerves in his left arm and losing its use. Years later, Field plays tennis with his left arm in a sling and serves by balancing the ball on his racket and tossing it up. He also plays golf and routinely breaks 100.

"All day long I have lots of pain, so if I happen to wince it's because I'm having 30 seconds of intense pain," he said. "But I stay busy and have fun and enjoy life. As long as I'm not thinking about it, I'm okay."

He credits his parents for his grit. His mother's nickname was "Sweet Sue" and his father was an entrepreneur.

"They were amazing, real entrepreneurs who never gave up," he said.

His father had a photofinishing business, and worked long hours. The business went sour and the bank called in the loans.

"He told my mother, 'If they don't let me off the hook, I have to go out of business.' He was turned down," he said. "I was a baby, and my mother took me and went to see the bank manager. She wanted to know why he would not lend her husband more money. The manager told her that he had no collateral."

"So she asked him, 'Who cleans the floors in this place? I'll sign a paper saying that if my husband doesn't pay you, I'll clean the floors or I'll work for whoever does the cleaning to pay back our loan.' He extended my father's credit," said Field. "And the business thrived until he retired."

Like his mother, Field never took no for an answer. After law school, he worked for a law firm specializing in real estate.

"I liked that business but knew that practising law wasn't for me," he said. "While I was a young lawyer, I began building houses with a cousin who was an engineer. It was fun and we made money. But, tragically, my cousin died."

Field's talent was spotted by a client, Toronto tycoon George Mann, and he hired him as an executive vice-president. He didn't stay long, and at 28 years of age plunged into the house-building business again and a land partnership with British-owned Bramalea Consolidated Developments Ltd.

By 1971, he was vice-president but wasn't impressed with the Canadian management. The company's controlling shareholder was insurance giant Eagle Star, in the UK.

"The English investors didn't know what was going on. The people in Canada were running around taking money for themselves. It was a mess," he said. "I was asked to squire around the head of Eagle Star in Toronto, and we hit it off. He invited me to see him in London, and when he found out that my wife's family had money, he said, 'Buy us out.' That started the process, but I never used any of my in-laws' money."

At the same time, Field had other business interests. He developed a photofinishing process, using neon light and fibre optics, that he sold for several millions of dollars to Kodak. Then in 1972, at 30, he took that money and joined with partner Richard Shiff to buy Eagle Star's controlling interest of Bramalea in a deal that was probably one of the first leveraged buyouts in Canada. Once inside, he realized that Bramalea had great land but nothing else.

"The executives were giving themselves bonuses when the roof went on a house, before it even sold. It was crazy. I was vomiting," he said.

In no time it was war. Management issued an ultimatum to Field and his partner and threatened to resign.

"We accepted their resignations and, before they had time to think about it, immediately called a Toronto newspaper to announce that I was president, Shiff was chairman and everyone had quit. We kept all the secretaries and locked everyone else out. I was shaking in my boots," he said.

In 1972, Bramalea had $125 million in assets and debts to match. By 1988, it had become North America's fourth-largest real estate company, with $6 billion in assets and $140 million in profits annually. The company built Toronto-area landmarks like the Four Seasons Hotel, the suburb of Bramalea and the downtown Hudson's Bay Centre.

Along the way, Field also acquired large chunks of oil companies Corvette Resources Ltd., Barrington Petroleum Ltd. and Coho Energy Inc.

In 1986, his partner fell ill, so they felt they had to sell to Trizec Corp., which was owned at the time by the Reichmann and Bronfman Edper group.

"I said to my partner, 'How could you do this to me?' Part of the deal was I had to run the whole thing, and I never liked Trizec. We had competed with them over the years and they were never nice," he said. "They were buying land at the height of the market, and I said to them, 'You can't make it pencil [you can't make the numbers work]. I'm out of here.' I also didn't like the way they treated people and how they used $1 billion worth of our credit lines and borrowed $1 billion more."

In 1989, Field cashed out for more than $100 million—just before the real estate recession felled Bramalea, the Reichmanns, the Bronfmans, Campeau and most others.

"It was heart-wrenching to see what happened. It was my baby," he said.

Field then benefited from the recession by investing his Bramalea windfall in RioCan, a real estate investment trust. It was buying shopping centres at fire-sale prices and pioneering the big-box store concept.

"It's been a 13% return for six or seven years," he said. "I'm also in the H&E REIT and was in O&Y's [Olympia & York's] REIT. I just loved the model."

Conversations with Field are always a treat. His enthusiasm is infectious and his outlook positive. He lives a frenetic life, enjoying work and visiting his three grown children and his grandchildren, who live in the United States.

"Life's a comedy and I love it all," he said.

WALLACE McCAIN

Wallace McCain is arguably Canada's most remarkable entrepreneur.

Beginning in 1957, he and his brother Harrison created global french fries and frozen food giant McCain Foods Limited, out of tiny Florenceville, New Brunswick. They also built Canada's largest trucking firm, Day & Ross.

But in 1995, Harrison fired Wallace, who was 65, when most people are ready to retire. Wallace McCain tried to buy out Harrison, but could not, and vice versa. So he did what comes naturally to a McCain: he built another giant. Now Wallace and his two sons operate Maple Leaf Foods Inc., which is larger than McCain Foods, and Wallace still owns one-third of McCain Foods.

"When he fired me, I said, 'I'm leavin' town,' and I began looking for another business," explained Wallace in an interview in his Toronto office in 2007. "My family and I decided it would have to be in Chicago—we love Chicago—or Canada or Australia. All my kids and grandchildren were going to move together."

Within months, McCain bought Maple Leaf, formerly Canada Packers Ltd., for $1.2 billion. In short order, he also acquired Schneider Corporation (JM Schneider Foods) for $515 million.

Harrison suffered from a lengthy illness, and by the time he died in 2004, the brothers had reconciled.

Wallace is now chair of Maple Leaf Foods and vice-chair of McCain Foods. Despite the brothers' feud, the McCain ownership structure did not permit forced buyouts or takeovers or liquidation to third parties. So nothing changed except that the two brothers stopped working—and fighting—together.

A McCain–Maple Leaf combination would be a food powerhouse that could realize some synergies and cost savings without causing product cannibalization.

"Should McCain go public? Yes. Will it? No. Should they merge? Yes. Will they? No," said Wallace. "I'd love to have someone convince the family, but I can't."

Wallace, like Harrison, is a stand-up guy with a short fuse. Both men, and two more brothers, were raised on hard work and the Bible. Suspicions are that their falling-out was probably a long time coming, given their competitiveness with one another.

Maple Leaf is Canada's 65th-largest corporation and in 2006 sold $5.89 billion worth of bakery and meat products all over the world. Its profits were $152.8 million, its assets $3 billion, and it had a workforce of 24,000. It is the largest frozen-bread baker in the United States. Wallace and his family own 33% of its stock. The Ontario Teachers' Pension Plan owns another 35%.

McCain Foods is Canada's 68th-largest corporation. Its sales were $5.56 billion in 2006, across 125 countries. The firm employed 20,000 people in 40 plants and sold 200 products. It has 75% of the world's french fries market and is the largest supplier to McDonald's globally. McCain's does not disclose its profits.

The only connection between McCain's and Maple Leaf is Wallace, and they are very different companies.

McCain Foods is 100% family-owned, but the only other family member involved in operations is nephew Allison McCain, who is chair. McCain's ownership is 33% Wallace, 33% Harrison's five children, and the rest divided among the nine children of two deceased brothers, Andrew and Robert.

By contrast, Maple Leaf, a public company, has three McCains firmly at the helm. Wallace's son Michael is CEO and son Scott, senior vice-president.

"McCain's has 15% of its assets in Canada and 85% outside the country, while Maple Leaf has the inverse, or 87% of its assets inside Canada and the rest outside," said Michael McCain in a separate interview with me in Toronto. "We are similar in size, but one is geographically diversified and product-concentrated and one is the opposite."

Michael had worked for the Florenceville outfit, but was also dismissed by his uncle Harrison while running its U.S. operations out of Chicago. He took over the helm at the moribund Maple Leaf 10 years ago and has turned it into a profitable, growing business. But it is a work in progress, notably due to the rising Canadian dollar.

"We are a Canadian-based, export-oriented manufacturer, and this is a challenge," he said. "So we are dealing with the currency issue, then we will, by 2009, be into acquisitions again."

Wallace, like Harrison, is a thoroughly gifted and energetic businessman. He is 77 years of age going on 30. He talks rapidly and has opinions on everything. When Wallace gets excited, every second word is a curse word.

"I learned how to swear milking a cow when I was a kid. Jesus. Just clean up the quotes for me, won't you?" he said during our interview.

Wallace and his family now call Toronto home and have a vacation spot in Nova Scotia. He does not miss Florenceville at all.

"I kept my house there but have slept there 4 nights in 12 years," he said.

Within months of leaving Florenceville in 1995, Wallace and his sons targeted Maple Leaf Foods, which was owned by British food conglomerate Hillsdown Holdings PLC. Initial negotiations were not going well until Wallace and his wife, Margaret, took a holiday in London.

"It was luck. Negotiations were going medium-rare and we were too far apart. I had no money. Remember, the [Ontario] Teachers' Pension Plan was willing to back me to buy McCain Foods, but that didn't happen, and all my money was tied up in McCain," he said.

"We were in London and going to the theatre in the afternoon. I was still licking my wounds and my wife says, 'Why not go to see Hillsdown?' She pressured me, to be honest. So I phoned the chairman—'Will you talk with me?' He said, 'Sure.' 'When?' 'Right now,'" he recalled.

The two discussed the deal all morning, then talks spilled into lunch. At 2 p.m., Wallace reminded the chairman that he had to take his wife to the theatre in the city, only to be assured he would get there on time.

"'She'll kill me,' I told him. He said, 'Relax.' Then he got his car and driver, drove me to the Dorchester Hotel, where we were staying, in time to go to the theatre. In the meantime, during the ride, I bought the company verbally," he said.

Michael was put in charge and rolled up his sleeves.

"The company was comatose and scared the hell out of us. We had only 24 hours to do our due diligence, but we figured we could fix it," said Michael. "It's been quite a journey, and we feel pretty good. Along the way we made 30 acquisitions in 12 years too."

The Schneider Corp. acquisition was complicated. Maple Leaf had launched a hostile takeover bid for the family company, lost it, then was able to buy it from the winning bidder.

This ability to roll with the punches distinguishes the McCains from others and was essential for success.

Wallace and Harrison's father, Baptist teetotaller Andrew McCain, exported seed potatoes. The two older brothers farmed, but Wallace and Harrison, the younger two, went to university. There were also two sisters, who did not work in the business.

"Harrison and I worked for the Irvings after we left college. After two years, we decided we wanted our own business and we looked at a lot of deals, such as buying seats on the Toronto and Montreal stock exchanges, but our brother Robert suggested we get into the frozen french fry business, which was just getting started in the States," said Wallace. "The idea came from him."

Going global was not the original plan, but it became a necessity.

"I'd be lyin' if I told you we had a vision to be a global company. We thought if we could sell across Canada, we would be doing really well," he said. "In our second year, in spring 1959, we harvested a bunch of peas and froze them. They were unsold and we were pretty squeezed and had to sell them. Somebody read in the newspaper that there was a shortage of peas in England. So Harrison made his first trip to England and sold them the lot, to a company called Eskimo. Our first french fries exports went to England too."

Export markets became a means of growing quickly, but they were also necessary in order to survive, the brothers discovered.

"The market was growing by 10% to 15% a year, and you have to move fast worldwide if you want to keep it. So we became consolidators," Wallace said. "We are still doing it and making dozens of acquisitions every year. Big ones."

The two brothers worked tirelessly and travelled constantly.

"One of us would start the business somewhere, buying to expand and buying everything we could get our hands on. We ended up in the loading, juice, dehydrator businesses, but are pretty much out of them all now," he said. "We went from country to country following customers like McDonald's or other opportunities."

They travelled so much that the company had two private jets. Every year Harrison ran a competition.

"He used to send me a note," Wallace recalled, "from the secretaries' travel information, that he called the 'away-from-home contest.' The winner was whoever had been away more than the other. We averaged 140 to 160 nights a year apiece. That didn't include day trips, to Montreal or Chicago or New York, in between."

Even so, the brothers managed to have nine children between them. I asked him how.

"Saturday nights," he shot back.

In order to manage their far-flung business from a tiny, remote town, the brothers decentralized the structure. They established free-standing entities in regions around the world. Local managers were deputized to buy rivals and grow the business at the same pace as the market increased.

"Florenceville was headquarters for Canada only. We ran the UK as a separate company and the same with the Dutch, French, Belgian, Russian, Polish, New Zealand, India, U.S. and Chinese operations. These are free-standing businesses, 100% owned by McCain," Wallace told me.

Rapid growth and acquisitions were financed out of profits, but the company was also "leveraged to the hilt," he said.

"We used the Bank of Nova Scotia exclusively. Ced[ric] Ritchie [former BNS chair] grew up seven miles away, and I used to call him my 'prize.' He did all our banking worldwide, and if we needed money we'd just call Ced," he said.

Naturally, there were currency and political risks, but the brothers escaped most catastrophes as a result of being in a rapidly expanding market category.

"Our first plant outside Canada was in England, and we decided to build another one there, to serve the Continent. We had two in Holland already. So we built a huge second plant. Then the currency [the British pound] took off and we couldn't sell our product to France. It was a hard squeeze on the British company, but the market in Britain grew so fast that it took up the slack and the plant worked out," he said.

The brothers' aggressiveness paid off in spades around the world, but so did other traits.

"My mother [Laura] was an Anglican who read the Bible every day, and that rubbed off. You've got to be ethical in all your dealings. Absolutely," he said.

The boys were also steeped in the Protestant work ethic.

"We always had something to do around the house," Wallace said. "Harrison was older than me, and he had a cow he made money with, so I wanted one. What a mistake. At 12 years of age, I had to milk that cow, half a mile away from home, every day, take the milk somewhere to hand-separate it, take the skim milk back to feed the calf and take the rest of the milk home—all before school started."

This upbringing imposed a personal discipline on the brothers that continued into adulthood.

"I made money, then I sold the calf and bought my first bicycle that way," he said.

The McCains and the Irvings played and worked together, but they also crossed swords in business.

"The old man, K.C. Irving, was personable—a real gentleman,

and a great salesman with an amazing memory," recalled Wallace.

Wallace went to university and was a pal of one of K.C.'s sons, Arthur, who was an usher at Wallace's wedding. They remained best friends until Arthur divorced his first wife, who was related by marriage to Wallace's wife.

There were also business tensions. Sparks flew after McCain dropped Irving as an oil supplier for its hundreds of trucks in the mid-1970s. In 1977, Irving lent millions to a McCain competitor, CM McLean Limited, so that McLean could expand in order to snare a McDonald's french fries contract. McLean was eventually gobbled up by the Irvings, pitting the McCains and the Irvings directly against each other. Irving also got into the trucking business in a bigger way.

The McCains fought back and in 1980 sued McLean for copyright infringement on its packages, forcing the Irvings to rename their brand. And in 1983, the McCain American subsidiary blew the whistle on the Irvings to Washington trade officials, sparking an inquiry into charges that Cavendish Farms was dumping frozen potatoes onto the U.S. market.

Today, the two empires have made their peace.

Allison McCain, Andrew's son, has worked around the world for the company. A diplomatic man, he replaced Harrison as chair of McCain's in 2002. Harrison's son, Mark, and Robert's son, Andrew, are also directors. None are officers.

"There's not one McCain in the company today," said Wallace. "We believe in getting the top management."

But the speed and alacrity on which the empire was built are missing, given the fractured ownership and the question of how to provide liquidity to heirs who want to cash out.

"Harrison and I made decisions quickly. We talked every day. There was no board, just the two of us. We would do our homework, but we had no board or partners. Public companies like Maple Leaf are slower, but it's easier to raise money, the governance is better and you have to show your underwear every day, so you had better be good. I'd love McCain to go public. There would be a lineup to buy its shares."

THE RICHARDSONS

In June 2007, the Richardsons of Winnipeg celebrated their family's 150th anniversary in business. This clan has become Canada's most enduring family empire and has been able to build without nepotism, squabbling or division.

"We're always putting the business and the people in the business ahead of the family interest," said Hartley Richardson in an interview with me in 2007.

Hartley Richardson became president and CEO in 2006 of the family's founding and holding company, James Richardson & Sons, Limited. A family member has run things since 1857, including a 27-year stint by Hartley's grandmother Muriel, who ran the empire until her two sons were old enough to take over.

"I describe my role as running a relay race," Hartley said. "You've been handed the baton and you run hard and you put a team around you because you want to finish the race ahead of where you started, and in the lead. That requires you to work with the best people you can find and support management. This keeps us focused on our guiding principles."

James Richardson & Sons is one of Canada's largest privately owned enterprises and is involved in financial services, real estate, resources and agriculture. In 2007, its total annual revenues were $3.5 billion, making it one of the country's 100 largest corporations.

"We're a Canadian business doing business globally in 50 countries, and we're still growing and see opportunities here," said Hartley.

The Richardson share of the grain business is still western Canada's largest privately owned segment, with 18% market share. The family's Pioneer Grain employs more than 3,000 people, who operate hundreds of elevators, terminals and a fleet of ships, and are involved in other agribusinesses.

In February 2007, the family launched a $1.8-billion takeover bid to buy Agricore Limited and merge its private grain business with the public company. But American rivals outbid them.

"We would have loved to acquire it, but in the end we're pleased. We acquired US$250 million of assets, grew our core business by 50% [in revenues] and retained 100% private ownership," said Hartley.

Family members who are directly involved day to day in Richardson business interests are Hartley, his brother David (international agriculture), cousin Royden (financial services in Toronto), cousin Jim (Tundra Oil & Gas), cousin Carolyn Hursh (non-executive chair of the holding company) and cousin Kris Benidickson (director and trustee of the family foundation).

By 2007, there were 11 members of the fifth generation, or G5s, as they call themselves, some fourth-generation members and 28 G6s. But this is a family business that is not run by family members. That is part of the secret of their success.

"We have independent directors on our parent company and all our operating company boards," said Hartley.

The family governance is a separate matter.

"Carolyn works at overseeing the family, and I work at running and overseeing the business. We work as a team. We talk a couple of times a week. She's based in Calgary but is here in Winnipeg a lot," he said.

Hartley's father was George Richardson, who ran the enterprises for years. Carolyn is the oldest child of the late James Richardson, George's older brother, who won three federal elections as a Trudeau Liberal, then eventually became disillusioned and sat as an independent.

The clan's longevity is unique and rooted in some effective guiding principles.

"We have non-family members running our operations," explained Royden in an interview in 2005. "This has been a good policy. Some families have problems because you can't fire a family member who's doing a poor job at running something. So we avoid that issue."

Besides such sensible governance policies, the Richardsons are also imbued with a dynastic ethos.

"Being a member of a family like this is about discipline, about responsibility, about suppression of ego. If not, it would blow apart," said Royden. "We have stuck together. Of course, that's not to say that we don't have disagreements from time to time."

The dynasty meets quarterly, coincident with board meetings, said Hartley.

"We believe in communication, the shareholders being family members. We have started holding a family conference, called the 'R Conference,' which brings together all generations. We host an interactive and fun environment over a weekend. Jim, Royden and I will make business presentations to update members," he said.

The Richardson fortune predates the country. The first James Richardson was an Irish orphan who immigrated to Canada in 1823. He apprenticed with a tailor in Kingston, Ontario, and, so the story goes, fell into grain trading by accident when his customers could not pay cash but would give him wheat, barley and oats instead.

He soon learned there was more money cutting grain-brokerage deals than cutting cloth. Between 1860 and 1864, he made his first fortune selling grain to upstate New York granaries during the U.S. Civil War.

In 1880—three years before the Canadian Pacific Railway reached Winnipeg—he sent emissaries out west to sign up farmers to grow grain for his business. Three years later, Richardson made the first shipment of western Canadian grain to Europe via the Great Lakes and the Welland Canal. His firm then sold its services through-out the Prairies and expanded into storage as well as shipping.

Winnipeg boomed before the First World War, and the Rich-ardsons were the world's biggest wheat merchants, exporting most of the grain harvested alongside the nation's spanking new railway. At the same time, the Winnipeg Commodity Exchange became big-ger and more important than Chicago's Board of Trade, thanks to the Richardsons and the other grain barons who lived in fancy mansions along the Assiniboine River in Winnipeg.

But the Depression changed all of that. Collapsed prices led to a farmers' revolt in Canada, as wheat plummeted to the same price as a bushel of sawdust. The Richardsons were resented, along with the other grain merchants. In the 1930s, the Canadian federal government established the Canadian Wheat Board to prop up prices so that farmers did not go bust. The monopoly purchase of all the country's wheat and other grains completely eliminated the grain trade that had made the Richardsons so wealthy. The Board also stored, handled, transported and exported grains.

Other grain merchant families, like the Gooderhams (who turned their grain into liquor), cashed in their chips, but the Richardsons remained and expanded into specialized grain-handling services and value-added products, plus other businesses such as investment banking.

In 1996, the family's traditional brokerage firm, Richardson Greenshields, was sold for $480 million to the Royal Bank of Canada's brokerage, RBC Dominion Securities. Then, in 2002, the family repositioned itself by launching Richardson Financial Group. Its CEO is Sandy Riley, an experienced executive from Investors Group, and it owns two entities. Richardson Capital Limited is a private equity firm with $1 billion invested in 14 Canadian enterprises along with partners such as Stephen Bronfman and Leonard Asper. The Group also owns a wealth-management firm, Richardson Partners Financial Limited, which it launched in 2004 and which by 2007 was managing $7 billion in client assets.

The family is also involved in the oil sands and in conventional oil production across western Canada through various public and private entities. And it is involved in real estate. Besides owning most of the buildings around Portage and Main in downtown Winnipeg, the Richardsons are investors in Kingstreet Capital, a large development company run by Jon Love, son of the Don Love who built Oxford Development into a giant. Kingstreet was bought by a pension fund after the real estate recession in 1989.

The Richardson longevity is unique and based on loyalty. For instance, Royden remained in Toronto after the brokerage firm was sold.

"Back in 1996, my three kids were happy in school in Toronto, and there are way too many Richardsons running around in Winnipeg. That was the bottom line. I figured I could add value to the family here, not in Winnipeg. So I stayed, and it's worked out pretty well," he said.

Hartley is based in Winnipeg for a variety of reasons.

"As long as we're actively engaged in the agricultural business, Winnipeg is a very good place to be. Our company Tundra Oil has operations in Winnipeg. Sandy Riley is based in Winnipeg. Private equity is in Toronto and Montreal. We find we can work very well from here, can attract good people. Being in the centre of the country, I can go to Calgary, Vancouver, Toronto, Montreal, New York, Chicago for the day. It gives us the opportunity to step back and really look at things without being caught up in the near-term issues," he said.

The result is that the Richardson story is unmatched.

"This is a sophisticated family," Royden said, "and we know we must stick together. That's been the secret."

LINO SAPUTO SR.

Emanuele (Lino) Saputo Sr., another exceptional self-made success, started a business in 1954, two years after emigrating from Italy. He bankrolled his father, Giuseppe, who was digging ditches in Montreal but had been a top-notch cheesemaker back home.

"I knew he could do much better for himself, so with my $500 I'd saved we started making cheese in a corner we rented at a downtown cheese factory," Lino Saputo Sr. said in a *Financial Post* interview.

Without formal education, Lino mastered the world of business and is now chair of the Saputo Group Inc., Canada's 92nd-largest corporation, with a market value of $5 billion in 2007, revenues of $4.8 billion and 9,500 workers.

Lino Sr. is also the family patriarch, with dozens of relatives who also share in the company's success as well as in other investments.

"My father is successful because he is very optimistic, has an incredible amount of energy and has street smarts and common sense," said Lino Jr., CEO of Saputo Group, in an interview with me in his Montreal offices in 2007. "I became CEO in 2004, and my father is chair. But he describes himself as my least expensive consultant."

Lino Sr. was the fourth of eight children of Sicilian immigrants. Their fledgling business boomed along with the population of Montreal's Little Italy. Initially, Giuseppe made 10 kilograms of cheese per day and Lino delivered them on his bicycle. Within the first few months, the family bought its first truck, and by 1957 the family owned a factory.

Worldwide, the Saputo Group is one of the 20 biggest dairy products producers and North America's third-largest.

"I have milk in my veins," said Lino Jr. "I grew up in the business, and at 13 years of age I washed the cheese vats, made deliveries. I love it."

Family is important to the Saputos. Lino Sr. had 7 siblings who shared in the business and helped in the early days. They, in turn, had 24 children, but most were not involved in the business as time went on.

"My dad was the driver, but he couldn't have done this without his family's help. But one of the big issues we had was that most family members had not been active for 20 years," he said.

"One of the fears was that if something happened to him, family members would have to jump back into the business, which would not have been good for the employees or management. Another issue was they needed a way to cash out if they didn't like the way things were run. So we went public. It was also an opportunity to put a really professional management in place," said Lino Jr.

The Saputo Group sold shares to the public in 1997, when it generated $500 million in revenues, or one-tenth the revenues for

2007. The stock has gone up 20% per year before dividends, which are paid to all shareholders annually.

Some family members have cashed out. In 2007, Lino Sr. and his three children—Lino Jr., Joe and Nadia—owned 34% of Saputo stock and the rest of the family 25%.

Joe owns the Montreal Impact soccer team and has been developing the sport throughout Canada for the past 20 years. Nadia owns a florist shop and is a party planner in Montreal. The rest of the cousins are also entrepreneurs.

"My father also formed Petra, which is a pension plan for the family which depends on profits from a different industry. In the 1970s and 1980s, it went into real estate," he said. "Various members of the extended family are shareholders with us in Petra."

In 2004, Petra, an operating real estate company, paid $240 million to buy 80% of Place Victoria, the Montreal Stock Exchange complex. It also owns 2 million square feet of industrial and office space plus three hotels.

Lino Sr.'s holding company is called Jolina Capital Inc. ("Jolina" is an acronym for Joe, Lino and Nadia.) Jolina owns TransForce, one of Canada's biggest trucking companies, which Lino Sr. helped turn around, and is now involved in the financially troubled lumber industry through Tembec Inc. and Arbec Forest Products Inc.

"Our dad has great financial backing and 50 years' business experience, so we don't question what he invests in, because he knows what he's doing," said Lino Jr.

Of course, Saputo has had challenges, notably in the 1960s, when there were allegations that a potential merger partner in the U.S. had links to organized crime. The press also said that Lino Sr. was reportedly beaten up in a restaurant one evening by unidentified individuals.

"These were exaggerated," said Lino Jr. "There were some scuffles and competition was tough in those days. Being Sicilian and successful always means to some people those links must exist, but my father just said to everyone, 'It means we have to prove ourselves,' and turned it into a motivation."

Lino Jr. is a handsome and friendly person who travels the world visiting the company's 46 plants in 5 countries and looking for new acquisitions.

"It's a great company, and it will grow quite dramatically in the future," he said.

The Saputo Group could accommodate a $2-billion takeover because its debts are so low and its profits so high, some $192 million in 2006, he said.

"But we are not motivated by becoming the biggest, but by the right asset, in the right place, which is the right size," he said.

The company has gone from making cheese to processing milk for other purposes as well. It takes about nine litres of milk to make one kilo of cheese, and the by-product is whey, which used to be discarded. Now whey is marketed as an ingredient used in infant formulas, yogurt, protein and lactose, a sugar replacement. Roughly 50% of Saputo's sales are retail or brand-name food and cheese items, and 50% are sold as private-label items or as ingredients.

Saputo has also benefited as a ranking member of "Quebec Inc.," with support from pension giant Caisse de dépôt et placement du Québec, the Société générale de financement du Québec and National Bank. For instance, Saputo Group garnered provincial help in obtaining the venerable Quebec-based Culinar Bakery, outbidding U.S.-based Interbake Foods, which makes Wonder Bread and Hostess Twinkies.

That 1999 deal took the company from being strictly a food processor selling to businesses (it makes about one-third of the mozzarella sold in Canada to pizzerias and institutions) to being a purveyor of consumer snack foods, soups, cookies and cakes.

In return, Lino Sr. and the family have been loyal to Quebec no matter which party is in power, and also philanthropic and community-spirited, supporting cultural and sporting events. In 2005, Saputo added former Quebec separatist premier Lucien Bouchard to its board of directors. The family stays out of partisan politics.

Lino Sr.'s advisor and confidant in these and other deals has been National Bank former chair André Bérard, who is on the boards of Saputo companies. Both men retired in 2004 but have been active ever since. They are also personal friends and can be seen often at Saputo's luxurious golf course, Golf Saint-Raphaël. Lino Sr. is also a charmer, comfortable in English, French and Italian. He collects vintage Cadillacs.

Roughly 35% of Saputo's sales are outside of Canada, and the addition of a large processor in Argentina enabled the company to export worldwide after it lost a subsidy case at the World Trade Organization following complaints by the U.S. and New Zealand.

"We needed subsidies to export to the United States from Canada because our supply management system makes our milk one of the most expensive in the world," he said. "So the way we exploit globalization is to buy platforms which do not need to be subsidized to export. So we bought Argentina."

"Exporting from our U.S. operations is difficult because milk prices there are volatile and trade on the Chicago Mercantile Exchange," he said. "We looked at Australia and New Zealand but bought in Argentina to supply those loyal customers we had developed in the U.S. at prices that were stable."

In 2001, Saputo acquired Dairyland, the largest western-based cooperative in Canada, which gave them procurement in Canada nationally.

"We are watching China closely, which is developing its dairy industry but is still a net importer, so it's a target market for us," he said. "Milk is heavily regulated around the world, and we are also growing our market in Europe through Germany."

The Saputo Group has created a winning formula that Lino Jr. describes as a "public entity with a family environment." He prides himself in knowing the first names of 80% of the 1,200 or so workers in the east-end Montreal plant.

"This is not an ego trip to me. I'm fortunate to have inherited a solid business and am a caretaker for the next generation—or the next CEO," he said.

RETAIL

Retail, farming and real estate often go hand in hand. In fact, some retail chains—such as Tim Hortons or McDonald's—are as much real estate empires and food conglomerates as they are fast food giants. This is because they decided, from inception, to own and operate the underlying real estate they occupied, rather than to merely pay rent. As their chains grew, so did their real estate portfolios, with locations on high-traffic intersections that have increased greatly in value over time.

Retail success, like real estate success, relies on traffic. But stores must do much more: they must be in the right place at the right time, mount smart marketing campaigns, then offer unique goods and services at fair prices. Costs must be controlled and, most importantly these days, retailers must be able to adapt quickly to meet fleeting consumer needs or wants.

Around 1986, the favoured retail model was the enclosed shopping mall, with big department store anchors and specialty stores in between. These monoliths were surrounded by parking lots for cars and, in addition to retail, contained outlets providing health care, beauty and government services. But in the mid-1990s, the anchors decided that they might be better off on their own, in free-standing buildings. This was the beginning of the "big box" retail parks.

The Internet has also had a profound impact on retailing. Most companies have adopted the bricks-and-clicks model to capture new, younger online consumers. Estimates in 2006 in the U.S. are that 80% of all purchases by under-18s are made online with credit cards. The same research suggested that by 2015, people of all ages will be using computers to the same extent as the younger generation. This will include e-shopping by baby boomers, who, for the most part, have to date been reluctant to give out their credit card information online to a website.

Already, the modern "shopping journey" includes searches on the Internet by consumers who will buy only in stores. They hunt for products or services by visiting competing retail websites, manufacturers' websites and consumer watchdog sites where products and providers are ranked, drubbed or applauded. The online shopping experience has broadened too, with the expansion of retail giants such as Amazon, which turned its bookstore into a virtual department store offering thousands more items. Another innovation has been eBay, which is really a retailer that sells goods by auction for a fee.

The vast array of offerings has, in essence, turned every consumer who surveys them into his or her own "buyer," in a professional sense. Buyers scour the world for new goods and services to put on their proprietors' store shelves. Today's e-shoppers can do the same and source the cheapest, best, most admired products from anywhere in the world, thanks to the Internet.

At the same time, people love to go to stores for experiences or to buy truly unique or heavily discounted goods. Wal-Mart has conquered the discount "space" in retail across North America and is also attacking the grocery and pharmacy businesses. This has forced many out of business or into the arms of consolidators, who must obtain the scale and reach of Wal-Mart's buying power in order to survive. In discount and grocery, size does matter, and Wal-Mart has used its clout to pioneer technologies such as electronic shelves that automatically send a signal to suppliers' warehouses when the weight of goods reduces, and to source from low-cost China.

Beginning in the 1980s, Wal-Mart, Home Depot, Costco, Sears, Gap and Nike moved aggressively into Canada. Their initial footholds were often obtained by acquiring established chains that were in trouble. But sometimes they just moved in and expanded rapidly. Whatever their tactics, they have triumphed over most large Canadian retailers, with the exception of Canadian Tire and three pharmacy chains. In groceries, the fight will be between newcomers Wal-Mart and Costco and established chains Sobeys, Safeway and Loblaws.

MARTHA BILLES

Martha Billes sits in the driver's seat of national icon Canadian Tire but lets professional managers do most of the steering.

And the journey has not been easy. She and her two brothers inherited a retail giant, but a series of succession battles have dogged the family for many years. Eventually, Martha Billes emerged as controlling shareholder, and the retail empire, on her watch, not only has warded off American rivals but has grown Canadian Tire into Canada's 44th-largest corporation, with $8.2 billion in sales in 2006, $5 billion in assets, $354.6 million in profits and 56,559 employees.

"We weren't the right mettle to be running a public company. My brother Freddy took business administration, but his personality wasn't appropriate for it. I took science, which was the wrong education. David's an engineer who is sought after, and excellent at it," she said to me in an interview. "None of us was cut out to run the company."

This realistic evaluation led to conflicts for a while but saved Canadian Tire from a fate that awaits most family enterprises when they share, then squabble or squander assets built by the first generation.

The company was started in 1922 as a repair garage by two brothers, Alfred J. and John W. Billes. They quickly expanded into selling tires, accessories and auto parts for do-it-yourselfers. In 1927, they incorporated their company and called it Canadian Tire because, according to Martha's father, Alfred, it "sounded big."

They eventually expanded by partnering with retailers across Ontario—some sold other products, and some took up the whole business model and adopted the Canadian Tire banner.

Going public followed, and several classes of shares were created with the IPO, resulting eventually in limited-voting "A" shares and voting "common" shares. The two brothers retained special voting shares to keep control.

The company now has 468 store operations. But Canadian Tire owns 75% of the sites (it rents the other 25% for lease to dealers), buys the merchandise and markets its brands. The company was also a marketing pioneer through the creation of Canadian Tire money, the first loyalty program in Canada to give customers coupons, with the look and feel of real money, toward future purchases.

While things hummed along in the stores and gasoline outlets, there were problems under the hood. The first crisis occurred in 1983 after Martha's uncle, John Billes, died and left his Canadian Tire shares to a series of charities.

"My brothers and I bought out the estate trust of my father's brother. My uncle, who had taken advice from one of Canada's financial institutions, made a huge mistake in his will by giving everything to charity but leaving only an income stream for his widow and kids as their inheritance," she said.

With each of Martha and her brothers, Fred and David, then owning 20% of the "common" shares, the siblings struck a shareholders' agreement that gave them each 20%, the dealers another 20% and the public 20%. The agreement stipulated that any change of control triggered a shotgun buyout for the remaining shareholders.

"When we had gone through that battle in 1983 together, I was of the belief—I was mistaken—that my brothers, at least Freddy, loved and really wanted to keep the company in the family.

I worked for that goal in 1983, then only a few years later, in 1986, he was marching to a totally different drummer," she said.

"Father had given us the shares for maintenance, not a free ride—to continue his job for him. So he was still alive, thrilled by the purchase of my uncle's shares, then devastated in 1986 when Freddy worked out a deal to sell the shares," she said.

Fred and David would sell some of their shares to the dealers' association but keep the total under 49%. It was an attempt to circumvent the 1983 "coattail" provision as well as the shareholders' agreement.

"In November 1986, the brothers signed the deal with the dealers, and my lawyer said, 'Martha you'd better climb on the bandwagon. You will be left with 20% out there and not even be on the board.' So I agreed to sell to the dealers," she said.

That December, the Ontario Securities Commission waded in and within a month had issued a stop-trading order against the dealers' offer.

"I was so elated by the OSC decision," she said. "The whole thing makes me seethe even now. That sale arrangement was just so wrong. The OSC decision said it was the most abusive transgression against shareholders' rights, motivated by cleverness and avarice to create an artificial transaction."

The attempted sale was triggered by the fact that David was uninterested in the company and its operations and Fred wanted out.

"It was a horrendous occurrence. My father was alive and living through all of this, and my dad said to me, at one point, 'Why don't you just sell and we'll start again.' This is a guy in his 80s. My dad said, 'I can get some of the boys together, the employees,'" she recalled. "I just decided to do whatever was necessary to keep the company going in the same direction."

The siblings sued one another and eventually signed a new shareholders' agreement. Just 10 years later, in 1997, potential problems started again when Fred decided to sell and Martha could not convince David to buy him out together with her in a manner that would be acceptable to the marketplace.

So she had to buy both of them out and she now owns 60% of the "common" special voting stock.

The siblings' relationship was strained after that. Fred died in May 2007.

"David's very aloof, [has] never gotten over what he calls my cheating him out of his shares in 1997," she said.

Martha was able to buy her brothers out because she had made money in the oil patch. She had left Toronto years before for Calgary's drier climate because she suffers from asthma and her son, Owen, suffers from allergies. She immediately got involved in Alberta's oil business and made a fortune in oil exploration. She also owned a half-interest in an oil-field-drilling servicing company at one point. She used that nest egg from those businesses, and borrowed funds, to take control of Canadian Tire.

"That was a huge turning point for Canadian Tire, because after I bought control, we had a much more focused board and the board caused management to, in turn, focus more clearly to create true strategic plans," she said.

A financial services arm had been created decades before and has grown into a profitable sideline. The retail design was further tweaked, taking into consideration competitors such as Costco, big-box warehouse stores, Home Depot and Wal-Mart.

"We had earlier tried warehouse stores but now concentrated on customer-service focus," she said. "Then we bought Mark's Work Wearhouse, a great company which has blossomed—a fantastic purchase."

Canadian Tire has also spun off an auto-parts chain, Part-Source, with 67 outlets, which is growing both through acquisition and internally, and the company remains one of the country's biggest petroleum distributors. But expansion attempts elsewhere are not in the cards.

"We had our nose bloodied twice in the U.S. and once in Australia. We came out of that [Australia] just barely whole but lost a lot of time and momentum with all three acquisition experiences. Canada has an awful lot to offer," she said.

Billes is active as a board member and is not exploring for oil any longer, but owns royalty-producing properties now.

"I am on two [Canadian Tire] committees but can't be on the audit or compensation committees because I'm controlling shareholder. I attend all the meetings, and have learned how to be outspoken and how to be quiet too," she said.

Her son, Owen, a member of the board, is going to be a Canadian Tire dealer and joined its training course in August 2007. Martha also has four stepchildren.

"Owen is of a perfect age to join the training for the other side of the game. We recruit guys in their late 30s and early 40s," she said.

Billes is also the driving force for Canadian Tire's philanthropy.

"One of the great pleasures of my life is to be chairman of our Canadian Tire Foundation for Families. We have programs which assist families in times of their greatest need, and in the past eight years we have disbursed $29 million," she said.

Martha stays quiet these days, after periods of unwanted publicity concerning several high-profile legal spats. But as one of the country's handful of female tycoons, she cannot disappear.

Perhaps taking on two brothers all her life helped hone her skills for the rough-and-tumble of the business world. But she credits the west.

"I went west and got involved in the oil patch. Someone asked about the fact that I was a woman on a board of directors, and the chairman replied, 'What woman? Martha's just one of the guys.' I've thought about this a bit, and I guess it's still a rather chauvinist society and you have to disappear into being one of the guys."

JEAN COUTU

It took 10 minutes for Jean Coutu to walk with me through his store on Ste-Catherine Street in Montreal because he stopped to talk with all the workers. We talked in a tiny upstairs office in June 2007, with windows overlooking the huge, colourful store. A pharmacist's smock hung on a coat tree, and he offered to put it on for effect. He's a marketer and made his offer with a wink.

Coutu is a very attractive, large personality who built his retail empire by combining the bedside manner of a kindly physician with the marketing savvy of a Madison Avenue professional. He is 80 but looks, and behaves, like a considerably younger man. His father, a doctor, lived to well into his 90s.

The Jean Coutu Group is Canada's 26th-largest corporation and in 2006 had $13 billion in sales, $6 billion in assets and $296 million in profits and was one of the country's biggest employers, with 47,115 workers. It dominates Quebec's pharmacy/convenience-store sector with 300 franchised outlets, and in 2007 it acquired 32% of Rite Aid Corp., with 5,100 stores in the United States and US$27 billion in sales. This chain became troubled in the latter half of 2007, but Coutu remained enthusiastic. However, many others predict that Rite Aid may bring about Coutu's downfall.

"Rite Aid is a strong third in the U.S., closing in on second," said the ebullient patriarch in our interview in the summer of 2007. "We've made about $500 million [capital gain] on the deal. Not bad."

By fall 2007, that gain had disappeared as sales and profits south of the border deteriorated. Coutu's mistake may have been to make a big acquisition. After all, his first entry into the U.S. marketplace had been successful because it grew organically. In 1986 he started with one store in New England and, through acquisitions and internal growth, built a profitable chain with 300 outlets. In 2005, Coutu Group took over the gigantic Eckerd chain but in 2007 swapped its 1,850 stores for 32% of Rite Aid in a deal worth US$3.4 billion.

"It was not what we wanted to have happen, and many people compare us to Canadian Tire or others that have failed in the U.S.," he said. "That's not true. We negotiated to buy Eckerd over the course of a year. It was a very good company, but what happened was during that time the competition hired away most of the good managers. So we did not get the staff we had hoped for. Now, with Rite Aid, we have a very good investment in the U.S."

Jean Coutu's story has always been about converting perceived setbacks into opportunities. His first challenge came during his second year of medical school, when he took on the dean of medicine after the grade required to pass was revised upward to 55% from 50%. Coutu took on the issue as a matter of principle on behalf of all the medical students—and lost. He said the dean flunked him because of his activism.

"They [the faculty] invited me to come back but I was cocky and said, 'It's finished.'" he said. "I was very hot-headed, but that was that."

He transferred his credits to the pharmacy faculty and finished in record time. Then he began working for small drugstores.

In 1953, his activism backfired again. He and three other managers in a chain of 18 outlets approached the owner to ask for shares, because they ran the most profitable operations.

"This was probably the most important thing in my business life," said Coutu. "He said, 'This is a family business and it will always stay a family business.' Three months later, the three of us left."

He sold pharmaceuticals for a year, then got into a 50-50 partnership with a pharmacist cousin. Jean would put up his time and the cousin, his capital. Two stores later, Coutu was putting in 75-hour weeks.

"My wife said I was not paid enough for all those hours and my accountant said the same, so I went to my cousin to ask for more. He refused," he said. "So I quit. My cousin ended up hiring three people to replace me."

He got $16,000 for his half and within days was offered a small pharmacy in Montreal. It had $17,000 in debts and gross revenues of only $73,000 a year. But Coutu's marketing moxie took over and he created promotions that immediately doubled revenues. By 1968, he owned eight stores.

"I bought more stores because, you see, I really like people," he said. "I could not keep increasing people's salaries with just one store, so I needed to buy more stores to promote them so they could make more money."

In those days, pharmacists not only filled prescriptions but handed out lots of advice as well. They also competed with physicians, who were able to buy drugs at a discount and sell them out of their own offices.

"Sometimes a doctor's diagnosis was related to what was in his cupboard," Coutu joked.

But an incident in one of his stores involving a doctor's discount and a good customer led to a new business model.

"This doctor came in and reminded me about his discount in front of one of my biggest clients," he said. "When he heard the doctor, my client said, 'I guess I'm too poor to get a discount.' That was the start of my realizing that pharmacies had to sell discounted drugs to everyone and to do this by offering self-service, no advice."

In 1969, he mortgaged everything to open his first super-size discount store with eight times the normal inventory.

"My slogan was 'Nobody gets a special discount. Everyone gets the same low prices,'" he recalled. "I was all in. It was go bust or make it."

The store was an instant hit, and crowds were so large that the fire marshal's office began restricting numbers, which created long lineups.

"So I set up a trailer for the people lining up outside and said, 'The coffee's on me,'" Coutu recounted. "And the lineups got longer."

By 1972, he began expanding through franchising and landed, as his first franchisee, Quebec's biggest drugstore, the Montreal Pharmacy. It was housed in a six-storey building, open 24/7, and had 250 employees. Hundreds more followed.

In 1986, he decided to tap into public equity markets, but not for the usual reasons.

"I wanted to have a boss, someone to report to," he said. "You can get pretentious, think you know everything, and I wanted the discipline of running a public company, with regulators and shareholders."

The initial $48 million raised was reinvested immediately in acquisitions to grow the chain.

"We have always reinvested profits," he said.

The 2007 Rite Aid deal was well received by the market initially. The Coutu Group is its largest shareholder: it holds 4 out of the 12 board seats, but must agree on all major decisions.

"Rite Aid has a great IT system, the right management and good locations," he said.

But there was controversy following the purchase of Eckerd, which led to Jean's return as CEO in 2005. He found retirement difficult and returned often to Montreal. He still has 89.8% of the company's special voting shares.

"It is very hard to fade away. I work because I like it," he said, adding with another wink, "I have to work because I have 5 children and 15 grandchildren."

He said the future of pharmacy is especially bright these days because of demographics, and an added bonus is the fact that 75% of clients are females buying non-pharmacy items.

"Pharmacies are convenience stores in the health and beauty area," he said. "There are still many opportunities, and we will go anyplace where good pharmacies are needed."

The next generation of Coutus is firmly entrenched in the business too. Of the 14 board members, 4 are family members, and sons Louis, François and Michel are executives.

Michel recalled starting in the business at age 10, with François, doing Thursday-night trash duty in the basement of their father's store.

"My father is a tough man—he's like a general of an army," said Michel. "He's a fair man, though, and he groomed us all our lives to become business-thinking people."

The family is close and shares a compound in Magog, outside Montreal. They are also loyal to Canada and are very philanthropic.

"I made my money here and I owe it to the Canadian people. Some people say I should go to the Bahamas. Why? Buy a big boat? Then what? Buy a big plane? Then what? A submarine?" Jean Coutu said.

He also believes that money isn't everything.

"It was the Depression and my father told me once he had a million dollars in accounts receivable. His waiting rooms were full but nobody could pay him," he said. "Both my grandparents had been rich and went bust. But my father, who struggled during the Depression, paid off all the debts of his father and said to me, 'I won't leave you any money, but I will leave you a good name.'"

GEORGE COHON

In 1967, McDonald's Corporation founder Ray Kroc pressured young Chicago lawyer George Cohon to get into business for himself and open a McDonald's in Canada.

Cohon did that, and then some.

Between 1967 and 2007, McDonald's grew in Canada to 1,400 outlets coast to coast. Then, in 1990, George took the template and conquered another northern clime. In January of that year, he opened the first outlet in Moscow's Pushkin Square, and by 2007 the Russian chain had dozens of stores—and the Pushkin Square outlet had become the biggest McDonald's in the world.

Cohon is the Lewis and Clark of fast food. Now semi-retired, he is the largest individual shareholder in McDonald's worldwide. In 2007, the corporation had a market capitalization of US$52 billion, 465,000 employees and operations in 120 countries.

He said in our interview at his Palm Beach mansion, in regards to his wealth, that he was once cited as the second-largest McDonald's shareholder who was an employee, after founder

Ray Kroc. In 2004, the Kroc estate owned US$2 billion worth of McDonald's stock.

"I don't talk about how many shares I have. A few," he told me. "Let's say I'm very comfortable."

Cohon is a thoroughly likable American from the heart of the Midwest. Tall, handsome and funny, he talks like a Gatling gun and serves as senior chairman of McDonald's of Canada and of McDonald's of Russia. He is also senior director with the Royal Bank of Canada and sits on the Astral Media Inc. board.

He and his wife, Susan, are friends of mine; the couple has two sons, Craig and Mark, and three grandchildren. Both sons are involved in not-for-profits. Craig lives in London and runs a non-governmental organization involved in Africa that is backed by BP PLC (British Petroleum) and other corporations. Mark is chair of the Ontario Science Centre and commissioner of the Canadian Football League. Both are movie-star handsome and Midwest nice.

Mark did business in New York City for years and Craig blazed a trail similar to his father's, by successfully opening up the Soviet Union for Coca-Cola products.

Cohon wrote a fascinating book about his Russian adventures, called *To Russia with Fries*, but his career in Canada was the launching pad and is also interesting.

It began in Chicago in 1967.

"I was pushing my son Craig in a stroller. I bumped into a lawyer friend of mine who said he had a client who wanted a McDonald's franchise in Hawaii and asked me if I could get to Ray Kroc to make this happen," he said.

"This led to a meeting I arranged for the guy with Kroc, but then Ray gave the Hawaii franchise to somebody else he met on a plane. So he offered the guy eastern Canada. The client said to me, 'I want Hawaii, not eastern Canada,' so he turned it down. I called Ray to tell him that and Ray said to me, 'You don't want to be a lawyer the rest of your life, do you? Get involved.' So I did and moved to Canada in 1968 and started the chain," he recalled.

The first store would be in London, Ontario, which has been a traditional test market for many retailers. Back then its demographics reflected the rest of the country's.

Cohon leased space in a strip plaza for the first outlet, and set to work. His launch plan was to donate half of the first day's proceeds to a charity, and he selected as his recipient the Society for Crippled Children, in London. But such philanthropical marketing was suspicious to Londoners.

"The board of the Society invited me to make a presentation about my plan at the London Hunt Club. Everybody wore a blue blazer. So did I, with a striped tie. Some guy asked me if it was a regimental tie, and I told him, 'No, sir.' Then they asked me what McDonald's was and wanted to know my intentions.

"I told them that McDonald's had sold enough hamburgers to go to the moon and back and enough ketchup to fill the Grand Canyon. One guy, who had fallen asleep while I talked, suddenly woke up when he heard the Grand Canyon reference and challenged it. I took out my notes and corrected myself, saying McDonald's had sold enough ketchup to fill the Mississippi River. By the end of the evening, they said they weren't sure whether they should accept the money. They didn't."

The opening was a hit anyway, and he invited founder Ray Kroc to come up to Toronto to celebrate.

"He saw how Toronto was booming," Cohon said, "and immediately offered me $1 million for the eastern Canada licence I had bought and my restaurant in London. My dad was there at the party and said I should consider the offer, but I said, 'I didn't come here to open one restaurant and sell out.' I turned it down."

His deal was for the exclusive and perpetual rights to eastern Canada in return for $10,000 for every restaurant opened. But it also required him to come up with $70,000 up front to pay for the first seven.

Cohon borrowed the money and had built 43 more restaurants by 1971. That's when he sold the rights back to the company in return for stock, which made him a significant shareholder. That allowed eastern and western Canada to be consolidated, and Cohon set about building a national chain.

Even after the brand had been established, there were skeptics in Canada, he said.

"I went to Schneiders [a meat company now part of McCain-controlled Maple Leaf Foods] with meat specs. They said, 'Why should we bother? We're Schneiders and we don't follow specs.' It turned out to be a huge mistake, and I told them it would be at the time. I said, 'Some day we're going to be huge and you will want our business.' That's what happened. Our meat supplier is now bigger than their whole company. Years later they came back to us to get the business and we told them, sorry, it was too late," he said.

Cohon took to Canada immediately and became part of the Toronto establishment. In 1975, he became a Canadian citizen, which back then meant giving up his American citizenship. And his gamble paid off. By 2006, McDonald's Canada was serving 2.5 million people daily out of 1,400 restaurants. It employed 77,000 people and had sales of $2.7 billion. This made it Canada's 136th-largest corporation, and bigger than Tim Hortons Inc. of Oakville.

Russia is also a giant. It started as a twinkle in George's eye back in 1976 during the Canada-Russia hockey series. That year, he treated a group of Russian VIPs to their first Big Mac and fries in a Canadian McDonald's. "They loved the taste, they loved the cleanliness and they loved the whole experience," said Cohon.

So he boarded a plane shortly after and began a 14-year journey to bring the franchise to the former Soviet Union. The challenges were daunting. There was no precedent in Russia for a North American–style corporation, and the country lacked laws or good business practices of any kind. Russians were indifferent employees at best and downright hostile at worst. They had no discipline, customer orientation or marketing experience. And Cohon had to operate within the ruble currency system to avoid risk, which meant creating a supply chain that could efficiently and properly produce everything from buns to patties and frozen fries.

Another challenge was to cope with the change in leadership that dogged the Soviets during the 1980s. But Mikhail Gorbachev's perestroika and glasnost had begun to bite, and by 1990 the first Russian McDonald's outlet opened. Months of training in Canada paid off, and the first Russian customers thought the staff members were Canadian because they smiled and greeted everyone warmly and quickly.

"Ultimately, Russia has become a great success story," said Cohon. "There are 168 restaurants and 18,000 employees serving 800,000 people each day. It is the best franchise in the world for McDonald's and is, I'm proud to say, now run by Russians. There are only 2 expatriates there. When I opened in 1990, we had to have 100 expats there to manage it. But they trained the locals, which was the mandate."

These days the Cohons commute between a farm in Ontario, their downtown Toronto townhouse and a magnificent home in Palm Beach, surrounded on three sides by water. Fittingly, a corner of its parklike garden is occupied by a full-sized statue of Lenin, bought for Cohon as a gift by late Toronto financier Ben Webster.

"Isn't it great? I love it," Cohon said as he escorted me to the site. "Ben gave it to me as a present because he was having some trouble getting money out of some Russians in a shipping deal. So I made a phone call for him to Gorbachev. He got his money, and Ben gave me the statue as a thanks. He dumped it on my lawn in Forest Hill, but I decided to bring it down here and tuck it away in the USA."

RON JOYCE

Ron Joyce grew up in a three-room bungalow in Tatamagouche, Nova Scotia, during the Depression. The only entertainment was Ron himself, who would sing and dance for his widowed mother, Grace, and siblings Bill and Gwen. But it was a life of hand-me-downs and humility, and by the time he was 16 years old he couldn't wait to get out. He boarded a train for Hamilton, Ontario, with $5 in his pocket.

"Poverty is a disease," he once told me. "It was just godawful."

But Joyce, accustomed to living by his wits, thrived, picking tobacco and working in Hamilton's steel mills as young kid to support himself. He eventually sent home enough money for his younger brother to join him.

It was a fitting apprenticeship for one of Canada's greatest entrepreneurs. He built the iconic Tim Hortons Inc. fast food chain, which was Canada' 192nd-largest corporation in 2006, with revenues of $1.6 billion, assets of $1.7 billion and profits of $259.5 million. I interviewed him for this book in 2007, but we have been friends since 1997.

Joyce bought out his partner in 1975 and in 1996 sold out to Wendy's International for $600 million worth of Wendy's stock and two board seats. A handful of years later, he had a falling-out with the founder of Wendy's, Dave Thomas, and eventually cashed in. Since then, he has made another fortune in the stock market and is now the second-largest shareholder in Shaw Communications Inc. after the family, and also on its board of directors.

Joyce is a big risk-taker. He signed on for a stint in the Canadian Navy during the Korean War "because I wanted the action," and after demobilization became a policeman in Hamilton. His first taste of prosperity, and of the food business, came when he worked for his Ukrainian in-laws during summers selling junk food on a beach on Lake Erie.

"Being a cop was the most boring job in the world. There's usually absolutely nothing to do," he said. He worked motorcycles and parking patrol, delivered a baby once with a partner and worked his way up to be an undercover morality-squad operative.

"I used to go out in my blue jeans and look for trouble," he said. "It wasn't hard to find."

Joyce supplemented his meagre police pay by taking on, as a favour, a struggling Dairy Queen operation. He worked both jobs and slept in the kitchen, but turned it around in no time. That's when Joyce answered an ad in the Tim Hortons store window and met the hockey player—and became his partner—in the flagging doughnut chain named after him.

Joyce quit the force in 1964 and took on this new task. He cleaned up operations and repositioned the chain as Canada's first 24-hour-a-day restaurant. This was a niche. As a cop, Joyce realized the need for round-the-clock eateries for people doing shift work. But he also realized the security issues, so he ensured the safety of patrons and workers in the late hours by offering free coffee to policemen in uniform. At any given time, night or day, there would always be a squad car or two parked outside a Tim Hortons outlet.

He also expanded while controlling quality by selling franchises to policemen and their relatives, and by policing the brand and the restaurants. Stories of his toughness with franchisees are legendary. For instance, in 1997, years after he sold the chain but when he still owned Wendy's stock, Joyce took me into a Tim Hortons in BC. He inspected the kitchen, made suggestions and refused free coffee and doughnuts.

"That's not your property to give away," he snapped at the young assistant manager.

In 1974, Tim Horton died in a car accident. Months later, Joyce bought out his widow. She later contested the purchase but lost. Joyce had 50 stores at this point, but running a bunch of doughnut stores was not how the fortune was made. It was made in land.

"I decided I wanted to control our costs. So we became a real estate company," he said. "We had been tenants, and one time my lawyer made a mistake and forgot to renew our lease within the six-month renewal period. So we were put on month-to-month at high rent. The landlord said, 'I gotcha.' There was a property for sale across the road, so I immediately put on my coat and negotiated to buy it."

The chain also evolved into a monolith out of necessity, he added.

"We were still small in 1970, and there were lawsuits around the country concerning suppliers and franchisees," he said. "So we started central distribution, warehouses, and got our own trucks. This gave us the ability to have direct buying power for flour, sugar, packaging, machinery, and we were able to get great contracts."

As the chain grew, competitors he dubbed "tagalongs" started to surface.

"The only way to stop these Mickey Mouse start-ups was to get bigger. So we started to open 150 a year and expedited everything. I called in my staff and said we were going to do this, but it would take a lot of sacrifice on everyone's part, time away from their families and so on," he said.

They went for it, especially Joyce's first cousin, Arch Jollymore.

"Archie said, 'Go for it,'" Joyce recalled.

They did, but not without plenty of risk.

"Our goal was 2,000 stores by 2000. By 1990, we had 500, 1,260 by 1995, and when I sold the chain in 1996, the goal was already met," he said. "I knew I had a winner. Alan Pyle [his lawyer] gave me a line of credit to grow the chain, but it almost destroyed me. Interest rates hit 22% and we were expanding and borrowing like crazy in the 1980s. I nearly lost the chain."

Could you have built this empire if you had not owned 100% of it?, I asked.

"I don't think so. I made a lot of my decisions in front of the mirror, shaving. I did not have to go to a board or committees. No, I don't think I would have," he said.

Joyce, born in 1930, left behind the day-to-day operations in 1996 and has enjoyed his massive wealth ever since. He travels constantly and owns several private jets, yachts and mansions. He also maintains a breakneck pace, businesswise. He started a charter airline business out of Hamilton Airport and invested $100 million in a magnificent golf resort called Fox Harb'r near his hometown.

"The golf course is a dog," said Ron in our book interview in his Burlington office. "I've put $100 million in it and have stopped chasing rainbows. I think it can break even soon. I've set aside $50 million, once I'm gone, to run it for five years."

Joyce is a tough and lovable energy force with a ready smile and a willingness to play for high stakes or just for fun. He's an indifferent golfer but built the championship course to spark some economic development in a moribund part of the country.

"It was about trying to get something to happen in that part of Nova Scotia," he said. "But I didn't get any grants from the government to do so, nor would they consider any, even though everybody else gets grants."

Likewise, Joyce was disappointed with his Wendy's deal. Joyce and Wendy's founder Dave Thomas had been golfing buddies and neighbours in an exclusive gated community in Fort Lauderdale. Thomas, who built his name into a household word through Wendy's ads, was a sharp operator who realized a good thing when he saw it. He needed Tim Hortons to bail out his troubled Wendy's.

Governance at Wendy's was poor. For example, Dave convinced his board to pay him a huge fee to use his name in TV commercials even after it had been used for years without charge.

"He got US$15 million to use his name, at the end, after the company spent millions making him a national icon," said Joyce. "It wasn't worth anything, and the company shouldn't have paid him. I thought we could build two great brands, but these people were a nightmare."

Fortunately, the Tim Horton Children's Foundation continues to thrive, in part through contributions from franchisees and customers. Joyce spearheaded the building of six magnificent camps where kids from poor backgrounds come for a special, life-transforming experience. The "guests" are sponsored by franchisees and can also move into camp counselling jobs, careers in the chain or scholarships. Joyce wanted to replicate a summer-camp experience he had once that was one of his happiest childhood memories.

"The camps have been important for the chain, for all involved," he said. "We did it for emotional reasons. I came from welfare, and so did Timmy."

DARYL KATZ

Daryl Katz grew up in the drugstore business and at a young age worked for his pharmacist father operating the cash register, stocking shelves and "taking care of the chocolate bars." Now he owns or operates more drugstores than anyone else in Canada, under the name of the Rexall family of pharmacies.

Katz is an aggressive Edmonton native who has built a huge retailing empire in less than a generation. He travels constantly and responded to my various e-mails within minutes no matter where or when he was contacted.

His business success has been impressive. In 1990, just shy of his 30th birthday, Katz scrapped his law practice in order to become a full-time businessman. By 2007, he was a billionaire and owned a chain of 2,000 stores in the U.S. and Canada with $6.5 billion in revenues. He also holds a portfolio of valuable real estate.

His business model from the beginning was to consolidate the industry by franchising as well as by buying small underperforming chains or mom-and-pop independents, then turning them around.

"I grew up in the pharmacy business, and I saw that the Canadian business was a pre-consolidation market compared to the U.S.," he said. "It's also an industry that grows by 10% a year. In other words, the growth that's baked in is so far ahead of inflation that you don't have to do anything but do leveraged buyouts of underperforming chains, then turn them around."

He makes it sound easy, but of course it was not.

He is an astute financier and added that owning 100% of his company has been an advantage. It has allowed him to move quickly, stealthily, and to reinvest all his cash flow back into the business without being slowed down by shareholder or stock market red tape. He constantly enlarges, rebrands and improves. In 2006, he brought the first drive-in pharmacy to Canada. Motorists can drop off prescriptions and pick up their drugs 20 or 30 minutes later by car.

He's also turning into a real estate player and has been buying sites, rather that always leasing store space.

"For the past five years, I have been acquiring as much real estate as possible, and we are building at the most convenient locations," he said. "This includes 50 acres in Sherwood Park [an Edmonton suburb]."

Katz may have grown up in pharmacies, but he acquired a taste for the business side. At 21, he bought the Alberta rights to Yogen Früz, a fast food franchise operation. He ran that while still in law school. Then, in 1986, he joined a law firm where he could also run businesses on the side.

"I knew I didn't want to practise law. I was an entrepreneur. I had trouble with law firms I articled with because they couldn't deal with a lawyer who had business interests. They wanted card-carrying partners who were committed to billing hours of service," he said.

In 1990, he made his first move when he heard that a franchisor in the U.S. called The Medicine Shoppe was about to sign over Canadian franchise rights to a small Quebec chain. He moved quickly, which is his signature style.

"I spoke with the CEO, and he said he was going to Montreal to finalize the deal. But I said we should talk, and that Edmonton was only a short flight from Montreal," he recalled. "Being a typical American, he didn't realize, until two hours into the flight and he was still in the middle of nowhere, that Edmonton was a long way from Montreal. I'm surprised he talked to me, but he did, and we did the deal."

Katz paid $2 million for the rights, then brought in Vencap, owned by the Alberta government, as an equity partner to help finance the deal. In three years, Vencap exited the business world altogether and Katz was able to buy its interest.

He then used the franchise concept to buy—and unite— small pharmacies into an entity that could realize economies of scale in accounting, marketing, sourcing and inventory systems.

In 1991, he began to make leveraged buyouts, buying stores with borrowed funds. By 1997, he was able to borrow in order to buy Ontario-based Pharma Plus and its 143 stores for a rumoured $100 million. He bought the underperforming chain from the Oshawa Group, which was owned by the squabbling Wolfe family, who sold their IGA grocery chain at the same time to the Sobeys.

Katz said he paid a premium over what rivals offered, but it was essential because the firm's size and success helped to put him on the deal-stream's radar screen. This meant that every investment banker or seller added him to their list of prospective buyers.

Of course, not everything has gone smoothly. He entered the U.S. market, buying the troubled Snyders Drug Store chain in the Midwest. Eventually, its underlying chain, Drug Emporium, was put into bankruptcy. But Katz was able to retain 150 drugstores in the U.S. Midwest. And U.S. expansion is unlikely, he said.

"The market down there is consolidated, highly competitive and huge. Walgreens opens 500 stores a year and has a market cap of US$50 billion," he said. "There's also a different mindset between Canadians and Americans. Down there it's eat or be eaten. That's why the Americans walked into the Canadian retail sector and have made a huge success of it."

But Canada was a different story. In 1999, Katz considered, then decided against, putting together a consortium to bid for Shoppers Drug Mart. Kohlberg Kravis Roberts & Co. eventually bought it.

"I would have had to bring in a big private equity firm. Maybe it was a mistake, in retrospect, but we'll get there," he said.

He now has more stores than Shoppers and has been busily gobbling up smaller groups and franchising. These included brands such as IDA, Guardian, Snyders and Herbie's (in the United States) and Medicine Shoppe. But he has also been creating a superbrand called Rexall. This is twinned in signage with the chain names and is also the chain's private-label brand for generic drugs, vitamins and other health products.

Besides "bricks," Katz also owns "clicks." He has a company that sells software and technology systems to pharmacies and owns Meditrust, Canada's largest mail-order pharmacy business.

Katz is a good marketer and has enhanced Rexall's profile through his $15-million purchase of the naming rights to Edmonton's hockey stadium, called Rexall Place, and $45 million for the tennis centre at York University, which hosts the biggest Canadian tennis championship every year. In May 2007, he made an unsolicited US$145-million bid to buy the Edmonton Oilers and has continued to up his price.

When asked why, he said, "Why not? When you grow up in Edmonton, you automatically become a hockey fan. I will pay whatever it takes to build a world-champion team here."

Businesswise, Daryl's strategy is to build on what he already has plus to pick up more mom-and-pop independent stores to flesh out his chain and spread overheads. He already has the first rights of refusal to buy 700 independent stores and will be doing so as the proprietors retire or sell over the next 20 years.

"We have 500 corporate stores that are 6,000 square feet, and we want to double that and continue to acquire independents," he said. "Until 1997, we focused on getting market share. Our chains were run by independent managements. Five years ago, we merged management and rebranded with Rexall and have created the second national brand in the industry."

Size also allows him to hire top-notch expertise.

"I wasn't able to hire world-class management, but now I can and do," he said.

Katz enjoys life in Edmonton and in California, for much of the winter. His dad, Barry Katz, is on the board of the Katz Group of Companies, which has invested in the stock market and in the oil industry. Daryl Katz no longer stays low-profile at home, and in 2006 completed construction of his eye-catching titanium-clad home nearly a football field in length on the west bank of the North Saskatchewan River. Reports in newspapers guesstimated that it cost $20 million to build.

"Edmonton is as good a place as any to come from and do business from," he said. "Everything's electronic today. You can be anywhere. My core executives are in Edmonton, but the last financing we did, which was one of the biggest in the industry, closed electronically in Edmonton, New York and Toronto."

Clearly, Katz loves what he does and sees a bright future in his industry.

"There is a potential for growth of 15% a year without acquisitions, doubling sales in 6¼ years," he said. "To some people, I'm an overnight success, but they just haven't heard of me. I've been at this since 1990."

BRANDT LOUIE

Brandt Louie's grandfather, Hok Yat Louie, immigrated to British Columbia from China in 1896 and worked all the hours in a day. He worked in a sawmill, grew vegetables and every morning before work took them by horse and cart to the city to be sold. While driving to market, he would study English.

"In 1903, he started a small general store, selling seeds and fertilizer to Chinese farmers," said Brandt Louie in an interview in 2007 over breakfast in Vancouver. "There were lots of Chinese here after the gold rush and after the railroad."

Louie's father, Tong Louie, built the modest business into a giant that is now in food wholesaling, drug retailing and real estate. H.Y. Louie Company Ltd. is British Columbia's second-largest private enterprise, after the Jim Pattison Group. Its workforce is roughly 8,000 and revenues are at an estimated $5 billion annually, so it is little wonder that Tong's nickname was Vancouver's "quiet titan."

"My dad was very hard-working and ran the company from 1953 to 1987," said Brandt. "He went to university, but it took him eight years to do four years. He would attend classes one year, then work the next to get enough money to study the following year. Business was hard. There was a lot of discrimination."

Today Tong's oldest son, Brandt, is a ranking member of British Columbia's establishment—ironic considering how badly Chinese immigrants like his grandfather and father had been treated in the province. They were ghettoized by racist bylaws and brutalized by Anglo competitors and banks that wouldn't touch Chinese-owned businesses.

Louie is now a director of Canada's largest bank, the Royal Bank of Canada, and various other public companies. He is also CEO of H.Y. Louie plus its subsidiary, London Drugs Ltd., as well as other family companies. In 2005, he became chancellor of Simon Fraser University.

Louie continues the tradition of being a "quiet titan," and his wealth is noticeable only by the fact that he employs a chauffeur to take him around in his Rolls-Royce to meetings and events.

The family fortune began with selling fruits and vegetables. H.Y. Louie died during the Depression and a brother ran the business. It struggled. In the early 1950s, Tong took over operations from his uncle and struck a deal to supply all the IGA stores in BC. Then, in 1998, the company became co-owner of a chain of 44 IGA and Market Place stores in the west, in partnership with the Sobey family of Nova Scotia.

The retailing fortune was extended in 1976 when the firm moved into drugstores by repatriating London Drugs from a near-bankrupt California company and converting its 10 small stores into 64 large operations across western Canada.

The family also owns charter airline London Air Services, a swanky fishing resort, and land developments from condos to shopping centres and apartment buildings.

Interestingly, the enormous influx of Chinese into Vancouver and other parts of Canada as well as the opening up economically of China itself have not piqued Louie's involvement in his ethnic community. He speaks Cantonese, but not well, he said.

"We are not involved in China," he said. "My dad went back in the 1980s and looked. He did not think the timing was right and did not think that being Chinese was beneficial. That was because there was resentment toward the lucky ones who got out."

But the Louies have become involved in charitable work. Brandt's grandfather came from a small village across the border from Macau, and in the 1920s he built a school and hospital there. Then, in the 1970s, the family rebuilt the school for the local people.

"There's a difference between making an investment and making a donation. If you make an investment, you need a return. If you make a donation to help the nation or a village, that's different," Brandt explained.

Louie's last visit to China was in 2000, when he visited Shanghai. But he remained unconvinced about doing business there.

"It was mind-boggling, and clearly this is the Pacific Century. But there are problems there, such as the issues of intellectual property rights and the rule of law. But the future is in China," he said.

"I'm not interested in doing business there because I'm busy enough here. My culture and education have been here. I'm a Canadian," he added.

Indeed, his family on both sides have been in Canada longer than most. His mother's grandfather predated the arrival of H.Y. Louie: he came to BC in 1852, looking for gold. He ended up repairing sails for ships in Port Victoria.

"Just because you are Chinese and might speak Chinese, it's not enough of a link to guarantee success there. The skills are not all that transferable. I don't view China as my country," Brandt said.

But his background has certainly made him sympathetic to the struggles of new immigrants.

"It's hard for immigrants to come to this country and do well. Very few make it in the first generation. I call it the Lost Generation. Business is done differently in Canada. But eventually the good news is that their children learn the system and that Canada is good to immigrants. Asians have done reasonably well," he said.

Louie's brother and sister are also involved in the family business. But his two sons are pursuing a different path. Both were educated in the United States, married American women and live there. One is a radiologist and the other a lawyer.

"I have a philosophy that you shouldn't force children to do something they don't want to do. I always said, whatever you do it has to be with passion, and if you have passion you will do well and eventually be rewarded," he explained. "Besides, you don't need a family member to run these companies today."

Times have certainly changed. He said his career path was determined by his father. He graduated from university, then became a chartered accountant in 1969. He moved to Montreal and worked for two years with accounting firm Touche Ross & Co. (now Deloitte & Touche), until 1972.

"But it was already expected that somebody would take over the family business," he said. "Today it's different: if you tell children anything today, they do the opposite. But that wasn't the case with my generation. So I joined the family business, and I learned to love it. At the time, it was suggested I do this. Yes. So I did."

Louie, in his 60s, now has lots of time to travel and to enjoy golf and other hobbies. And there are no plans to expand operations, such as retailing, beyond western Canada.

"It's a regional market we understand. I'm not sure you have to be national. Ontario's a tougher retail market and Canada's not a homogeneous country. You can't take the same model and just place it east," he said.

It also helps that BC, Alberta and Saskatchewan are becoming the most prosperous part of the country because of vast resources, free-enterprise governments and the escalation of commodity prices.

Louie's extracurricular activities include regular annual visits to the World Economic Forum in Davos, Switzerland—the most high-octane gathering of business leaders. He likens it to "university without having the exams or the homework." He also enjoys sitting on various corporate boards, which he also regards as educational.

"It's interesting to watch how people manage their companies. There's no right or wrong—it's all just different," he said.

One of the reasons why H.Y. Louie and its divisions have prospered is because Vancouver's and BC's economies have improved. Mining has returned, population growth by retirees has increased and tourism is growing, all of which supplement the slowly declining forestry sector.

"One-quarter of all dollars spent in the province used to be forestry. Now there is hardly a blip if there's a downturn except in small communities dependent on a mill," he said.

Louie remains committed to private ownership and is a philanthropist who earmarks funds principally for scholarships and educational institutions.

"It's more fun to run a private company. You don't have to worry about all those silly rules," he said.

"And personally," he added, "we live simply and believe that, as my father and grandfather did, if we are successful, we have an obligation to give back to the community where the wealth came from. It's a responsibility, but it's also a lot of fun."

THE SOBEYS

The Sobeys celebrated their corporate centennial in 2007 in tiny Stellarton, Nova Scotia. But it was a muted, Presbyterian Scots–style party.

The Sobeys are one of Atlantic Canada's four enormous business groups, along with the Irvings, McCains and Jodreys. For four generations they have done business far from Bay Street, and prospered in a region that mostly exports people.

The Sobeys own Canada's second-largest grocery-store chain and its second-largest movie-theatre chain and, through various real estate entities, are also the largest landlords in Atlantic Canada. They also own Halifax's skyline and most of its downtown retail and millions of square feet of real estate across the country.

Sitting atop it all are the Sobey brothers and their Empire Company Limited, publicly listed but 80% owned by the family. By 2006, Empire had become Canada's 25th-largest corporation, with revenues of $13.42 billion, assets of $5 billion, profits of $296 million and 36,786 employees.

Brothers David and Donald Sobey sit on Empire's board, as do four members of the next generation: John, Robert, Karl and Paul Sobey. Dave's son is Paul, who is CEO, and Dave's brother Donald is chairman emeritus.

If you met any of them on the street, they would, like the Jodreys or Irvings, look just like any other middle-management, middle-aged Maritimers. Dave and Donald were both inducted into the Business Hall of Fame in Toronto in 2007. Both are droll but have a twinkle in their eyes. I lost a bet to Donald years ago, about whether there was a Scottish currency (there is), and he collected on it by flying me to speak at a Dalhousie University fundraiser for medical research. I have golfed and fished with Dave, Ron Joyce and others off the coast of Nova Scotia, and Dave is quiet but loves to laugh.

In 2007, the family restructured its holdings. Early in the year, it spun off Crombie Real Estate Investment Trust for a market value of $1.6 billion and retained 49.5% of its units. In April, Empire privatized Sobeys Inc. and paid more than $1 billion to buy the 29% of shares it did not already own.

"We have 1,300 stores in total—plus a chain of convenience stores in Atlantic Canada and drugstores," said Dave in an interview in 2007. "We have franchised stores and smaller ones, and in Quebec and Toronto we are introducing Sobeys Express [prepared foods to go]."

Sobeys is half the size of Loblaw Cos. Ltd. but bigger than third-place Métro-Richelieu. Its stores operate under the brand names of Sobeys, IGA, Foodland, Thrifty Foods and Price Chopper. In 1998, it expanded greatly when it paid $1.5 billion to buy the Oshawa Group, with its IGA stores and other assets, from the warring Wolfe family. This gave the firm great locations and brand-name recognition outside Atlantic Canada.

Ironically, the family's huge real estate assets were not created by design, but out of necessity, similar to the reasons why Ron Joyce of Tim Hortons bought and retained the underlying property beneath his franchises.

"We got into real estate because it was the only way we could get locations. Dominion Stores [owned by Toronto's Argus Corp.] was the biggest retailer across Canada and always had first preference on locations," said Dave.

Not surprisingly, Dave and Ron Joyce are close friends, and Ron was on the Sobeys board for a number of years.

The Sobeys have also done business with the Jodreys for decades. Jodrey heir David Hennigar is their broker and sits on the Crombie board of directors. But in 1994, the Sobeys bought out the Jodreys when it took over Halifax Developments and its 2 million square feet of Halifax that included landmarks such as Scotia Square, Barrington Tower, Cogswell Tower, Duke Tower, the Trade Mart, CIBC Building, Barrington Place Shops and the Delta Hotel.

Empire also retained ownership of Sobeys sites and owns 4.4 million square feet of retail space, plus the family owns 36% of Genstar Residential Development Partnership (bought with Fred DeGasperis and Carlo Fidani, Toronto developers). These involve lucrative properties and lands in both Ontario and Alberta.

"It was started by our grandfather J.W. Sobey," said Dave. He is chairman emeritus of the now-private grocery chain Sobeys Inc. "My grandfather's dad had a farm in Pictou County. It was an old Scottish tradition that everything was willed to the oldest son, who happened to be out west. My grandfather worked on the family farm, but when it was willed to his brother, he moved into town and worked in the mines as a carpenter. He didn't like it so he opened a meat store. All farmers had to be good at carpentry and also handy with the meat."

J.W.'s store was in Stellarton, but he lived in Glasgow. The area is comprised of a cluster of 5 towns with about 45,000 people.

The biggest growth spurt for the company was brought about by Frank Sobey, who died in 1985 at the age of 85. His sons were Dave, Donald and a third, Bill, who died in 1989.

Today, there are two dozen Sobeys in the fourth generation, and many work directly in the family's businesses. Dave has a daughter, Janice, and his son, Paul, is heavily involved. Donald has three children. His son Robert is president of Lawtons Drug Stores Ltd. The late Bill Sobey had four children; his son Frank is chairman of Crombie REIT. There's also another branch of the family: the late Frank's brother, Harold, who has sons in the business.

"Our brother Bill died at 61 in 1989," Dave Sobey said. "He had been president of Sobeys, then I was, then we hired a professional president, Bill McEwan. Then I became chair and Donald was CEO of Empire. We reorganized our holdings in order to have a better way for the family to continue to retain control of Sobeys Inc."

The 2007 buyout will mean that the family owns 80% of the entire empire and the public only 20%. Eventually, the family will likely privatize Empire Co.

So far, the Sobeys have remained successful by getting along and being united in their strategy.

"My brother Bill went straight into Sobeys from school," said Dave. "But it was still a small business. When I came along three or four years later my dad thought, one son's enough. So he persuaded me to go to college. I took engineering but always wanted to get in the food business. I worked there when I was a kid. I enjoyed it. It was fun."

Some time later, Donald, the youngest, joined the firm too, and the three brothers and their father really put their shoulders to the wheel and built a giant.

"It was a growing family business. How did we get along? We had our differences of opinion and so on. But we always had sit-down meetings with Father and usually ended up in my brother Bill's office over a round table," said Dave. "We got along for a couple of reasons: we each focused in different parts of the business and, secondly, we each had a high respect for each other's opinions. That helped us to talk. And our father, well, he wasn't the easiest guy to follow."

Bill focused on real estate and Dave on store operations.

"I was more in the merchandising and operations, and Donald went to Queen's University, then went into Empire," he said.

The Sobeys are philanthropists, principally in Nova Scotia. Saint Mary's University's business school is named after them, following a multi-million-dollar gift.

But even today they live a modest lifestyle in Stellarton and, sometimes, Florida.

"Dad didn't like to show off," says Donald. "I remember he would take a new car and run it though puddles so nobody thought he was getting a big head. I guess it was his Scottish upbringing."

The Sobeys face a challenging future, along with Loblaw Companies, with the entry of aggressive Wal-Mart and Costco into the grocery sector.

"Loblaws were the ones that took the position to come up with a vehicle that would compete directly against Wal-Mart," said Dave. "Wal-Mart Supercentres have the complete range and are a food and general department store combined. They've had quite an impact on Loblaws in Ontario after only opening six or seven of these stores."

Dave said the Sobey strategy will be to focus on food.

"We know food better, have been in it for 100 years, and that's our business and that's what we're going to focus on. We have good-looking stores, focusing on variety and service and quality. We also feel location is a factor. Our stores are smaller, which means it's easier to place them in convenient locations for the consumer."

Besides, competition is not new in the food business, he added.

"There were lots of small stores in small towns years ago. Now there are fewer, but bigger, stores and millions of dollars of installations with thousands of products," he said.

Like so many dynasties, the Sobeys take a long view of the world, and of their businesses, just biding their time and making money for decades. May it continue in future.

THE WESTONS

The Westons are one of Canada's richest families, and their current patriarch, Galen Weston Sr., has a decidedly entrepreneurial bent. He and his late brother, Garry, inherited their father's sprawling international conglomerate, established in the late 1890s, and grew it into a dramatically larger business empire.

A third brother, Grainger, left the family business in the 1970s, moved to Texas and bought a small bakery called Grandma's Cookies, which he sold to Frito-Lay in 1977. After that, he developed resorts throughout the Caribbean. There are also six daughters—Miriam, Nancy, Gretchen, Barbra, Wendy and Camilla—who are all important Weston shareholders.

Their father, Garfield Weston, raised his nine children mostly in Britain, at their home, Wittington House, near Henley on the Thames River. They moved frequently as Garfield combed the world for business opportunities. The English estate was eventually given by the family to the Salvation Army.

Wittington is also the name of the family's private holding company, which is controlled by Garfield's nine children. By 2007, the various companies controlled by Wittington Investments included George Weston Limited, Loblaw Companies Limited, Holt Renfrew & Co., Associated British Foods and Selfridges.

In 2006, George Weston Limited was Canada's largest family-owned enterprise, with $32 billion in revenue, $18.6 billion in assets, $121 million in profits and 155,000 employees.

Associated British Foods PLC owns various manufacturing operations in Britain and Europe, making Ryvita, Ovaltine, Mazola oil and Twinings tea, among other brands, as well as upscale grocer Fortnum & Mason. In 2007, Associated had a market value of £7.3 billion, revenues of £6 billion in 60 countries, and 60,000 employees on its payroll.

Meanwhile, the next generation is actively taking the reins. In 2006, Galen Jr. was appointed executive chairman of Loblaw Companies Limited. Garry's son George is chief executive of Associated British Foods, while son Guy is chairman of Wittington Investments UK.

Galen Sr. is an energetic, optimistic man. He was the youngest of the nine, born in 1940. He juggles global responsibilities and commutes between his Toronto and London offices as well as a

Windsor, Florida, residential development. He is chairman and president of George Weston Limited; chairman of Holt Renfrew, of Brown Thomas Group, in Ireland, of Selfridges and of Wittington Investments; and a director of Associated British Foods.

The family business was started by George Weston, Galen's American-born grandfather, who at age 12 became a baker's apprentice. In 1882, he purchased a bread route from his employer and went on to establish a successful biscuit and bread business in Toronto.

His son Garfield, born in Canada, was an enterprising man and an anglophile who expanded his father's bakery business into an international conglomerate. In the 1930s, Garfield moved to Britain to build a chain of biscuit and bread factories, in the hope of establishing a new export market for Canadian wheat in the midst of the Depression. During the Second World War, he served as a British member of parliament and worked full-time assisting in the food supply chain from North America to England.

During the war, Garfield refused to move his children back to Canada, despite the aerial bombing of London, out of loyalty to his constituents. He also refused to send them to posh boarding schools. The nine grew up a close-knit bunch, steeped in the Methodist values of hard work, temperance and charity.

Garfield also personally handed over millions of pounds to England's Chancellor of the Exchequer to help restore St. Paul's Cathedral after a bombing attack and replaced 16 Spitfire planes lost during the Battle of Britain. He was even asked to become a director of the Bank of England, but telexed back, "There must be a mistake. I'm a baker, not a banker."

Galen Weston Sr. was born in Britain but is a Canadian by choice. A good-looking man, he attended a number of schools while his father moved, buying and selling various companies. He went to the University of Western Ontario but left one credit shy of a degree in order to go to Ireland to start working in his father's grocery business there. He eventually established his own chain, Quinnsworth (sold in 1997 to British giant Tesco), then took an existing Dublin fashion retailer and turned it into a chain of four outlets called Brown Thomas. He met his glamorous wife, Hilary, there, when she was one of Ireland's top fashion models. They married in 1966 and have two children, Galen Jr. and Alannah.

Galen Sr. moved his family from Ireland to Canada in 1972 to rescue a flagging Loblaw Companies Limited. He engineered and led a successful turnaround over the course of the next 20 years. In 1986, Galen purchased Holt Renfrew and appointed Hilary as deputy chairman. She immediately began the revitalization of this luxury Canadian retail brand. When she was appointed in 1996 as Ontario's lieutenant-governor, she transformed the role from an honorary and ceremonial position into one that supported many meaningful community initiatives and charities across the province.

Several years before Galen became head of Loblaw Companies, Garry moved to Britain to run operations there. The two were opposites: Galen is a natural marketer with flair, and Garry was more conservative.

A project near and dear to the hearts of the Westons is their 200-home development in Vero Beach, Florida, which is now largely completed. The project represents new thinking in the context of upscale urban development, incorporating, through planning and design, a true sense of local community.

Galen Jr. and Alannah Weston are entrepreneurial like their parents and run a number of businesses. Galen Jr. is married to a granddaughter of Tom and Sonja Bata, Alexandra, and leads Loblaw Companies Limited as executive chairman. Alannah is married to architect Alexander Cochrane and is the creative director of Selfridges.

Despite their British pedigrees and connections, Galen and Hilary Weston are actually very Canadian. They are at ease anywhere and are often seen walking, hand in hand, along Toronto's Bloor Street to inspect their Holt Renfrew flagship or talk to colleagues at one of the many Loblaws supermarkets. I have socialized with them, was a guest at their son's fabulous engagement party and thoroughly enjoy their company.

"I enjoy business and creative, dynamic executives who are, at the same time as they are operating companies, reading, travelling, experiencing and able to challenge themselves," Galen Sr. said in an interview with me. "I still spend three to four months a year travelling, and I insist my senior guys do the same thing. I hire contrarians and those with a breadth of experience. To me, that's what's important."

The Westons are gifted business people who continue to thrive despite their involvement in highly competitive businesses in Canada and Britain. Loblaws remains challenged by Wal-Mart—and is countering with the launch of a new budget clothing outlet called Joe Fresh—and by a price war with all its competitors. Profits fell in 2007, along with stock prices, and there was concern whether the appointment of young Galen as executive chair was warranted and would impair earnings going forward. He addressed this in fall 2007 with analysts.

"Our organization is far too complex, not agile, and inconsistent," Galen Jr. said at a special presentation outlining the results of the company's 100-day strategic review, taken after two years of increasing turmoil, supply-chain stumbles and a management upheaval last fall that saw exiting president John Lederer succeeded by the family scion.

"We have too many management layers and too many colleagues with confused accountabilities," Weston said, with considerable duplication between head office and the regions. Even worse, he admitted, the company had missed the boat with customers by being overpriced and out of stock on goods too much of the time.

"We are not delivering the right value for money," he said. "Our actual prices relative to Wal-Mart are significantly higher than we thought."

The Westons have proven to be talented business people in the past, but often with the help of professional managers, not family members. This latest challenge is formidable, but the family's patriarch has been a turnaround specialist in the past. He may have to be one again.

FORESTRY

Canada remains a significant producer and exporter of forest products, from pulp and paper to lumber and building products. The Forest Products Association of Canada estimates that the industry employs 900,000 people directly and indirectly. But the industry struggles due to a high Canadian dollar, U.S. protectionism, the American housing recession and global competition.

The result has been that giants such as Domtar and Abitibi have fallen on hard times and merged with foreign competitors. Hardest hit have been producers in Ontario, Quebec and Atlantic Canada who operate mostly small mills and who have high labour costs and depleting forests. The industry is healthier in British Columbia and Alberta because foresters there manage larger tracts of Crown-owned land, which has justified the construction of huge, efficient downstream milling operations, some with roofs as long as several football fields.

Even when the timber rights are owned—not leased from the government, as is mostly the case—there are serious problems. New Brunswick's Irving family is losing money on its freehold forestry operations. In a rare interview with the *Globe and Mail* in November

2007, Jim Irving said they were down to the "bare bones" in terms of cost-cutting or investment in improvements due to the soaring Canadian dollar, and were still losing money. The number of publicly listed forestry companies in the U.S. and Canada decreased from 44 to 14 in one year by fall 2007.

Struggles mean that the sector will continue to downsize and be consolidated in order to realize cost savings, but two billionaire forestry families are profiled here. Both are in British Columbia. In addition, other Canadian billionaires have significant interests in the business, such as the Irvings; the Saputo family in Quebec; Brookfield Asset Management, with timber rights; and Vancouver's Jimmy Pattison, who owns 25% of Canfor Corp., the largest lumber producer in the country.

THE KETCHAMS

West Fraser Timber Co. Ltd. is one of three forestry giants in British Columbia that have not been felled after two decades of softwood lumber disputes with Americans and of industry consolidations. The others are Canfor Corp. and Tolko Industries Ltd. All three are well positioned in BC and Alberta, well capitalized and modernized, unlike their competitors in eastern Canada.

West Fraser is a Canadian giant owned by an American family who have gone from operating one sawmill in 1955 to owning the world's second-largest lumber producer. West Fraser went public in 1986 and is now Canada's 110th-largest corporation with, in 2006, $3.7 billion in revenues, $4 billion in assets, nearly $400 million in profits and 10,000 employees.

West Fraser's CEO is Hank Ketcham, an aw-shucks American who grew up in Seattle and who operates this slickly run giant out of an office building in the downscale district of Vancouver near GM Place, the city's hockey arena. He is also a Canadian citizen.

West Fraser's growth has been impressive. In the past 20 years, sales have gone up tenfold, as have assets, but shareholder equity has

WHO OWNS CANADA NOW

jumped from $218.9 million to $2 billion. The Ketcham family as a whole owns nearly 40% of the stock. The next highest shareholder is Montreal money manager Jarislowsky Fraser Limited.

If you invested $100 in West Fraser in 1986 and reinvested dividends, your stake would have been worth $693 by 2007, representing a 10.2% compound rate of return.

"There is a continuing strong commitment by all three sides of the family toward the company," said Hank in an interview in his spartan Vancouver office. "We have no shareholder voting commitments [the Ketchams don't vote as a bloc], but the company has always been part of the family and that's the expectation going forward. We have a strong emotional attachment to it."

The Ketchams got into lumber in the 1920s when Hank's grandfather, also Henry, left the east for Seattle to start a wholesale trading business.

"He barely held on during the Depression," said Hank Ketcham.

Henry had three sons—Bill, Peter and Sam—all of whom served in the U.S. military, two during the Second World War and one in Korea, then attended college under the GI Bill before joining their father's Ketcham Lumber.

"My dad, Peter, was a real entrepreneur and immediately began looking for something more exciting than trading lumber," said Ketcham. "So he said to his brothers, why not buy a mill? So the three of them one weekend just got in a car and went north to buy one."

They bought a sawmill that had 12 employees for US$45,000. Then they decided that the youngest brother, Sam, should move to Canada to run it.

"Sam was unmarried and so he was the logical person to go up to BC and run it, then look around for other opportunities," said Ketcham.

Success was rapid. This was due to the fact that the brothers got along and had complementary skills.

"The underlying success was due to two things: Sam was a tremendous people person. He died a few years later in an accident, but if he had lived he would have become one of the great names in Canadian business. He had such a compelling personality," said Hank. "His personality inspired loyalty in employees, which allowed the business to grow."

Secondly, all three were great businessmen. "My dad, Peter, was the entrepreneur, always pushing for opportunities, but, as a trio, they were also a great management group—very conservative. They took chances, but always hedged their bets too," he said.

This alacrity and risk-taking allowed them to survive the booms and busts of the forestry business, with fluctuating prices and government policies. They not only survived but acquired new operations along the way to spur their growth. Then there were acquisitions of timber rights.

"In the 1950s, 1960s and 1970s, the BC government was making more timber available and there were lots of little timber rights holdings around. So we became consolidators—so did other companies—and bought up these rights," he said.

By 2007, West Fraser had grown into dozens of mills, manufacturing operations and marketing distribution systems that now fan out across the United States, Canada and elsewhere. The company also has an enviable land spread of timber rights and owns a small retail business.

Ketcham grew up, as did all of the cousins, in Seattle, even though the family business was in Canada. He ducked service during the Vietnam War by pulling a draft number that wasn't called, then immediately headed north.

"I was lucky as hell missing that draft. So in 1974, I joined the company. At the time, it had only two good sawmills and a few building-supply stores," he said. "But every couple of years they bought another sawmill and modernized facilities. They also were expanding into retail and buying timber rights."

Ketcham fell in love with the business working summers in British Columbia's scenic interior.

"I didn't study forestry, but I studied sociology in university during the Vietnam War. I had a different outlook on many things back then. My dad stayed in Seattle and Uncle Sam was up here running the company. But I got to love the business and the people," he said. "And I certainly never thought it would get to this size."

Hank's uncle Bill is the only surviving founder. He lives in Seattle and is on West Fraser's board of directors.

When asked how a bunch of unconnected Americans from Seattle could build something that dwarfed Canada's giants like MacMillan Bloedel, Hank paused.

"You know what? They could see there was a special opportunity here, which is why they came," he said. "Why didn't the others? Where was MacMillan Bloedel and these other guys? They were focused on the coastal big trees. That's all they were interested in, and others like us didn't have coastal operations. We had a different attitude and looked for niches, because in the U.S. Pacific Northwest most opportunities had been gobbled up already by established companies. But up in Canada they could see there was still a vast opportunity.

"The timber we have here is the best in the world. We have huge challenges with the pine beetle, which will significantly reduce the timber available. But even so, Russia and Canada have the best trees in the world," he said.

In 2006, West Fraser expanded significantly into the United States and bought Weyerhaeuser's 13 mills for US$325 million. This will add greatly to production and be a hedge against future softwood lumber disputes by American rivals who have convinced Washington to impose everything from export taxes to quotas.

"It's been very unfair. But we have been living with trade sanctions from the U.S. since the mid-1980s and thrived anyway," Hank said.

But the Weyerhaeuser deal is good for the future.

"We now have a solid base in the U.S. and view ourselves as being very good at making lumber," he said. "We stay inside North America. We were in Uruguay but sold that. But you never know— we may look farther afield in future."

In world terms, West Fraser is a smallish player, but it's considered one of the best-managed in the industry.

"I like to make sure we are number one in shareholder return and making money. Number one in size is not an object: best-run is," he said.

As with other family businesses that are publicly listed, succession is an issue. With the Ketchams, there's the added concern that few in the family live in Canada or work in the business, and all face daunting estate taxes south of the border because they are American citizens.

"That's the problem with this family business. We have complicated cross-border tax issues because we are Americans. Estate taxes are significant, so we have to plan for succession, and often this requires share sales. Of my eight cousins, only two are in Canada."

"This company's not like Al Thorlakson [Tolko] or Jimmy Pattison [controlling shareholder of Canfor]. We are now second-generation, and not as entrepreneurial as the first, and most of us live in the U.S.," he said. "But we're committed and have a great team."

ALLAN AND JOHN THORLAKSON

Vernon is a bucolic town in British Columbia's Okanagan Valley with a population of 30,000. It is hardly head-office country.

But Tolko Industries Ltd., the world's fourth-largest lumber manufacturer, with annual production of 2 billion board feet and an estimated $2 billion worth of assets, is headquartered here. It employs 5,000 people and markets lumber, paper, veneer, plywood and oriented strand board in 22 countries. Its mills and other operations are scattered across Canada's four western provinces.

Tolko is privately owned by the Thorlakson family, and its name is an acronym of sorts.

"It is every second letter of my surname," said CEO Allan Thorlakson in an interview with me. This cryptic name, the firm's location tucked away in a tiny town and a general practice of declining interviews have allowed the Thorlaksons to stay out of sight.

Thorlakson agreed to this interview as a favour to a mutual friend, Peter Bentley, chairman of lumber rival Canfor Corp.

Tolko is a giant that has quietly become one of three major forestry players left in British Columbia and the only privately held one. Canfor and West Fraser Timber Co. Ltd. are publicly listed but controlled by Jimmy Pattison and the Ketcham family respectively.

Allan is Tolko's CEO, and his brother John Thorlakson is executive vice-president. A third brother was bought out years ago by the other two. The brothers are in their late 60s and both have sons working in the business. Allan has three sons and John, one son and one daughter. That generation are all adults, but most work outside the family business.

"All the kids have worked here," Al Thorlakson said, "but there is in place the discipline of professional management. We don't tolerate nepotism."

The Thorlaksons are of Icelandic descent. The brothers' grandparents met in Winnipeg in the early 1890s, then headed first to Alberta and then to British Columbia.

"We like it in Vernon. I'm six minutes' walk from work. Most of our people walk or ride a bicycle to work," he said. "It's a great place to run a business. The only person who must sacrifice is the CEO: I travel like a yo-yo—extensively."

Despite its remoteness, Vernon is a desirable locale and recruitment is easy.

"It's a family-oriented community with great amenities. It's one of the best addresses in the forest industry you can get," he said.

His father, Harold Thorlakson, founded the company in 1956 after working in the petroleum industry. Just 25 years ago, Tolko had only one sawmill. By 2007, it was building its 19th facility.

"My dad left that oil company in 1947 and went farming for a couple of years. Farming was in his blood. The good news is he recognized the farm economy had little future. So he got into logging, then bought a planer mill and that led to a sawmill," said Allan.

"His forte, his ongoing strength, was marketing. He did a reverse vertical integration from marketing into manufacturing. He understood something that we still maintain, which is that we are very customer-oriented," he said.

Both Allan and John are mechanical engineers and hands-on managers. All the mills report directly to Allan, and he is known for being a tough taskmaster. There is no middle management. Allan regularly drops into mills unannounced to inspect operations and encourage workers.

"I'd say engineering is helpful. Obviously, it's a discipline, but lots of engineers don't have business aptitude," he said. "My brother is more analytical than I am."

Like many family firms, the brothers have had to sort out their differences and build a loyal team.

"Tolko was my father's gift to his three sons," said Allan. "We have operations in all four western provinces. We have been successful because we have good people, good planning and, obviously, a contrarian strategy compared to many of our competitors."

Years before others did the same, Tolko aggressively embarked on a diversification out of British Columbia. "We looked at the storm clouds gathering. So we spent the better part of 15 years investing outside of the province," he said.

Tolko also steered clear of stock markets, despite being wooed for years by investment houses eager to take the company public.

"We've been courted hundreds of times, but we are committed to staying private. That may change. The next generation will now be making those decisions," he added.

But remaining private has given them a competitive advantage, a theme that runs throughout business.

"You can be more strategic if you are private. You can go slower. It's a real advantage to be private. We have none of that governance BS that the public companies have to put up with."

But Tolko's board of directors does embrace governance principles that public companies have had to adopt. Both brothers are on the board, but so are three outside directors.

"We have taken the best of public company governance and left out the excesses and negatives," Allan said.

Allan lives an ordinary life in a home located in a subdivision in the ranch country of Coldstream, near Vernon. He also owns a modest condominium in downtown Vancouver, which is in his wife Marlene's name, as is a home in Kelowna. He skis at the family's $400,000 chalet at the Silver Star ski resort.

"A number of people skiing Silver Star have been surprised to hop on a chairlift and discover that the person sitting beside them is Al Thorlakson," said Vernon mayor Sean Harvey in a *Vancouver Sun* interview.

The brothers value their privacy. There is "no percentage whatsoever" in publicity. "It only creates problems," Allan said.

Tolko, for instance, does not belong to the industry's lobby group, the Council of Forestry Industries, and Allan has often found himself off-side with the consensus over how to handle the Americans, damaging softwood lumber obstacles or other policy matters.

Now that the softwood lumber issue has settled down for a few years, the biggest challenge is to remain competitive in the face of the increasing Canadian dollar and of increasing competition from South America.

"Lumber is a global commodity, and we are seeing product from South America," he said. "Canada has to be careful. If the Canadian dollar hits US$1.25, I'll be looking for a job in the oil and gas business."

Another sore point has been that while forestry makes huge economic contributions to Canada's living standards, it is a political orphan.

"We don't get half the attention of the auto industry," he said.

Even so, Allan does not show any signs of slowing down just yet.

"I ski and my retirement project is golf. I go to Hawaii one week every spring and one week in the fall, but the summers here are beautiful. I'm having more fun than I've had in a long time. When things are good, it's not as much fun. The fun times are during the tough times when you have to be preoccupied with figuring out strategies."

ENERGY

I n 1941, Calgary had a population of 87,000. Then oil and natural gas discoveries turned Cow Town into a financial capital with more than one million people and more head offices than Vancouver or Montreal. Calgary and Alberta now vie with Texas for prominence in the world's "oil patch." This is not only because there is oil and gas there, but because Canadians have developed technologies and engineering techniques that allow them to economically explore and exploit energy in the hostile Arctic, the deepwater offshore and the gooey, remote oil sands.

As a result, Alberta's prospects could not be brighter. Living standards, on a per capita basis, are already the world's highest for its 3.4 million residents. The provincial government is debt-free, and low income tax and sales tax rates have made Alberta Canada's tax haven. If oil exports reach 6 million barrels a day by 2020, Canada will be the world's third-biggest exporter, behind Russia and Saudi Arabia. Then there is natural gas, also in abundance in all three western provinces, the Northwest Territories and the arctic offshore.

The downside is that oil and natural gas prices have always been cyclical and may turn again one day. Price volatility has dogged the region forever, and its industries have been repeatedly clobbered. Calgary stagnated during the 1980s, hit by Ottawa's tax grab in 1980, then by OPEC's price collapse in 1986, from US$36 to US$18 a barrel. These flattened fortunes and drove companies out of business. Prices then fell to US$11 a barrel in 2002, before the world's supply-demand situation changed. In 2003, prices headed upward, and by 2007 there were plenty of oil billionaires in Alberta and hundreds, if not thousands, more Albertans who had become extremely wealthy.

Even so, Calgary has fewer billionaires than does Montreal, which has a considerably smaller economy. This is because wealth in Alberta has been more widely distributed, due to the unique nature of Calgary's oil sector. Until the 1970s, the industry was dominated by huge, foreign-owned multinationals such as Exxon and Shell. These companies snapped up leases and sat on them until Premier Peter Lougheed imposed drilling requirements on those holding deeper rights. This forced them to divest, which created drilling opportunities for small Canadian companies. But these "juniors" had no money and were able to entice talent away from the multinationals only by offering generous stock options and equity ownership positions. Often they had to pay drilling contractors or engineering consultants with stock.

"For 15 or 20 years, Canadian oil and gas companies gave stock options to all their employees, even those in the field. Or they had stock participation plans," said retired investment banker Wilf Gobert in an interview with me in spring 2007. "The value of their oil stocks, at US$60 a barrel, was 28% of the Toronto Exchange, which meant there were unrealized capital gains, mostly in Calgary, of 1.5% of value, or up to $7 billion. Now oil is nearly US$100. The math is incredible—there are thousands of options worth billions."

J.C. ANDERSON

It took a couple of hours and a rugged four-wheeler to drive with J.C. Anderson across his spectacular spread on the outskirts of Calgary.

"I have done enough travelling in my life, so I even stay all winter here," he said in an interview in his kitchen. "It doesn't get better than this . . . Calgary, Alberta, and the piece of land I have here."

Picture windows across the back of the house face the Rockies in the distance. Rolling fields with livestock and barns decorate the landscape.

A lower-level recreation room houses a big-screen television, a poker table for a dozen, pool and shuffleboard tables and a giant, fully stocked bar. A bachelor now, and a jock, Anderson hosts weekly card games and gatherings to watch football and other sporting events.

He started off life thinking he wanted to be a high school football coach, and all of his children were interested in competition too. All became world-class equestrians, and two represented Canada in the Olympics.

Anderson was a middle-class kid from the American Midwest. But in 1970, at 40 years of age, he discovered one of the biggest natural gas finds in Canada's history, a field called Dunvegan. By 2007, it had produced 1 trillion cubic feet of natural gas, and it still had many years of capacity left.

This find became the backbone for Anderson Exploration Ltd., which had, in 2001, an enterprise value of $7 billion and was Canada's fourth-largest natural gas producer. That year, Anderson sold the company for $5.3 billion and he sold his 6%, a stake worth $310 million.

But since then oil prices have rocketed. Anderson now owns Anderson Energy, which has been buying land positions and junior oil companies. He also owns a 3,000-acre ranch just outside the city limits of Calgary near the Spruce Meadows horse park. Anderson started accumulating ranchland back in 1976 and now, in Calgary's urban "shadow," he owns one of Alberta's biggest and most valuable ranches. Values here have skyrocketed, along with oil prices and everything else.

It's an operating ranch with 265 cattle, 250 calves, 10 bulls and dozens of horses, along with a riding ring and stables. J.C. loves the farming and horse businesses and is involved in managing everything from buying livestock to building facilities. Both his grandfathers were farmers from Sweden.

J.C. (John Carl) Anderson, a big, burly man, was born and raised in tiny Oakland, Nebraska, 58 miles south of Omaha.

"My dad was a cashier at the local Farmers and Mechanical Bank," he said. "All I knew was sports, and I started out to be a coach. One day I said I'd stay here in Oakland and work because I didn't know what to do, but he said, 'Go to school and it'll come to you.'"

"I also looked at all the starving coaches in small towns and decided I didn't like that," he said. A high school geology teacher spotted Anderson's intelligence and encouraged him to go to the University of Texas, where he studied engineering.

Anderson came to Alberta in 1965 when a colleague in Texas refused to be transferred there by Standard Oil of Indiana (now Amoco).

"I went to his farewell party, and the next week he came in and said he wasn't going after all because his wife refused to move to Calgary," said J.C. "So I went. I could kiss him now."

The first year was rough. Calgary was a provincial town with a population of barely 200,000. The winters were brutal, especially for an American engineer who was used to working in the field in Texas or out on rigs offshore from Louisiana.

"I drove across the border with everything I owned. I was an assistant chief engineer," he said. "It was 35 below, and I'd never experienced that kind of cold."

For the first few months he stayed in the Calgary Inn, at $11.75 a night, frequenting, along with other lonely fellow travellers, the legendary Owl's Nest bar, where oilmen gathered nightly.

"In those days the bars had 'ladies and escorts' sections, and the bars were for men. It was terrible," he said.

But it didn't take long for the gregarious, party-loving American to meet all the oil-patch players. In August 1968, he left his employer and launched Anderson Exploration with $300,000 raised by his brother, a lawyer in Texas who happened to have wealthy in-laws.

"We needed this to pay rent on an office, buy data [on geological information] and do deals," he said.

Finding oil and gas is like investigative journalism or police work, a tedious process of picking through data and documents in order to find tidbits or keys to unlocking geological secrets. It's also a matter of doing deals with other detectives, to share costs and intelligence.

In short order, Anderson got a piece of a nice discovery, then he became intrigued by the logs showing a fault, or structure, deep underground in a productive area in northern Alberta known as the Peace River Arch.

"It looked like a fault in the Gulf [of Mexico] coast, but it looked terrible on the logs," he said. "We did 13 wells, and some had gas. I was intrigued. This was an enigma, and I spent months studying and theorizing about where this gas was."

In 1970, he decided to drill back into an old "dry" hole in a certain section, just because the section number matched part of his own licence plate number. That well was being tested the same night as Anderson and his dad were down in the southeast corner of the province testing another well in a place called Manyberries, Alberta.

"I'll never forget that night," he said. "We made two discoveries. It was one day before my 40th birthday. At 10 p.m., my tool pusher [rig hand] shows up drunk as a skunk so I had to babysit and test the well myself. It was an oil discovery," he said. "My dad was so excited he couldn't sleep. I said to him, 'Dad, I'm a millionaire.' Dad was 75 years old at the time.

"The next morning, after being up all night testing that well, we went into the hotel and called the guy looking after the well up north, and he confirmed we made the bigger discovery up north the same night. I knew right then that there was a chance that would be a huge gas field."

That discovery was enormous. Called Dunvegan, it contained a gas storehouse 17 miles long and 4 miles wide and has been producing ever since. Next, J.C. did a financing deal with a pipeline outfit to bring the gas to markets, which gave his company instant cash flow.

But luck did not always accompany him. In 1981, he decided to go public, and he amalgamated all his companies and holdings to do so. But plans were aborted because of the negative effects of the 1980 National Energy Program (NEP) and due to the depression in oil and gas prices. Under the NEP rules, he also had to Canadianize the company (bring in Canadian partners, because he and his backers were Americans) to get federal government drilling grants, so he and his brother sold a chunk of their company to BC Sugar as a partner.

Then more bad luck struck. In 1987, he was poised to take his company public on the very day that stock markets crashed catastrophically—Black Tuesday. He withdrew the public offering. Had he already gone public when the downdraft started, the company's shares would have sunk disastrously low.

"In July 1988, we gave a huge dividend to BC Sugar's shareholders in the form of Anderson stock, which is how we went public," he said.

With cash flow from Dunvegan and other discoveries, and with equity from the public, Anderson then went on a buying spree and became a major consolidator in the industry, snapping up financially limping entities such as Ulster Petroleum, Home Oil and Numac Energy.

Like other entrepreneurs, Anderson has an aptitude for focus and flexibility. But unlike others, he credits a stint with U.S. Army Intelligence for his instincts. In the 1950s, he was drafted into the army and plucked out of boot camp, after a test, to be a member of the Counter Intelligence Corps in Washington.

"I was just a pup, but it was great training. We obtained the background checks to provide clearance for top-secret positions and worked with the FBI. That taught me how to get in anywhere, deal with people on a different, senior level and get answers out of people. Those interrogation skills helped me learn how to think."

MURRAY EDWARDS AND AL MARKIN

Murray Edwards is one of the richest oil men in the world who isn't a sheikh, monarch or dictator. He's a middle-class boy from Saskatchewan who has built one of the world's largest independent oil companies, in terms of market value, in just 20 years.

Edwards is as big as a linebacker, as aggressive as a Wall Streeter, but a low-key person who has meticulously avoided the media. Nonetheless, he granted me an interview for this book in spring 2007, and he's a very engaging, articulate fellow.

Edwards's rise to riches began in 1987 when he was 28 years old. He was practising law and enjoying life, then suddenly he lost a close friend, of roughly the same age, to brain cancer.

"It caused me to look at myself and do what I really wanted to do, which was to try business," said Murray in the no-frills penthouse offices of his holding company, Edco Financial, in Calgary.

"After he died, I left law practice and went from making a good living to no salary," he said. "I did a joint venture with Peters & Co. [a Calgary investment bank] and two partners, Jim Grenon and Ron Mathison, to do deals. After five years, we split up. In January 1989, we started Canadian Natural Resources Ltd. with Al Markin with $100,000 and also started Ensign Resource Service Group later that year."

By 2007, Canadian Natural Resources had also become one of the biggest players in Canada's oil sands. Edwards's companies pump out more oil every day than some OPEC countries, and production by 2015 will soar as oil sands production comes on stream. The company has budgeted, over that period, $25 billion for oil sands projects, which consist of converting the sands into crude oil. For years to come, Canadian Natural will operate the largest construction site in Canada: in 2007 it employed more than 7,000 engineers and construction workers. Current production is 600,000 barrels of oil a day, and by 2020, oil sands production should add another 400,000 barrels per day—a total of 1 million barrels daily, which is equivalent to 40% of Canada's exports to the United States.

Edwards also helped to build Penn West Petroleum, a public energy trust, and owns 18% of Ensign Energy Services (Canada's second-largest oil service company) plus 30% of Magellan Aerospace and 40% of Imperial Metals, the second-biggest mining operator in British Columbia. On top of all that, he owns 18% of the Calgary Flames and a ski resort at Lake Louise.

Edwards is a soft-spoken individual with a king-sized stature. He is six feet, two inches tall and has a broad, friendly face. He grew up in Saskatchewan, the middle child of three.

"My grandparents all immigrated from Wales. One was a blacksmith and another a homesteader," he said. "My sister is an optometrist in Regina and my brother a doctor in Calgary. I always had an interest in politics. Then I figured out that most politicians were lawyers, so I went to law school. I took a business degree at the University of Saskatchewan, then went to the University of Toronto law school. But I found out that I liked business more than politics."

After graduation in Ontario, he headed straight for Calgary and a job at one of the city's biggest law firms, Burnet, Duckworth and Palmer.

"I liked law. I liked Toronto, but felt a calling back to the west. Out here the economy allows you to succeed on your own merits, rather than success based on your family background," he said.

He formed his investment banking partnership, then struck out on his own. The rest, as they say, is history, and he has parlayed thousands into billions of dollars of value by becoming the oil patch's chief consolidator, scooping up smaller companies as well as the Canadian subsidiaries of multinational oil giants that wanted out of Canada.

He has also built the company by democratizing ownership, which incorporates loyalty and ambition into the corporate culture.

"Canadian Natural Resources is one of the largest independent oil and gas companies in the world and its management [with employees] has the largest ownership position among such companies, at about 15%," he said.

"We started it in January 1989 with a market capitalization of $1 million, a stock price of 7 cents a share and 400 barrels a day of production. Now it produces 600,000 barrels a day and has an enterprise value of C$48 billion," he said. "It has been hard work. We were a consolidator and made strategic acquisitions: Sceptre Resources in 1996, Ranger Oil in 2001, Rio Alto in 2002, the private acquisition of BP Amoco's Canadian oil assets in 1999 and Anadarko Petroleum Corporation's Canadian assets in 2006."

Al Markin declined to be interviewed for this book by deferring to Edwards. "He can tell you everything you need to know. You don't need to talk to me."

Markin had a string of successes in the oil patch prior to his partnership with Edwards. He became a star at Merland Exploration Ltd. during the 1970s, then left to run Poco Petroleum Inc. from 1983 to 1987. Most years were good, and the stock went from $1 to $20 before fizzling out in the oil "depression." In 1989, Markin teamed up with Edwards.

One of the keys to Edwards and Markin's success has been not only consolidating the industry but keeping the people acquired along with the assets.

"Anadarko was a 100% exit from Canada, so all the key people came with the deal. BP [another acquisition] kept their natural gas assets, so only some people came over to us," said Edwards. "Every worker gets stock through savings plans or options. This creates an alignment of interest."

Canadian Natural has a flat organizational flow chart. A management committee of 14 people runs the operation and meets often. Members include those who run marketing, exploration, finance, accounting, production, exploitation, land and corporate development as well as the chief operating officer, Edwards, and Markin, who's the chair.

The company has also devised creative solutions to get skilled workers to work in its remote oil sands project hours north of Edmonton.

"We are running direct flights to the oil sands site from Deer Lake, Montreal, St. John's, Moncton, Winnipeg, Vancouver, Kamloops. We have weekly flights that take them directly to the site, within 5 hours tops, and in 15 minutes they are at work," he said. "We also have services. A Tim Hortons on site, for instance. Some of our employees have moved to Fort McMurray."

Besides manpower issues, Canadian Natural must deal with the reality that it is a "price taker" not a "price maker." This means cost controls, innovative ways to save funds and avoidance of excess debt.

"There's a lesson as to how fleeting things are. You must always be looking for the next opportunity. People tend to get complacent with success. But you have to earn it every day—it's not a given right," he said.

Dealing with failure is also necessary. Edwards counts as a "turning point" his first dry hole.

"We capitalized Canadian Natural and hired operating management. We bought land and drilled our first well," he said. "I was convinced we would find something, but it was a dry hole. I was humbled but realized that you drill dry holes in life, so you must have a plan B."

The current optimism that China and India will ensure high commodity prices for years is not something to go to the bank on, said Edwards.

"Is it different this time? When people start to say this boom will last forever, that's probably a sign that we are close to the end. There's a pause in western Canada right now. People are more prudent. Leverage can be your undoing. Euphoria is cause for concern.

Government intervention and environmental issues are a concern. Price volatility is a worry, so you have to cautiously manage leverage," he said.

The cyclicality of the oil business led Edwards to diversify. In 1993, he got into the aerospace business, which he considers counter-cyclical to oil prices, and, in 1995, mining. When prices for oil are high, aerospace is hurt, because airlines must pay more for fuel, which is roughly one-third of all their costs. Conversely, when fuel prices drop, aerospace profits should theoretically rise, because airline costs go down and profits can go up.

"We acquired Magellan Aerospace as a diversification from oil and gas. Its customers were planes and they burned fuel, so it was counter-cyclical. But it's been challenging. It's a real work in progress and breaks even. It has taken additional time for me. My view is that if you persevere with a business and have fortitude and liquidity to work through problems, hopefully one day you will see profits. There are two positives: airlines are picking up and ordering aircraft, and Canada is starting to spend more on defence."

The company makes parts and landing gear and employs 3,500 workers around the world.

His mining venture, by contrast, has been another home run.

"I bought Imperial Metals when it was cheap and nobody was building mines in Canada anymore. But we got involved with Sumitomo Canada Ltd. and built a mine in 1997. Then acquired a second one. We're the second-biggest mining operator in BC."

Edwards is obviously a smart operator and negotiator. There are also other elements contributing to his enormous success.

"You have to be lucky to be good, but you also have to be good to be lucky," he said. "There was a radical change in the [Alberta hydrocarbon] basin. There was a wholesale departure by multinationals such as Shell, Exxon, Texaco, BP. Their opinion in the 1980s and early 1990s was that Canada was a mature basin, the cost structure was too high and opportunities were too small, so many left. We aggressively captured their assets as they left—proactively. Then oil price increases helped."

For instance, Edwards and his team swooped down on BP Amoco in 1999 immediately after the company sent out a tentative press release talking about possible divestitures.

"We met with them in jeans and cowboy hats during that year's Friday Stampede Parade Day and hammered out a deal over the weekend when nobody else was working," he said.

Edwards still works constantly but now is married and has a baby son. He enjoys hockey and reading, and watches political manoeuvres with a keen eye.

Never one to rest on his laurels or anyone else's, he also has a unique take on his success.

"Have I been successful? I guess it depends on how you define 'success,'" he says. "Whether you are a teacher or a social worker or a businessman, everyone has his or her own metrics. It's about personal satisfaction and the difference you can make. That's how I define success."

But Edwards is also an optimist about his region.

"Look at this city or western Canada. This is a real success story, a wealth-creating engine. We have resources: uranium, potash, oil, gas, coal. I would argue that agriculture is not that far behind in terms of importance in global trade, as feedstock for energy and as the breadbasket for Asia. So western Canada is well positioned," he said.

THE MANNIXES

Ron Mannix ascribes to his father's philosophy that the only good publicity is no publicity. Some say his father, Fred, used to pay public relations specialists to keep the family's name out of newspapers. The fact is, the family's late patriarch, F.C. Mannix, rarely gave interviews. As a result, he was rarely mentioned in the press and didn't need staff to keep it that way.

The Mannixes still live quietly. They are involved in many public causes, and I have socialized with Ron Mannix and his wife,

Nancy, at the World Economic Forum in Davos. But I have only interviewed Ron once for this book, and it was on that occasion that he shared the reasoning behind the familial reticence.

"In my personal opinion, you don't give interviews because it takes too much time, work and attention. I don't believe, for me, there's any real value in publicity," he said.

The family's shyness has been facilitated by the fact that their companies have, with two exceptions, been privately held. They have also been in the B2B, or business-to-business, category, never dealing directly with the public.

The empire began changing in 1997, and by 2006 the family had divested their largest holdings, in part for succession-planning purposes. Ron and Fred have a sister, Maureen, who moved back to Calgary in 2006. The three have 12 children collectively, and the family's Carthy Foundation supports many worthwhile causes. But the siblings conduct their own philanthropy as well.

Fred has concentrated on the issue of the demilitarization of Canada, or, put another way, the proclivity on the part of Ottawa to let the Americans defend North America. He is also on the board of the Fraser Institute, among other organizations.

Ron is a director and financial backer of the Canadian Council of Chief Executives. He travels extensively and is concerned about helping Canadian economic and political leaders understand the environmental challenges and what is happening in China, India and elsewhere. His Norlien Foundation deals with disadvantaged children, environmental matters, music, and health/wellness and addiction.

In 1997, the Mannixes sold all the assets that they jointly owned. These included Pembina Corp., an oil and gas pipeline company, and Manalta Coal Ltd., the country's largest coal miner. The assets were worth about $1.6 billion.

Fred operates the Mancal Group of companies, which includes an operating oil company called Mancal Energy Inc., which owns 25% of a huge natural gas discovery made in 2004 by Shell Canada Ltd.

Fred is also involved in commercial real estate. His most notable holding is Calgary's Nexen Building, which stands among the city's core of oil-company head-office towers. The Mancal website, which enumerates the firm's holdings, highlights an interest in global business opportunities, including activities in the United Kingdom, Kazakhstan and Barbados.

Fred has been an honorary colonel in the Calgary Highlanders, where, before retiring in 1994, he was known affectionately as "Colonel Fred." Like his sister and brother, he grew up working in the business. At 15, he worked in a coal mine. At 16, he operated a bulldozer at the Brazeau Dam, then held a succession of project management jobs. So did his brother.

Ron operates through Coril Holdings Ltd. He also owns Loram Maintenance of Way, Inc., a private railway-maintenance company with superb technology that is headquartered in Minneapolis but operates globally. In addition he runs a development company that built the plush Hyatt Hotel in downtown Calgary, a favourite meeting place of the city's business community.

The fortune was launched by their father, Frederick Charles Mannix, who expanded from construction to pipelines, oil and gas, coal and railway maintenance. The Mannix construction companies were involved in huge infrastructure projects such as the Trans-Canada Highway, the Toronto and Montreal subway systems, Calgary's and Edmonton's light rail systems, Quebec's James Bay Project, the St. Lawrence Seaway, big power dams around the world and Arctic artificial islands for oil exploration.

Ron's father's lifelong pal, and lawyer, was former Alberta premier Peter Lougheed.

"He was like a brother to me, and we travelled the world together," the late Mannix told me in an interview years ago.

The Mannix coal assets, the biggest in western Canada, were sold to Luscar Ltd., which was taken over by Sherritt Gordon Limited (which became Sherritt Inc. in 1993). Some assets are now part of Fording Canadian Coal Trust.

Fred, Ron and Maureen's grandfather, also named Frederick,

started the Mannix enterprise, but his only son—their father—grew it to unimaginable heights. He learned the business at his father's side and travelled with him from camp to camp. His father built hydroelectric dams but realized Alberta was running out of cheap, accessible energy-rich areas to exploit, so he started buying coal mines.

Hard times hit in the early 1940s during the war, so the Mannixes sold 51% to their archrival, the Morrison-Knudsen Company of Idaho, the world's biggest earth-moving contractor. The proviso was that young Mannix would still run operations on behalf of both owners. But in 1951, after two major oil discoveries in Alberta brought a rush of business, the Mannixes were able to buy back the firm. Their father had also learned all about Morrison-Knudsen's earth-moving techniques.

The oil discoveries in Alberta led to opportunities and the Mannix firm became pioneers in "big-inch" pipe. They ended up owning the Pembina Pipeline Corporation.

The 1950s were a boom time, and the railway maintenance business arose out of construction contracts with railways. Loram Maintenance has patented and designed custom-made machines that crawl along railway lines, grinding railheads, ditching, ballast cleaning and changing out old rails for new ones—at up to 15 miles an hour.

No longer in construction, the brothers operate some businesses, invest their capital, do their philanthropy and live quiet lives on huge ranches outside Calgary. Their father died in 1995.

Fred, the oldest, is a pilot and avid outdoorsman who hunts around the world. A capable administrator, Fred once confided in a rare interview in the 1980s that heavy lies the mantle of management.

"Altogether there are 132 companies. It can drive you out of your mind," he told a local reporter. Today there are only a few dozen left.

Ron had a different take about family businesses when we chatted in 2007.

"Family business is the best business there is when it's done right, and it's the worst business when it's done wrong," he said. "That's because when it's done wrong, it can destroy both the family and the business. When it's done right, it can improve the family and the business and the community."

CLAY RIDDELL

Oil billionaire Clay Riddell would have gone bust in 1983 if there had not been a fire one weekend at the huge Syncrude oil sands plant in Fort McMurray.

His Paramount Resources Ltd. was caught in a squeeze: he was a small independent natural gas company—had discovered lots of it, but could not sell it because of a downturn in economic conditions.

"I had contracted my gas to Pan-Alberta [Gas Ltd.]. Trans-Canada PipeLines and other pipeline companies were not buying from independents like me. So I sold my gas and was all ready to produce it," he said in an interview in his Calgary offices. "I had ordered nine compressors [to get the gas into the pipeline] at $1.5 million each, but I didn't have the cash to pay for them. I just figured the bank would finance me."

But one phone call made it clear to Riddell that getting a bank to finance the compressors had suddenly become impossible.

"It was a Friday when Pan-Alberta called and said their purchase of my gas would be delayed by one year. That was a disaster. I had no way to pay for those compressors, which meant that the company was basically bankrupt," he recalled.

As luck would have it, the very next day—Saturday—Riddell read about a huge fire at Syncrude's oil sands plant, which had destroyed five compressors just like the ones Riddell had bought.

"So I called them up to sell my compressors and on Monday they bought them, for a 50% price uptick [50% more than Riddell had paid]," he said.

Riddell said this is not the only lucky break he, and others like him in the oil patch, has had. Sitting down with him in his Calgary office in 2007 was a treat. He's a Prairies guy, polite and friendly, modest and very direct. There is no irony, sarcasm or passive aggressiveness out here and that's refreshing.

"I have stretched farther in business than I ever should have, several times. I have been very aggressive. I did this because early on, I had made enough wealth so I would never be destitute. This meant that betting the whole thing never bothered me. I had enough assets and just wanted to compete. It was sort of a game I played against the majors [big multinational oil companies] to see if I could build a big company," he said.

And he won the game. Riddell is CEO and chair of Paramount Resources, which is 50.1% owned by Clay and his family. His son, Jim Riddell, runs Trilogy Energy Trust, which the family owns 25% of; his daughter Susan (Sue) Riddell Rose runs Paramount Energy Trust (50.1%); and his son-in-law, Mike Rose, runs Duvernay Oil Corporation (15%) and North American Oil Sands (33%). In April 2007, North American Oil Sands was sold to Norway's Statoil for $2.2 billion.

For fun, Riddell is also part-owner of the Calgary Flames hockey club, along with Murray Edwards and Alvin Libin, as well as of Calgary's Big Rock Brewery.

"I never expected to have the portfolio I have. My advisors and brokers say I have the worst portfolio in the world, having mostly oil and companies which I control," he said. "But it has been a slow and steady growth for 30 years with continuing reinvestment in energy."

Riddell and children Jim and Sue are all geologists. Daughter Brenda is a lawyer and entrepreneur and Lynn runs Paramount's computer operations. All are business-oriented. In 1990 Jim and Sue joined the firm, and both hit the ground running, Clay Riddell said.

"Both sat around the dinner table, as did the other two, and sort of followed events. They got a feel for the industry. Sue worked for Shell Canada for five years, which was good training. Once the two of them were on board they got very aggressive," he said.

Brenda owns a breeding operation and runs the Alaris Fund, which "buys" cash flows from companies so they can become public companies.

"It's one-of-a-kind and allows management to continue or else be bought out or expand," said Riddell.

Riddell's wife, Violet, is a nurse but also sits on Paramount's board of directors. The two met in Edmonton. In 1959, Clay had been transferred there as a young geologist working for Chevron Corporation.

Riddell grew up in Winnipeg with two older sisters and inherited his entrepreneurship and aggressive risk-taking attitude from his father, Cecil Riddell.

"My dad did everything and anything. He had a farm in southwest Manitoba and he lost it during the Depression. Then he ran a grocery store for years and finally went to Winnipeg in 1940. He decided he'd never been anywhere, so he lied about his age—he was too old—and joined up to fight in the war. The military found out in the UK he lied, so he was parked there for four years and never saw any action," he said.

After Cecil returned to Manitoba, he worked odd jobs, sold vacuum cleaners and owned a hamburger joint, "which was a dump," said his son.

At 13, Riddell decided to find a job and remembers a conversation he had with his father about working.

"My dad came home and said, 'How'd it go? Got a job? No? Where'd you go? Nowhere?' Then he said to me, 'An employer won't walk in here and offer you a job. You've got to go out and find one.' He told me there were always jobs around for those who looked," he recalled.

Riddell's interest in exploration came about in 1950, when one of his sisters became a geologist and got him summer jobs in the bush with Manitoba's mines department.

"So I went into sciences," he said. "I was a bush geologist every summer for 15 years. In the winter I learned other stuff. Then I began consulting to pay the bills, so I could learn more stuff. I ran a little company for [Vancouver stock promoter] Murray Pezim. When I started, oil was $2.56 a barrel and gas 10 cents a thousand cubic feet."

He mastered the art of acquiring land positions and financings, and in 1975 he launched his own firm.

"I started Paramount as a private company. No partners," he said. "I think having partners is probably the worst idea. I've seen so many breakups. I think it's better to do it yourself and learn yourself."

Riddell eventually took his companies public, thus acquiring partners, but rejected the use of multiple voting shares to control his empire.

"I control my company the old-fashioned way. The use of multiple voting shares was suggested to me, but I wasn't interested," he said.

His decision to split Paramount up into two income trusts was tax-driven but also management-driven.

"I don't think I'm smart enough to manage a company the size of Anderson [Exploration] or EnCana. So breaking it off into bite-sized pieces was appealing as well as tax-efficient," he said.

The future for energy is very positive, and big Canadian independents like Riddell's will continue to be consolidators, acquiring assets and companies.

But like so many other Alberta tycoons, Riddell is friendly, with a down-to-earth style even though he and his family have a king-sized income from trusts, estimated at $150 million a year. He is often seen standing in line with other Paramount workers at a coffee shop near the company's headquarters. He also owns several high-end restaurants, breeds horses on his 400-acre estate southwest of Calgary and avoids publicity.

But he and his family are quietly philanthropic and have targeted mental illness and education among their causes. Politics is another passion, and Riddell helped bankroll Preston Manning and his fledgling Reform Party following Ottawa's 1980 National Energy Program debacle.

He remains a fiercely proud westerner and worries about Canada's future political fragmentation.

"Gradually, we are getting some financial power in the west. The two biggest pipeline companies in North America are here and other important head offices. But we need a bank," he said. "I worry about the dithering in the east. They lost control of Inco and Falconbridge.

"Fortunately, free trade has been a great boon. Without it, we would have a 50-cent dollar. It has brought more competition, and industries like forestry struggle. I have never been a western separatist, but am still very much opposed to the complete domination of government by eastern Canada. All the power's in the east and still is. I worry about that."

THE SOUTHERNS

Industrialist Ron Southern likes nothing better than to read books about Churchill, Montgomery and medicine. *Gray's Anatomy* sits on a bookshelf in his office, and the *Merck's Manual* guide to pharmaceuticals is usually beside his desk.

"He's a closet doctor," explains his eldest daughter, Nancy Southern, CEO of ATCO Group. "Everyone in the office goes to him for medical advice."

That is because Ron, ATCO's chairman and the son of British immigrants, wanted to go to medical school as a young man. Instead, he came up with a different prescription for success. He and his father, S.D. Southern, a Calgary fireman, invented portable industrial housing in 1948 in their family garage.

Today, the Southerns own a global manufacturing company that dominates a niche and are also the only family in Canada to own a power utility.

In 2006, ATCO Ltd. was Canada's 125th-largest corporation, with $2.86 billion in sales, $7.69 billion in assets, $207 million in profits and 8,000 employees. The family owns 82% of voting stock. Canadian Utilities is 74% owned by ATCO and in 2006 had $2.4 billion in revenues, $6.9 billion in assets, $359.7 million in profits and 6,374 employees. It provides power for the northern two-thirds of Alberta, including the gigantic oil sands region.

ATCO began after the Second World War. Ron saved the tips he made working summers at the Banff Springs Hotel and combined that with his father's $2,000 demobilization pay from the RCAF, and the two started Alberta Trailer Hire beside a service station.

"We adapted U-Haul trailers from the States and invented workforce housing that didn't consist of just putting up a tent," he said in an interview in his Calgary office.

From that modest grubstake, ATCO became a world-beater, its orange and aluminum cubicles home to everyone from scientists in the Antarctic to construction workers in Greece, pipeline welders in Argentina, oil explorers in Sumatra, missile trackers in the Indian Ocean, highway builders in France, miners in Nigeria and smelter workers in Australia.

ATCO is the world's largest manufacturer of construction-camp shelters, but it has also shipped schools to Saudi Arabia, portable hospitals to Vietnam, and entire towns to Algeria. In addition it is a huge land-contract drilling and well-servicing company in Canada.

This is a uniquely western Canadian business, forged by the needs of Alberta's infant oil industry. ATCO began by building housing for oilmen to live in when drilling in empty wasteland, where roads, good weather and accommodation are scarce. That is in part why the company became the world's first, and pre-eminent, builder of prefab structures that can be disassembled quickly and transported over roadless glaciers, tundra or deserts.

In 2007, ATCO remained the only global player in this lucrative niche.

"We just did a project in Indonesia for 4,000 workers building an LNG [liquified natural gas] plant," said Nancy, CEO of ATCO and Ron's oldest daughter. "Now everyone wants a better camp because they are competing to attract people. There's a flat-screen television in every room; there are single rooms, recreational basket-ball courts; one camp has a one-kilometre running track suspended above the camp; they have pubs, restaurants, theatres. These are mini towns."

ATCO also has a wartime contract division, ATCO Fron-tec, providing housing, canteen, maintenance, communications and sanitation services. In addition, the division runs the North Warning System in Canada and Alaska for the two countries, an expertise that arose out of its utility's ability to run and control unmanned power plants in remote and hostile locations.

From the beginning, ATCO housing has been a huge suc-cess. But it was also dependent upon resource exploration and extraction, which meant it was a cyclical business. In 1980, Ron bought a plodding regulated power monopoly in Edmonton called Canadian Utilities.

It was a hostile takeover, and an ugly battle ensued with Cal-gary Power, the hydroelectric utility. Ron put the whole company on the line.

"It cost $350 million to buy control. For a little trailer builder, it was a big reach," said Ron. "But I wanted a non-cycli-cal business to build a stable future. Everyone in Calgary said to me, 'What's wrong? Lost all your courage? Why buy a utility? Why not take a chance?'"

But Ron nearly lost everything months after buying the utility.

"Interest rates went to 23%. The National Energy Program crippled the oil industry. I had a few sleepless nights," he said. "In 15 months, we would have had no money left. We knew that to renegotiate with lenders was not on—they were all panicking. I took our 5-year plan and threw it away and said, 'It means diddly-squat if we're not in business.'"

He and his team of 55 managers from around the world met monthly for years until the balance sheet was restored.

"We learned our lessons and turned it around. We put the right people in the right jobs, and that became the foundation of what ATCO is today," he said.

The power utility presents the biggest challenge in the future.

"We currently handle 13,000 megawatts of power and have to double that amount in 10 years," said Nancy. "It's phenomenal. But project-execution risk is what I worry about—people taking shortcuts, or a debacle due to inexperienced people. I don't see where we're going to find the people, either."

Other challenges include the competition for assets against pension funds and private equity pools of capital.

"This represents an unlevel playing field. We pay taxes and want to maintain our credit rating and are competing against tax-free entities or leveraged-buyout artists," she said. "Our mentality is to protect our reputation so we can grow our companies and protect shareholders. The private equity mentality is take C$1 billion, put together a fund, use junk debt, then buy, strip and sell off pieces."

ATCO is very much a family business but is committed to rewarding entrepreneurs within its ranks. It also stands uniquely alone as Canada's biggest clan led by a woman. Nancy is CEO; her sister, Linda Southern-Heathcott, is on the ATCO board but runs the family's successful Spruce Meadows equestrian centre, theme park and championship series. Their mother, Marg, has also been a full-fledged partner in the building of all these businesses and serves on a number of corporate boards in her own right.

"I was always fascinated with business. I was a child of commerce," said Nancy. "I played in the factory and on the trailers. Also, Mom was such a big part in the company that dinner conversation every night was about business."

Half of Nancy's executive committee of six are female and roughly her age, in their mid-40s. Nancy ran the company with her father for three years but now is the boss.

"We work well together, and he's still involved and important," she said.

Nancy feels that being female is obviously not a disadvantage for her but says there is a glass ceiling for other women everywhere, including at ATCO.

"Being a woman is an advantage for me. In this organization there isn't the usual prejudice, partly because R.D. [Ron] had no sons," she said.

Nancy and Linda seem to handle their business and family responsibilities just fine. As for the next generation, each sister has three children who are too young to know whether they want to join the family businesses in some capacity.

"Just as my sister and I had the opportunity to do what we wanted to do, we will want them to do what's best for them," said Nancy.

Going forward, ATCO's business model is pretty secure, although there is a Chinese competitor now.

"We are in workforce housing, then got into drilling, then repatriated Canadian Utilities. It's a sound model, and I don't see us deviating much from that. We have triple-A credit rating and are culturally entrepreneurial. We have a 40-60 split between our two businesses in either direction and are comfortable with that," she said. "If we see the non-regulated operations grow out of range, we will look at acquisitions on the utility side or growth on that side. But we will not do a big bolt-on."

Nancy attributes the success of the empire to her father's intellectual aptitudes—and grit.

"I had a drinking problem," said Ron, who stopped in 1970. He said he took up riding with his daughters as a "substitute for drinking, and all the extra energy and time went into that."

This energy and mental curiosity are key ingredients to his and ATCO's success, said Nancy.

"He's always hungry for knowledge and reads some 12 to 15 newspapers a day before he leaves the house," she said. "They come from around the world—the *New York Times*, *FT*, *[The] Times* of London, *Herald Tribune*, *Washington Post* and all the Canadian and local papers. He's forever circulating articles around the office. He sees trends very quickly and then is at the forefront to act or correct. He also works on his network of colleagues around the world. Then, when he makes a decision, he demands thorough analysis—the what-ifs. He's a big fan of negative thinking."

Ron once explained ATCO to me by writing down several key phrases on a blackboard in a Spruce Meadows meeting room: "The plan must be simple: Easily communicated and transparent. There must be a determined execution—guts, skating and back-checking. We must have the spirit to win. A firm grip. We don't get knocked off the puck easily. That's ATCO."

MINING

Mining built Canada and has quietly continued to grow in size and importance. As of 2007, Canada remained one of the world's biggest exporters of metals and minerals and Toronto raised more money for mining financings than any other city. More mining companies are listed on the Toronto Stock Exchange than elsewhere, and Canadian mining expertise is respected—and sought—worldwide, from geology to drilling and engineering. Canadians also dominate the world of specialized legal and accounting mining services.

As testament to its prominence, every year the world's mining executives descend on Toronto for the Prospectors and Developers Association of Canada international conference. In 2007, the confab attracted a record attendance of 16,000 participants from around the world. The conference features panels, lectures, displays, schmoozing and awards events. So does Vancouver's mining conference, called Roundup, which that year drew a record 6,000 attendees.

But mining in Canada has not been everyone's cup of tea. It is a rough business populated with colourful characters. Its boom-

and-bust nature makes it risky but hugely lucrative, and also very susceptible to fraud. Criminality has been easy because news or rumours of a discovery, real or imagined, can create fortunes overnight. By the time the dust settles, and the rumours or discovery is debunked, the liars have cashed in. Contributing to this culture over the years was the absence of securities laws in Canada, until in 1963 a gigantic insider trading scandal besmirched dozens of companies from across North America and led to imprisonment for some CEOs. Securities laws were put in place in 1964, but the shenanigans continued for years because many scoundrels simply shifted themselves and their operations to small, poorly policed exchanges in Vancouver and Calgary.

Scandals dogged the western exchanges but were peanuts compared to what happened in 1997. The world's biggest gold swindle involved Bre-X Minerals Ltd. of Calgary. About $9 billion in stock market value eventually evaporated following the alleged suicide of its field geologist, who was reported to have jumped out of a helicopter in Borneo on his way to explain why independent drilling had failed to verify his massive gold discovery. Independent consultants later determined that his assays had been "salted" with gold from another location and that the announced results were a total fraud. Around the same time, a second salting scandal occurred, involving another junior company in Canada. The Bre-X scandal and others resulted in tougher rules governing mining disclosures and assaying and in the closure of Canada's small exchanges in Vancouver, Calgary and Montreal.

Bre-X made headlines around the world and contributed to a mining depression that lasted a number of years. Fortunately, by the time metals prices began to improve in 2003, Canada had cleaned up its act and its mining sector was able to participate in the opportunities that higher prices began to yield. Exploration jumped, bringing about discoveries; mines expanded and new ones were commissioned. Another boom had begun, this time fuelled by escalating prices for everything from copper to potash, coal, zinc, gold, nickel, lead and uranium. Some today talk of a super-cycle of prices because of world economic growth rates and Asia's industrialization and infrastructure investments.

Investors inside and outside Canada have been flocking to the sector, and in 2006 foreign takeouts began, further driving up prices of stocks. In one 12-month period, ending in spring 2007, foreigners gobbled up four of Canada's biggest mining corporations. But this only freed up more money for other Canadian mining companies, who remain at the forefront of global exploration, dealmaking and growth.

ROBERT FRIEDLAND

In the 1970s, Chicago-born Robert Friedland lived in a cave in India as a mendicant. By 2007, he was a billionaire a few times over. He now owns homes in many countries plus a lavish Boeing 767 jet with a bedroom and gym. Even so, in some ways he still lives like an ascetic, minus the vow of poverty. Friedland doesn't indulge in the usual luxuries, works out rigorously every day and never, ever stops working. His life consists of time zones, cellphones and endless meetings in dozens of countries with heads of state, geologists, mine workers, engineers, financiers and investors.

"I basically live on an airplane," he told me. "We know countries like we know stocks."

Friedland's holding company is Ivanhoe Capital Corp., in Singapore, which controls two Vancouver-based public companies in the mining sector: Ivanhoe Mines Ltd., with a market value of US$5.3 billion in 2007, and Ivanhoe Energy Inc., worth about US$500 million. Friedland privately holds stakes in many other enterprises, as do both Ivanhoe companies.

During any given year, Friedland visits four dozen countries and logs enough miles to circumnavigate the globe a couple of dozen times. But his business trips are not about wining and dining clients. He immerses himself in the culture and power structure of a country in order to determine who to do business with and how.

Friedland, 56, is sandy-haired and boyish in appearance. He looks half his age, and is lean, fit and palpably intense. He can engage briefly, but mostly interacts by "mining" conversations for nuggets of knowledge, insight or anecdote.

He also holds court like a guru. Typical was a conversation we had in Beijing's swank China World Hotel complex. I arrived from a dinner party at the Canadian ambassador's residence, and Friedland sat cross-legged on a chair in the corporate lounge after a workout. It was 2 a.m. and people came and went. Robert listened, asked questions and made observations.

Friedland's father also had a remarkable life. He survived Auschwitz and ended up in Chicago working as an architect for Frank Lloyd Wright. The Friedlands even lived in Wright's Wisconsin commune for a while, then Robert went to a tiny liberal arts college in New England. He transferred to Reed College in Oregon, where his roommate was Steve Jobs, founder of Apple.

The two headed to India to work for a non-profit helping the poor. Friedland stayed longer than the two-year stint, learned Hindi and became a spiritual seeker. He refers to this experience as the "India years."

He returned with a wife and children. After working as a tree farmer in Oregon, he came up with a simple business proposition—and his pal Jobs grubstaked it.

"Trees grow 9% a year at absolutely no cost to the owner, so we bought lots of timber rights and made money," he said. "Then I fell into mining by accident."

Around 1981, he immigrated to Vancouver.

"The appeal was multiculturalism and the fact that it was very neat. When I came it was pretty quiet. Boring, actually," he added. "But mining companies are registered in Canada like ships are registered in Liberia. It's a large land mass that is incredibly well endowed in mining resources. Mining is much smaller in the U.S. than it is in Canada, where it is 10% of the economy."

Mining was his métier. He has also made fortunes in other

ventures, from timber to XM Radio and Internet portal Sina.com in China, but nothing compares with his track record in mining.

Exploration is always a gamble—guesswork by scientists as to what's valuable underground and where to drill. Explorers have to kiss a lot of frogs before they ever find a prince. The difference is that while some never do, Friedland's found more than most.

His geologists, financed by his ability to raise lots of money from investors, have found lots of stuff but, more importantly, have made two world-class discoveries: a nickel deposit in Labrador and a gold/copper find in Mongolia that may become the largest in history.

"Robert Friedland is a genius," said Norman Keevil, chair of gigantic Teck Cominco Limited of Vancouver in a 2007 interview for this book. "He's great at all aspects of the mining business."

Friedland's first billions came in 1996, when he sold Diamond Fields Resources Ltd.—and its nickel discovery—to Inco Ltd. for $4.3 billion. Teck made $350 million on the deal.

That same year, Friedland was sued by the U.S. Environmental Protection Agency (EPA), which alleged that he should be solely liable for environmental cleanup costs at an abandoned mine site in Colorado. The EPA tried to seize Friedland's Canadian assets, but he won after the company hired by the EPA to clean up the site was indicted by a U.S. grand jury for not doing the job and thereby defrauding the EPA.

That whole affair tainted Friedland south of the border, but he was already mostly living in and concentrating on doing business in Asia.

"We went to Mongolia in 1996 after the country adopted a Canadian-style mining law that guaranteed tenure," he said. "Then we acquired a large land position of 33,000 square kilometres"—half the size of New Brunswick.

But by 1997, his biggest hopes were pinned on Indochina Goldfields, which had staked claims in and around an alleged giant discovery of Canadian exploration outfit Bre-X. In May of that year, Friedland raised $375 million to commence drilling there, just days before Bre-X's geologist leaped out of the helicopter near the mine site in Borneo. Weeks later, investigators determined that it had been the biggest gold swindle in history.

In hindsight, Friedland's timing turned out to be fortunate. Bre-X brought about a drought in mine financings that lasted for years, and Indochina was flush. Friedland renamed it Ivanhoe Mines and deployed its cash in Mongolia.

"We were lucky we raised the money before the music stopped," he said. "God was thinking about changing her mind and decided to make us lucky."

Ivanhoe spent $8 million and five years drilling dry holes in the Gobi Desert until Friedland met Gramjev, a Mongolian anthropologist and geologist who is a direct descent of Genghis Khan.

"He said, drill on Turquoise Hill and you will find gold," Friedland recalled.

That hill—Oyu Tolgoi in Mongolian—was where Tibetans 5,000 years ago mined turquoise for jewellery. Turquoise happens to be oxidized copper, and copper is often found with gold. The result was that Ivanhoe's hole #150 tested gold and copper in astounding quantities.

"We're not talking about finding a mine here," he explained. "This is the world's first new gold/copper province—not a mine or a field, but a province. If I have a genius at all, it's to create a corporate culture that listened to a guy like Gramjev."

Even sweeter, Friedland had taken the land off the hands of BHP Billiton Limited, whose geologists had given up. Now, as of 2007, further drilling has shown that there's more gold and copper in this deposit than on the books of BHP and the Rio Tinto Group combined.

Since then, the Mongolia play has been pure Friedland: he has mastered Mongolian geology as well as the nuances of Mongolian nomadic culture and politics. His team dominates the economy and has been building both a charitable presence and a huge camp in the desert at the mine site.

His investment hasn't abated despite the fact that both sides have been trying to negotiate a final development agreement for years. In 2006, London's Rio Tinto Group committed at least US$1 billion to gain an option for up to 40% of Ivanhoe, and represented a vote of confidence in the project.

"This is Mongolia's shot to be an important, prosperous country," said Friedland. "We get it and are continuing work. We also realize that any deal must be fair, and philanthropic, in order to create a sustainable development franchise in the nation."

Friedland's other far-flung operations include mines in Tasmania and Kazakhstan. He is involved in oil and mineral exploration in China as well as a small gold mine operation there, the first licensed to foreigners. There's also the commercialization of a process to convert oil sands bitumen and heavy oils into light crude without using fuel or emissions, and a top-secret project in Russia using nuclear power for excavation.

Robert Friedland has become the embodiment of the global economy. He moves to the action, and he recognized China's potential years before others did.

"China will improve the world. The Chinese believe in hard work, achievement, respect for elders," he said. "They are acquisitive and have a strong desire for material goods. The world is divided between consumers like us and the Chinese, and those in the other world, like the terrorists who drove the planes into the World Trade Center. They're the enemies of the system. The Chinese are our best friends because they are consumers."

"I have never encountered corruption there because we deal with large parastatal entities like PetroChina. In that country, you get a bullet in your head if you're caught being a crook," he said.

Personally, Friedland will roam the world until he cannot and shows few signs of a slowdown or of aging.

"Twenty years ago, we realized that we were a company that never sleeps because we operate in all time zones," he said. "We have Canadians in every country imaginable working for us today. This is the new world. Most don't get it."

NORMAN KEEVIL

Norman Keevil spent a boyhood staking claims with his dad around the family cottage on Lake Temagami in Ontario. Eventually, they made a copper discovery, which led to the creation of Temagami Mining Co. and also to his father's departure from his life as a professor at the University of Toronto.

In 1962, young Norman was also headed for academia. He had graduated with a PhD in geophysics from Berkeley University in California and headed off to a university job in Utah. Then his mother called.

"She asked me to work with my dad. I didn't want to, but she said, 'We really need you,'" Norman recalled. "So I joined."

And in the next 45 years, Norman Keevil took his family's small copper producer in Ontario, started by his father, who was also a geophysicist named Norman Keevil, and turned it into mining powerhouse Teck Cominco Limited of Vancouver, the world's sixth-biggest mining company and Canada's 62nd-largest corporation.

Teck mines 1 million tonnes of rock per day around the world and throws off $50 million worth of cash a week. By 2007, it had attained a market value of $16 billion and had $4.8 billion cash in the bank despite paying the highest dividend of any major mining company in the world.

Teck is one of Canada's biggest coal producers and operates the world's biggest zinc mine, in Alaska. In July 2007, it snapped up Aur Resources Inc. for $4 billion, and the cash-rich giant owns pieces of dozens more mining outfits. Teck has also moved into the lucrative oil sands, in partnership with Petro-Canada and others. Its share of reserves totals 1 billion barrels of oil, and by 2010 its portion of production will be greater than that of oil sands pioneer Suncor Energy Inc. of Calgary.

Keevil agreed to an interview and brought notes. We went to lunch in summer 2007 outside on the patio of the Pan Pacific Hotel, overlooking Vancouver's Coal Harbour. He spoke so softly that he was barely audible over the seagulls and the café chatter.

He has very blue eyes and looks like the British aristocrat that he is supposed to be. His grandfather was due to inherit a fortune in Britain but instead accompanied a shipload of horses to Canada and never left. Norman's father was eccentric and brilliant but easily distracted. Norman, by contrast, is steady and resilient to the ups and downs of his father's focus as well as to those of mining. The result is that he has created one of the country's greatest corporations.

"In my wildest dreams I never expected this," he said over lunch. "Five years after I joined Temagami, we bought two companies, Teck-Hughes and Goldfields, from Joe Hirschhorn. These were small companies which had 20 million barrels of oil, which was worth US$1 a barrel in those days. Today, we have 15% of a tar sands project and our share is 1 billion barrels."

Getting from there to here has been a journey and then some. But he describes himself as a "prudent risk-taker" and faithfully ascribes to his mantra of "first building good reserves, then finding the right people, and thirdly getting enough money."

"The first turning point for our company," he said, "was in 1968, when I hired Bob Hallbauer as CEO and a team from Placer Developments. We had worked together, and Placer was the best mining company in the world back in the 1960s."

Hallbauer seized the opportunity, then outlined the challenges to Keevil and his father.

"He said, 'You want to create a major mining company? You've been exploring for years and haven't found a mine. We have to pick up some ore reserves. You have no money, and none is available.' He was right. Finding isn't that easy. It takes years of effort and always involves a bit of luck," said Norman.

At that point, the company had three small underground mines with only two years' worth of reserves left to mine.

"So he had a point," he admitted.

In 1969, they bought control of two companies for $2 million and merged with both. That brought the total value to $20 million—small compared to Canada's biggest at that time, Noranda Ltd., with

$1 billion in shares. Noranda's assets have since disappeared into the balance sheets of mostly foreign mining companies.

Keevil hired even more top engineers, then moved operations to Vancouver and concentrated on mining projects that could be financed by banks. Unfortunately, by 1972 Teck still had a value of only $20 million, due to deteriorating prices for all metals and minerals and to the election in British Columbia of anti-mining New Democrat Dave Barrett.

"After the Barrett election, we put everything on hold but kept working on improving reserves in our projects, so that when the market turned we were sitting on lots of reserves," he said. "We also had half a dozen key employees that were the best in the business. We had more engineers per mine in head office than anybody else. We had talent, and the banks recognized that."

His mantra—reserves, people, money—was in sync, but then along came the recession of 1974. Keevil was in trouble and had to bet everything to keep going.

"My personal loans were bigger than my net worth, but nobody noticed," he said. "I took out the loans to buy my own stock."

He protected the company from bargain-hunting giants by creating dual-class shares.

"Without dual-class shares would I have lost the company? Yes. We had built up reserves which were not appreciated by the market for a while, and Noranda would've gladly grabbed us," he said.

The recession lingered, Barrett stayed in office and stock prices lagged, but Teck was still able to open three new mines by 1977. Next came entry into the coal business, in tandem with Stephen Roman's Denison Mines Ltd., which built a coal port on BC's coast. But Denison left in a sea of losses, while Teck has prospered for 20 years.

"Denison and the Japanese were betting on prices, so they negotiated market-price contracts," Keevil said. "We negotiated fixed prices with escalators. My approach, as a prudent risk-taker, is to make deals to keep the mines open for 20 years and to make sure the banks are paid back in the first four years. The result was that Denison couldn't afford to mine anymore when prices dropped."

Teck's BC coal success led to partnership in the Elk Valley Coal Partnership, the second-largest coal shipper in the world. It also invested in Robert Friedland's Diamond Fields, netting Teck a profit of $350 million, and invested that in a gold mine called Antamina in Peru.

"We were crucified by the stock market for a couple of years after we took Antamina on. It was during the middle of the Asian crisis, it was unclear whether we could finance it and it was risky because Peru was dangerous. It was also a mine in the high Andes, which had never been done before," he said.

Peru became a homer, then Teck acquired Canadian Pacific Limited's Cominco, with its giant Alaskan property. It became the world's biggest zinc mine.

In 2003, commodities began to jump in price as China and India gained economic steam. This tide lifted all mining boats, but Teck's more than most. By 2005, worldwide consolidation began sweeping the mining industry, first in gold, then in base metals.

"Inco did not have the right mentality and was not run by miners," said Norman. "These guys [Inco and Falconbridge] stared at each other for 30 years and should've been together for obvious reasons. We went to Inco and they thought buying Falconbridge would make us and everyone else go away because they would be too big."

Inco bid for Falconbridge, then Teck made a hostile $16-billion offer for Inco, in cash and shares. When the dust settled, Falconbridge was owned by Xstrata PLC, out of London, England, and Inco by Brazil's CVRD. Each buyer paid huge premiums.

"Inco had a combination of old production, which we felt we could improve, as well as new long-life reserves under development. But the financial capacity side of my mantra [reserves, people, money] also led us to pass when the bidding got out of hand," he said. "Do I regret not getting Inco? Yes. Do I regret not getting it by paying too much? No."

Teck remains on the hunt to explore and is immune from hostile takeovers. Keevil has voting control over the control block of multiple voting Class A shares. Other Class A shareholders are Quebec's Caisse de dépôt et placement du Québec and Japan's Sumitomo Metal Mining Co.

Symbolically, Teck's boardroom table is round, but, added Keevil, "We always sit in the same chairs."

Keevil has two daughters, a son and nine grandchildren. His son, Norman Keevil III, sits on the board, has a PhD in robotics and is chief operating officer of Triton Logging Inc., which manufactures unmanned harvesting submarines.

Keevil's father, who died in 1989, was constantly inconstant.

"Every time he'd get a new wife, he'd retire for a while," the younger Keevil said. "He was busy. We eventually found out he had five more children we didn't know about."

The Keevils are also, dating back to the errant grandfather, an important family in Britain.

"My grandfather was the oldest son and heir to a large food company, the biggest food wholesaler during the Second World War. His brother was Sir Ambrose Keevil," he said. "But my grandfather was a black sheep who came over in 1907 with a herd of horses, got seasick, went to Saskatchewan and stayed there."

Keevil is in the office every day, but stands back from the fray somewhat. His CEO is Don Lindsay, a veteran investment banker who specialized in mining financings.

"Eyes on, hands off. If you are involved in building a company, it's hard to keep your hands off. But that's meddling. I'm a non-executive chair," he said.

Clearly, Teck is going to become even bigger because it's rich enough to be an eater and impossible to eat. Much depends, however, on commodity prices.

"We are probably into a super-cycle now—the aspirations of the Chinese and Indians, and three billion people are involved here," he said. "The world needs new capacity."

On the list eventually, he said, is some participation in Robert Friedland's massive gold/copper discovery, Oyu Tolgoi, in Mongolia.

"I would do that in a minute," he said. "Friedland is a genius."

In the meantime, as usual, Teck has stakes in dozens of promising junior exploration companies, its farm team.

"Guys out there have as big a dream as we did, and markets are in better shape than they were for us to grow our company," he said. "Canada, and Teck, will remain in the game in a bigger way in the future. That's certain."

ROB McEWEN

McEwen Capital occupies a funky loft overlooking a parking lot and Toronto's bank towers.

"I didn't want to be in those towers, because I've spent my life in them," said proprietor Rob McEwen in an interview in 2007. "This is more fun."

McEwen is as unorthodox as his surroundings, and is a meticulous financier—and goldbug—who began charting the market performances of stocks for his dad when he was only 10 years old.

By 2006, he was owner of the largest stake in the world's second-biggest gold mining company, Vancouver's Goldcorp Inc. Goldcorp had a market value of $20 billion and in 2006 was Canada's 167th-largest corporation, with revenues of $1.9 billion, assets of $20.9 billion, profits of $463 million and 9,000 employees.

McEwen was CEO until 2004, when, at only 50 years of age, he suddenly quit as CEO and planned his exit. By 2006, he was fully gone—and had moved on to a new mining challenge, and to philanthropy and medical research.

"In 2004, my sister and mother died within months of one another, which means I met someone I hadn't met in a long time: it was Mortality," he said. "We had been a family of six—me, three sisters and my parents—and now there were just two of us left. So I shuffled my priorities."

McEwen grew up in Toronto's rough-and-tumble penny stock market milieu. He gravitated toward mining investments early in his career and has combined the curiosity of a geologist with the financial engineering of an investment banker. He is also a very common-sense guy and, at the same time, thinks completely outside the box.

For instance, he turned the world of mining exploration on its head—and found 6 million ounces of gold.

He also may be the first businessman in Canada to reap billions in profits from a nasty strike (46 months long), then convince the strikers—180 of them—to decertify their union.

His talent has not been as a mine finder. He's a balance-sheet finder, or a trained money manager, whose talents include an instinct about the market and an aptitude to effectively communicate with other investors or shareholders.

McEwen ran a closed-end mutual fund with his dad in the 1980s. The fund snapped up control blocks in several mining companies, and McEwen combined them into one entity in the early 1990s. Eventually called Goldcorp Inc., the company had a market value of $60 million and was producing 53,000 ounces of gold a year at the time.

In 1991, he had also converted the closed-end mutual fund into a merchant bank and was approached to become a white-knight bidder for a gold mine.

"The Red Lake Mine was a terminal case and was not expected to survive," he said. That's why the price was rock-bottom. McEwen took over its flagging mining operation, which was considered nearly depleted, having yielded 3 million ounces of gold over decades. Then he merged it with his other mining interests.

But Red Lake's asset was the fact that it was beside "sister" mine Campbell–Red Lake, which had produced 10 million ounces, or more than three times as much as Red Lake, and was still going strong.

"We had 1,400 feet unexplored right next door to a giant mine, so in 1995 we set aside $10 million for an exploration budget. Sure enough, in 1996, after drilling nine holes, we discovered ore grades that were 30 times higher [richer in gold] than our existing ore grade," he said.

During this process, he also turned mining on its head with his Linux approach.

"I would say to my geologists, 'So how big is the ore body?' They'd say, 'Don't know.' 'How long will it take to find out how big it is?' They'd say, 'Don't know.' So I held a two-day brainstorming session and behaved like a fly on the wall for five minutes, then said, 'Stop,'" he recalled.

"I asked the youngest guy there, the person with the least tenure, to tell me about the last idea that any one of them had had that was shot down. Then I said, 'If anybody looks at you like they are going to fire you, I'll fire them.' That way I destroyed the hierarchy in one statement, which broke the logjam. New energy came out of that meeting," he said.

Following that, McEwen happened to attend a course at MIT and had a sudden epiphany. His team loved the idea, and he announced a worldwide contest worth $500,000. He wanted ideas as to where to drill next to define his ore body, and he released onto the Internet all his company's data and drilling records. Two separate Australian geoscience firms shared the prize money, identifying the same drilling targets. They hit gold.

"We tapped the intellectual capital of the world, and this gave us more confidence in our targets. We found gold at the bottom of the mine that had been there for 50 years," he said. "We monetized what was in our filing cabinets. Now the area is the most active exploration area in the world."

The richness of the discovery made the company one of the world's lowest-cost producers, at only US$65 an ounce, or roughly 8% of prices in 2007. Even better, there were no new buildings to build, staff to hire, permits to wait for or roads to build.

During this time, McEwen also went for the gusto by marketing the stock over the radio and to individual Americans. He voluntarily swapped his 44% multiple voting stock for only 6.5% of the regular stock to make it more attractive to the Americans.

"The U.S. market turbocharged our currency," he said. "We listed on the New York Stock Exchange in 1995 and American investors went from 5% of trades to 58% of the volume."

He was on a roll, and in June 1996 was able to benefit from a nasty strike.

"I had death threats—had to put bulletproof glass in my home in Toronto. It went on for 46 months, but we kept finding more gold, so the share price went up even though gold prices went down. The union was confused as to why we wouldn't settle, but I didn't want to waste money on production or wages, but to spend it on exploration," he said.

In May 2000, the union members kicked out the United Steelworkers and accepted $30,000 worth of stock options each.

Next came management-level change. "In 2004, I felt the company needed a new CEO. We did a search and found no one. I noticed a company called Wheaton River Minerals Ltd. and we bid, offering a 7% premium. We proposed to them to combine the companies and they'd manage it; we'd move the head office to Vancouver and split the board. They loved the idea."

The merger was stalled until 2006, when Goldcorp became a takeover target. Eventually, Goldcorp bought its predator, Wheaton gobbled up another company and all four merged.

McEwen immediately became involved in another gold venture. He controls two junior exploration companies in the U.S., worth more than US$1 billion, plus a dozen more involved in 20 exploration plays. These may be the next Red Lake Mine, because they are near mines where massive amounts have already been mined and more may be found.

"I think like a chess player. Most people are reactive, and I try to be a few moves ahead. Travelling around the world opened my eyes," he said. "After I graduated from university, I travelled for five months in a converted army truck from London to Kathmandu. I've always been curious about the unknown or the exotic."

PETER MUNK

Peter Munk says his grandfather was a chocolate tycoon in Hungary before the First World War, then had become a real estate magnate and the biggest taxpayer in Budapest by the time the Second World War began. Peter's father, Louis Munk, was a ne'er-do-well who mastered cards and tennis and liked fast cars and faster women.

Obviously, business brilliance in the Munk family skipped a generation. Peter Munk is one of the world's most versatile and successful entrepreneurs, and has proven able to adapt to many businesses, as did his grandfather.

"My dad was an athlete and great card player," said Munk in an interview in 2007 in his exquisitely furnished Toronto home. "I am a lousy golfer, but I am very good at business. So I've always done a lot of business."

The Munks fled the Nazis for Switzerland, and in 1947, at 19 years of age, Peter immigrated on a student visa to Toronto to study electrical engineering. There, at a Diana Sweets restaurant hangout, he met rich kid David Gilmour and they began a partnership that would span decades.

"We are lucky people, quite able," he said. "We are hard workers, are self-confident and learned from our failures and successes. We have also changed with the times, and David is a gifted salesman, a great marketer."

Munk is chair of the world's biggest gold-mining company, Barrick Gold Corporation, with a market value in 2007 of around $28 billion. It was Canada's 59th-largest corporation in 2006, with $6.39 billion in revenues, $24.8 billion in assets, $1.7 billion in profits and 20,000 employees. He started the company with Gilmour, who sold out, and Peter owns "1% or 2%."

Until 2006, Munk was also chair of Trizec Properties, which was sold for US$8.9 billion to Brookfield Properties and a U.S. partner.

David Gilmour permanently left Canada in the early 1960s, and now lives in New York and Palm Beach and owns Fiji Water, one of the world's three largest bottled-water companies—bigger than Evian.

But the two cut their teeth in 1953, when they scraped together $4,000 to start a colour television manufacturing company called Clairtone. Nine years later, it was taken over by a Nova Scotia Crown corporation, but not before the two took on the world's giants.

"It was nine fantastic years and taught us more than any Harvard MBA would have," he said. But, he added, "In the end, we were fired."

The two left Canada and started South Pacific Hotel Corporation, which ended up being the largest hotel and restaurant chain in Australasia in the 1970s.

"Clairtone had reached a market cap of $20 million at its peak, but three years after we were fired from Clairtone our hotel company was listed on the Hong Kong Stock Exchange with a $100-million market cap," he said. "We ordered lots of champagne. We couldn't believe that, just three years later, we had a company with a market cap of $100 million."

In 1980, they sold out for $100 million each and formed a three-way partnership with Adnan Khashoggi, Saudi Arabia's oil minister.

"I decided to come home and get into natural resources," said Munk. "Gilmour went to the Bahamas. He said his family had paid high taxes in Canada for five generations and he was sick of it."

The three—Munk, Gilmour and Khashoggi—launched Barrick Petroleum with great fanfare. Munk and Gilmour staged a press conference in Toronto to show off their famous partner and announce their comeback. Oil prices were riding high, at US$36 a barrel, thanks to the oil cartel, and they set about looking for opportunities in Alberta.

"We were chasing oil deals here in competition with every German dentist [highly taxed German professionals enjoyed tax breaks if they invested in oil anywhere] and U.S. underwriters. Gilmour refused to come back and pay taxes, so I had to do the slogging," he said.

Munk wanted to raise his children in Toronto, but when the National Energy Policy ruined the business in 1981, he shifted course.

"By 1982, we had changed the name to Barrick Resources, then Barrick Gold," he said. Their first investment was a small Alaskan mine producing 3,000 ounces a year. Then, in 1984, Munk got lucky.

"We bought a wounded giant, Camflo, in Quebec and its claims in Nevada were the turning point and became the most successful mine in our generation. With Camflo, we also got [late] mining engineer Bob Smith, who was brilliant," he said.

In 1984, Camflo's mine was producing 40,000 ounces a year. By 2007, the mine had produced 20 million ounces and still contained 25 million more.

With Smith at the technical helm, Munk devised creative financing techniques, including hedging gold by forward selling. This added an additional US$2 billion over a 13-year period, until Munk stopped hedging as prices began escalating.

Barrick's profits were invested in developing successful mines in Africa and South America. In 2000, Barrick bought Homestake Mining for US$2.2 billion, and in 2006, Placer Dome Inc., making Barrick the world's largest gold producer.

In the 1990s, Munk came across another "wounded giant" that became a huge winner. He cashed in most of his 40% of Barrick stock to buy Trizec Properties. Barrick shares were owned by his holding company, Horsham Corporation, and a merger took place that turned Horsham into a real estate giant.

"We bought Trizec [which had been jointly owned by the Reichmann and the Peter and Edward Bronfman empires] when it was in the dumps," he said. "We did a deal with the bank, put half a billion dollars into the company to get control and converted Horsham into Trizec. Barrick stayed on its own. Trizec became the holding company, and in 2006 it became a U.S. REIT, which we sold." (Ironically, the buyer was, with an American partner, Brookfield Properties, which is run by Jack Cockwell and the management team that ran the Bronfman empire, which once shared control of Trizec.)

Munk and his wife, Melanie, are jet-setters who commute among their stunning homes around the world, including a mountainside chalet in Klosters, Switzerland, and socialize with the rich and famous. They have five children and four grandchildren.

Despite a glamorous social life, Munk remains a serial entrepreneur. In 2000, he stepped down as Barrick's CEO, but as its chairman fully supported its two giant takeovers. Then, in 2006, he was upset that Barrick did not get into the bidding war for Inco Limited.

"Inco, Falconbridge and Noranda all disappeared within 18 months. It was tragic for Canada. I wished we'd bought Inco. I would have bought Inco, but I was no longer the CEO of Barrick," he said. "The beauty about buying Inco, even for a lot of money, is that the day you took it over, you immediately got huge cash flow."

The loss of such mining head offices is a national tragedy, he added. "We have the best mining engineers, best mining market here. Thirty years ago you came to the TSE for full value. Legal, title, specialized accounting, 20 of the top consulting engineers were here. This is an enormous amount of expertise," he said. "But companies are disappearing. You have to be competitive. You must wake up every day trying to figure out how to be the biggest and the best."

He still does. While on an annual yachting trip with his family in the Mediterranean, Munk came across another wounded giant, an abandoned naval shipyard in Montenegro. In 2006, he obtained a 99-year option for US$90 million to turn the yard into a high-end yacht basin and tourist gaming destination.

"There used to be 600 yachts cruising the Med every year, and now there are 6,000," he said. "That's a huge opportunity."

He also moves in A-list circles. He introduced, for instance, Russian oligarch Oleg Deripaska to Magna Corporation's Frank Stronach, which led to a US$1.5 billion purchase, by the Russian, of 40% of Stronach's voting control block in Magna. And through Brian Mulroney, who has been on the Barrick board since leaving politics, Munk has had access to heads of state for both social and business or mining-claims purposes.

A globalist, Munk remains loyal to Canada and Switzerland, which accepted his family as refugees during the war. He has not gone offshore for tax purposes, as other wealthy entrepreneurs have done, and has given away tens of millions of dollars to Canadian educational and health care causes.

"You make your money here, you ought to pay tax. Canada is a great environment for business. It has a satisfactory health plan. Its rule of law is solid and reliable. This makes up five times for the taxes you pay. Switzerland is the most successful country in the world even though it has no natural resources. Both are successes, but both must always foster entrepreneurship. That's how a country moves forward."

SEYMOUR SCHULICH

Seymour Schulich's greatest business success came out of a desire to be able to write off skiing and poker trips to Nevada.

"After 19 years, this idea [of doing business in Nevada] evolved into our group owning 30% of one of the largest gold-mining companies in the entire world," he said in an interview with me in his Toronto office in 2007. "I call this the law of unintended consequences."

Schulich has always loved any excuse to go to Reno to play poker, so he and his partner, Pierre Lassonde, hunted in Nevada for mining investment opportunities. This is how they ended up finding a motherlode that they swapped in partnership with their shareholders for a huge stake in Denver's Newmont Mining Corp. in 2002. The deal was valued at US$5 billion at the time, and by 2007, the overall value of Newmont had doubled in value to US$30 billion, with 28,000 employees and with exploration lands equal in size to Britain.

The result is that Schulich is one of Canada's richest men. But he's also one of its most interesting and philanthropic. Since 1995, he has given away $210 million to health and educational institutions. He feels it is an obligation.

"It's important that people do something," he told me. "You

have to leave a legacy: why were you here, and why did you make all this money? You have to make it mean something."

Schulich is the son of a Hungarian dress designer and was raised in a Montreal apartment. He still stretches a dollar as though he had been raised in the Depression. He and his wife, Tanna, live in the same home they bought in 1977 and he drives a 12-year-old Lincoln Continental. He often goes to Swiss Chalet for lunch in Toronto and uses coupons to pay.

Schulich describes himself as a "nerd" and was a big fan of westerns as a kid. His favourite movies are *Revenge of the Nerds* and *The Wild Bunch*, starring William Holden as a gunslinging hero. His office in Toronto is decorated with western memorabilia from Nevada, and in a corner is a pile of his favourite videos and books that he likes to give to friends and visitors.

Schulich has a good sense of humour and a Runyonesque flair for colourful language and colloquialisms. He reads several books a week and e-mails reviews to his pals. In 2007, he compiled an entertaining book of his own aphorisms, accompanied by cartoons, and called it *Getting Smarter*.

Until 2007, Schulich was chair of Newmont Capital Ltd., Newmont's merchant banking arm, then mostly cashed out. His partner, Pierre Lassonde, is now vice-chair and heading back to Forest Hill to live in a magnificent 20,000-square-foot mansion. Schulich left because of litigation risk and other red tape south of the border.

"U.S. lawyers' fees amount to 3% of GNP. The S&P 500 profit is 6% of GNP," he said. "There should be loser-pay laws. If you lose the case you pay everyone's legal fees. Class actions are constant. The company has had 1,700 lawsuits, and 800 are still outstanding after 10 years."

"The Sarbanes-Oxley thing [an act introducing tougher regulations on public companies imposed after Enron's collapse] was an overreaction too. Newmont saw its audit fees go up from US$1.2 million annually to US$6.5 million. Its insurance for directors and officers climbed to US$4 million from US$2 million," he said.

Schulich and Lassonde remain good friends and are the odd couple of mining. They met in 1980 while working together at money-manager Beutel, Goodman & Co. A couple of years later they left the firm and launched penny stock Franco-Nevada, with its unique business concept.

"It was called 'Franco' because 'Pierre' is French and 'Nevada' because Nevada is where Schulich loves to play poker and ski," explained Pierre to me in an interview. The pair's plan was not exploration plays but to buy royalty interests, or cash flows, from existing mining operations. They once described themselves as "miners in loafers with tassels."

Lassonde combed the world for deals, and Schulich masterminded the operation. Then in 1986 they made their biggest score. "Four months after we decided to do this, one of our guys was reading a local paper in Reno, Nevada, and there was a royalty [rights to earn the royalty in future in return for a price] for sale, US$2 million," said Lassonde. "That's all we had in the bank, but I bought it. I called Seymour and said, 'The good news is we bought our first royalty, and the bad news is we have no money left.' He went crazy thinking I spent too much. But that US$2 million has given us US$500 million so far. Who knew then?"

The mine, called Goldstrike, shared with Barrick Corporation, eventually became one of the world's richest. Schulich also cashed in on Robert Friedland's Voisey's Bay nickel discovery in Newfoundland and many other discoveries in the oil industry.

Franco-Nevada became Canada's best stock investment, with gains averaging 43% a year. With this new venture, Schulich and Lassonde turned $3.5 million in market value into US$5 billion during 18 years of flagging gold prices, industry malaise, scandals and skittish gold-stock markets.

Now Schulich is giving the money away. There is the Schulich School of Business at York University, the Schulich Heart Centre at Sunnybrook hospital, the Schulich School of Medicine & Dentistry at the University of Western Ontario, the Schulich School of

Engineering at the University of Calgary, the Schulich School of Music at McGill University and hundreds of scholarships.

"I've hit gold mines and oil wells," he said. "I'm a guy with a lot of luck in the golden age of discoveries. These times will never occur again."

Schulich is as good-hearted as he is outspoken and funny. In 2006, he told the *Montreal Gazette* why he gave so much to the music program at his alma mater, McGill. He said he and a friend used to perform Kingston Trio songs.

"I had a repertoire of 200 songs—I didn't say I was good," he said. "For the first song, there was a big crowd around us. By the second, most of the girls were gone. By the third, we were alone. It didn't really have the effect we were hoping for."

Schulich was born in 1940, a child of the shmatte, or garment, industry, as were fellow Canadian billionaires Barry Sherman and Ned Goodman. Their fathers toiled in a business that was highly competitive, low-paying and dependent upon the whims of fickle consumers. This obviously honed special skills.

"My father always said to me, don't be too tough or too smart," he said. "People don't like too tough or too smart."

Schulich took sciences in university, but loved business history, finance and statistics. In 1963, he started with Shell Canada Limited. Then he won a $2,000 scholarship toward an MBA. He paid his tuition and gambled the rest on oil stocks. He said it was the most important $2,000 of his life.

From there, he worked for three years at a small brokerage, then joined Beutel, Goodman as an oil analyst. He left for Toronto with the firm in 1977.

"We got three times more business in the first year we were in Toronto," he said. "People didn't want their money managed in Quebec. We went from $300 million in money under management to $1 billion in the first year. It skyrocketed. It was fabulous."

In no time, Toronto overtook Montreal in financial importance. Schulich had loved his hometown, but he would never return.

"Quebec has finally integrated into the country, but Quebec is not a multicultural meritocracy like Ontario," he said. "My advice to my sister's grandson is to get out of Quebec because he'll never make it in Quebec. *Pur laine*, or being French, is all-important there still."

The establishment is alive and well in *la belle province*.

Besides his Newmont stake, Schulich is the largest investor in Canadian Oil Sands Trust and invests in other oil stocks as well. In fact, of the 15 companies he's made huge profits on, 12 were in Alberta. In 2006, the Tory government attacked income trusts like Canadian Oil Sands with a 31.5% proposed tax and Schulich attacked back. He bankrolled an organization to fight the decision and embarrass the government.

"I'm on tilt," he told me right after the government's tax was announced. "This is like treating a hangnail by chopping off the finger itself. It's sheer stupidity, and I'll never vote Tory."

Schulich has been busy promoting his book and travelling around the world. He is a frustrated—and accomplished—writer who e-mails diaries of his trips to friends. And his insights are quite interesting.

His approach to philanthropy is also time-consuming. "With all the due diligence you have to do to make sure your gift accomplishes what you want it to do, it's easier making the money than giving it away," he said.

PHARMACEUTICALS

The world's shifting demographics have catapulted health care in general, and pharmaceuticals and pharmacies in particular, into the business big leagues. Unfortunately, Canada has not built a Pfizer or a Merck with tens of billions in sales. In 2007, Canada was dependent on drug imports. Some blame the failure to create global pharmaceutical champions—despite important inventions here such as insulin and heart stents—on effective lobbying by American and European pharmaceutical giants in Ottawa.

But their efforts did not always work. In the 1970s, the Canadian federal government decided to encourage a homegrown industry—and the production of cheaper generic drugs—by removing patent protections more quickly than elsewhere. This made it possible for Canadian outfits to start, which led to the growth of two sizable Canadian entries, Apotex and Novopharm.

The new companies thrived in Canada and began exporting around the world. But their good fortune was somewhat short-lived. In the late 1980s, the big drug lobby won its way back into the hearts of Ottawa politicians—and their legal protection. During free trade negotiations, the Mulroney government bowed to pressure from Washington to extend patent protections to match American durations. Despite this setback, three Canadians have continued to grow their businesses and make personal fortunes under the shadow of these giants.

LESLIE DAN

Leslie Dan came to Canada as a wartime refugee. He survived the Holocaust as an adolescent, by assuming a false identity, and in 1947 he got out of Hungary to Toronto and a new life. Fortunately, his parents and sister got to Canada too, later.

"I was 18 years old, all alone and had nothing. I became a busboy at the Silver Rail Tavern [in Toronto] for 18 months so I could go to high school, learn English and prepare to get into university," he said in an interview in Toronto in 2007.

As things turned out, Dan not only overcame a hideous childhood, along with his loved ones, but has enjoyed a charmed life ever since. This is, he believes, because he gained some unique strengths as a result of his ordeal.

"It made me more flexible in my thinking, less hung up emotionally on things. It made me stronger. Some people who went through the war were weakened. I was lucky," he said.

Dan is shy in person, but is an aggressive entrepreneur. He created a generic drug powerhouse, Novopharm Ltd. At its peak, his company employed 3,000 people in 3 countries and had sales of more than $750 million annually. In 2000, he sold to Israel's gigantic Teva Pharmaceuticals Industries Ltd. for a rumoured US$450 million, becoming Teva's second-largest shareholder. The stock, which he kept, quadrupled in value by 2007. He also owns Viventia Biotech Inc. of Toronto, a cancer research company into which he has invested $130 million. When asked how rich he was, he said, "I don't divulge that."

It all began with his dream to become a pharmacist.

"I had a natural attraction to pharmacy. I was one of the lucky

ones who knew what I wanted to do. Others are lost for a few years,"
he said. "It's a clean, honourable profession and helps sick people get
well. I couldn't sell booze because it would be against my moral principles. We are here to help people rather than destroy people."

He finished high school, then took pharmacy at the University of Toronto. Like most graduates, he then worked in a drugstore, but he had a different plan.

"After two years I realized that retail was not for me. I never
wanted to open a store. It was not in my blood. Manufacturing was,
but I had no money to get started," he said. "Pharmacists make a good
living, but pharmaceuticals became a huge multinational industry."

By 1956, he had saved $500 and "eased into distribution." He
started a specialty clearing house that sent medicines from Canada
across the country and then to Europe. He called it International Pharmacy, and its business model was really a combination of his newly
acquired profession and his father's occupation as a wholesaler.

International Pharmacy filled prescriptions in Canada, but not
Canadian prescriptions: these were written in other languages by
foreign doctors, and International sent the drugs back to patients in
Europe, where medicine was in short supply. Dan employed trans-
lators and sent tens of thousands of parcels abroad.

"For instance, there was demand after the war for drugs to
treat tuberculosis. Many people got sick during the war, and even
in the 1950s there was still a lot of the disease there," he said.

From this base, he created Interpharm Ltd., which distributed
creams and ointments made in the U.S. to Canadians and others.
Then, in 1965, he opened manufacturer Novopharm.

Like his archrival, Barry Sherman of Apotex, in 1969 Dan
cashed in on favourable legislation in Canada that made it possible to make products under licence and pay royalties to the patent
holders. Novopharm's revenues in its first year totalled $165,000
but soon it would be in the millions.

"The government in Canada did this compulsory licensing
because it wanted to establish a better health care system, with medicines available at moderate prices," he said. "The multinational drug

companies were up in arms over it. Of course they did not like it, but who cares?"

The laws put him in the right place at the right time, but Dan also credits his success to other traits.

"I have always had focus and great industry and, to a certain extent, luck, and other traits that apply to every business, such as determination, people skills and integrity," he said. "I also have found very talented, hard-working people."

But his kind of success also requires guts.

"I have had sleepless nights," he said. "In 1995, I borrowed substantial sums to expand the company—$250 million—and if we had stumbled, it would've sunk the company. But if we hadn't expanded, we would have been too small to compete."

Dan works in stark contrast to Barry Sherman. "We are opposite personalities. He's bombastic, litigious, and I'm more subdued and compassionate," he said with characteristic generosity. "My way is successful, and his is too. I remember reading a book written by management guru Peter Drucker, who said some people are short and some people are tall, some are old and some are young, some fat and some skinny, but all of them can do the right things and become successful."

During those early years, Dan also found personal success. He met his wife, Judith, through some fraternity brothers. They married in 1958 and had two sons, Michael and Aubrey, and a daughter, Andrea Dan-Hytman, who runs Viventia with her father. Judith died in 1995 and he remarried. He now has nine grandchildren.

"Michael was a neurosurgeon for 15 years, but is now an investor. So are my other two children," he said. "They are all on their own."

None of the children was interested in running Novopharm, which led to his decision to sell.

"My kids didn't want to run it, and they weren't the right people. It's an exception when children continue to successfully run a company anyway. You need highly trained people," he said. "There are often a lot of fights among children. Look at what happened to the Steinbergs. Their fighting resulted in the company going down the drain. It was hard to sell, but I talked myself into it."

Another alternative would have been to take the company public, inviting investors as partners, but Dan did not want to do that. So he put out the word, and plenty of buyers came forward. Novopharm was very profitable.

"Going public is too much of a hassle," he said. "Being private is much better. I decided I had to sell in April 2000 to have continuity. We had 1,200 workers in Canada and 3,000 worldwide. Teva was the best choice. I checked it out carefully."

Dan received cash and Teva shares. He will not say how much he received exactly, only that it was "hundreds of millions of dollars in cash and shares." "The shares have gone up four times," he said. "It's worth a lot. But that's private information."

These days, Dan is busy at Viventia and also with philanthropic activities.

"I still work 12-hour days. If you want to live long, you have to be active," he said.

His huge donations rescued the Faculty of Pharmacy at the University of Toronto and financed the establishment of several chairs in medicine. He also put up millions to build the impressive glass Pharmacy Building for the university, across from the Ontario legislative building. And he is a benefactor for other causes in the arts, health care and educational spheres.

"Canada is one of the best countries to live in," he said. "It's liberal and protects human rights. I arrived with little and built a future and have lived peacefully. The government is as open as it can be. It's a highly desirable country. It has a good economy, resources, and is intellectually advanced. I was a refugee after the war, and my Canadian passport is the only passport I've ever had."

Leslie Dan is a remarkable man who overcame struggles that few people can imagine, then scaled the heights of free enterprise. What is interesting about a conversation with him is that there is no detectable anger or bitterness about what happened in Europe decades ago.

"So what if those things happened? They should not influence your moral values."

EUGENE MELNYK

Eugene Melnyk's favourite boyhood activity was blocking shots as a goaltender from guys 20 feet away on cold, dark nights at an outdoor rink in Toronto's west end.

"We didn't have proper face masks in those days, so you just stood there and took the shots. It made you a little tougher," he said in an interview with me.

Such tenacity and stickhandling ability has helped make Melnyk very rich. He is the founder of and largest shareholder of Canada's biggest public pharmaceutical company, Biovail Corp., which had a market capitalization in 2006 of $4.3 billion, $1.2 billion in sales and $237 million profit. Melnyk and his family now own 18% of the company.

Melnyk personally has made US$1.5 billion since he invested $5 million in Biovail's unique technology 20 years ago. Four years after that, after the election in Ontario of a New Democrat government, he moved offshore to Barbados for tax purposes. However, he continues to donate millions to Canadian causes. He absorbed a loss of $30 million in order to save the Ottawa Senators from bankruptcy in 2004 (the team made it to the Stanley Cup Finals in 2007). He has also given money to help support several Ukrainian orphanages and is now chairing a campaign to raise money for Canadian Olympic athletes.

"I decided to get out of the business world in December 2006, when my brother died at 51 years of age," he said in 2007 in the great room of his magnificent Lake Simcoe cottage in Ontario. "Now it's my family, hockey and horse racing."

Melnyk resigned as chair of Biovail in 2007 after taking quite a few pucks to the face in the business world. In 2007, he settled with the Ontario Securities Commission by paying a $1-million fine for offshore trades he did not disclose but said he knew nothing about because independent trustees handled such matters. He is also negotiating a settlement with the Securities and Exchange Commission, which takes a dimmer view of offshore trusts.

He says Biovail has fallen victim to ruthless hedge funds that drub corporate reputations in order to make fortunes on shorting their stocks. Biovail has sued 22 U.S. hedge funds and financial analysts for US$6 billion for libelling and slandering the company related to short selling. When the first of the negative reports by defendants regarding Biovail started a few years ago, the stock was at $55 a share and fell to $13. In December 2007, it was around $14 a share.

"Canadian companies listed down there have no one to protect them," he said. "Fortunately, I have good lawyers and the investigative TV show *60 Minutes* took on the case to show how we were victimized by these hedge funds."

Melnyk is a very competitive guy. Medium-height and well-built, he has Slavic good looks, and has recently become a huge fan of cricket. He also owns a 1,000-acre thoroughbred operation in Florida, where he raises and trains 500 racehorses. He installed closed-circuit television in his Caribbean home to watch events live.

"I used to go to the racetrack with my uncle Leo when I was six years old or so," he said. "My dad didn't approve, but I loved it."

Risk-taking was a family trait. Melnyk's parents each escaped from Ukraine after the Second World War and found their way to Canada, where they met. His father was a physician who died when Eugene was 17 and in his last year of high school. Melnyk took a year off to play keyboards and sing in a band called the Studebakers, then tried university.

"I went to a business class and said to myself, 'They don't know how to teach me to make money,' then I went to an economics class, saw all the numbers and walked out," he said. "I was 19 years old and that was that. So I joined a company up the street from school."

Beginning in 1979, he sold giveaway items and educational materials to pharmaceutical companies, which would then hand them out to physicians in the hopes they would prescribe their drugs. By 1981, he had his own marketing agency doing the same.

"One year later, the Canadian Pharmaceutical Association banned giveaways, so I started a medical publishing company," he said.

In 1982, he launched Trimel Corp. to help physicians who were inundated with information from the plethora of journals and medical information. Trimel condensed research and published a digest version for each specialty.

"For six years, I wrote the editorials, sold the sponsorships—I read everything. There was no Internet, so I would tap into medical librarians for information," he said.

His publishing venture expanded into 40 journals per month, each sponsored by a well-heeled advertiser. In 1987, he took Trimel public and one month later sold his control block to Thomson Corp. for $5 million.

In 1989, he, with a partner who had worked for a German pharma giant, entered the pharmaceutical business. They bought 50% of struggling Swiss start-up Biovail SA, which had developed the world's most efficient drug "delivery" system—a controlled-release technology that allowed patients to take their medication once a day instead of many times daily.

This was a breakthrough in the field of patient compliance, and something that Eugene knew about first-hand, from when he was growing up.

"I used to have Sunday lunch with my grandmother, and I used to use coloured magic markers so she could identify which meds to take at what times of day through the week. She couldn't keep track," he said.

By 1991, he owned 100% of Biovail and had paid $5.5 million for the technology.

"It was a big bet, all my capital," he said. "I threw out the old business model of doing contract research with large drug companies in return for cash and small royalties. I said, 'Rather than being dependent on these companies, let's target four or five products that will be off-patent [their patents will expire] six years from now, develop the product and license it at a late stage.' This is the cornerstone of our business philosophy."

Melnyk worked constantly running his public company and financing its research through sources such as Investors immigrant funds, vehicles created to help would-be immigrants invest in Canada to qualify for entry.

"I worked a string of days, other than Christmas, of 411 in a row. I tapped into immigrant funds and raised $37.5 million that way. I paid every nickel back, and it funded all our research and development," he said.

Biovail's first big hit came in 1996, involving a hypertension drug called Tiazac, which Biovail enhanced through its delivery-system technology. A pharma giant paid US$20 million cash up front for the new improved version, plus a 35% royalty, and bought 20% of Biovail stock at a premium. Eight more such product enhancements followed, and by 2006 the company had reached $1 billion in sales, employed 1,600 people and had nine plants producing products and innovations.

Another delivery innovation was FlashDose, which consisted of pills for the elderly and the young that need not be swallowed because they liquify on the tongue within five seconds.

Biovail also markets products itself and buys brand names of top-selling drugs where patents are about to expire. It enhances the drugs with its various delivery systems, then re-markets them using the old brand name.

"Drug companies just walk away from brands they have built over years. Can you imagine Crest toothpaste or Maxwell House coffee doing that?" he said.

Of course, the only reason a brand is sold to Biovail is because the pharmaceutical is reconstituted and improved. For instance, Biovail relaunched the hugely popular anti-depressant Wellbutrin in 2003, in partnership with its creator. The drug had been improved by adding Biovail's timed-release technology so that patients needed to take only one tablet a day. Better yet, this gradual, continual dosage eliminated one of the drug's negative side effects, that of sleeplessness.

This type of innovation and partnership has allowed Biovail to cash in on global brand-name drugs, inherit massive promotional goodwill and produce successful drugs after the drugs' patent protections have elapsed.

Melnyk clearly loves the game in all its forms. He still plays the real thing too—hockey (although not in Barbados)—and enjoys his thoroughbred horses. He flies by private jet, but has a "five-day rule": he's never away from his wife, Laura, and their kids for more than five days. The two met in 1991 when she was an accountant with Deloitte & Touche.

Until 2004, when he resigned as CEO, Eugene was a virtual CEO—a unique situation that he credits with allowing him to think out of the box.

"The benefit is to be able to look at the cultural psyche of business people in various countries," he said. "The Canadian inferiority complex truly does exist. Canadians are less aggressive. I see how our U.S. counterparts truly play to win. They view business more as war than as a process."

As for his own success, Melnyk points to Louis Pasteur and other great pharmaceutical inventors.

"One person sees a mould and another sees penicillin," he said. "It's luck, awareness and knowledge."

BARRY SHERMAN

Self-made billionaire Barry Sherman said he spends more than anyone else in Canada on legal fees—an estimated US$100 million a year.

"It's the cost of doing business in pharmaceuticals against these awful multinationals who gouge the public," he said in an interview in his office, north of Toronto.

Sherman and his four grown children own 95% of the Apotex Group of Companies, Canada's largest chemical manufacturer and largest generic-drug manufacturer, with an enterprise value of US$5 billion, 7,000 employees, US$1.5 billion in sales and more than 400 products. Key managers own the other 5%. He also owns 70% of Cangene Inc., listed on the Toronto Stock Exchange, plus 5% of Barr Laboratories in New Jersey. He sold 75% of Barr in 2005 for US$1.5 billion.

Sherman is a scientific genius with an appetite for a fight. He is central casting's version of an egghead, complete with thick glasses and unruly hair. He is also a major philanthropist and self-confessed workaholic who met me for several hours on a statutory holiday in 2007.

"I work 24/7. I do 50 peoples' jobs. I'm head scientist; chief inventor, with 100 patents; head lawyer. I find ways around patents and find ways to litigate," he said.

These are the traits that have propelled him into the pharma big leagues in a relatively short time. Rivals call him "the shark" because of his aggressiveness and fearlessness in a game run by gigantic pharmaceutical bullies who use the legal and political systems to keep out competition. Lawsuits are part of the cost of doing business in that sector.

"Drug companies are monopolies, make outrageously high profits and do anything they can to protect their privileges," he said. "I have fought hundreds of cases and lost only one or two. Lawsuits are usually frivolous against us, and they sue for patent infringement, sue because we use the same or similar techniques. They even sue because they allege the pill is the same size, shape or colour."

But they have picked on the wrong guy. Sherman's shrewd tactics, his clashes with U.S. regulators and his unrelenting court battles with the world's drug giants have given him legend status.

During the 1990s, Apotex was involved in 100 different court cases. It also has a long history of challenging big drug-makers before their patents expire. In 2001, Apotex made copies of Bayer's antibiotic Cipro, and in 2004 Sherman sold a low-cost version of the anti-depressant Paxil before GlaxoSmithKline's patent expired.

"The system is being screwed up by greedy people who see this big pot to be split, and they have no interest in consumers, who get screwed by paying more than they should for medications they need," he told a U.S. newspaper at the time.

Gouging is apparent: U.S. prescription drug sales in 2006 totalled US$252 billion. Generic drugs accounted for 56% of prescriptions filled and a mere 9% of sales in dollars.

In 2007, he pulled off his latest manoeuvre, which was to flood the American market with a copycat version of the top-selling blood thinner Plavix. The dust-up that followed pitted Sherman against industry giants Bristol-Myers Squibb and Sanofi-Aventis Groupe.

"We challenged their patent extension and sold US$1 billion worth of product in competition with Bristol-Myers in the first two weeks before we were enjoined in court," he said. "In the U.S., if you are the first to challenge a patent, you get to sell the product for six months. Then, if you lose, you must split your revenues 50-50 with the pharmaceutical company you are challenging. In this case, we have challenged first, shipped US$1 billion worth of product in six months, and if we win we keep US$1 billion and get damages. If we lose, we get to keep US$500 million of the sales," he said. "So our minimum upside for the year is US$500 million and our maximum upside is US$2 billion."

These challenges are testing a patent system that should be reformed. For years, pharmaceutical giants have routinely reapplied for patent extensions, thus depriving consumers of generic-drug bargain prices. To Sherman this is as much a worthy cause as a business model.

Barry is likely a genius. His dad was a zipper manufacturer who eked out a living and died when Barry was only 10 years of age. His mother was an occupational therapist, and he and his sister worked from early on to help their mother make ends meet.

He was a gold medallist at the University of Toronto, then won a full scholarship to MIT, where he completed both a master's and a PhD in engineering in two and a half years. Friends say that while he was a student, he was so brilliant he found mistakes in textbooks and would bring them to the attention of instructors. That's a talent that he now applies by finding loopholes in legal cases and patents in order to bring generics to market.

"Am I a genius? I think I'm just focused," he said. "I was always good at sciences and math, and I always took what was most difficult, which is why I took engineering in university."

He came back to Canada in 1967, after graduating, and bought his late uncle's business from a trustee before it went bust.

"I bought the company for $100,000. It was nearly insolvent and was run by a trustee because my uncle's kids were too young to run it," he said.

Sadly, those cousins launched a legal action in 2007 against Sherman, on the basis that their father's company was the predecessor to Apotex. He dismissed this as "preposterous" because he sold that company in 1973 and then launched Apotex. That case is still before the courts.

The name Apotex stands for "apothecary technology," and the company took years to break even.

"My plan was to invest as little as possible in plant and equipment and to make just one type of tablet—a simple compressed pill. Our first generic hit was in 1980, and we took 80% of the market," he said.

After that, he built the company aggressively and was helped along by Canadian compulsory licensing laws that allowed generics into the market.

"Then, in the late 1990s, the Mulroney government changed the rules. We haven't made money in Canada since, and the market has been handed over to multinationals which don't create jobs or do research here," he said.

Fortunately, Sherman had diversified outside of Canada in the early 1980s and had bought financially troubled Barr Laboratories. It was an inspired transaction.

"Barr was in trouble so we bought 80% of the company for US$1 million, and over the years we have reduced our interest to 5% and made US$1.5 billion doing so," he said. "Barr was tremendously successful, and it would have been impossible to build Apotex without the success at Barr."

Now Apotex is a global player with plants and sales offices around the world. But Sherman keeps research at home in Canada and is a fierce Canadian nationalist.

His prodigious workload is partly motivated by this and is all the more remarkable given that he suffers from chronic fatigue syndrome.

"I always did, even as a kid. My fourth-grade teacher nicknamed me 'Grandpa' because I was always tired," he said. "I find it difficult to function, but I drive myself. I'm often here at the office until midnight. I'm a late riser. I don't sleep well. I may be in bed for 10 hours, but I'm not sleeping. I have a paper and pencil nearby and make notes during the night."

Sherman and his personable wife, Honey, have three daughters and one son. Their eldest daughter is an entrepreneur who runs the family's portfolio investments. Their son is studying engineering, one daughter is in pre-med and another is still in high school.

Succession is an issue, but Barry already has a team of 50 key managers, including president Jack Kay and his sister Sandra's husband, chartered accountant Michael Florence.

"I have to deal with the issue of succession because I'm 65. Jack Kay is 67. Both of us plan to stay another 30 or 40 years, and we consider ourselves at the halfway point," he said.

He plans to give away all his wealth and is not motivated by money. The Shermans live modestly.

"There are only two advantages to being extremely wealthy as far as I can tell," he said. "After you are wealthy, you start getting invited to a lot more parties. Secondly, you have an ability to do things for other people."

An "avowed atheist," Sherman's ambition is to add $1 billion to his charitable Apotex Foundation, which is currently $300 million in size.

"I explain to my kids this is not their wealth—this is in trust to you, and it is for the country and the community."

HIGH TECHNOLOGY

I n 2007, Canada's biggest corporation, in terms of stock market value, was high-tech darling Research In Motion, creator of the BlackBerry. Like other tech companies, RIM's software and hardware have had to constantly evolve in order to corner a piece of a ruthless marketplace. Business is hard enough, but the high-technology business is perhaps the toughest in the world. Software takes years to develop and has a shelf life roughly equivalent to that of yogurt. Competition is global and the only barrier to entry is IQ.

To succeed, companies must reinvent themselves constantly by fostering corporate cultures dedicated to innovation and science. They must also attract and retain talent through stock options that match other companies' stock options, then build teams in recognition of the fact that successes are based on intelligence and collaboration in clusters of excellence.

This creates its own tyranny as newcomers or imitators poach or overtake products and people. Stock prices rise and fall based on these events. When they rise, talented people stay. When they fall, those people go elsewhere, triggering more falls in value. Stock market excitement led to the dot-com bubble—then flame-out—which created more challenges for this sector. Some of Canada's most stellar entries, such as Nortel Networks, JDS Technologies and Mitel Networks, soared, then were drubbed or disappeared along with hundreds of others.

These vicissitudes have led to consolidations, to reincarnations and foreign takeovers (including that of ATI, profiled here) and to a further brain drain. Even so, important companies remain and thrive, along with a handful of important venture capital incubators. It is also interesting to note that, like those in real estate, three of the people profiled in this chapter—Mike Lazaridis, K.Y. Ho and Sir Terence Matthews—were born outside Canada. Two—Robert Miller and Charles Sirois—are businessmen from Quebec who have made fortunes in the sector. Sirois used other peoples' money to briefly consolidate a chunk of the world's telecommunications industry, while Miller has built from scratch a distribution company that controls most of the world's semiconductor and capacitor markets.

JIM BALSILLIE AND MIKE LAZARIDIS

Research In Motion Ltd. is the high-tech giant that invented thumb-typing and the ultimate cellphone with e-mail, otherwise known to the world as the BlackBerry.

In fall 2007, the value of stock owned by its two founders, Jim Balsillie and Mike Lazaridis, totalled $4 billion each despite their stunning philanthropy. But being rich at the Kitchener-Waterloo giant is nothing unusual. Many of their employees are millionaires many times over, and also work hard and live relatively modest lifestyles. Money is not their object, it would seem. To underscore this, for several years Balsillie has had a standing rule that any employee caught looking up and discussing the company's stock price has to personally buy doughnuts for the company's entire staff of several thousand.

"It messes up a company to concentrate on stock prices. It's the worst thing," said Balsillie in an interview in 2005. "It costs about $800 to buy doughnuts for the whole company. It's happened a few times."

In 2006, the two partners shared the *Financial Post*'s prestigious CEO of the Year award. At that time, Research In Motion was Canada's 108th-largest corporation, with $3.4 billion in revenues, $3.6 billion in assets, $722 million in profits and 4,784 employees. Its market capitalization reached US$25 billion in 2006, then hit US$70 billion by 2007. Roughly 20% of its stock, or US$14 billion worth, was owned collectively by management and employees.

RIM's success has defied the 1999 technology market meltdown. The company is run by technological geniuses who, since 1992, have stayed focused on creating their wireless winner and constantly improving it. Their technology has always been one or two steps ahead of the pack.

"I've always been asked, 'Do you look back at competitors?'" said Lazaridis in an interview with the *Financial Post* in 2006. "Why should I look back? We invented this market."

This happy state of affairs is due to the fact that this is a perfect "marriage" of two very different individuals with complementary skills: the technological expertise of Lazaridis and the smart financial-engineering and business-development knowledge of Balsillie, a chartered accountant.

The two are also an odd couple in the sense that Balsillie is a gregarious jock from small-town Ontario and Lazaridis is a nerdy, egghead immigrant from Turkey.

Balsillie describes himself as a "guy's guy." He owns several golf courses, has been trying to snag a National Hockey League franchise and enjoys the rough-and-tumble of playing a good hockey game after a 12-hour day.

Lazaridis, by contrast, was born in Istanbul, Turkey, to Greek parents. In 1966, when he was five years old, the family immigrated to Canada with three suitcases, eventually settling in Windsor, Ontario, where his father joined the line at a Chrysler factory and his mother worked as a seamstress.

Both Balsillie and Lazaridis are devoted family men and loyal colleagues. Lazaridis has dinner every week with his parents. The company's chief operating officer is Doug Fregin, a childhood buddy since grade 6 in Windsor. Both entered science fairs and tinkered with ham radios. Balsillie still plays hockey with guys he grew up with.

Lazaridis studied electrical engineering at the University of Waterloo, but left a few courses before graduation in 1984 after he landed a $600,000 contract to develop a display system for General Motors. In 1987, another lucrative contract followed, this time from Cantel, to research wireless devices.

By 1992, he was working on a "wild" scheme to link the technology of pagers with that of computers in order to create wireless e-mail. At the time, Balsillie worked for an engineering outfit that eventually hired Lazaridis and his small engineering firm to conduct contract research. When Balsillie's employer sold out to a European company, he took his severance and savings, took out a small business loan as well as a mortgage on his home, and invested $250,000 in Mike's firm. He also took a pay cut of 60%.

"I have a different view of risk," said Balsillie. "I think we are trained to perceive more risk than there really is in the world. It keeps insurance companies happy. I also came from not having a lot, so I was not worried about not having a lot."

The division of labour was easy. Balsillie stickhandled the business plan, strategy, marketing and financing. Money was needed to undertake research, development and marketing.

"We raised US$600 million [C$1 billion] in 2000 and we happened to be the last big deal before the tech bubble collapsed. One week later and we would have missed the window. We're like an Indiana Jones movie," he said.

Balsillie earned his CA, then an MBA at Harvard University, before joining the automotive industry. Harvard, he said, was an important, defining experience.

"It took me a while to strip away the Canadian predisposition of shyness. The most shocking thing was the first day in a class when all the Harvard students were complaining to the professor that his process and curriculum were not what most of them needed or wanted," he said. "I was in disbelief at their demands. The point it made to me is that power is more apparent than real, and is negotiable. I also learned that the American culture is different. People are very promotional. There is an aggressive predisposition toward that."

He took unconventional courses at Harvard to "see things from a different direction" and always knew that he wanted to apply conventional business practices to entrepreneurship.

"If you know exactly what you want you have a higher probability of success," he said. "But sometimes blind squirrels do find nuts."

Research In Motion has benefited from the booming capital markets but, unlike other businessmen, its founders were not tempted to grow too quickly or to diversify.

"We've stuck with the same engine," Balsillie said. "Half our job is saying no to polite investment bankers who want to load us into satellite or to buy dumb companies. They flatter you and can be persuasive, but we rely on our own analytics and trust them."

Diversifications are restricted to technological add-ons and regional expansion.

"Perception was that we were just a niche with an interim, limited future," he said. "But we have grown through depth and providing more, and now our customer base is growing rapidly."

The company has plenty on its plate and has launched dozens of bells and whistles to its core product. What's interesting is that during the 1990s the team devised a business strategy that is counter-intuitive: Balsillie describes the company as a "middleware partner." This means that their device can be used anywhere and its software licensed by anyone because it has been made to be compatible with any cellphone, any telecom carrier and any customer's internal e-mail system, anywhere. This has enabled the company to steer through the shoals of competition by imitators and by gigantic entities such as Microsoft, British Telecom and Nokia. Balsillie calls it a "Switzerland" strategy: the BlackBerry is a small "neutral" entity that can do business with all the "superpowers."

The company is one of many offshoots of the University of Waterloo, Canada's Harvard or MIT. The region has been traditionally entrepreneurial, and the university was started by two industrialists who wanted to encourage enterprise by allowing professors and students to develop technologies and patent them.

"A region like this needs primers. It needs someone to prime it. You can take it on yourself. You say, this is an area that has huge potential and you start it, and once you start it, you gotta help it. Then, eventually, if you find the right people to run it and if you give it enough nurturing, it starts running on its own," said Lazaridis in an interview in 2006 with the *Financial Post Magazine* when he and Jim won CEO of the Year.

The two founders were unusually enterprising as kids. Lazaridis excelled in school, and at 12 years of age won a prize at the Windsor Public Library for reading every single science book in the library.

"I had five or six paper routes," said Balsillie. "I also sold greeting cards at eight years of age door to door. People used to say how adorable my sales pitch was. I used to say, 'Buy now and beat the lineups at Christmas.' I would sell the cards for $10 or $15 and make 20% commission. I bought my own bikes and clothes."

An example of his gift of the gab occurred a few years back. He had told a group of investment bankers in a New York restaurant that the brand name BlackBerry was chosen after a professional product name search. But when this explanation fell flat, he concocted a better story, saying he named the device after the favourite fruit of a buxom *Penthouse* magazine centrefold.

"The guys in the restaurant began to chant, 'BlackBerry, BlackBerry,' and my CFO said to me, 'Good save,'" Jim recalled, adding, "Never let the facts get in the way of a good story."

Naturally, there have been some hiccups along the way. In spring 2006, the firm forked out $700 million to settle a patent-infringement case, without admission of any liability. The lawsuit didn't hurt the company, but Balsillie described its duration as "like a train wreck in slow motion." In 2007, Balsillie resigned as chair (remaining co-CEO), apologized and set aside $5 million with Lazaridis to pay for extra auditing costs for some accounting errors involving US$250 million in stock options paid to other employees.

Besides running their business, the two each finance and run ambitious philanthropic projects. Balsillie put $30 million into the Centre for International Governance Innovation. Lazaridis and the provincial government put in millions more, and a neighbour, academic John English, runs the initiative. It aims to devise ways to enhance governance among global institutions.

"The UN system was set up out of crisis, and there's not lots of research as to how to do this better. We have to," Balsillie said. He also gave $100 million—the largest-ever donation in Canada in the social sciences and humanities as of 2007—for the Balsillie School of International Affairs, a collaboration between his centre, the University of Waterloo, and Wilfrid Laurier University.

Lazaridis earmarked $100 million of his own money to establish the Perimeter Institute for Theoretical Physics, with help from governments and millions from Balsillie and Doug Fregin. Research areas include quantum theory, quantum gravity, superstring theory, particle physics and cosmology. There are dozens of resident researchers and plans to host hundreds of scientists to present papers.

Lazaridis said his institute probably won't yield any significant breakthroughs for at least 50 years, but no matter. Progress, he said at a press conference, depends on a combination of patience, focus and an enduring respect for the cornerstones of knowledge: reading, mathematics and basic scientific research.

Both men are twice exceptional. They have created an incredible global business, but also are committed to fostering important global legacies.

KWOK YUEN HO

The stunning lobby of ATI Technologies Inc. is pure feng shui, possibly the only one of its kind to be found in a Canadian corporate headquarters. The building is atrium-style and its focal point is a fountain of rocks, flora and fauna with a gigantic indoor perpetual flame that soars 20 feet high out of water. Feng shui is the ancient Chinese practice of arranging space to achieve harmony and to beneficially affect health, wealth and relationships.

There is little question that all these benefits have been achieved by ATI's founder, former chair and former CEO, Kwok Yuen (K.Y.) Ho, along with partners Benny Lau and Lee Ka Lau. All three men have become rich in Canada since immigrating from Hong Kong in 1983. And reports are that they are living happily ever after. He declined an interview for this book.

In 2006, ATI merged into a private entity called Advanced Micro Devices in a deal valued at US$5.4 billion. At the time of the merger, ATI was Canada's 127th-largest corporation, with sales of US$2 billion annually and 3,300 employees. It invents and manufactures high-performance computer chips that create three-dimensional video characters and other high-end graphics featured in video games, computers, cellphones and digital TVs.

"In the last 20 years, Canada has become much better for entrepreneurs," said Ho in an interview with *Canadian Business* magazine. "It was extremely difficult because there was no venture capital in Canada and the banks would never lend you money. At ATI, we used an overseas bank at first, not a Canadian bank."

Over the years, Ho has declined interviews with the media. His quotations that follow are all from *Canadian Business* magazine, *Toronto Sun* and *Globe and Mail* interviews.

Canada has been good to him and his partners, and he has been good to Canada. The three young men in their 20s arrived in Canada together as tourists in 1983, then decided to stay. Despite their education and experience in the high-tech world, they couldn't find full-time jobs. Ho hired himself out as a consultant, but then the three decided to pool their resources and their meagre savings to launch Array Technologies Inc. (later shortened to ATI Inc.), a graphics company designed to sell components to the nascent personal computer market.

The company immediately took off, creating a cash-flow crunch. Canadian banks were uninterested in lending, and venture capitalists were few and far between. Fortunately, Ho was able to convince an Asian bank to give their business a loan of $300,000.

By the end of its first year in business, the fledgling company had posted $10 million in sales of graphics technology, which was sold to enhance Commodore and Tandy computers.

Growth continued to soar, and within eight years Ho took the company public. His reasoning was unusual and ironic. He felt that the transparency requirements would end rumours propagated by his rivals that the fledgling company was in deep financial trouble and would not be able to meet its commitments to customers.

The three men worked closely together on strategy, but Ho ran the corporate operations, raised money and smoothed out the disagreements that arose in a company employing scientists, mathematicians and technical experts. They also socialized together. Most Saturday nights were devoted, with spouses and children in tow, to dinner parties, and the group even vacationed together occasionally.

Their success has been due to solid customer relationships and great suppliers, mostly in Taiwan, where Ho went to university. These networks have given ATI cost advantages and have created a culture of customer service that requires flexibility and quick adoption.

The ability to shift direction rapidly is essential to survival in this world. In 1994, for instance, ATI bet on the wrong technology platform and lost business when Intel unveiled its Pentium computer chips. Its stock collapsed in price by 75%. But ATI recovered two years later by inventing its own chip, which won contracts from the world's major manufacturers.

Fleet-footedness and flexibility have characterized Ho's life.

His grandparents had been wealthy until the Communist revolution. He was born in 1950 in a small village in mainland China. At 10 years of age, he was shipped off to join his father in Hong Kong. Eventually, most of the clan got out of mainland China. Ho worked as a boy in China and Hong Kong to help the family make ends meet, by growing and selling vegetables and fruits.

"When I was 9 or 10 years old, I grew vegetables. A lot of people liked to buy from me at the market because I was a kid. One time, a lady showed up wanting to buy veggies, and I looked at her and it was my mum. So she bought veggies and also got the money. I started doing handicrafts when I was 7. I made hats. I made a comparably small amount of money, but it was important to our family," he said.

He was a good student, and the family scraped together enough to send him to university in Taiwan.

"When I was at university, I was involved in an awful lot of activity that turned me a lot toward becoming a businessman. But my family was so poor that there was no way to make a dream to become a businessman, so that's why I wanted to be an engineer. To make a living," he said.

He returned to Hong Kong and worked in high-tech manufacturing for a while before taking a trip to check out North America. He settled on Canada but said once, in an interview, that it doesn't really matter where one goes.

"Some people may say they want to go to the U.S. because there are opportunities and there aren't in Canada. Or they go to Canada because there are opportunities and there aren't in the U.S. They don't understand. Everywhere has opportunities," he said.

By 2000, Ho was ready to retire, and had begun to do charitable work with the Chinese community and in the health and education fields. But new challenges kept cropping up at work. Then, in 2003, he was hit with allegations by the Ontario Securities Commission that he, his wife, Betty, and two employees and their spouses were guilty of insider-trading violations. The other four settled out of court for relatively small fines, but the Hos stood firm.

Sadly, the charges were levelled against the Hos following a charitable transaction in spring 2000. They had sold several millions of dollars' worth of ATI stock, then donated the shares to three charities. But their stock sale came just before an announcement that the company's forecasted earnings would be disappointing. This announcement triggered a 45% plummet in share prices.

In other words, the couple never benefited personally from the stock sale and had never intended to. In 2005, Ho retired and left operations to Dave Orton, a personable American executive who came on board after his California company had been acquired by ATI a few years earlier. I interviewed Orton and had a tour of operations in 2005. He commuted between his California home and ATI in Toronto and helped Ho stickhandle through the OSC and marketplace challenges after the other founders had left.

In October 2005, Ho and his wife were completely vindicated by an independent panel appointed by the Securities Commission.

"The evidence of K.Y. Ho stood the test of cross-examination and we accept it," the panel wrote in its 22-page finding. "[Also] there was no submission made by [OSC] staff—nor could there be on the evidence—that the gifts of shares by K.Y. Ho to the three charities were other than gifts made in good faith."

The decision removed a cloud over ATI's and Ho's heads but left a bitter taste for the immigrant who had built a huge company in Canada.

"My family and I are very pleased with this result," he said in a prepared statement. "While I have the greatest respect for the work of the OSC staff, I have always strongly believed that the allegations of wrongdoing against me were entirely without merit."

Later on, in a newspaper interview, he elaborated. "How could I settle? I wanted to clear my integrity and get justice. I suffered long and hard, but in the end I got the truth."

In 2006, he told *Canadian Business* magazine that retirement suited him but was long overdue.

"The high-tech industry is so dynamic you always have something you want to fix before you go, and it drags on and on. It never ends. I planned to retire in 1999. I wanted to retire by the time I was 50. I failed. I wanted to retire before 55. But I'm glad I still achieved it at 55 so I don't have to change another number," he said.

"In the last 20 years, I owe my family too much. I spent 99% of my time on ATI, ATI and ATI and the other 1% on my kids and life. Right now, I should spend some time with my family, take care of them, but also take care of a lot of other interests."

He still lives in Toronto but travels to Asia, where he hopes to invest in high-end tourist destinations to tap the growing Asian market. He's also involved in philanthropy.

"When you're poor, you're always looking to get wealthy, to get money," he explained in an interview. "Why do I do charity? Because in the early days, when you don't have money, you definitely want to work hard to make money. But after you get money, you should remember how you suffered and how you now have a chance to share your fortune with other people."

SIR TERENCE MATTHEWS

Sir Terence (Terry) Matthews is the world's only Welsh billionaire and Canada's greatest high-tech entrepreneur.

Matthews is the son of a coal miner and was born in tiny Newport, Wales. He's a rambunctious, brilliant, fun-loving former rugby player who joined the wave of hundreds of thousands of Britons who immigrated to Canada in the 1960s to get out from under the country's then-deteriorating economy.

Since then, Matthews has launched dozens of start-ups and has been the only Canadian entrepreneur to build two tech giants from scratch: Mitel Networks and Newbridge Networks, with sales between them of more than $1 billion. Both were sold.

Those successes, plus more, place Sir Terence at the top of the high-tech big leagues. But his companies do not sell high-profile consumer products like the BlackBerry. They sell B2B, or business-to-business, products that provide the components or networks for the brand-name products that consumers buy.

What's distinctive about Matthews is that he has proven time and again that he has the Midas touch. A goateed dynamo, he puts in 14-hour days, 7 days a week, and is involved in many projects, and many companies, at the same time. Little wonder that the motto on his Celtic House Venture Partners website is "Luck has nothing to do with it."

Celtic House is a side investment of Matthews's, an "incubator" or "angel" venture capital firm started in 1994 with partner Roger Maggs. Since then, it has raised hundreds of millions, from Matthews and others, to invest in start-ups, mostly in the United Kingdom and Canada. Between 1997 and 2007, Celtic invested in 50 technology companies in the optics, software, systems and semiconductor subsectors of the technology sector.

"There have been 16 successful exits worth over US$5 billion and Celtic House seed-funded 12 of these," said the Celtic House website in May 2007.

Unfortunately, Matthews declines interview requests, so information has been compiled from periodical and market information.

Atop Matthews's personal business empire is Wesley Clover, with offices in Kanata (outside Ottawa), Wales and Australia. Matthews is chairman and oversees Wesley investments in three sectors: technology, real estate development and leisure.

The company's principal real estate holding is Kanata Research Park, with 1.7 million square feet of commercial space and room for another 2.3 million square feet on 566 newly acquired acres.

Its leisure group owns Celtic Tech Jet, which charters executive jets and offers aircraft maintenance and management services plus two five-star resorts and a film production company. Its flagship is Celtic Manor Resort in Wales, a 19th-century castle with a hotel and conference centre on 1,400 acres. Celtic Manor's championship golf course hosts many tournaments and will be the venue for the Ryder Cup in 2010. It also has an executive course, spa, health club and four restaurants. In Canada, Wesley Clover owns the Marshes Golf

Club in Ottawa and the Brookstreet resort with its spa, health club facilities and restaurant.

The underpinning for the Wesley portfolio is made up of 15 technology companies, some public, most private. These enterprises are involved in next-generation networking and telecom and deploy a cluster approach that consists of maximizing synergies and utilizing team problem-solving to win global markets.

The linchpin is Mitel Networks Corp., Canada's 491st-largest corporation, with sales in 2006 of $450 million and 1,500 employees. Mitel is 100% owned by Terry Matthews and in April 2007 paid US$723 million to buy Internet-based telecom provider Inter-Tel Business Communications, of Arizona, with revenues of US$458.4 million. The acquisition more than doubles Mitel's size, marking the creation of Matthews's third billion-dollar baby.

Other Wesley Clover companies include the Waterloo, Ontario, Sandvine Corp., which went public in 2006 on the AIM exchange in London; March Networks Corp. in Kanata; Ubiquity Software Corp. in the UK; and NewHeights Software Corp. in Kanata.

What's important to note is that the Mitel that Matthews currently owns is not the original Mitel that made him his first fortune. The original Mitel was sold in 1985, and he bought back one of its divisions in 2001, then poured US$211 million into research. For several years, the company lost money, but he did not lose sleep over it.

Matthews explained this financial fearlessness in a *Financial Post* interview with Kevin Restivo in 2005. "I am an enthusiast. It is not only about money. I am not saying money is not important. But you have to enjoy what you do as well. I like laughing. I like going around to customers and talking to them. Most of all, I enjoy beating up on my competitors. I really enjoy that!" he said.

His business model has been simple.

"I bet on markets, then I introduce the technology to address the market. There are at least 20 companies I have investments in now," he said.

When asked how his smaller companies compete against the

giants of the world, he said, "The most successful companies some-times have the least amount of people. If you went in to get brain sur-gery, would you be happy if 50 people were operating on you? No. You want the best brain surgeon in the world to operate on you."

Clearly, the technology stars must have been shining down on Wales when Terry Matthews was born in 1943. As a kid, he could fix everything from televisions to radios and clocks. At 15, he was handpicked by British Telecom for an apprenticeship in its research and development department.

He spent a decade there, earning a university degree part-time in engineering, then, in 1969, at age 26, he and his wife, Ann, came to North America for a look. He landed a job in Ottawa with an affiliate of Nortel Networks Corp. and they cashed in their return tickets to set up house.

At Nortel he met another bright British engineer, Michael Cowpland. In 1972, the two decided to get into business together to produce hotel fire alarms. Matthews took out a $5,000 home-equity loan to rent office space, Cowpland put up some money, but the product was a dud. Next they decided to export electric lawn-mowers to the United Kingdom. They called the company Mitel, an acronym of Michael, Terry and Lawnmower.

Shipping and handling problems sank the venture, and they hired themselves out instead as high-tech consultants to firms that had sprung up in Ottawa's Kanata suburb, around the National Research Council and Nortel. At its peak, Ottawa's high-tech sector employed 80,000 people, or 10% of the region's workforce, and there were direct daily flights between Ottawa and Silicon Valley's San Jose, California.

Matthews and Cowpland were part of this mix. Shortly after they started consulting, they commercialized a technology outlined in Cowpland's engineering PhD thesis, involving Touch-Tone phones. It was innovative and became a business success, turning Mitel into a chip manufacturer ahead of the pack in a niche market.

In 1985, British Telecom bought Mitel for $322 million and the two men went their separate ways. In short order, Matthews launched Newbridge Networks Corp. and also spun off CrossKeys

Systems Corp. and TimeStep Corp. Newbridge became a leader in telecom-networking and data-communications products, notably ATM (automated teller machine) devices and routers.

By January 2000, Newbridge employed 6,500 and had revenues of $1.8 billion. In May of that year, France's Alcatel bought it in a stock swap worth US$7 billion. Matthews did not want to sell, but his shareholders did. Matthews's portion was US$1 billion, and his Alcatel stock made him its single biggest shareholder. Even so, Alcatel's management made it clear that he was not welcome to work in the company. Shortly after the purchase, when the tech bubble burst, Alcatel's stock retreated.

Matthews was still hugely wealthy and returned to Wales for a while. Within months, he returned to Ottawa as CEO of Telexis, a four-year-old spinoff from Newbridge, then renamed it March Networks Corporation and redirected its efforts into video surveillance systems.

Terry, his wife and four children guard their privacy, but one of his children, Owen, is CEO of Matthews-owned NewHeights. Owen Matthews learned from a master. In an interview, he explained how his father refused to let Mitel distribute his son's products until they had proven their merit.

"[My father] won't blow his reputation over his son's company unless he thinks it's a bloody good company," Owen told a Canadian newspaper. "Now, he actively promotes the company and is comfortable providing all kinds of introductions. He's more conservative with this company because it's me and he's adverse to his son failing."

Terry's also adverse to failing himself, but he has nerves of steel. In 2005, he happily reported that Mitel was finally doing well against giant rivals.

"Mitel now generates about 80% of revenue from brand-new products. What it tells you is the changeover to solutions built using Internet Protocol [a tech standard] is quite dramatic. Now, of course, I am feeling very good about my investment. But two to three years ago it was not so obvious. It was a pretty ugly time but I decided to keep investing."

ROBERT MILLER

My hours of conversation with Montreal entrepreneur Robert Miller have been the most unusual, comprehensive and interesting interviews of my career. He refuses publicity, but we met for long stretches twice in the summer of 2007 for this book.

"I will blow your mind," he said. And he did. Not only is he a rare individual, but he is also a brilliant business strategist.

Miller is sole proprietor of Future Electronics, a global distribution giant, based in Pointe-Claire, Quebec, that sells high-tech components, specializing in semiconductors and capacitors, which drive the world's industries.

Future Electronics employs 5,000, including many salespeople and engineers in 167 offices located in 39 countries, and operations are open around the clock. The company's revenues exceeded US$3 billion in 2007. The company has no debt and an estimated enterprise value of several billion dollars. Miller also jointly owns a real estate development business in Naples, Florida, with his ex-wife, Margaret, that is probably worth US$1 billion. His reticence about publicity is rooted in a concern about personal security as well as in the fact that Future Electronics is not, nor ever will be, a public corporation.

"There's no point for getting publicity. I'm an ordinary guy but wealthy. Wealth breeds jealousy, jealousy breeds hatred, hatred breeds haters and haters breed problems. I want my sons to live a normal life and not be bothered," he said.

Miller was born in 1945 and raised in Montreal. He studied business, but wanted to be a radio broadcaster. There's a vintage radio microphone on a credenza in his huge Montreal office.

Miller is very spiritual and survived a close brush with mortality a few years ago. He suffered from atrial fibrillation, which usually results in fatal strokes or heart attacks. Two years ago, he underwent a process known as cryoablation, which freezes heart tissue to stop arrhythmia of the heart muscle. It worked. Hockey player Mario Lemieux underwent the same procedure for the same condition. Miller had read about Lemieux's problem in newspapers and tracked him down. Both returned to full speed, and Miller intends to double the company's size by July 1, 2010, through six revolutionary initiatives. "I'm a poor man because I only have 24 hours to live each day," he said.

Miller gives away millions to worthy individuals, charities and causes. The public does not know, for instance, that the company opened its doors to hundreds during the Quebec ice storm of 1998, as it had its own generators and a sophisticated food services operation.

"More than half our profits are given away. You have to give till it hurts," he said.

"My life is based on trust. I was taught to be cautious. I drink the truth serum every morning. I'm big on making a contribution to society. The Dalai Lama's religion is kindness. My religion is generosity. I have a unique style, but it is nothing mysterious," he said. "My drive came from my sparse beginnings and my desire to have security and to make an impact on society."

"My rivals play checkers. We play chess," he said. "This is an unusual company with enormous potential. No one understands business the way we do. Our approach is simple, logical. We have a unique win-win philosophy."

Miller and his team have set Future Electronics apart from others by moving quickly, which they can do because it is a sole proprietorship, but also by investing heavily in a seamless global technology platform. Components, prices, orders and shipments are traceable, in real time, everywhere. This "dashboard" provides Miller with a huge competitive advantage: a window into global trends and the supply-demand relationship of every high-tech widget worldwide.

In other words, Future Electronics understands the future. And Miller carefully watches and charts this market intelligence to foretell supply-demand scenarios.

"He is able to chart which components will be in huge demand in the electronics industry and when commodity prices will begin to take off. He always seems to be one year ahead of the competition," said Miller's friend Gerry Duggan, who came out of retirement in 2007 to be a full-time consultant after being Future Electronics' president when Miller was ill.

Miller says the next economic transformation will be the acceleration of Asia's industrialization. He estimates that, in a handful of years, two-thirds of the components he sells, which underpin such development, will be bought in Asia, up from the 45% demand currently. So his plan is to make Future Electronics a consolidator in a hurry.

"First of all, we have no debt, and cash is king," he said. "We intend to invest in, merge or acquire 30 companies in the next three years. Most of these intended transactions will not require integration, as we will allow them to operate independently. In many cases, we will purchase a 50% ownership of these companies. In Asia, it is important to have a local face, but more important, our business partners will then have skin in the game, and a shotgun buyout two years later if they want out."

By contrast, companies usually buy out small players, then absorb or shut them down. Miller's strategy is to ensure their survival by becoming their partner.

"I tell them, 'I will never allow independent distributors like you to disappear.' I tell them I will help them stay in business, because we have 400 suppliers and they have only 15 or so," he said. "I will give them advice. They will make more money. I will be generous. We will teach them everything we know and share with them our systems. We will give them our expertise in engineering, and they will help us in return."

Besides external changes, Miller has also devised unique approaches to improve Future Electronics' internal operations. "People talk about the science of medicine and the art of selling. I believe medicine is an art and selling is a science," he said. "Everyone wants to be rich, but not everyone wants to work hard," he added. "So we teach them where to go, what to do, how to do it, and then measure them because what gets measured gets done."

Future Electronics deploys what Miller calls the Z Strategy—

Z for "making zillions of dollars"—which is designed to leverage sales and engineering so that they are more productive and make more money. For instance, when Miller returned as president on October 1, 2005, he said that the company's 260 certified engineers in the Advanced Engineering Group were seeing an average of one customer per week. He has subsequently introduced a lot more discipline, and the Advanced Engineering Group engineers are now seeing at least 10 customers per week. All advanced engineers must leave a daily voice-mail message of up to 5 minutes duration. This message must include what they did that day and what others may need to do by way of follow-up. This information is circulated to 8 or 10 others who are involved, and they must fill in the engineering information log indicating that they have listened to the voice mail and when they heard it. This confirms that it was received.

"So it means you better have done something every day," Miller said.

Miller believes in Friday business discipline. He explained, "I never leave the office on Friday afternoons, because purchasers want to clear their desks and place all orders then. Research shows that 61% of orders of our customers are placed on Fridays. So we have a roll call at 4:45 on Friday afternoons so that we know we are calling customers when all the other guys are sleeping or playing golf."

Miller is also transforming the overall marketplace through Future Electronics' Stop Manufacturing Program and Inventory Exchange Program.

"For instance, Cisco in 2001 wrote off US$1.5 billion in unsold components [semiconductors and capacitors], and Nortel Networks, US$1 billion," he said. "This is a waste, and waste is a sin." Manufacturers who have signed on to the Stop Manufacturing Program are given information about current and future demand for components so they don't overproduce. And those customers who sign on to the Inventory Exchange Program can buy others' excess inventory or sell their own through Future Electronics at fair market prices, thus avoiding write-offs. This is a huge virtual aftermarket opportunity in a semiconductor marketplace that was worth US$250 billion in 2006, of which 8% to 10% was written off.

The germ for the idea for this brilliant business niche came out of Miller's concern about pollution, environmental degradation and the exploitation of finite resources as a result of throwing away all these unsold components.

"We have new, dynamic strategies in place and every angle covered," he said. "If it all hits, we are going to make billions of additional profit in the next several years. Now we are getting bigger stakes, better positioning—and position and relationship is what it's all about."

Miller's business smarts have been passed along to his two entrepreneurial sons, Frederick and Rodney, but his own father was bowled over by Miller's good fortune.

"He was in the car business, groceries, retail, and once owned an antique store. When he retired, he worked at Future Electronics, and his job was to open the mail," Miller said. "Everyone loved him and he was very friendly. He was great with his grandchildren, a nice man. My mother died at 55 years of age. My dad died much later, in 1985."

Miller lives in Montreal's Westmount and jets around the world visiting operations and closing deals. At work, he regularly appears in its auditorium to rally the troops and to update them on the latest Future Electronics strategies. He is committed to very open communications within the company. He despises politics in business and defines business politicians as "individuals who make decisions which benefit them but which do not necessarily benefit the corporation."

He got into electronics when he returned to Montreal from Rider Business College in New Jersey. "I got involved in radio and thought that's what I would end up doing, but I got back to Montreal in 1967 and met this guy who wanted to hire a university graduate. It was a small specialty electronics wholesaler. He drove a big luxury car, so I joined," he said.

Miller learned the business and in 18 months left with the owner's son, Eli Manis, to start up Future Electronics. Miller bought out Manis in 1976 and he has owned 100% of this private enterprise ever since.

"I did one really smart thing, which was I took a three-year technical course in electronics at the Montreal Technical Institute," he said. "This helped me. I have always understood the latest in component technology and how to use it—gave me a definite edge."

This is why Miller invests heavily in semiconductor and related technology education for his employees. Future Electronics' Montreal headquarters houses extensive training and education facilities. Its cavernous sales floors look like newsrooms: a sea of desks surrounded by low-rise dividers, computer monitors and people with headsets. Employees use the subsidized cafeteria by accessing it with an e-card payment system, and also have on hand a dry cleaner, fitness facilities and access to the hotel pool next door. The company just hired several English teachers to upgrade employee language skills.

"We should have done this 20 years ago, and it will make us a fortune," he said. "I spent years learning French but I cannot understand the nuances of contracts and so on, and employees are held back if they do not really understand English well enough."

Miller is a self-confessed workaholic who still never stops, but much more of his time is now spent on non-business projects.

"I once worked 765 days in a row, without one day off," he said. "I'm not proud of that. It was a mistake. I was never home before 11 at night except Saturdays. when I got home at 8 p.m."

Today he believes that his staff should work a 40-hour week, 8 hours daily, so that they can enjoy their families and friends. He is very charitable toward employees and their loved ones, sending them for expensive medical treatments, buying their children puppies or mentoring. He helped in the development of tennis star Greg Rusedski, as well as Chicago Blackhawks right winger Martin Lapointe. He also mentors prominent politicians, academics and business people around the world.

"He loves training people," said Gerry Duggan. "Robert is a good friend who has been wonderful to my family, and there is one word to describe this guy, and it's 'love'"—unusual praise for an unusual person, who even describes his ex-wife as "a special friend and a brilliant businesswoman." The two separated amicably after many years of marriage and have been business partners ever since.

"My goal is to run out of money and breath at exactly the same moment," Miller said. "My kids understand this. It's my money, and I'll decide where the money will be given away."

CHARLES SIROIS

At an early age Charles Sirois mastered the art of using other people's money in high-risk ventures.

When he was 10, he said in an interview with me, "My dad gave me a portfolio of penny stocks, worth $1,000, and said, 'Those are your assets. Now make them grow. So in secondary school, when other kids were reading the sports pages, I was following my stocks in the newspapers. My dad was a heavy speculator and played in risky businesses."

So has Sirois. It took him only 20 years to parlay $200,000 of his uncle's savings into a highly leveraged telecom empire worth $10 billion by 2000. Then he cashed out, for an estimated $1 billion, and left BCE, the Caisse de dépôt et placement du Québec, National Bank and others holding the bag after the 2001 telecom meltdown.

"Charles is a friend of mine and he's a master salesman," said billionaire Stephen Jarislowsky, whose Jarislowsky Fraser Limited of Montreal manages $60 billion of other peoples' money. "I wouldn't have invested with him, but others did. He's a very convincing guy."

Sirois learned how to handle risk from a master, his father, who ran a number of businesses in Chicoutimi but also played the high-risk commodities market. One day, he watched his father lose everything, but move on.

"It was 1970 and I was a kid. He lost $200,000 in one morning, which was a lot of money in those days," said Sirois. "I was in his office and he had all these brokers on the phone. He looked at me and said, 'What should we do now?' I was white. I couldn't speak. So he said, 'I think we should eat our losses.' He hung up and just said to me, 'Okay, we have to make something else work now.'"

It was an important lesson.

"If you take risks you sometimes lose, so you have to swallow, turn, snap back and go again," Sirois said.

Sirois attended Université de Sherbrooke and took finance because of his love of mathematics and physics. He then obtained a master's from Université Laval in finance.

"I had no interest in business. My father was discouraged because I was not interested in being an accountant. In school, I discovered finance and models, lots of math, so I decided to go into that," he said.

Working in a small town running many different small businesses did not suit him. He stayed for 18 months, then struck out on his own, using a different business model.

"My dad was a regional entrepreneur, which means when he got to a certain size in a region, he'd start a completely different business. So he was involved in a rest home for the elderly, a credit information system, publishing, paging and telephone answering."

Paging was an intriguing business, and Sirois decided to become a consolidator.

"I asked my dad to sell his paging business to me. He put a price of $200,000 on it and said, 'Pay me in preferred shares. Then you can buy them back when you have enough money and give the money to your [two] sisters instead of to me,'" Sirois recalled.

By 1979, the paging business had grown to revenues of $180,000 a year and $60,000 in cash flow. So Sirois began his career-leveraging climb. He bought another paging company, in Quebec City, for $1 million, borrowing $300,000 from a bank and $200,000 from his uncle. The other $500,000 would be paid to the seller over five years, at no interest.

Sirois then moved to Quebec City and began buying all his competitors with bank borrowings. By 1984, his company, now called Telesystem Limited, had borrowed $7 million and had equity of only $300,000. Naturally, his bank—the Royal Bank of Canada—was nervous.

That's when he convinced the Caisse de dépôt et placement du Québec to buy 30% of Telesystem for $2 million. This allowed him to reduce his loans to $5 million and switch to National Bank, Quebec's hungriest lender. With those two, Sirois had enlisted Quebec Inc. on his side, as have so many others.

"The Caisse liked my model of consolidating all the mom-and-pop paging companies, so between 1984 and 1986 I bought 22 companies across the country and created the largest paging company by far. We had 100,000 customers, and the next one in size had only 30,000 customers," he said.

By the time his shopping spree was over, he was $65 million in debt and had only the $2 million in equity that he had obtained from the Caisse. So he took the company public, called it National Pagette and raised enough equity to pay down $20 million in loans. Then he enlisted BCE, another Quebec establishment pillar.

"The next new business I wanted to get into was the cellphone," he said. "Rogers Communications Inc. was the king, through Cantel. So I met with Bell [BCE] and convinced it to merge my paging assets to create an integrated paging and cell business. We did this in 1987, called it Bell Mobility, and I owned 15%."

Weeks later, in 1988, at only 33 years of age, Sirois became chair and CEO of Bell Mobility. But his lack of interest in management and his tangles with the Bell bureaucrats led to his decision after two years to leave. But during that time, the stock ran up to $40 a share from $8.50.

His next move involved international wireless.

"I decided to go into emerging markets. New countries would go directly into wireless and not build all those telephone poles and wires. So I obtained licences and built an international cellular company," he said.

In 1992, he pulled off a coup by convincing archrivals Rogers and BCE to join his hostile takeover bid for Teleglobe, Ottawa's long-distance international monopoly. They put up all the money, and he ended up with 20% and the jobs of chair and CEO.

For the next few years, the booming telecom stock market propelled Teleglobe stock from a market capitalization value of $500 million in 1992 to $10 billion in 2000. That year, BCE's CEO, Jean Monty, a friend of Sirois's, agreed to pay $9.6 billion in BCE stock and $1 billion in cash for the 77% of Teleglobe it didn't already own.

Almost immediately, the shares in both companies crashed. Sirois was paid out $800 million for his 20%. But Jean Monty resigned and BCE wrote off $8.5 billion. Sirois blames BCE and Monty for Teleglobe's cratering.

"BCE made mistakes," he said. "They fired the entire management team, and none of them understood the international marketplace. If you fire the guy in Africa, your competitor will hire him and take all your traffic. The biggest mistake they made was strategic: when Global Crossing and others collapsed, they should have consolidated the market at 10 cents on the dollar. They had the money and no one else did. They would have owned the world because nobody else would add to capacity at 100 cents on the dollar."

"The only mistake Jean Monty made was in the selection of the CEO for Teleglobe, and by the time he discovered his mistake, it was too late. A major strategy was missed, and nobody became a global consolidator," he said.

Teleglobe was eventually sold out of bankruptcy protection to India's Tata Group.

But Sirois made another $150 million from the Caisse de dépôt and a private equity partner for a content company he owned. And he made another $100 million in 2005 when he refinanced and sold Telesystem International Wireless to Vodafone and others. He had run that company in partnership with Rogers.

By 2007, Sirois was still operating through Telesystem, but now it is a private company involving his father, sons and his uncle.

It controls several companies in the entertainment, health care and technology sectors and manages $600 million worth of venture capital portfolios in the U.S. and Canada.

In Africa, he bankrolls entrepreneurs and works with his son, François-Charles Sirois and a cousin, Denis Martin Sirois. The three have created a $20-million foundation.

"I believe strongly that the only way an emerging country can get out of poverty and remain out is through the private sector. It's impossible to do it through governments, which you can't keep honest. Government cannot create wealth," Charles Sirois said.

Charles lives well. He has two children by his first marriage and five grandchildren. He and his wife, Susan, have homes in Montreal, Paris and Florida.

"I did not know I would make this much money, but I know I own it," he said. "It is fun. But making it was also a little bit stressful."

ENTERTAINMENT AND MEDIA

P erhaps it is because of Canada's long, dark winters spent mostly indoors. Or the need for music or comedy to brighten the climatic gloom. Whatever the reasons, Canadians are really good at entertaining themselves, as well as others, and are disproportionately represented in Hollywood, on Broadway, on television, in the media, in the music business and in online gaming. Many Canadian performers have become household names around the world, such as Céline Dion, Anne Murray, Keanu Reeves, William Shatner, Michael J. Fox, Donald Sutherland, Mike Myers, Jim Carrey, David Cronenberg, Sarah McLachlan, Paul Anka, Alanis Morissette, Bryan Adams, Leonard Cohen, Martin Short, Dan Aykroyd and Eugene Levy. They have made millions, but the seven Canadian businessmen profiled here have made a billion or more building or running entertainment empires. Three started as performers themselves and did not continue. But all seven have certainly mastered the art of showbiz.

Content distribution, not content creation, has been the secret to making money in this sector, through ownership of newspapers, broadcasters, cable companies, popular websites, museums, radio

stations or sports franchises or through exclusive deals with theatre promoters. This is how these entrepreneurs have become billionaires and why others profiled have added this sector to their
portfolios. If you were to include those owning media and sports
franchises, the list would extend to conglomerateurs and investors
such as Paul Desmarais, Paul Hill, Jimmy Pattison, Ted Rogers and
J.R. Shaw, as well as sports-team owners Larry Tanenbaum, Al
Libin, Eugene Melnyk and Murray Edwards.

THE ASPERS

Izzy Asper was a breath of fresh air in the very stuffy world of
Canadian business. He was not a buttoned-down suit from a fancy
school or a fancy family. He was not a name-dropper or a corporate climber. To everyone and anyone, he was just plain Izzy, a boy
from the Prairies, where people are bred to be modest, self-reliant
and neighbourly.

Izzy was also Canada's last Renaissance man and had more
career successes in more fields than a dozen *Who's Who* entries.
He was an accomplished lawyer, politician, broadcaster, columnist,
financier, philanthropist and musician.

He died in 2003 but left behind a business empire, CanWest
Global Communications Corp. Canada's biggest media group owned
in 2006 about $5.6 billion in assets in Canada, Australia, the United
States, Britain and Turkey. It employed 10,656 people around the
world in its television and radio stations and in Canada's largest
newspaper chain.

CanWest is controlled and run by Izzy's three children, Leonard, Gail and David. All are lawyers, directors of the company and
trustees of the Asper Foundation, one of Canada's 20 biggest foundations, with more than $112 million.

Leonard is CEO of CanWest, Gail is corporate secretary and
runs the family's philanthropic interests, and David is executive
vice-president of CanWest, chairman of the National Post and

involved in real estate and special projects. In 1992, convicted murderer David Milgaard was released after David argued the appeal of his 1970 conviction before the Supreme Court. His efforts also resulted in finding the guilty party. In 2007, David earned a master of law degree from the University of Toronto.

Leonard, born in 1964, is the youngest; David, the oldest, was born in 1958; and Gail was born in 1960. All have very different personalities. Their three eloquent eulogies at Izzy Asper's huge funeral in Winnipeg reflected their unique relationships with their father. Hundreds attended and the assemblage included tycoons such as Ted Rogers, former prime minister Jean Chrétien and Reform Party founder Preston Manning.

Despite access to Canada's highest echelons, the three Aspers are all down-to-earth. They are also comfortable in their corporate incarnations. Izzy's health had been an issue for years—he had a quadruple bypass 20 years before he died—and he began handing over the reins, and defining roles that his children would play, years before it was necessary.

"Izzy's feeling was that I had the best skill set for this job," said Leonard in an interview at his Toronto office at Global Television in the summer of 2007. "Gail took herself out of the running. David said he didn't want it. David and I thought about being co-CEOs, but he likes projects with a beginning, middle and an end.

"I love this job but there's never an end. That's why I compete in sports. You can't say you won in business, because the season is never over. There's no piece of silverware on the mantle. You can have your best year of profitability and the stock tanks because its price is based on perceptions about future earnings," he added.

The three siblings get along well and hold family meetings quarterly, out of the fray. Winnipeg is headquarters, but Leonard moved in 2006 to Toronto, where the investment, business, advertising and media communities are clustered. He commutes between the two cities.

Gail has been travelling constantly and has raised $200 million—and is on her way toward $300 million—from governments and the private sector to build the Canadian Museum for Human Rights at home in Winnipeg. It is the first federally financed museum outside of Ottawa.

"At our family meetings we talk about major topics or deals, like Alliance Atlantis, Australia or CanWest board appointments, and then there are issues like who's using the house in Florida for Christmas vacation," said Gail. "Our goals are to achieve strong shareholder values, us included. And as for the future size of Can-West? We need to be as big as we need to be."

Growing up in a family where debate was encouraged has led to a consensual management style.

"I like to get smart people in a room with ideas, and the guy with the multiple votes makes the decision. I call myself a consultative decision-maker," said Leonard. "[With the family] I have a casting vote on CanWest matters. We work together. David and I do a lot of collaborative decision-making. But we have a shareholders' agreement and can be split up easily."

Since Izzy died, the company has been very active, making takeovers, restructuring and culling properties to prune debt. But his children are not in any hurry to make CanWest even bigger than it was, having watched their father build it over many years.

"Izzy tried many business ventures that naturally didn't work out. He used to say, 'If at first you don't succeed, join the club,'" said Leonard.

Izzy started his first business venture in the 1960s, while he was still practising law. He put together a consortium of 15 investors to launch a distillery in Manitoba.

"He saw Sam Bronfman and told him he'd be bigger in 30 years than Seagram," said Leonard. "He learned the business and went to Kentucky. He had a 30-year plan, but 2 years later it was bought out and they doubled their money."

Izzy was also fiercely political. He was elected to the Manitoba legislature and served as leader of the Manitoba Liberal Party from 1970 to 1975. Politics led to interest in the media and its influence. He left public life but had bought a North Dakota radio station for about $750,000, dismantled it and shipped the equipment to Winnipeg to get a Canadian broadcast licence.

In 1976 he bought struggling Global TV with two partners, and in 1977 he launched merchant bank CanWest Capital, with Toronto private equity giant Gerry Schwartz. Both were lawyers from Winnipeg. Their firm was a pioneer.

"It was a 10-year closed-end fund, and he worked with Gerry, who had learned everything about private equity and merchant banking at Bear, Stearns in New York, with Henry Kravis and others in the 1970s," said Leonard. The two eventually had a falling-out over philosophical issues, and Gerry went to Toronto and started his own firm, called Onex Corp., now Canada's 15th-biggest corporation.

In 1989, Izzy parted company with his Global partners too. The divorce was litigious, and Izzy ended up owning the network after an auction was held. Two years later, he took those assets (held in CanWest) public and then invested the proceeds outside the country.

"We were doing a co-production with a New Zealand partner and found out about a bankrupt national network there," said Leonard. "We bought it from the bank for $8 million and got the rest of New Zealand for $100 million. By 2007, we had received $400 million in dividends out of there. Also, the same bank owned another channel in Australia, which was another $51-million bet. So far, we have received $900 million in dividends from Australia, and it's worth $1.3 billion. Both were spectacular investments."

In 2000, Izzy emerged partially successful in a takeover bid for WIC (Western International Communications Ltd., a west-coast broadcast property) and was able to buy it for $800 million after Shaw Communications and CanWest agreed on how to divide the assets. Then, days later, he made a deal with Conrad Black to buy Canada's largest newspaper chain, Southam, for $3.2 billion.

"We went from 800 to 8,000 employees in one month," said Leonard. "It started because Izzy wanted to buy [Southam's online site] Canada.com or do a 50-50 deal for it with Conrad. Then Conrad issued a press release saying all his small papers were for sale, so we had a management meeting and decided to try and buy Alberta and Saskatchewan papers. Then we ended up buying them all," he said.

By 2007, CanWest was digesting two more acquisitions: the broadcast assets of Alliance Atlantis, which tripled its number of specialty channels in Canada, and a chain of radio stations in Turkey. Buying traditional media outlets is somewhat controversial, but Leonard pointed out that regulations vary from market to market.

"People for the next 20 years will still be turning on radios. Nothing happens as quickly as people think it'll happen, with television or any media," he said. Besides, countries vary greatly. For instance, only 2% of Turks have multi-channel [cable] television, and 25% of Australians. So there are opportunities to grow conventional businesses in differing markets, he said.

There is also the world of new media, populated by websites and portals and young consumers. CanWest's strategy here is to look for acquisitions but also to digitally build out its existing brands. Conventional media developed with digital media is a powerful combination.

"YouTube did not exist 18 months ago. MySpace could be gone in 18 months. These are like hot nightclubs. Take Facebook. Lots of people are leaving it because there are too many politicians on it," he said. "I believe that no one executive has the vision to know the future, so you must create a culture which captures these fish when they float by."

Clearly, the tricky part for CanWest going forward will be retaining family solidarity, something that has eluded many other well-heeled Canadian clans. Leonard credits his father's foresight and tutoring with their success thus far. This preparation included establishing good lines of communication, setting out partnership rules and distributing assets along the way.

"You have to start giving children assets in their 20s so they are not demanding dividends or fighting over business strategy," said Leonard. "Everyone has nice houses; nobody has obscene wealth. A cottage, maybe. And all of us have personal foundations to do good things with. If kids are asset-rich and cash-poor, the squabbling begins. Izzy understood this. So do we."

CALVIN AYRE

The world's largest computer facilities for online gaming are nick-named MIT, which stands for the Mohawk Institute of Technology, not the Massachusetts Institute of Technology. It's a giant "server park" inside Kahnawake, a Mohawk Indian reserve just across the St. Lawrence River from Montreal and on the U.S. border.

This is where Canadian entrepreneur Calvin Ayre first obtained a gambling licence, and where he located his computers. But his idea was not to build another casino inside an Indian reserve. It was to create a virtual casino on the Internet using an Indian-reserve gambling licence.

The result is that Calvin Ayre has become wealthy in short order. But his success is controversial: he went from growing up on a pig farm in Saskatchewan to attending the prestigious University of Waterloo, where he earned a science degree on a scholarship, to being a wealthy jet-setter in a risky—and risqué—business.

"It was character-building to grow up in Saskatchewan, get up in the dark, feed the pigs and go to school with pig shit on your boots in minus-40-degree weather," he said in an early-morning interview in summer 2007 in Toronto's hip SoHo Metropolitan Hotel. "We used to do our chores, walk half a mile for the school bus, then come home in the dark. It was tough."

The family moved to BC when Calvin was 11. Ayre later went east to university, then ended up back in Vancouver in the real estate business, then the stock market. Then he was already on to his next gig. He launched a back-office business service bureau working with high-tech companies, then began to realize the future of online gambling.

By 1993, he had crafted a business model based on jurisdic-tion-shopping, a legal term for picking locations that would allow gaming, optimize opportunities and minimize taxation. He called his new enterprise Bodog ("for no reason at all").

For instance, his Mohawk-based computer servers are doing nothing illegal and, besides, are out of bounds to Canadian and American gambling or taxation regulators. His gaming licence is legitimate too, because it was granted by an Indian reserve, which is exempt from gaming laws. Bodog's marketing and software operations are in Vancouver, but he avoids problems by not soliciting bets from Canadians.

He also avoids problems with the U.S., where taking bets by phone (though not placing the bets themselves) is illegal. He accepts bets from Americans and anyone else, but these are placed through call centres located in offshore havens that permit gambling. On top of it all, he and his company are residents of Antigua, which is a gambling-friendly tax haven.

"We weren't avoiding the laws by designing operations this way. We always went to jurisdictions that allowed us to operate this kind of business," he said. "That's because I didn't want to waste a lot of money on lawyers."

Even so, Ayre has to be careful and has avoided travel to the United States since 2006, when American officials began a crackdown on Internet gambling. The FBI has arrested several executives from Britain and Canada even though they were working for companies in Britain, where gambling is legal.

"We don't advertise in the U.S. and haven't targeted Americans since then, but we do take bets from Americans," said Ayre. "There is no legal reason we can't do business with them, because the transactions are done outside the country. But I stopped going to the U.S. before all this stuff [the arrests] because the jurisdiction had made its viewpoint well known."

The Washington-led crackdown caused the collapse of several companies on the London Stock Exchange and has shrunk the American market.

So far, Ayre's only "punishment" has been that *Forbes Magazine* dropped him from its 2007 list of the richest billionaires in the world, after putting him on its 2006 cover. He said he was removed because he refused to be interviewed by the magazine after they misquoted him the year before. But he said the magazine audited his operations to verify his wealth.

"Forbes based the $1-billion 2006 value on Bodog's $200-million-a-year revenues [profits from bets], which they sent in auditors to verify. Now revenues are 50% higher and I feel richer," he said. "We've got to be worth US$1.5 billion, I would think."

Paradoxically, all the notoriety has been good for business, he said. That's because the business is marketed to young males, and Bodog's branding strategy is to portray Ayre, on its websites and videos, as the Hugh Hefner of the online world. Good-looking and in his 40s, Ayre's appearances are book-ended with beer and beautiful, scantily clad women. He also broadcasts videos of daredevil stunts (as does Richard Branson of Virgin airline fame), part of extending the Bodog brand to the promotion of extreme fighting events, rock bands and testosterone-laced videos.

Up close, however, Ayre is a brainy, soft-spoken and buttoned-down entrepreneur who's a dead ringer for actor Matthew Perry from the TV show *Friends*. He showed up for our interview in a suit and tie, and his candid answers were refreshing and thoughtful.

"Don't get me wrong—I like to have fun—but I don't sit around every day with girls on each arm and a beer in my hand," he said. "I couldn't run anything at all if I did that."

All this has paid off handsomely. In 2006, he was featured in *People* magazine as one of the world's most eligible bachelors. This drives traffic to his Bodog sites and events.

Equally helpful, he said ironically, was a newspaper report in Canada about his father's conviction in 1987 for trying to smuggle marijuana into Canada from the Bahamas. The report repeated an allegation that Calvin should have been implicated, and also discussed his problems in 1996 with the BC Securities Commission.

When I asked him about this after our lengthy interview, he responded by e-mail: "The [drug-smuggling case] was two decades ago so I don't remember much, but I do know that I was never aware of anyone saying I was involved until I read it someplace [in the *Vancouver Sun*] recently. I was not involved, so if someone said this, then they were mistaken."

When asked why he didn't correct the record by demanding a retraction, he wrote, "Lawsuits aren't typically my style. Being in the Gambling, Fighting and Rock and Roll business, these inaccuracies actually give me 'street cred' and increase the value I offer to the brand. They are actually making me money, so in a way I don't really have that big of a reason to contradict them. I'm much more interested in what the people who work with me think."

He said his new blog, CalvinAyre.com, is aimed at correcting the record, both past and future, because "I have learned no media is above putting words in my mouth."

On the topic of his skirmish with BC's securities regulator, he was also blunt: "First it was never a criminal case. I settled at a point where I could not afford to fight. Thankfully the demise of the Vancouver Stock Exchange makes the entire situation only a media issue, as the settlement only applies to publicly-listed companies inside BC, of which there are none."

Despite a clear conscience, he added that "it was a valuable lesson."

Ayre is a strategic thinker, something that he attributes to his education. He loved sciences.

"Physics is a way of problem-solving. You must figure out which of the laws of science pertain and then apply them," he said. "Also, understanding how things work in the world allows you to avoid the crazy things people tell you."

He took science and played defence for the University of Waterloo's hockey team but found the place difficult and "lonely." His proclivity was toward business, and he eventually obtained an MBA while selling real estate, then stocks, in Vancouver.

After his brush with trouble in the stock market in 1991, he opened his own business, called HQ Vancouver, which provided office space and services to small companies. This introduced him to online gaming, software development and a network of practitioners in that new space.

"I marketed HQ's services mostly to Vancouver tech startups," he said. "Then that whole world opened up to me."

He used his HQ office, equipment and services to research, then launch, Bodog. He hired teams to create gaming software, then paid for their efforts by licensing the software to gaming websites and providing those sites with office backup services. Finally, he launched his own site, Bodog.

Without doubt, Calvin Ayre is an unusual but gifted entrepreneur. Some could describe him as a modern-day Sam Bronfman, skirting the edges and unable to pass the smell test in some salons. But then again, passing smell tests isn't exactly something that a boy from a pig farm in Saskatchewan could ever accomplish.

GUY LALIBERTÉ

Urchins and unusual people populate Cirque du Soleil stage productions around the world, re-enacting the grittiness that Guy Laliberté experienced as a young street busker.

Laliberté is the world's greatest impresario and also a longhaired, chain-smoking party animal who hangs out these days with the rich and famous. A close friend was the late Beatle George Harrison, who shared his love of Formula One racing and helped him get the rights to the Beatles' songs that became the Cirque's latest hit show, *Love*. Laliberté travels constantly and also squires around some of the world's most beautiful fashion models.

Guy Laliberté was born in Quebec City in 1960. He left Canada after high school to wander Europe with buddies who were mostly artsy performers. More than once, he slept on a park bench. But he eked out an existence by playing his accordion, fire-eating and juggling for tips.

Back then, in 1982, he was a penniless daredevil. Today he is a billionaire daredevil who owns 95% of Cirque du Soleil. The

Cirque was his brainchild and has become a global brand name and a permanent fixture in the sparkling Las Vegas firmament.

"The dream at first was about entertaining people, being able to get to people and to travel around the planet. In a certain sense, I was hoping to entertain as many people as possible. On the other hand, I never suspected that it would become quite this big financially. I never really strived for that—it was more about entertainment. I suppose it is a little surprising," he said in an interview in 2006 on *The Business*, a California radio program on the entertainment industry. He declined an interview for this book because he had no time in 2007.

His first Cirque in 1985, an animal-free circus, involved a cast of 73 people. By 2007, there were 3,500 employees worldwide, including 900 artists. In its Montreal head office, Cirque du Soleil employs 1,600 workers who are drawn from 40 nationalities and speak 25 languages. Some 50 million people have seen one of the Cirque's many productions around the world, and there are five Cirque shows permanently featured in Las Vegas theatres and in Disney World in Orlando.

Cirque du Soleil is a seemingly bottomless content provider, creating distinctive shows that incorporate world-class gymnastics, choreography, staging, costumes, music and marketing. Current plans are to open permanent shows in Tokyo and Macao and, in 2008, to roll out a new production based on the music and life of Elvis Presley.

Laliberté bought out his co-founder, Daniel Gauthier, and now reinvests 40% of profits annually into creating new content, which he says is equivalent to research and development. Mounting theatrical productions is a very risky business: one show can cost up to $200 million to develop and produce. Cirque du Soleil also extends its brand by creating original content for television, DVD and film and by selling merchandise.

The Cirque was invented by Laliberté and Gauthier in the 1960s. They combined the talents of their peer group and fused circus arts and street musicians into a production for tourists near

Quebec City. Rather than renting a theatre, they created venues for their shows by organizing street festivals.

The next idea was to buy a massive tent to house their Cirque. With hair down to his waist and a two-pack-a-day Gauloises habit, Laliberté called on conservative bankers to try to get financing so his troupe could tour in a tent beyond Quebec.

"The first 50 bankers who we went to see just laughed in our faces," he said on radio, adding that it wasn't funny, because "we weren't wearing red noses or funny hats."

But their big break came two years later when Quebec government officials took a flyer by giving him $1.5 million to stage a street show to celebrate the 450th anniversary of the arrival of Jacques Cartier in New France.

The tent fell down the first day, and there were other logistical problems, but the audiences loved it. They even made a profit of $40,000, which convinced the two to grow the concept.

"I knew something was right artistically. Very early on, I knew that we needed more shows if we were going to sustain our growth," he said to the *Financial Post* in 2006.

In 1987, with financial backing, he took Cirque du Soleil, tent and all, to a Los Angeles arts festival.

"I bet everything on that one night," he later said. "If we'd failed, there was no cash for gas to come home."

Crowds packed its tent and the Cirque caught the eye of Las Vegas promoters and others. Soon its troupe was touring everywhere.

"The first Las Vegas group that approached us [in 1991] was Caesars Palace. We had developed the premise of *Mystère* for them, but their board turned it down. The second group that was interested was the Hilton, but that fell through as well. Then Steve Wynn of Mirage Resorts called us asking if we had reached a deal with any one of his competitors. The answer was no from our end, but I didn't think Steve would be interested. He was already producing the best show in town with Siegfried and Roy. I remember him flying up to Toronto to see our tent show, *Nouvelle Experience*. That's where we shook hands and made the deal. He invited us to perform in the parking lot of the Mirage and, in parallel, to start creating *Mystère* for his Treasure Island," Laliberté told the *Financial Post*.

Making the transition from a tented tour company to staging musicals in theatres was not easy, but Laliberté had targeted this long ago.

"You have to imagine what Las Vegas was about back then. It was all about gaming," he told the *Post*. "Entertainment was not what it is today. With *Mystère*, we were planting a flower in the desert. It was a big risk and a beautiful creative challenge. We had to learn a completely different type of production, but we knew we had the creative ability. I wasn't worried, but Steve Wynn sure was. At one point, he wanted to change some artistic aspects of the show, saying we had created a German opera. I just reminded him that our agreement included a clause that gave us complete artistic control, so he couldn't intervene. He looked at me and asked, 'Did I sign that?' Right up till opening night, he was swearing and wondering what he had gotten himself into. But *Mystère*'s success speaks for itself. It's been running for 14 years [since 1991]," he said.

In 1998, Cirque opened its aquatic show called O. Then in 2000, Wynn sold out to MGM Grand and the new owners decided to emphasize entertainment over gaming because it attracted more people. So the Cirque was commissioned to do more, and in 2003 opened a burlesque, cabaret-style show called *Zumanity*. It was very controversial because of its depictions of sexuality.

"Was it a risk? Yes. Was it a moral risk? No. *Zumanity* is about love and humanity and tolerance. It was also perfect for the New York New York Casino and distinctive from all of our other productions," he said in a newspaper interview. "The controversy happened before the launch, when people were trying to understand it and the media were blowing things out of proportion. Once it was launched, people understood what we were saying about love and tolerance."

In 2004, *Ka* followed.

"It is an epic tale by the world-acclaimed writer and director Robert Lepage. It has pushed the boundaries of innovation and technical accomplishment for theatricals to a scale never before seen," he said.

Then in 2006, Cirque du Soleil launched *Love*, a US$150-million production based on the music of the Beatles that followed a tortuous set of negotiations involving two widows and the two living Beatles, Ringo Starr and Sir Paul McCartney. The production came about as a result of Laliberté's friendship with George Harrison.

"George attended one of my Grand Prix party events, and we just had a good time talking. He was jamming with the musicians and taking in the whole creative ambience. A few weeks later, he invited me to London. We pursued our discussion and decided that we wanted to create something together," he said.

"Fifteen years ago, Las Vegas was 90% gaming and 10% entertainment. Now it's 60% entertainment and 40% gaming. That's our contribution. As long as our shows remain distinctive, there is room to explore new ones in Vegas. But we are looking at other venues. We'll open a permanent show at Tokyo Disney in 2008. We should be opening at least one in Macao, and we're always looking for options in London and New York. I believe that, if we can change Las Vegas, we can do so elsewhere in the world," he said.

Along the way, he has lost collaborators. His creative director, Franco Dragone, left to produce Céline Dion's *A New Day* show at Caesars Palace and a water-themed extravaganza.

But Laliberté's biggest disappointment occurred in May 2006, when controversy dogged a $1.2-billion casino project in a dilapidated part of Montreal and he pulled out.

In an interview with Radio-Canada, he pulled no punches: "It [systematic protest] is becoming a trend, the 'brand' of our society . . . It's unfortunate because Montreal is recognized internationally for its joie de vivre, as a destination, and instead of building on those assets, we continue to fight within the family. Meanwhile, other cities in the world continue to grow. We continue to lose ground [culturally], sort of like we have [lost ground] to Toronto from an economic and business point of view."

Laliberté is certainly his own man but obviously has a talent for creating and sustaining a huge enterprise with tentacles everywhere. He has turned down buyers and has said he cannot operate as a public company because it would slow down his decision-making.

He lives a bohemian existence even today, but also enjoys a glamorous and flamboyant lifestyle. For instance, in June 2006 he combined the celebration of his parents' 50th wedding anniversary with the opening of his Beatles show. He flew in 75 family members to see his parents, Gaston and Blandine Laliberté, renew their vows at a Bellagio Hotel chapel, then moved everyone to a fancy restaurant for the launch party of the show.

"I am what I am from them. This is my gift to them," he told the *Las Vegas Journal-Review*.

The party cost a mint, but that weekend a Vegas gossip columnist reported that Laliberté had won more than US$500,000 in 30 minutes at a high-end gaming salon.

JOHN MACBAIN

Rhodes Scholar. Harvard MBA. Married into the well-connected family of Paul Desmarais. Brilliant business strategist. Self-made billionaire. And now international philanthropist.

Such are the life and times of John H. McCall MacBain, a middle-class boy from Niagara Falls, Ontario. In 2005, he gave $1 million to his hometown for a community centre to be named in his parents' honour. His father was Al MacBain, Queen's Counsel and member of parliament for many years. His mother, Viola, was also active in the community.

"I am always reminded of my roots no matter where I travel," he told the local newspaper.

Today, however, MacBain's idea of "community" is the global village. He lives luxuriously, and relatively tax-free, in Geneva, Switzerland, giving away money around the world out of proceeds from a business empire he created in 20 countries.

He became the King of Classified Ads and acquired hundreds of free buy-and-sell magazines around the world that sold ads in a diversity of markets, products and platforms. His Trader Classified Media NV was sold, reaping him more than US$1 billion personally.

MacBain's rapid rise to riches started when he left home for McGill University, where he studied economics. His superb work landed him a Rhodes Scholarship to Oxford University, which was followed by an MBA at Harvard University.

He was not just a great student, but an entrepreneur as well. Niagara Falls residents reminisce about the summer when MacBain missed out on a job as a swimming instructor, working for the local government. Undaunted, he organized his own private swim school, renting pools at 25 private homes to teach kids how to swim. He even bought insurance to cover the cost to homeowners or himself.

But his educational trajectory in three countries turned him into an internationalist even though he returned from Harvard to Montreal in 1984. He had landed a job there in marketing, for Power Corporation. He also "landed" his first wife, Louise Blouin MacBain, who was related by marriage to his bosses, the Desmarais. Her sister is married to Paul Desmarais Jr.

MacBain's Power connections in Canada and Europe were helpful, and in 1987 he and Louise bought *Auto Hebdo*, a classified advertising publication for cars in Quebec. MacBain did not invent the business model, but he certainly led the way in taking it to new, global heights. "We view ourselves as Pac-Man, eating the daily newspapers from the back," he once said.

These publications unbundled journalism from advertisements. They zeroed in on the revenue-generating part of the media business and saved the cost of providing editorial content. In fact, in these publications the advertisements *are* the content, and the publications gather together more ads than could be found in local newspapers collectively.

MacBain started off with an auto seller, then quickly realized the model was a huge win. He eventually gobbled up 570 publications in 20 countries, advertising autos, jobs, real estate and general merchandise.

He did not respond to an interview request, and declines most interviews, but John Francis, owner of Trader Media Corporation of Mississauga, which published *Auto Trader* and other publications in Ontario, says MacBain is a hard-driving businessman.

"We had Ontario, and he went elsewhere in Canada," said Francis in an interview with me in 2007. "John [MacBain] left Canada about 1989 because he ran out of things to buy here. Then in the early 1990s, he also exited, for tax purposes, out of Canada, way before he sold the business in 2006. We sold our business too—to Yellow Pages, a few months before he did."

John MacBain's edge came from his comfort in foreign jurisdictions, his aggressiveness and his ability to attract favourable financing. Those traits allowed him to become the sector's global consolidator, even taking on high-risk markets such as Russia and the Eastern bloc.

All this was possible through his financing salesmanship. In the early days, he forged a 50-50 partnership with Torstar Corporation, owner of the *Toronto Star* and Harlequin publishers. With its money, he gobbled up publications in North America and Europe. Better yet, MacBain was given favourable terms, a free rein and lots of money to invest without strings, something unheard of in financing circles. He bought Torstar out, then found another sugar daddy—a rich European family who gave him money on exceedingly generous terms.

By 2000, he had consolidated all these assets into one entity in order to go public. And his timing was fortunate. That spring, he sold shares in Trader.com and capitalized on the frothy high-tech bubble by emphasizing the digital, or website and Internet, potential of his publications. The stock sold at $28 a share, or 12 times revenues. In a major coup, he beat the market meltdown. In a handful of weeks, Trader.com shares were fetching only $6 apiece.

"He nailed it," said Francis. "He had the guts to make some big bets. He is very astute and made a lot of money out of markets no one else wanted. He also kept going further and further afield to find the cheapest money, which allowed him to have a lot more latitude. He made a fortune mostly through acquisitions, then he would consolidate, hack and slash."

He also adapted a business model created in North America to Europe and elsewhere. It was not always easy. Such foreign deals took time, were complicated and required partners with patient capital.

"Doing deals in Italy, Hungary, Russia, China—that's where he was able to shine," Francis added.

MacBain and his wife, Louise, split along the way, and he eventually bought her out for hundreds of millions of dollars in 2004. They have three grown children. She lives in London, where she runs a fine-arts publishing business and is familiar to tabloid readers because of her jet-setting and her hobnobbing with Britain's royals and elite.

In 2007, John was made CEO of Trader.com, officially called Trader Classified Media NV and based in Amsterdam.

Trader Classified Media NV "kept stakes in Car News (Taiwan), Shou di Shou (China), Netclub (France and Canada), and Trader Media East," said Yahoo! Finance in June 2007. "Company co-founder John McCall MacBain (president and CEO) controls the company [and] bought out the stake of his ex-wife, Louise Blouin MacBain, in 2004."

MacBain has lived in Geneva on a magnificent estate overlooking the Alps since 2003 with Marcy, his second wife. She was born and raised on a farm in Goderich, Ontario. She went back to school to study public health management and has spearheaded, along with advisors, the family's "investments" in helping Africa.

The two give away scholarships and have pledged to hand out $1 billion to help sub-Saharan Africa.

The website of his McCall MacBain Foundation, in 2007, had a mission statement: "To support charitable programs in the health, education, social assistance and the environment on an international level, in particular by contributing to such programs in Africa as well as to hospitals, schools, universities and non-profit organizations in North America, Asia and Europe (including the United Kingdom)."

"Your goals change as the roof gets higher," John MacBain told the *Globe and Mail* in an interview in 2003. "At the beginning you say, I'd like to put my family through school and get a nice house, but when you've passed that, you say, the marginal utility of money is zero in the end. You can't eat it. You can only sleep in one bed. We don't have those extravagant needs. We're far past the stage where we can live quite comfortably, so we want to give the balance away."

ALLAN SLAIGHT

Broadcast billionaire Allan Slaight lives in a house in Toronto that is not what it seems to be. And that is the way he likes it. It is a former dry-cleaning factory located on a back alley behind stores and the trendy North 44 restaurant in suburban Toronto. But inside is a marbled and multilevel space surrounding an atrium garden filled with art treasures and with large rooms for entertaining. It is the residential version of the art of deception—the perfect Slaight of hand.

I've socialized with, interviewed and worked for Slaight. He talked with me in 2007 from his home in Florida for this book.

Slaight is a magician who just happened to make a fortune in the radio business. In April 2007, Astral Media Inc. paid him $1.1 billion for the broadcast chain he had begun building in 1985. He had bought it from Conrad Black's Hollinger Inc. for $196 million and a down payment of only $18 million. And he pulled the deal out of a hat.

"Mine has been success pushed by poverty. The greatest thing that ever happened to me is I quit CHUM Radio after eight years because it was time to move on. Then I did pirate radio, called [Radio] Caroline, in Britain. I came back and turned around Maclean-Hunter Radio. Then I quit when its chairman, Don

Campbell, got out of his sickbed with flu to go to a convention in Toronto and announced that I was making too much money. So I quit on the spot. Then I started hanging around to see what would unfold," he said.

He took a holiday with friends who worked with Conrad Black.

"I was in Florida on a cruise with one of the directors of Hollinger. As I was going down the gangplank after the cruise, I suddenly looked at him and said, 'You should sell me Standard Broadcasting.' He said, 'Let's have coffee at your place at 8 o'clock tomorrow morning.' It turned out they had decided to sell," Slaight recalled.

Slaight was tired of working for employers, after skirmishes with penny-pinching Maclean-Hunter and an irascible Izzy Asper, among others, at Global Television.

"I mortgaged my house and borrowed money at 22% interest rates," he said. "I said to my backers I would use my best efforts to go public in 18 months. I borrowed money from the Ivey family [of London, Ontario], [broadcaster] Gordon Sinclair, Roynat and a few others."

Then magic happened. Slaight had been a hard-driving operator who picked a team carefully. But he always loved parties, and his annual CFRB shindig in Toronto was the hottest ticket in town, complete with singing stars and dance bands. After the festivities, Slaight would squire a hand-picked posse, often including myself, to go to dance clubs until the wee hours of the morning, then show up at work by 8 a.m. He thinks on his feet and talks like a jackhammer. Always unorthodox, Slaight required all applicants to submit to a handwriting analysis before hiring them.

He is also hyperactive and loves to listen to music and write books about magic. Most of his friends are magicians or musicians, including Gordon Lightfoot, not businessmen.

"I don't belong to any of those downtown gentlemen's clubs," he said. "I have no interest. I don't want to drive downtown and have lunch with a bunch of guys."

Slaight's first passion was magic. He has also turned Gerry Schwartz on to the "black arts."

"Before Christmas 1939, my parents took me with my brother to Eaton's Toyland to pick out a present. I was absolutely captivated by a middle-aged guy doing tricks and selling magic kits. I didn't want a train or a plane, but I wanted that $1 magic kit. I still have it," he said.

Young Allan perfected card tricks and mentalism, or mind-reading, then got into journalism.

He grew up in Galt (now part of Cambridge), Ontario. In 1946, the family moved to Moose Jaw, Saskatchewan, after his father bought the city's *Times-Herald* newspaper.

"Galt was 14,000 people and Moose Jaw 25,000, so I thought I was going to the big city," he said. "My brother was entranced with newspapers, but I wasn't. When dad and his partner bought a radio station, I fell instantly in love with radio."

He married and moved to Edmonton to be a radio reporter on a bigger station. Fortunately, he was able to supplement his young family's income by doing magic shows.

"In 1950 we moved to Edmonton, and then my wife and I had three kids quickly, so she couldn't work," he said. "I worked six days a week as a news reporter, making $160 a month. Our rent was higher than what I made. So I did magic on my one day off— Saturdays—and travelled around northern Alberta with a suitcase full of tricks. I eked out an existence."

He graduated from reporter to disc jockey, then sales manager, and eventually wound up as a station manager in western Canada.

"My formula was to play top-50 music, stage zany promos and have good news coverage," he said.

In 1958, he returned to Ontario as general manager for Toronto radio giant CHUM, a job he held until 1966. Gigs elsewhere in Canada and in Britain followed, until 1985, when he was ready for his big gamble. He assembled well-heeled friends, who became backers, and some money he had salted away himself over the years. He also got a good price for Standard Broadcasting, because Conrad Black was uninterested in broadcasting assets. After paying $196 million to Black for the company, he all but erased its debt of $178 million by quickly selling its only television station, in Ottawa. He never looked back. He got the company for virtually nothing.

"We built Standard from 7 to 51 stations and have more radio properties than any other group in Canada," said Allan, who handed over the reins as CEO in 2000 to his eldest son, Gary Slaight. He has another son, Greg; a daughter, Jan; and a total of five grandchildren.

The family still owns a large outfit, InStore Focus, which conducts supermarket samplings and other market research.

"It turns a handsome profit," he said. "How did we get in there I can't even remember. Fluky. It seemed to tie in with radio."

Gary had been the driving force at Standard, but he also talked his father and siblings into selling.

"He was getting a little bored—he's been doing it so long," Allan said. "It pleases Gary. Besides, Greg was reporting to his older brother, and that is not the most ideal arrangement. Greg is semi-retired and lives in St. Catharines, and my daughter moved to Australia with her family a few years ago."

Essentially, Slaight is a showbiz guy who has never been that comfortable in a suit. But radio, like magic, is about providing entertainment at a profit. The two were a fit, as was Slaight's decision to get into sports.

In 1993, he paired up with Toronto's Bitove family, who owned many restaurants and a catering business, to woo a National Basketball Association franchise to Toronto. They beat out other contenders and called their team the Raptors. The team has been a sell-out success since its launch in 1995.

But the partners bickered, and in 1998 Slaight bought out the Bitoves, then sold the team and its new downtown arena to a Bitove cousin, Maple Leafs owner Steve Stavro—and for a lot of money, a rumoured $200-million profit. The team, along with the hockey franchise and the Air Canada Centre, is now owned by the Ontario Teachers' Pension Plan in partnership with construction tycoon Larry Tanenbaum.

"Let's just say I did extremely well," said Slaight. "I sometimes shake my head at how well everything has gone. Radio has been a great deal."

Slaight is as eccentric as he is successful. During a 2005 visit to his home, I noticed a few stray cards stuck to the vaulted ceiling of his living room. They had been thrown up there as part of a trick performed by one of his dozens of professional-magician friends at a gathering a few days before.

Slaight entertains lavishly and often, usually ending the evening with a dazzling magic show by his pals. He also houses one of the best magic libraries in the world in his second-floor den. That's where he practises his tricks, in front of a three-way mirror.

In addition, he authored a compendium of a magic maven's tricks—a lowly factory worker and sometime postman named Stewart James from Courtright, Ontario, which is near Sarnia. Slaight grew up as a fan of James, memorizing his tricks out of magazines. He eventually tracked him down a few years before his death and compiled his magic for the sake of posterity.

"He was a genius. He devised mathematical games for *Scientific American*," said Slaight.

The James File, with 2,700 pages of tricks, decorates the foyer of his home. It is a compilation of thousands of known and unpublished tricks using everything from rope to math and cards.

"These guys like James are very intelligent," he said. "It doesn't translate into anything else, although magicians in ancient times used it to gain power and prestige. But the fact that you can shuffle a deck of cards doesn't make you a good CEO. That's about something else."

These days, he is starting to chip away at other projects, but not magic. Or golf.

"We published 2,700 pages and it sold very well. I haven't a sequel in mind," he said. "But I'm starting to write a book about my rather weird life with somebody else. I'm barely getting underway.

"And golf? Absolutely not. I stopped playing when Gary started beating the hell out of me at 16 years of age. Magic's my main hobby, but I love to do crossword puzzles and reading. I'm relaxed and very content. I'm the new, improved Allan, or so they tell me."

THE THOMSONS

The richest Canadian family is the Thomson clan. Their fortune, estimated at $29.3 billion, began with $500 invested during the Depression in a radio station in northern Ontario.

Roy Thomson turned this stake into a business empire—and into the last hereditary peerage granted in Britain. In 1964, Roy was named Baron Thomson of Fleet. By the time he died in 1976, he owned more newspapers than anyone else in the world.

His son, the late Ken Thomson, was also a gifted business-man and an art connoisseur. He died in 2006 at age 82, having repositioned his father's conglomerate from a mixed bag of news-paper, oil and travel enterprises into the world's biggest electronic information provider for professionals.

Only one year after Ken's death, the latest Lord Thomson, David, proved his mettle by initiating one of the biggest deals in Canadian history: merging with Reuters Group PLC in a deal worth US$17.6 billion. The new combined entity, Thomson-Reuters, will be the world's biggest news and financial data company once all approvals are official in 2008. And the Thomson clan will have controlling interest.

At the end of 2007, the combined entity, Thomson-Reuters, had 50,000 employees worldwide, great brand-name franchises and a combined market value of $30 billion, generating profits of $1.5 billion annually. The Thomsons also own 40% of CTV-globemedia Inc., which owns CTV and the *Globe and Mail* in Canada.

Despite such high-profile holdings, David Thomson is as reclu-sive as his father and grandfather were. The day after his huge Reuters deal came down, he spent only 96 seconds on the global conference call staged by the company for media and financial analysts.

"I would like to say that my late father was more than familiar with this dream," David said. "He believed it was all about opportunity; it was all about possibility. If my grandfather were here, I think he'd be—the word 'ecstatic' I think is appropriate."

Naturally, David declined an interview, as his father did back in 1986. Ken Thomson remained an extremely cordial fellow at social gatherings in Toronto and occasionally wrote me (and, I'm sure, other journalists) fan mail if a column struck his fancy.

The Thomson-Reuters merger will seal the family's success. The Thomson interest, held on behalf of the family by the Woodbridge Company Ltd. in Toronto, will be diluted to 53% from 68.5%. It still represents solid control.

Woodbridge is a private holding company co-chaired by David and his younger brother, Peter Thomson. The third generation's legal advisor is vice-chair Geoff Beattie, a talented lawyer plucked from a big firm in Toronto by John Tory Sr., who was Ken's *consigliere*.

Roy, by contrast, operated as a lone wolf and became an acquisitor at a relatively mature age, in his 40s. He was tight-fisted and money-oriented, coining such famous aphorisms as "News is what fills the space between the ads" and "The only difference between rape and rapture is salesmanship."

His patrician son used to soften these bon mots by protesting that "people don't understand that my dad was just a kidder."

The family fortune was rooted in Roy's aggressiveness and acquisitiveness. Roy Thomson invented the reverse takeover (in which a smaller company buys a larger one by borrowing against the value of its future cash flow) and became a billionaire as a result of a North Sea oil discovery. In 1971, when Thomson was already established as a press baron, American oil baron J. Paul Getty talked him into betting $20 million on an oil well at a dinner party. He tried to find a way out of the commitment but did not want to be thought of as a "piker" by Getty and others. Against his better judgment, Lord Thomson hustled up the money, and the well came in. Other wells followed.

His son, Ken, began his career as a newspaper reporter but quickly thought better of it. Gentle and cautious, he could handle his aggressive father and heed smart advice from others.

"Roy was a sucker for deals," said former Thomson executive Michael Brown in an interview with me in 2002 in New York City, "and he would talk to anyone about anything and then get us involved. I remember once he left for Lebanon because there was a television station for sale. We told him just to look at the station and not look at anything else.

"He said okay. He came back with the station, but it took two weeks more before we finally prodded him into admitting that he had bought something else: an orange grove."

Naturally, the Lebanese orange grove did not go into the public company, but the anecdote illustrates why the Thomson empire has been so eclectic and why Brown was hired by Ken to repurpose the empire. He did, and led the Thomsons into a massive sell-off of newspapers and positioning in electronic media catering to captive audiences like doctors and lawyers.

"We like biblical products," he said. "We don't want to be in television, films or trade books. These are off-limits to us. We're looking for very solid franchises that are going on forever, like the Bible. Consumer magazines and trade books [jargon for non-educational, non-reference books] are sold through gimmicks and froth. We like essential or serious educational, reference books. What's most desirable are products which are not paid for by the user but by the employer."

That shift in strategy converted Lord Thomson of Fleet into Lord Thomson of Cyberspace. And the family has prospered ever since, adding to their portfolio and now capturing Reuters.

The family wealth is shared among Roy's three offspring—Ken and two sisters—and their seven children. But in 19th-century fashion, Roy Thomson's will stipulated that only a male heir could run the business. This meant that Ken was in charge of the second generation's business affairs and that in this generation, it is to be left up to Ken's two sons, David and Peter, who happen to be Roy's only male grandchildren. (Ken also had a daughter, Taylor, and Roy's two daughters have had four daughters in total.)

In his autobiography, Roy Thomson was very clear in this directive to his heirs: "David, my grandson, will have to take his part in the running of the organization, and David's son, too. These Thomson boys that come after Ken are not going to be able to, even if they want to, shrug off these responsibilities."

Such glimpses into the Thomson mentality are rare but always interesting. For instance, David granted an interview in 1993 for the book *Old Boys*, an oral history of Toronto's elitist private secondary school Upper Canada College. David attended the school and reportedly loathed it.

"I learned at a very early age that people did not give a shit about me, and when they did, they wanted something," he said. "It was as basic as that. I lived, for so many years, feeling a sense of helplessness. Now I am extremely self-sufficient and rather overly aggressive, I suppose."

In 2002, however, he made it clear in an interview that he embraced the challenge of being heir to a business colossus.

"The business is in my blood. I would spend countless hours with my grandfather in the mid-1970s, and I have been intimately involved in the strategic direction of the company, working with its executives, and have a very strong sense of it," he said.

Similarly, Thomson sightings are rare, although family members do not have to hide. This is because their success at avoiding photos and publicity means that they can move freely in Toronto and elsewhere. Of course, annual meetings are a different matter. In 2002, Ken retired as chair and David ascended, and both spoke emotionally.

David paid his respects to his father's stewardship and noted that he had transformed it from a $500 million company in 1976 to a $20 billion one by 2002.

"As a shareholder, I am delighted with that record," he said. "As my father's successor, I am humbled."

At that same meeting, Ken related an anecdote about Roy

after he had snagged Britain's last hereditary peerage. Fellow Canadian peer Lord Beaverbrook had just died, and his son, Max Aitken, had declined to accept the title.

"[Max] said, 'There will only be one Lord Beaverbrook,'" Thomson related to the shareholders. "But there were reasons. There were frictions there. But there were no frictions between my father and myself, that is for sure.

"Dad got me in the car—Dad always used to throw these things at me when I was driving him in the car—and he said, 'Ken, young Max has turned down Lord Beaverbrook's title. I want you to promise me you will not turn down the title.' I said, 'Well, Dad, it's kind of naughty of you to make a person promise something like that but' . . . I made the promise."

Ken took the title in 1976 but never sat in the House of Lords, because he did not want to lose his Canadian citizenship. As the eldest son, David is now the third Baron Thomson of Fleet. However, he and his brother co-chair the family holding company, Woodbridge.

David attended Cambridge University and started his business career at an investment bank, then moved on to a Hudson's Bay store in 1979, when the family owned the gigantic retailer. By 1987, he had become president of the Bay's Zellers, a retail discount division, and then joined the Thomson Corp.

He collects art, as his father did. Just before his death, Ken Thomson donated his entire collection of 2,000 pieces, worth $300 million, to the Art Gallery of Ontario.

David is no slouch either in the art world. He owns one of the world's biggest collections of the work of 19th-century English landscape artist John Constable, and in 2002 paid a record price, rumoured to be $120 million, for the Peter Rubens masterpiece *The Massacre of the Innocents*. He gave it, as a present, to his father.

David's brother, Peter Thomson, started his career as an apprentice news photographer. He shares the Woodbridge chairmanship and will also be a director of Thomson-Reuters. But he operates privately as a venture capitalist and has also been a rally race-car driver since 1986. Their sister, Taylor, lives in the United States.

These days, David has surrounded himself with a talented team of financial and legal experts. He lives a jet-set, but quiet, life, commuting handily between Canada, the United Kingdom and the head office in Stamford, Connecticut.

By most accounts, the brothers are as modest and easygoing as was their father, and David eulogized what he described as his father's real accomplishment.

"If the definition and measure of a human being are the lives that are touched, he touched them in such a unique, genuine and open manner," he said.

CABLE

mericans invented the coaxial wires that replaced the rabbit ears over television sets and were able to provide surefire television reception. But it was Canadians who took the fledgling industry to greater heights. This was because most Canadian homes could only receive one or two homegrown television channels. Those who lived a few miles from the U.S. border, without physical obstructions, were able to capture American television airwaves via tall antennas perched atop their homes. But most Canadians could not do this, nor could they guarantee good reception.

In 1970, Ottawa passed the Broadcast Act and then carved the country up into cable licence areas. People were invited to tender for these monopolies, and entrepreneurs flocked to the business. The beauty of cable licences was that they prohibited any competition and also represented a great opportunity because the licence itself was a "bankable" asset. This meant licensees could borrow money from banks to build a sales force, install microwave receivers to get signals, and use teams to install wires in as many homes and offices as possible. Once subscribers were signed up, their monthly fees covered all costs, making the business a licence to print money.

The fastest-growing, best-financed and more aggressive quickly embarked on strategies of consolidation, buying up as many ma-and-pa cable licences across the country as they could. By the 1990s, three cable giants emerged. They were well capitalized enough to diversify into other businesses and to merge their cable services with high-speed Internet and telecommunication in order to offer "bundled" packages to consumers. Groupe Vidéotron took over most of Quebec (and then André Chagnon sold to Pierre Péladeau's Quebecor), then Ted Rogers and J.R. Shaw divided most of the rest of the country.

TED ROGERS

In 1925, Edward Rogers Sr. invented the world's first alternating current (AC) radio tube, which enabled radios to be powered by ordinary household current. He then made the world's first electric radio.

The technology pioneer died in 1939, at only 38 years of age. His son Edward "Ted" Rogers Jr. was only 5 years old at the time but went on to carry the family tradition to new heights. Rogers Communications Inc. is Canada's 40th-largest corporation, with a market value in 2007 of $28.7 billion. Revenues in 2006 were $8.8 billion, assets $14 billion and profits $622 million, and the company employed 21,000 people.

Ted began as a lawyer, something his mother encouraged.

"My mother said, 'You'll probably be an entrepreneur, to get the family name back in the communications business, and you may go bust. So you should go to law school to have something to fall back on,'" he said in an interview with me in 2007. "It was a great experience, and I learned about corporate and tax law and how to be disciplined in my thinking."

He ran radio stations while still in law, and ever since has aggressively, and steadily, borrowed huge sums to build a conglomerate that straddles related sectors, from telephones to cable television, broadcasting and publishing. He also owns the Blue Jays baseball club and its stadium.

"I've worked for Ted on and off for years, and he's pretty amazing," said Paul Godfrey, CEO of the Blue Jays and former CEO of Toronto Sun Publishing, which Rogers owned briefly in the 1990s. "He's usually first and ahead of the pack."

Ted attends lectures and high-level conferences with a note-book in tow. His diligence has made him a pioneer like his dad. He jumped first into the fledgling cable business, and is now Canada's largest cable company, with 2.5 million customers. He also single-handedly challenged the telephone monopolies, because he foresaw that cable and telephone would eventually compete for users. He was first into wireless telephones, and he has built up a content division that includes print, broadcast and the Blue Jays.

But it's been a high-wire juggling act of massive debts and smart tax avoidance. He said he has never missed a night's sleep, but his bankers probably have. Now Rogers is in great shape, debt-wise.

"You never avoid taxes—you just postpone them, and we've built the world's finest team of tax-loss experts," he said.

Luck and speed have also played roles.

"Licensing of wireless was a turning point, and our acquisitions, which made us 60% a wireless company. We bought a ticket to the future, and it had 'wireless' written on it," he said. The other 30% of the assets are cable, and 10% is content.

"From a business standpoint, losses in baseball and all, our media companies promote all our businesses, which adds tens of millions of dollars in value," he said. "It means the Rogers name is sunk deeply into the community. Am I a fan of baseball? I have to be, and I've had an expensive education."

Ted and his wife, Loretta, live in Toronto, where they raised their son and three daughters. Both are energetic and unassuming in manner. He's tall, with a thatch of reddish hair, and is very gregarious and always brimming over with questions at social events. He's a genuinely curious man. Loretta, on the other hand, is more reserved and is an astute judge of character.

Their son, Edward III, is president of Rogers Cable, the largest division. He is as quiet and unassuming as his father is mercurial and bombastic. When I asked him in an interview in 2003 about his father's legendary temper and how he handles it, he replied coolly and calmly, "I prefer to call it 'passion.'"

At the time, Edward, born in 1970, presciently discounted the speculation that his father would retire shortly. Back then, Ted's departure was rumoured to be imminent. But it's been postponed a few times and may never occur.

"It's fun to work with him," said Edward. "The team works well too. Ted will continue to do what he does and what he loves: improve the Rogers group. When he feels he can't do that, he'll think of other things to do. He's very sharp."

The family controls 92% of voting shares and 32.5% of the company's total equity. But the governance is interesting: the chairman of the Rogers Communications board is not a family member but an independent director. In fact, independent directors have been given the power by Ted in the bylaws to appoint the CEOs of the various divisions and holding company.

This means that Edward passed muster to become a president. He joined the company in a marketing capacity in 1994, after a stint at a U.S. cable company. His three sisters also play various roles in the organization.

"We act as part of the team, and the company executives treat us that way," he said. "I always thought I'd work for the company. I was never sure for how long. I don't feel like work is work."

Edward's corner office has the usual corporate memorabilia, but it also contains photographs of his young daughter and a telltale teapot. His maternal grandfather, Roland (Jack) Robinson, an undefeated member of parliament in Britain for 33 years, became Lord Martonmere and eventually governor general of Bermuda. His mother, Loretta, was born in Britain and raised mostly in the Caribbean, where his parents met.

Edward clearly inherited an interest in politics from both sides. Ted is a long-time (Progressive) Conservative, and Edward studied political science in university. An understanding of the political process is key to the future of the Rogers empire because of the role regulators and politicians have played in its creation and will play in its continuation—from ownership rules to licences, protectionist policies to keep out foreign market players and postal subsidies for Rogers's magazines.

"I think Canadians should have real alternatives to the Liberals at the federal level. It's healthier when at least there are two strong parties. It makes us all sharper, whether it's our company or our country, when there's choice," said Edward.

Edward is hard-working like his father, putting in between 60 and 70 hours a week while still finding time to co-parent his daughter and dabble in photography and video.

"When you have a daughter, you have lots of reasons to take photographs," he said. "She's the passion in my life."

Thus, despite the demeanour and manner of a more mature man, Edward is still a Generation-X'er with a totally different perspective on life.

"I don't speculate about the future," he said. "But I'm not planning to be looking at channel lineups when I'm 70."

Ted's entrepreneurial bent surfaced while he was still a student at York University's Osgoode Hall Law School. In 1960, he bought his first radio station, and by 1965, while articling, he had snagged one of the first cable TV licences in Toronto. By 1967, he had begun a strategy as a highly leveraged industry consolidator gobbling up small "cablecos." In the early 1970s, he pulled off two reverse takeovers and bought cable companies that were both larger than his own operation. In 1980, he took over an American outfit and was, briefly, the world's largest cable operator.

He cashed in his American chips, then reinvested the proceeds in the telephone business. He realized that "bundling," or offering multiple services to customers, was the name of the game. He offered telephone, cell, cable and high-speed Internet. By 2007, when Ma Bell was on the block, he was uninterested. Its stock had stalled for five years while Rogers's had gone from $5 a share in 2004 to $42 in 2007.

"We should just keep doing what we're doing and not get distracted with this highfalutin' stuff," said Rogers after his annual meeting, where he announced a tripling of dividends.

It was clear that Ted's strategy worked, and the debt reduction, which began in 2000, was paying off in dividends for all shareholders. He could sit back and watch it all work beautifully, but he won't. He still runs the show and is delighted that after a leveraged buyout, his archrival BCE will have three times the debt Rogers has.

"If they want to start a price war with all that debt, we're here to finish it," he chuckled.

In 2007, he and Loretta gave $15 million to Ryerson University in Toronto, which named its business school, the largest in Canada, the Ted Rogers School of Management. This is the second-largest donation by them to that school (the first was for its broadcast faculty). The Rogers's commitment was in large measure due to the fact that 70% of Ryerson's students are the first in their families to attend a university.

"We are thrilled to support Ryerson's management school," said Ted at the ceremony. "Loretta and I believe strongly that education is a great enabler. Education can remake a country, a city, a community into a different place. For almost 60 years, Ryerson has combined academic rigour and relevant practical experience with accessibility and diversity to produce so many graduates who have contributed to the fabric of this country. It is our pleasure today to support the Ryerson management school and its students to help ensure even greater accessibility for many of Canada's business leaders of tomorrow."

J.R. SHAW

Les and J.R. Shaw grew up on a farm outside Woodstock, Ontario, but both made their fortunes in the city. Les built the family's pipeline business into a world-beater, and J.R. became king of the cable business in western Canada.

"Our dad, Francis Shaw, was a great entrepreneur," said J.R. in an interview with me in 2007 in Calgary. "He started off with a small cable partnership in Woodstock, and my brother and I just couldn't see the cable business as a good one to be in."

But the two brothers ended up growing both businesses.

J.R. is controlling shareholder and chair of Shaw Communications Inc. of Calgary, Canada's 132nd-largest corporation and its second-largest cable company, with $3 billion in revenue in 2006, $7.5 billion in assets and 9,000 employees. He also controls the 373rd-biggest company, Corus Entertainment Inc., a broadcaster with $726 million in revenues, $1.8 billion in assets and 2,000 workers. The two companies made a combined total of $493 million in profits. Before he died in January 2007, Les built ShawCor Ltd., a pipeline manufacturer, into Canada's 280th-largest corporation, with $1 billion in revenues in 2006, $1 billion in assets, profits of $92 million and 5,000 employees worldwide.

Despite huge success, the two remained modest guys whose riches did not distract them from their Protestant work ethic and down-home values. But they were a remarkable partnership. They worked together since the 1960s, sat on one another's boards, talked almost daily and owned minority interests in one another's companies. They also have two sisters, who have shared in the profits of the pipeline manufacturer every year.

"We went public in 1968 with the pipeline, and our dad stipulated that we paid our sisters every year and, if we didn't, they could take control," said J.R.

Both men started out working in the pipeline-manufacturing business. Their father had benefited from the network and relationships he made as a friend of American industrialist C.D. Howe, who came to Canada during the Second World War. The company found a niche selling specialty pipe to large oil-exploration companies around the world.

"I graduated from university in Michigan and went straight into the business," said J.R.

J.R. worked for ShawCor throughout the 1960s in Ontario,

then set up shop in Edmonton to sell pipe in Alberta's booming oil business. Once settled, he quickly realized why cable television, which his family had neglected in Ontario, would be a winner. Cable technology had been invented in the United States. His father brought it to Canada, but J.R. and Les were uninterested in the small, slow-growing operation.

"Woodstock and most of Ontario's population was along the U.S. border, so people could get the Canadian stations and most of the American ones too," he said. "But in Edmonton, miles from the U.S. border, there was no American TV, and there were only two channels. So I decided to bring cable in."

In 1968 the Canadian Radio-Television Commission (now the Canadian Radio-television and Telecommunications Commission) was created, and in 1970 the Broadcast Act was enacted— and J.R. jumped at the chance to get one of the new cable licences. The country was carved into franchises in Canada because of the capital cost involved in cable. Millions had to be invested in linking homes by coaxial wires connected to microwave towers strung across the landscape from the United States. These towers captured and transmitted American broadcast signals.

Cable penetration grew faster in Canada than elsewhere in the world because of the appetite for U.S. programming and the paucity of Canadian offerings. J.R. fought for the Edmonton franchise against a dozen others and landed a licence to provide two more stations to half of the city's territory.

"I was disappointed I didn't get the whole franchise, but I said, 'That's fine, because any kind of licence will help me get more licences and more stations down the road," he recalled. "I was like everybody else. I just wanted choice [on television], and so did other Canadians who were living more than 60 miles from the border."

Months later, he and his wife bundled their four tots into a recreational vehicle for a vacation in British Columbia. But along the way, J.R. did business.

"We took a motor-home trip with our four little kids, and

I came back with cable rights to Kelowna, Penticton and Revelstoke," he said.

He raised $10 million from banks and from partners John and George Poole, who founded construction giant PCL, based in Edmonton. In 1972, J.R.'s company went public. "We sold cable services by going door to door, and in 10 years built the base up."

As penetration—and profitability—grew rapidly, many other players jumped into the business, snapping up franchises and gobbling up small cable outfits.

"I said, either we were going to be the eaten or be the eater," he said. So he devised a strategy of consolidation.

He targeted the ma-and-pa cable companies and grew by swapping Shaw stock for their ownership. This gave them tax advantages, liquidity and an exit, but it also bolstered Shaw's values and replaced growth by debt with growth by equity. Many of the smaller players remain Shaw shareholders.

"If you were a small cable guy, it was better to be part of a bigger company with Edmonton cable assets rather than own 100% of the Hat [Medicine Hat] and go up and down depending on what was happening in local factories or local industries," explained J.R.'s son, Jim, who is Shaw's CEO. "Probably 30% of our shareholdings represents what was swapped to other cable operators over the years."

J.R. retained control through the use of multiple voting shares. He controls 79% of votes and 10% of the stock.

What's unusual is that all four of J.R.'s children play important roles in his enterprises. Jim is CEO, his sister Julie is an architect and runs real estate operations, Brad is senior vice-president of operations for Shaw Communications, and Heather is executive chair of Corus.

J.R.'s two sons, then, are on Shaw's board and his daughters are on Corus's, which is run by CEO John Cassaday. Also on Shaw's board is Ron Joyce, a friend of J.R.'s who built Tim Hortons Inc. and who is the largest shareholder in the company other than the family. Ron, J.R. and Les all met while building their businesses in southwestern Ontario, outside Toronto. Tim Hortons started in Hamilton and is now based in Oakville.

In 1987, J.R. diversified into content when he bought a radio station in Red Deer, Alberta. Twelve years later the Shaws owned dozens of radio stations and spun these off in as a separate public entity called Corus. By 2007, Corus owned over 50 radio and television stations, a book publisher, television series and other intellectual properties.

But J.R.'s cable business became a huge player in 1994 when it was approached to act as a white knight by Maclean-Hunter Limited in order to fend off a hostile takeover by Ted Rogers and his cable giant.

This led to a series of asset swaps between Shaw and Rogers Communications. Rogers owns most cable assets in Ontario, and Shaw those in western Canada, except for Regina. Like Rogers, Shaw acquired U.S. cable assets but cashed out.

"We did not have good partners there. Twice," said J.R.

In 1995, J.R. moved the company's headquarters from Edmonton to Calgary, where it now occupies a high-tech building on the edge of downtown, within walking distance of J.R.'s penthouse condo along the river.

These days he spends weeks each winter in Hawaii with his children and 12 grandchildren. He is also an active member of Calgary's business establishment and served as chair of Suncor Energy Inc. for 9 years.

Besides cable and content, the family has also been investing in real estate and recreational properties. J.R. has built one golf course and is developing a resort with three more courses and condos in Radium Hot Springs, BC, three hours' drive from Calgary.

What's remarkable about J.R.'s offspring is their work ethic, given their wealth. "We grew up on a ranch," said Jim. "We had to do chores every day, no excuses. When I was 16, I'd go out with my friends and my dad wouldn't give me a curfew but would say, 'The later you stay out, the earlier you have to get up.' He'd get me up no matter what time I came in, and then I'd wonder why I would sleep through lunch."

Jim, the oldest, worked at various jobs after quitting university, then joined the family firm at the bottom as a cable installation guy. The experience of working himself up through the ranks gave him operational insights and helped him stick with priorities but also tempered strategies, given the distracting and fast-paced nature of change in the entertainment delivery sector.

"I always wanted to be the CEO, but I didn't stay in university until the end because it was too much structure for me. Now there's structure but it flows. It's entrepreneurially grounded," he said. "I don't think, as a CEO, you ever stop working. You wake up at night and can't stop thinking. You travel a lot. There are time zones to deal with. Last week, I was in New York to meet with big shareholders, strategic partners, possible candidates for directors and to discuss future plans. It was exhausting. It takes me weeks to recover."

The future of the cable industry long-term is up for grabs as wireless technology now allows computer content to bypass cable and go directly onto home television screens. Debates also rage within the industry as to the importance of convergence between cable, telephony, computers, satellites and more exotic technologies.

Said Jim Shaw, "I am focusing on what the consumer is all about: convenience, not convergence. 'How can you make it easy for me? I have enough problems and I don't want to have to solve my own technology problems. I want to watch what I want to watch, when and who I want to watch it with.'"

No matter what the future holds, J.R. and his kin are fabulously wealthy as a result of success and of a special bonus that is baked into the company's bylaws. Les's heirs are also wealthy, but the two brothers differed in terms of their succession planning.

"My brother went offshore [for tax purposes] in 1995 in Barbados," said J.R. "But I won't. I made it here. I live here, and I'll pay the taxes here."

FINANCE/
MONEY MANAGEMENT

erhaps it is the Scottish tradition of thrift, but Canada has built one of the world's most stable financial sectors. And stability is critical to economic development. Strong financial intermediaries are the gatekeepers of entrepreneurship and success. When they work as they should, they take deposits or investments from the public, then reinvest them in businesses and individuals with good ideas or with favourable prospects that will grow the economy. A country is only as successful as its financial intermediaries are solvent, smart and fair.

In the past, favouritism, nepotism and intolerance blighted Canadian banking practices, but the 1980s explosion of savings rates led to a proliferation of investment and investor alternatives in the form of private money managers, pension funds and mutual funds. Until then, Canada's banks and insurance companies were dominant and intimidating. Branch banks were run for the most part by Anglo-Saxons and occupied oversized granite buildings with pillars and marble. Today, banking has gone online and most branches have disappeared or morphed into other usages. The oldest bank building in the city of Toronto, for instance, now houses the Hockey Hall of Fame.

Another change occurred in the late 1980s, when brokerage-firm trading fees were deregulated. This opened up competition but reduced profits. At the same time, banks were lobbying for expansion opportunities, and eventually they obtained the right to buy investment banks. Within a handful of years, the mainstream banks owned virtually all of the investment banks, then began to move aggressively into the mutual fund area. Now banks dominate both businesses.

Change to bank ownership was another matter, one Ottawa has not considered. By law, no single entity, foreign or domestic, can own more than 10% of a chartered bank's shares unless that bank is a small start-up. This stricture came about in the 1970s to prevent New York's Chase Manhattan Bank from buying the Toronto-Dominion Bank.

For a period of time, a provincially chartered trust-company sector grew under the shadow of the federally chartered banks. Trust-company ownership rules allowed individuals to own 100%, but these institutions were restricted to lending mortgage money. This sector disappeared, following a number of frauds and mismanagement scandals in the 1980s. The banks took over.

Canada also invented another financial intermediary to meet a special need: the credit union was created during the Depression to prevent farm foreclosures. This form of people's capitalism has given rise to many entities across the country, but none as large as the Desjardins Group in Quebec, which, along with other Quebec financial intermediaries, has financed local enterprises and entrepreneurs. Credit unions, and their cousins the cooperatives, have also become aggressive players nationally and have often joined forces with entrepreneurs and private corporations. Likewise, the country's gigantic pension pools, led by Quebec's Caisse de dépôt et placement du Québec and the Ontario Teachers' Pension Fund, have adopted the roles traditionally played by investment bankers as equity partners, traders and dealmakers.

But the most globally successful financial intermediaries have been Canada's insurance giants. These consolidated Canada's sector, outperformed most foreign competitors at home and now variously operate in dozens of countries. They also have expanded into the mutual fund and money-management fields. Canada's three largest—Sun Life, Manulife and Great-West Life—are now among the ten biggest life insurance companies in the world.

G. RAYMOND CHANG

Mutual fund king Ray Chang likes to say that he's Jamaican by birth, Chinese by heritage and Canadian by choice. He went to Rensselaer Polytechnic Institute in Troy, New York, but at 17 years of age transferred to engineering at the University of Toronto in order to save on tuition and living expenses.

"I knew I wanted to take engineering just for the mental discipline. I'm lazy. I knew I needed that discipline and push," he said in a 2007 interview in his Toronto offices at CI Financial Income Fund. "I took solid state physics, which is the backbone of transistors and chips today. But I made up my mind in engineering school I would not be involved in technology too much. You end up with blinkers. I wanted to be able to *use* technology."

Chang grew up in a prosperous business family, and so was drawn toward finance and accounting. That, plus a chance meeting with a family friend, led him into the world of mutual funds that took off in the 1980s.

By 2006, he was trustee and chair of CI Financial Income Fund of Toronto, the country's third-largest, with a market value of $3.6 billion, revenues of $1.3 billion, assets of $2.8 billion and profits of $308 million. The company manages more than $81.6 billion in mutual fund assets on behalf of clients, manages institutional money for pensions and corporations and also owns Assante Wealth Management (Canada) Ltd., with 1,000 financial advisors across the country. Sun Life Financial Inc. owns 36% of CI and added its captive sales team to the mix.

"You don't measure life by the money you accumulate, but by what you do with it," Chang said.

Chang is a big man with a broad smile and a laid-back Jamaican manner. He is still involved in CI but not in its day-to-day affairs. He's a philanthropist, and is also a venture capitalist involved in new technologies, medical research and energy processes.

On top of it all, he's a benefactor and chancellor of Ryerson University in Toronto. He gave $5 million for Ryerson's continuing education programs, and also established a chair at the University of Toronto in internal medicine and a fellowship for West Indian doctors at the University Health Network.

In 2007, the G. Raymond Chang School of Continuing Education at Ryerson announced that it will collaborate with the University of the West Indies to set up online and video-conferencing programs in order to distance-train nurses.

"I got a good education, and you can't put a value on that," he said at the time of the announcement. Chang has been a blessing to the school not only financially but also in his spirit, which is genuinely warm and down-to-earth, and in the standard he's set for dedication to continuing education. I have socialized with him and he is a dedicated family man who has retained his friends, and ease, from Jamaica.

Chang was one of 12 children reared by Gladstone and Maisie Chang in Kingston, Jamaica, during the 1950s and 1960s. Five of these "siblings" were actually orphaned cousins. But it was one big, happy family. He said his childhood was idyllic and shared with not 11 but 30 siblings and cousins in 5 houses on the same street.

Chang came by his business smarts from his father and uncle, who owned Consolidated Bakeries back in Kingston. The two men were also involved in construction and packaging businesses and employed hundreds of people.

Chang's grandparents had left China to be indentured labourers in the Caribbean, as did thousands of others from Asia. His family speaks a dialect of Chinese known as Hakka, which means "guests," and which is also the name of a Han people probably originally from the far north of the country.

Chang left Jamaica to go to university but always assumed he would return home. But Jamaica was economically ravaged by poor politics. So in 1970, when he graduated in electrical engineering in Toronto, he went immediately to work for an accounting firm in order to get his chartered accountant status.

"I worked in mining audits while studying for accounting," he said. "It was good because I would go away to remote parts of the country to mines to do these audits, which meant there was nothing else to do. So I had to study."

His three-year stint was valuable because he learned about financial engineering and taxation.

"Unfortunately, business is a lot about understanding the tax system," he said.

In 1973, he got his CA and took over a small Toronto factory that made high-end furniture. He employed 8 craftsmen and soon grew his talented workforce to 32. Recruitment became a problem because too few skilled workers were available. Then the 1974 recession hit the company hard. Sales fell. He hung on until 1980, then sold it.

"I like craftsmanship but soon realized the problem was replenishing the craftsmen," he said. "It was not a good business to be in."

He decided to return to his accounting firm, Coopers & Lybrand, and run a small-business practice for the firm.

"I spent 90% of my time doing workouts and negotiating refinancings for small businesses. I'm happy to say none went into bankruptcy," he said. "But it was more interesting to build businesses than rescue them."

The burgeoning mutual fund business was not something he knew much about until he hooked up with a family friend back in Jamaica.

"Bob McRae was a commercial pilot from Canada who used to be in Jamaica on two-day layovers. He was a part-time journalist for the *Financial Post* and came to our family business to write about the bakery because we were the largest importer of Canadian wheat," he said.

But Robert McRae was also a pioneer and owned a small mutual fund in Canada called Universal Group of Funds. In 1983, he asked Chang to help him organize the back-office functions of the business.

"It was an administrative mess, and he also had another problem which I was able to figure out," Chang said. "He had problems hard-wired in his software which needed fixing. So I corrected it. Then the stock markets took off for the next few years, and funds did well. But I'm not a marketer, so I continued to run his back office, and we found Bill Holland to run marketing," he said.

Chang and Holland have been a great team. Both men bought into Universal Funds and set about creating a new, unique business model. They discovered some niches in the marketplace that would differentiate them from the competition: they would provide an opportunity for Canadians to invest outside North America and would hire independent portfolio managers from other countries to find opportunities.

"In the 1980s, everyone in Canada was selling Canadian and U.S. funds. We went beyond that. Bob [McRae] had a buy/sell agreement with Mackenzie [Financial], who managed our North American funds. So we launched the first Latin American fund. At one stage, we had the third-largest Latin American fund in the world," he said.

The two also targeted the less populated regions of Canada to sell their funds.

"This was our second reason for success. Everyone marketed Toronto, Montreal and the big cities, but we went outside the big cities. There was loads of money there," he said.

Then they devised another way to sustain their success. One of the obstacles they faced was they could not afford to pay the incentives to brokers or advisors that competitors could and still make a profit. So they kept costs low to match incentives, which included taking no salaries, only stock options.

"So we ended up with so much equity that way," he said.

The two divided tasks, with Holland in marketing and Chang running operations. In 1986, Chang's engineering and technology background paid off for CI Financial. The firm's technology was outdated and expensive, and for the next three years Chang oversaw the design and construction of a state-of-the-art technology platform. Not only did this prepare them for massive growth, but their efficient and advanced technology actually helped attract acquisitions. So the company became industry consolidators.

In short order, they bought three major rivals, then Assante, with its advisors. In fall 2007, CI made a takeover bid, unsuccessfully, for Ned Goodman's Dynamic mutual fund empire. The company is clearly still on the hunt.

"We became the lowest-cost producer of mutual funds in Canada, comparable to the low cost of U.S. funds," Chang said. "Our administration costs at CI were 0.19%, and others were at 0.27%. We charged 2% management fees like everyone else, but we guaranteed the lowest cost and said to our investors, if our costs were further reduced, we would lower their costs even more."

Chang has two children from his first marriage and continues to enjoy visits back home in Jamaica and with his family scattered across Canada, the U.S. and Britain. His uncle continues to run Consolidated Bakeries, which still has 150 employees. And Chang has gotten involved down there in business development. For instance, he has helped Jamaican farmers and others develop food export businesses. President's Choice jerk sauce is one of his products.

But Jamaica continues to struggle. Only 2.5% of Jamaicans are non-blacks, and Chang saw Jamaican politics shift to what's known as "black man time." This meant that minorities were not included in the power structure.

"The country's a mess, but I still have interests down there," he said. "I have always intended to go back home. But I never will."

NED GOODMAN

Ned Goodman used to pass long nights in the wilderness as a geologist by whittling figurines out of wood. These days, he is surrounded by large-scale sculptures and works out of an office tower in Toronto.

"I have a piece of wood in my log cabin in the Laurentians that I'm going to sculpt. It's on two horses, and the tools and lights are all set up to work on it. But I never seem to be able to get there and start it," he said to me in an interview in 2005.

How a workhorse like Goodman could ever hope to have a hobby is beyond imagining. He studied geology but went from rocks to stocks and now spends 12-hour days, most days a week, honing Dundee Corporation into an even bigger resource, real estate and money-management powerhouse than it already has become.

Dundee is Canada's 268th-largest corporation, with $1.1 billion in revenue, $3.5 billion in assets and $98 million in profits. But it also controls huge underlying companies, Dundee Wealth Management Inc. and Dundee Real Estate Investment Trust, among others. In September 2007, Scotiabank bought 18% of Dundee Wealth Management and other assets after Dundee's bank hit heavy weather due to its overexposure to subprime mortgage credits from the United States. The bank's purchase sparked a takeover bid by Ray Chang's CI to buy the entire business, but Goodman had already made up his mind. The future, however, is another matter, and he and his four sons may sell to one of many interested buyers who began hovering around by late 2007.

The clutch of companies are all named Dundee after the city in Scotland where investment trusts were invented. Dundee also has ownership in Canadian resource companies. All in all, Goodman's companies employ about 4,500 people.

"I don't like to think about that," he said in an interview in his Toronto office. "It scares me. I don't feel rich and I don't talk about it. It does me no good. I just love what I do. I still take work home."

Goodman is a rugged Montrealer with a no-nonsense manner. He's also a pussycat, and a sucker for a good, or a hopeless, cause. He gives to charity quietly.

We met in spring 2007 for an 8 p.m. interview in Dundee's corporate headquarters. He had been there since 7 a.m., and when we finished, he left with a briefcase. He does not like the media and avoids interviews. He is a loner by nature but works with people all day long.

In 1960, Goodman left geology because of a mining recession that year that convinced him to get a graduate degree in business instead. His dad had been in Montreal's garment business as a fashion designer.

"My dad left Ukraine in the back of a hay wagon. He was hard-working but not too successful," he said. "I played football and basketball but loved physics, math and chemistry. When I told my parents I wanted to be a geologist, they said, 'What's that?' My dad didn't know anything about science or business, but he taught me to be nice to people no matter what circumstances you—or they—are in."

Goodman got into the money game after he earned his MBA at the University of Toronto (his geology degree was from McGill University) and joined a brokerage firm as an analyst. Next came a partnership with money manager Austin Beutel, called Beutel, Goodman & Co., which also ended up employing Seymour Schulich as a partner.

In 1976, money fled Montreal after the election of separatists, and so did the firm's clients. So Beutel, Goodman relocated to Toronto and grew quickly, but the partners eventually split and did their own thing.

Goodman formed Dundee Capital, which comprised Beutel's family of mutual funds called Dynamic. It also owned a merchant bank that owned shares in International Corona, a mining company controlled by flamboyant Vancouver mining promoter Murray Pezim.

In 1981, Corona launched an audacious $3-billion lawsuit against Lac Minerals Ltd., alleging that claims bought by Lac belonged to Corona. By 1987, Goodman had taken over Corona because Pezim had driven it financially into the ground. Goodman kept financing the litigation.

Then in 1989, Corona won the case and was awarded the mining claims. Its stock jumped tenfold within minutes of the decision, and Ned made hundreds of millions of dollars. The claims became the basis for the gigantic Hemlo mine, which is still producing. But Ned cashed in immediately.

"I couldn't see me having 90% of my net worth in a gold-mining company trading at well beyond what it was worth," said Ned.

He invested his profits in Dundee Corporation, which he modelled on the Pennsylvania-based Mellon Bank, a wealth-management entity providing well-heeled clients with investment advice. It became a giant version of Beutel, Goodman.

"Its largest investment of $1 billion is in DundeeWealth, which, in turn, has $33 billion in Dundee Securities under management and $25 billion in Dynamic Funds," he said. "It has 1,800 financial advisors, 600 offices and $1 billion in revenue a year. It's a key asset. But I'm still in resources, have done well and will be involved. But it's my weekend job."

Goodman controls 21% of Dundee Precious Metals, 24% of Breakwater Resources and 100% of Western Resources.

"We third-party manage some small resource companies, and my son Jonathan runs Dundee Precious Metals," he said.

Jonathan is Ned's oldest son and is a geologist with an MBA; David is a lawyer and is CEO and president of DundeeWealth; Mark runs two junior resource companies on his own; and Daniel in 2007 decided to set up his own investment counselling business, leaving Dundee as an advisor.

"He's going to be a competitor," said Ned proudly about his son Daniel. "I work with all of them."

On top of rocks and stocks, Ned also started his Dundee real estate division from scratch in 1996. It now has more than $4 billion in assets and a market capitalization value of over $1 billion.

"We like industrial buildings in Quebec and are the largest office-building REIT [real estate investment trust] in Canada. We don't buy trophy buildings. We have 10 buildings in downtown Calgary that are less than 20 storeys high," he said.

His Dundee Bank of Canada opened for business in 2006 and

caters to financial advisors on behalf of their clients. It does not have branches and only takes deposits from financial intermediaries. Changes to the Bank Act, which Ned lobbied for, allow 100% ownership of a bank with up to $1 billion in capital and 65% ownership up to $5 billion. Goodman's bank now has $1.5 billion in assets. Unfortunately, its debt problems led to the sale of 18% of the empire to Scotiabank in fall 2007.

Also in 2007, Ned decided to step back from day-to-day trading and money management to concentrate on building the real estate portfolio. He is also the founder and benefactor of the Goodman Institute of Investment Management at Concordia University.

Goodman is a loyal Canadian but is concerned about the country's future. He believes that both banks and pension pools of capital enjoy too many privileges and keep out new players.

"In the past 20 years, the banks have become much more powerful. They are controlled by nobody and are just coining it. Guys who spent five to six years as president of the bank retire with C$250 million and nobody complains," he said. "They sell perpetual preferred shares at 4.5% coupon [dividends] and run 20% return on equity. They are 50% of the mutual fund industry and put the trust companies out of business. They will get insurance too."

As one of Canada's biggest investors, Goodman bemoans poor management. "The management of large companies in this country is abysmal. We had the best ore body in the world owned by Inco. It was a meteorite of nickel which fell from the sky and is easy to mine. It was owned by two companies. One was for sale, and did Inco buy it? At $20 a share? No. It was widely held and run by Scott Hand, a second-class lawyer from New York. His attitude was, why roll the dice? And he didn't. Eventually Falconbridge was sold for three times that money and Inco was taken out by Brazil's CVRD."

Goodman controls his business empire through multiple voting stock.

"Take Teck Cominco and Dr. Norman Keevil. He's built a huge company taking risks because of multiple voting shares.

Likewise, I wouldn't do this if I couldn't have multiple voting shares. It isn't worth the hassle," he said.

He's also convinced that Canadian resources are the country's trump card.

"Venezuela, Bolivia, Ecuador are all closing up shop to resource extraction, so it's now Eastern Europe and Africa and Canada," he said. "And there are three billion people in the world who want indoor plumbing, and they're going to get it. So half want plastic, copper, zinc and other commodities, and countries with half the mining commodities in the world are refusing mines. So supply-demand means higher resource prices. It's as simple as that."

He also believes that Quebec will never leave Canada and that Canada may end up joining the U.S. unless its taxes and the number of foreign takeovers decrease.

Our interview ended around 10 p.m., and as we left he opened a book of Bill Reid sculptures.

"This stuff is great, isn't it?" he said. "I really have to finish some sculptures. I will one day. But work is so much fun."

HAL JACKMAN

Financier Hal Jackman has the only business card in the world that delivers a lecture.

"In 2005, the average CEO in the United States made 411 times more than the average worker, up from 1980, when the multiple was 42," it reads. Following that is a quote from Roger Martin, dean of the University of Toronto's Rotman School of Management: "I find that life on boards is biased towards pro forma conversations, shallow discussions, management stonewalling and procedural matters of limited utility."

The last few years have been spectacular for the Jackman empire, which is based on investing other peoples' money wisely as well as their own.

"There is easy money—too much money—and this is why

there are huge excesses," he said in an interview with me in 2007. "Money supply is out of whack by governments, and the private equity and hedge funds have unlimited access to funds."

Jackman is 75 years old and chair emeritus of E-L Financial Corp. Ltd. of Toronto, Canada's 151st-largest corporation, with $2.195 billion in revenues in 2006, $7.35 billion in assets, $372.5 million in profits and 1,683 employees. Its subsidiaries are the Empire Life Insurance Company, based in Kingston, Ontario, and the Dominion of Canada General Insurance Company, and it also controls United Corporations Ltd. and Economic Investment Trust Ltd., both closed-end funds. CEO is Hal's son Duncan, and the control block is owned by Jackman's five children.

The family also shares, with the Jodrey family of Nova Scotia, control of Algoma Central Corp. of St. Catharines, Ontario. Algoma is Canada's 445th-largest corporation, with $548 million in revenues in 2006, $514 million in assets, $42 million in profits and 1,400 employees. It started out as a railway and has become the largest Canadian shipping company on the Great Lakes and St. Lawrence Seaway.

But all this empire-building has never gone to Jackman's head, even though he is proud of it, and of Duncan's business acumen.

"I was born in 1932. I don't believe this [stock market] prosperity. My birth year was the pits, the absolute economic bottom. And I rode it all the way up during my lifetime. To do well, you don't have to be good, just not be stupid," he said.

Hal Jackman is one of the most well-read businessmen in Canada. He is also a paradox: a maverick born into Toronto's elite, and a man who thinks nothing of driving a beat-up car, and one who enjoyed the pomp and circumstance of being Ontario's lieutenant-governor for eight years.

He has guided the business empire he inherited from his talented father, Harry, who was a legendary Toronto money manager. But he has also taken time out for frivolities like playing table war games with his former partner, the now infamous Conrad Black.

And he has been the embodiment of noblesse oblige—running for public office, serving as chancellor of the University of

Toronto and giving away four times his annual income to charities every year. He has given $30 million to the University of Toronto and $5 million to the Four Seasons Centre for the Performing Arts, the opera house in Toronto.

Duncan, his second son, took over the reins in the late 1990s. He has the same fierce eyebrows and height as his dad and has also dabbled in politics, as a backroom boy behind the success of the Reform Party and the united Conservative movement.

In 2007, Duncan threw his father an elegant surprise birthday luncheon, to which I was invited. About four dozen of us were feted at the Toronto Club. We came from a variety of backgrounds, mostly the Canadian military reserves, Bay Street or childhood pals. It was an eccentric Jackman moment.

Duncan asked his dad to make a few remarks off the cuff after lunch, then asked him to wait while he summoned two tall uniformed soldiers to march in with flags. Helmeted and handsome, they took positions on either side of Hal, like matching bookends. His speech was vintage Jackman, both dry and acerbic.

E-L's stock has outperformed many others in the business of underwriting and investing. Hal's father, Harry, made a fortune during the Depression by fearlessly buying up penny stocks, with underlying values, that no one else wanted. Jackman himself went to law school but ran the business and eventually bought out his three siblings.

"I have five kids, and Duncan runs the business. All he has to do is not lose it and keep the confidence of his siblings. They can throw him out if they gang up on him. My siblings tried to do this, so I had to buy them out," said Hal.

Besides Duncan there are Victoria, Consuelo, Trinity and Henry. Hal's wife, Maruja, is an academic.

Our interview took place over lunch, and Jackman came prepared.

"In 1986, when you wrote the prequel to this book [*Controlling Interest: Who Owns Canada?* in 1986], E-L Financial stock was worth $45 a share," he said. "Now [spring 2007] they are worth $700. Back then, dividends were 50 cents a share, and now they are 50 cents a share. So our dividend policy represents a huge compulsory savings in our case."

Jackman and his family were one of the 32 families profiled in my 1986 book *Controlling Interest*, and one of the few dynasties who made it into this one. At the time, he predicted most would fail.

"One of the biggest risks for rich families is that these sons have very dominating fathers and most are scared stiff of them. I was intimidated by my father," he said. "What happens is many feel they must prove their value and become suckers for con artists or shifty advisors. This is a huge danger."

Jackman became a friend of Black's in the 1980s after Black bought control of Argus Corp. from the two widows of the controlling shareholders, Bud McDougald and E.P. Taylor. Black invited Jackman to swap his Argus stock in return for 16% of Black's private holding company, Ravelston. Jackman blamed McDougald for the problems that plagued Black after the takeover.

"I knew [Argus chair Bud] McDougald. He was not a nice man. E.P. Taylor, his partner, was a remarkable man. McDougald was a sybarite, an anti-Semite who did nothing. By failing to do anything, he allowed Massey-Harris [the tractor maker] to go bankrupt and did not look after [grocery chain] Dominion Stores," said Hal.

Shortly after, Black bought out Hal, but the two remained friends. They were the scions of wealthy men, had attended Upper Canada College, and loved literature, military history and war games.

But their paths diverged. Black moved to Britain in the 1980s after buying the prestigious *Telegraph* newspaper. Eventually, the friendship became distant, then ended after Jackman publicly—in one of my columns—criticized Black's business practices.

"To me, Conrad is a tragedy. So highly intelligent and so carried away with his lifestyle. It's absurd. There was a disconnect between his intelligence and the way he lived," he said. "I read Conrad's book on FDR. It was good. I read the whole bloody thing, 900 pages. That's what he should be doing. He's a very good writer."

Equally puzzling to Jackman was Black's pursuit of a peerage in Britain and his collection of assorted celebrities as trophy directors.

"All these fancy people, Lord Carrington and Henry Kissinger. They are interesting people but made no contribution to the company. Never did. He could have had access to these people anyway if that's what he wanted . . . good conversations," he said.

Hal has been a governance watchdog for years. In 1977, he sold National Trustco to the Bank of Nova Scotia but crossed swords with fellow bank directors after he was automatically put on its board.

"I didn't want a seat, because I have never been a big fan of our banking system or banks," he said. "They don't compete. They don't treat the little guy properly. They take a cheque, hold it for eight days and make interest off the float while they hold it. It's not right. Big sophisticated customers make other arrangements for cash-management purposes with these same banks."

Even so, he stayed on the board for five years but quit in a huff.

"Peter Godsoe [former Scotiabank chair] railed against the proposed merger of the Royal Bank of Canada and Bank of Montreal in 1998, but then in 2002 he proposed a merger with the Bank of Montreal. All the directors voted for it, and I was consistent, and against mergers, so I quit. It was stupid. I was also the only director to refuse to take stock options or to go on their junkets."

Clearly, Hal Jackman is one of a kind. For years, he has been Bay Street's chief scold but, more importantly, he and his family have never taken advantage of their positions and have steadfastly stewarded other peoples' money. The next generation of Jackmans—his five children, led by Duncan—are likely to do the same.

STEPHEN JARISLOWSKY

Stephen Jarislowsky should have been a professor, or the male equivalent of television's brash, irreverent Judge Judy. But he became a billionaire instead, by carefully looking after other people's money as well as his own.

Despite his track record as a smart stock-picker, he is more academic than pinstriped and has become the country's chief investment and corporate governance gadfly.

Since 1955, his firm Jarislowsky Fraser Ltd. in Montreal has managed pension and personal assets for the biggest, richest companies and individuals in the country. By 2007, its 125 professionals managed $60 billion in pension and other assets.

Jarislowsky is curt, bordering on rude, and has the manners of a Prussian and the sculptured looks of a patrician. He's self-deprecating and neurotic. His office is a tangle of neglected plants, and he has never owned a cellphone or computer and never will. And Stephen's personal life is also an extension of his profession.

"I don't know how to spend, much less waste, money," he said over lunch with me in Toronto in 2007. "I know how to accumulate and invest, but I am very frugal. I am a Depression child."

Jarislowsky has lived in the same house in Montreal since 1972. His indulgences are really investments, or "accumulations," as he calls them. He collects wonderful art, which he learned to appreciate from his first wife's family, who were dealers in New York City.

With his second wife, Gail, he owns a picturesque farm on Vancouver Island and a pristine 2,000-acre island off the British Columbia coast called Marina, which could be worth nearly $400 million alone. But he does not even have a cottage on the island, nor does anyone else.

"It has 15 miles of beautiful, unspoiled beach, and in the islands people are paying $500,000 for 100-foot frontage," he said with a gleam in his eyes.

Jarislowsky leads a spartan lifestyle considering his wealth and the high-tech business he is in. He is very 19th-century in terms of technology and also has the moral convictions of a Victorian.

"I don't like technology. When they invented those things, I was already working 12 hours a day, so how could I have become more productive? Technology brings too much information today. People don't have the time to understand and think through things. A lot of the decisions today are made by people who have no understanding and haven't thought things through," he said.

His lifestyle has been decidedly different from the lavish one lived by his father, a rich Berlin industrialist and banker who died short of his 30th birthday in 1930 when Jarislowsky was only 4. His mother went back to work to salvage the empire, which was ravaged by family disputes, and Jarislowsky and his two siblings were sent to the Netherlands to live near an aunt. They were raised alone by nannies and servants.

His mother, a lawyer, remarried in Paris and had two more children, and in 1941 they fled the Nazis. They reunited with some family money in New York City that had been salted away years before by Stephen's late father.

Jarislowsky was raised a Lutheran but also attended Jesuit and Episcopalian boarding schools. "I'm against religion and its leaders. Anyone with a direct line to the Almighty and no sense of humour is a very dangerous person," he said.

Jarislowsky is undoubtedly a genius. He speaks four languages and mastered English in weeks, well enough at age 18 to finish a four-year engineering degree at Cornell University in just two and a half years. He went into the army, mastered Japanese as an intelligence officer, then came out and earned a master's at the University of Chicago in Far Eastern studies and an MBA at Harvard University.

"I'm overeducated, not the norm in the world of business," he said.

In 1949, he joined Alcan Inc., moved to Montreal and sped up the ladder as an investment analyst. In 1952, he moved to Manhattan to work with his in-laws in their art dealership, and still has recurring nightmares about being lost in a huge, canyon-like city.

"I hate Manhattan. I hate big cities, always have," he said.

In 1954, he returned to Montreal and joined forces with another money manager, Scott "Scotty" Fraser, and others.

"We started with $100 and made $500 writing an article in *Fortune* magazine about mining fraud called 'How to Run a Moose Pasture,'" he said. "It paid for our incorporation. We also developed a research method for clients, then I did field research on Canadian companies for a Chicago investment firm."

Calling on Canadian companies brought attention to Jarislowsky and led to contracts to manage corporate pension funds.

Today, Jarislowsky's family holds 50% of the voting shares of the investment firm, and his partners the rest. A board of seven, which changes every six months, directs activities and hands out bonuses. Jarislowsky controls three seats.

"I own all the shares that have assets and pay dividends," he said. "Will my family sell when I'm gone? It's up to them."

Jarislowsky has two sons, two daughters and four grandchildren. His long, healthy life so far has been fulfilling, but he talks about mistakes with characteristic bluntness.

"My greatest crime, and biggest regret, was the terrible effect my divorce had on my two sons. They never had a chance. I also regret marrying my first wife," he said.

When separatist violence struck Montreal in the late 1960s, Jarislowsky stayed calm and stayed put even though some clients and rivals like Beutel, Goodman headed to Toronto. This was partly loyalty and partly inertia, and he does not gloss over the cost to the province of two generations worth of political turmoil.

"The separatists did not ruin the economy, but terrible management and the domination of the unions did. One in four people in Quebec works for the government, and they make $100 a week more than the other three workers. We have 40% unionization, the highest in the world. We give away education for free so people can be taxpayers somewhere else later, because they leave Quebec," he said. "The infrastructure has deteriorated, and we are the highest taxed except for Newfoundland."

He has a unique, odd take on the reasons behind Quebec's malaise.

"It's the weather and the church," he said. "So these poor bastards for 250 years have frozen their butts off every winter, had nothing fresh to eat every day, had 16 kids, gave their money to the greedy church and hoped one of their children would look after them when they were old. They got used to that, which is pretty awful to get used to, and so they naturally feel that suffering is okay. Now they are suffering under the unions."

Despite problems, Jarislowsky has never considered leaving for any reason, including lower taxes.

"I could save millions a year, but what for? I have all the money I need. I don't know how to spend money," he said. "I have a sense of accumulation, but not greed. I'm reasoned, not emotional."

In public policy, his passion has been corporate governance. In 2001, he and Claude Lamoureux, former head of the Ontario Teachers' Pension Fund, which is the country's second-largest pension, launched the Coalition for Good Governance. The organization identifies problems and works with companies behind closed doors. This was needed because in Canada there has been little or no countervail in courts or laws to combat corporate malpractice.

"The owners of the companies [investors] never took an interest in how the companies were run and what the CEOs were doing. They didn't do their fiduciary jobs, these money managers," he said. "The buy side [money managers] had too many conflicts of interest."

Conflicts meant there were no checks and balances. Money managers treated companies gently in order to get coveted pieces of new issues or else to get business in the form of lucrative investment-management fees to run company pension plans. Conflicts existed not only among professional managers of pension funds, but also among mutual funds.

"In fact, they were the worst," Jarislowsky said.

In the U.S., mutual funds also vied to be in a company's good books so that they could get defined-benefits pension plan inclusion or management fees, or be approved as an investment in a company's employees' 401Ks—U.S. pension shelters for which employers put up some money but decide what stocks or funds the 401K invests in.

"Canada has been no better," he added. "Canada's thieves are one-twelfth the size of America's thieves because we are one-twelfth the size of that country's economy. The Enrons here are just smaller. The same looting went on at Nortel and JDS. And look at the mess involving BCE and its Teleglobe, media and South American cellphone investments."

He believes that the problem is human nature, which is why governance models must be strengthened.

"We've had 5,000 years of laws and it hasn't stopped crooks. You need checks and balances and good people. Now the buy side can all hide behind the Coalition to do the right thing. They were a bunch of cowards before," he said.

The Coalition for Good Governance puts pressure on companies to behave properly, from directorship choices to compensation, disclosure and financial reporting.

"There is no protection for shareholders here [in Canada]," he said. "We must change the business and investment laws. Investors never had any input into these laws. There should be an outside committee looking at these laws from the buy side. We have 13 securities commissions and fill in 13 sets of forms, and none of them are any good. I wrote letters to the Ontario Securities Commission for years about Conrad Black and about trailer-fee rip-offs in mutual funds. It took Americans to get these things in the courts. Imagine a Bre-X [$9-billion fraud] and no one in jail."

"The police know nothing about white-collar crime. Commissions can only slap fines. But many of these matters should be criminal, and the RCMP is underfunded and stands no chance," he said. "So-called self-governing doesn't work. The Toronto Stock Exchange is interested in more listings, and the IDA [Investment Dealers Association of Canada] is interested in the bottom line of investment firms."

At the heart of all the scandals and malfeasance, he said, is when boards of directors allow executives to be paid so much they are "led into temptation."

"We should know human behaviour by now. It's even in the Lord's Prayer: 'Lead us not into temptation.' If you give an executive 1 million share options and for every dollar the stock increases he makes $1 million, that's too much temptation. He will do everything he can to get the stock as high as possible. Such options do not line the executive up with the best interests of investors. That's why they are totally wrong."

He's also been an outspoken critic of double-dipping by executives and of multiple voting shares that award control of companies to people who have not put up the lion's share of the capital.

"The chairmen and founders of Magna Corp. and Shaw Communication Inc. get an override of pre-tax profits on top of a salary and share benefits," he said. "These two guys [Frank Stronach and J.R. Shaw], plus their families, are making more than enough money for normal human beings. I think it's immoral. If they get rich because the stock goes up, I have no objection, because everyone else has a chance to buy the shares. But I have no respect for these double-dippers." (When asked about this, J.R. Shaw said, in our interview in 2007, that he has waived such overrides because it has caused too many "hassles.")

Multiple voting shares are an obscenity that facilitates these arrangements, he said, and should be grandfathered. Jarislowsky led such a move when he was on the SNC-Lavalin board.

"Everyone was scared the company would be taken over, but nobody has done so," he said. "No new multiple voting companies should be listed on stock exchanges," as is the case in New York.

Jarislowsky began slowing down in 2007, and has been taking off 10 days each month to travel. He also is involved in his pet project, the Jarislowsky Foundation, which has established nearly two dozen university chairs in a range of subjects. Each chair is chosen from among the best candidates from around the world by a committee of two university representatives, two from the academic field, and Jarislowsky.

"We get world-renowned people, and then that helps change the culture in the university too," he said.

He's also busy memorizing by heart all the classical music ever written. He took a course on orchestral conducting in Europe.

"I'm basically a college professor and intellectual. I know music and memorize it. I have another 300 years to go," he said. "I'm sort of miserly in my own actions and like living a simple life. I never tried to build an empire like what my family did in Germany."

MICHAEL LEE-CHIN

Michael Lee-Chin is the Tiger Woods of Canadian business: a man from a racially mixed background with a huge grin, great physique and impressive wealth.

Lee-Chin is a Chinese-African Jamaican who has made a fortune in Canada. He grew up in a village, is the oldest of nine children and made it to Canada to study engineering.

He owns AIC Ltd., which is Canada's 17th-largest mutual fund company, with $8.5 billion in assets under management. It is a private company, and profits are not disclosed. Until June 2007, he also owned its distribution network, Berkshire-TWC Financial Group Inc., with its 238 offices and a sales force of 700 independents. He sold that company for $200 million to Manulife Financial Corp. in a private deal, according to Bay Street sources.

He also stepped down as CEO of his mutual fund company in 2006, and it may eventually be sold. This may be because Michael and his family have political ambitions for him back home in Jamaica. He has certainly been turning his business attentions toward that region for a few years.

He owns about 70% of one of Jamaica's largest financial institutions, the National Commercial Bank. He bought it in 2001 and turned it around by modernizing operations and bringing in strict financial controls. He also owns Total Finance (now called AIC Financial Ltd. [Trinidad]) in Trinidad and Tobago and Columbus Communications in Barbados.

Personally, he owns 250 acres of beachfront property in Ocho Rios, Jamaica, and estates in Canada and Florida.

Meanwhile, AIC's performance has been lacklustre compared with many mutual fund rivals. Its assets under management have steadily decreased from a peak of $12 billion to a 2007 total of $8.5 billion.

Even so, Lee-Chin has been an incredible builder, and his story is right out of Horatio Alger. He did not return calls about being interviewed for this book.

What Lee-Chin has been quoted as saying is that his mother was an orphan of Chinese extraction and he was born in 1951 out of wedlock. She married and had eight more children. His parents were lower-middle-class and lived in scenic Port Antonio. But life was a struggle of multiple jobs and entrepreneurship.

Lee-Chin was a good student and able to win a scholarship to go to high school. He said he worked on a cruise liner and at an aluminum plant to earn money for college. In 1970, he left to study engineering at McMaster University in Hamilton.

He came back briefly during that time, when his savings were whittled down to $600, and was able to obtain a grant to finish from the Jamaican government. But this required him to return home to build roads.

He graduated in 1973 and returned to Jamaica, but not for long. The country had continued to deteriorate economically due to the anti-capitalist policies of its leaders.

He came back to Hamilton looking for an engineering job and worked part-time for $2.50 an hour as a bouncer in a bar near McMaster University's campus. Then, in 1977, he bumped into a buddy in the bar who was bragging about making $400 a day in the burgeoning mutual fund business.

The chance barroom meeting convinced him to take the Canadian securities exam, which you needed to become licensed to sell mutual funds. Lee-Chin proved to be a natural salesman, a savvy image-maker and an astute investor, so his career soared. So did the growth of mutual funds as a whole, fuelled by demographics, good stock markets and low interest rates.

By 1983, he had become an established financial planner with many clients. He then decided to take a big risk personally. He borrowed $500,000 to buy stock in publicly listed mutual fund outfit Mackenzie Financial Corporation.

"The stock went from $1 to $7 in four years, so my $500,000 became $3.5 million. That gave me my financial base," he told U.S. business magazine *Black Enterprise* in a 2002 interview.

In 1986, he was ready to start his own mutual fund business, so he bought Advantage Investment Council, a fund company with only $800,000 under management. He became chief salesmen and money manager, and the firm grew. Within 10 years, AIC was managing $1 billion of other peoples' money, and 2 years later, $12 billion.

"No fund was as focused as ours was. Our philosophy, of owning a few businesses and holding them for a long, long time, was unique," he told the magazine.

But privately operated mutual funds in Canada were beginning to be outmuscled by gigantic Canadian banks and large insurance companies that used their sales forces and marketing budgets to get into the game.

Lee-Chin became one of the casualties, in part because of mediocre performance, in part because he did not strategically align himself with another mutual fund company (or several of them). By 2007, AIC's assets under management had fallen to $8.5 billion. Lee-Chin stepped down as CEO but remained executive chairman, involved in the investment strategy of AIC's 30-odd mutual funds.

Like other immigrants, he may have been distracted by business and political issues back home. His mother is now a successful retail-chain entrepreneur, as are other relatives. And the continuing political problems have concerned him along with many others.

His roots, from poverty and obscurity to wealth, have never left him. This was clear in a comment he made to *The Globe and Mail* concerning his 2001 bailout of the Jamaican bank.

"When I was sitting in the Minister of Finance's office on the verge of giving him a check . . . the thought flashed through my mind," he said, "how is it possible for a son of an orphan to now be buying a bank? All this is possible because I am the product of many factors I had nothing to do with. I was blessed to have been born to parents that nurtured me and gave me a strong value system. I am who I am because of my experiences. Had I been born 200 years earlier, I would have been a chattel."

Lee-Chin learned as a kid how to work hard and sell. His mother sold Avon cosmetics, and as a teenager he helped an uncle sell sewing machines door to door. He also turned some of his perceived disadvantages—a proclivity toward flamboyance and his West Indies accent—to advantages. One of his first moves as a rookie mutual fund salesman was to buy a BMW he could not afford. He enjoyed fancy cars but also reasoned that people liked dealing with successful salesmen. In no time, he was leasing a Rolls-Royce.

"What do I do with this darn accent?" he once told a magazine. "So my conclusion was, the best person I can be is me. The accent comes with the attitude, and I just have to be me."

Lee-Chin's investment role model was Warren Buffett, and he named his holding company Berkshire after Buffett's considerably more successful Berkshire Hathaway. He adopted his motto: "Buy, hold and prosper." He restricted the number of investments to only a few "great" companies, then charged slightly higher management fees than most mutual fund outfits. With slightly higher fees, he was able to recruit and retain a motivated sales force.

"I think most successful people . . . are fervent, are courageous, are passionate, are consistent in their behaviour, are transparent. They walk the talk because they have a purpose, and they think long-term," he told a Burlington audience in 2004.

Lee-Chin owns 90% of AIC and has always operated in Burlington, Ontario, away from Bay Street. AIC's lobby is symbolic of Lee-Chin's style: lavish and Caribbean. For years, he has entertained guests with two exotic parrots whose vocabularies consist of two words: "buy" and "hold." And there's a helipad out back.

Besides his own chopper, he owns a fleet of luxury cars and the same model of corporate jet as Microsoft founder Bill Gates. He has a yacht anchored at his mansion in an exclusive gated community on an island off Miami's coast. He also lives on a lavish estate in Flamborough, Ontario, once owned by Michael DeGroote of Laidlaw Corp. fame. He has been married twice and has five children.

Lee-Chin has been generous both in Jamaica and in his adopted Canada. He donated $30 million to the Royal Ontario Museum for its dramatic addition, called the Michael Lee-Chin Crystal, which was designed by famous architect Daniel Libeskind. He has also given $10 million to the University of Toronto's Rotman School of Management and millions to other causes. Whether he stays or eventually returns to his native Jamaica as a tycoon or politician or both, he has left several important legacies. He created opportunities for himself and others, from employees to investors and suppliers. He is truly a Canadian success story, and a Jamaican one. He has proven that smarts and hard work, plus timing and an aptitude for good publicity, can trump background or poverty in Canada's new meritocratic society.

THE INDUSTRIALISTS

Canada's industrial base has grown by adding value to its resource base, such as sawmills, smelters or refineries. But heavy, metal-bashing manufacturing mushroomed during the Second World War as part of the military effort. After the war, Canada got into the auto business in a big way with the formalization of the Auto Pact with the United States. This treaty was mutually beneficial: Canada had a small automobile manufacturing sector but was a sizable vehicle market for the Americans. So Washington and Ottawa inked a deal that linked auto jobs for Canadians with the percentage of Detroit's car sales that Canadians represented.

The innovation was that border tariffs would not be imposed on parts or vehicles as they travelled back and forth between the two countries for assembly or sale. In other words, this was the first maquiladora—an agreement to suspend tariffs in order to tap cheap labour on the other side of the American border.

Auto-assembly plants sprung up in Ontario to be near cheap electricity, existing manufacturing, steel mills, Detroit's head offices and the massive American marketplace. These operations employed tens, then hundreds, of thousands of Canadians. By 1986, General

Motors of Canada had become one of the country's 10 largest corporations, along with Ford Canada and Chrysler Canada. Their growth was swift because Canada's lower labour rates, lower currency and cheaper power provided significant competitive advantages.

As these branch plants expanded, so did their Canadian suppliers. The removal of border tariffs plus just-in-time manufacturing created a huge, vibrant auto-parts and supplier sector in Canada, employing thousands more and generating billions in export earnings. By 1989, when the Free Trade Agreement replaced the Auto Pact, Ontario's auto industry was one of the province's principle economic cornerstones and a bigger export dollar earner in many years than any one of its resource sectors.

But the invasion of foreign cars into North America began a slow, steady slide for Detroit's automakers. Chrysler nearly failed, then revived, only to be merged with Daimler of Germany to avert another financial catastrophe. In 2007, Daimler cashed out and left the company in the hands of a private equity firm that has begun to prune and sell off profitable pieces.

The difficulties were caused by many factors. Foreign competitors built models with better gadgets and enhanced fuel efficiencies. At the same time as revenues were grabbed by superior rivals, American and Canadian unions obtained expensive benefits from pliant, comfortable managements, thus adding to overhead costs. All had led to a steady downsizing of auto manufacturing in North America.

Interestingly, CIBC World Markets chief economist Jeff Rubin believes that lost auto and manufacturing jobs are not a disaster and that Canada is doing just fine. "The [manufacturing] sector lost 275,000 jobs since the war and another 200,000 will be lost this decade as the Canadian dollar rises. [But] this will simply match the U.S. [manufacturing-job] levels of 10% of the total employment," wrote Rubin in 2007. "The fate of manufacturers was sealed when tariffs were dropped. The fact is, the job losses have turned out to be nothing more than a footnote in a Canadian labour market that has seen the creation of 1.5 million jobs."

This shift is global, and deindustrialization will continue except in those areas where Canada has special advantages or technologies. Tellingly, four of the country's largest fortunes have been made in traditional manufacturing but only two have some production in Canada, while two do not. In addition, Gerry Schwartz's Onex has invested heavily in various manufacturers in North America and around the world, but Schwartz is profiled in the conglomerate section of this book.

THE BATAS

Tom Bata Sr. stared long and hard at the runway where we were standing in 1992 while watching an acrobatic air show in Czechoslovakia. He didn't say anything for a long time. This is where his father's airplane had crashed on a foggy morning 60 years earlier, leaving Bata, only 18 years of age, fatherless and heir to an industrial empire.

In those days, his father, Tomas Bata, was one of Europe's biggest industrialists, mass-producing shoes and wooden crates, cartons, machines, tools and small aircraft in 45 factories in and around Zlin, in what is now the Czech Republic.

"My father was a business aviation pioneer," reminisced Tom, "and, like many of them, he died doing it."

For two days I travelled with Tom, and his wife, Sonja, to inspect the forests and buildings that his parents owned but that had been seized by the Nazis, then by the Communists. He had been given them back by the new Czech government in return for investing money in its fledgling economy. The Batas are friends of mine.

Tom is a patriarchal figure who speaks English with a British accent and has a thatch of white hair and a jolly, dignified manner. Sonja is a stunningly beautiful woman, 12 years younger than her husband, and has travelled the world with him as a full-fledged partner. She is a Swiss-born architect who was in charge of Bata's shoe and store designs.

Both are remarkable business people with a keen sense of

public service. "Bata" remains in Africa and India the generic term for "shoe." The multinational employs 80,000 worldwide, is in real estate development and retailing in India in a big way, and makes a million pairs of shoes every working day of the week.

Now the CEO is Tom Jr., a Harvard MBA who operates out of a tiny office in Lausanne, Switzerland. Gone is Bata's stunning glass headquarters in Don Mills, Ontario, near Eglinton Avenue. It was abandoned and boarded up in 2002, giving many the impression that the family is on the financial ropes. That's simply untrue. Tom Jr. has decentralized the operation and created mini head offices around the world wherever they sell shoes. The Bata headquarters in Don Mills has been sold to the Aga Khan, who is building a magnificent museum and prayer hall there on behalf of the world's 15 million Ismaili Muslims, many of whom have prospered in Canada.

But creative disruption, and dramatic innovation, has been embraced by the Batas, which is why the empire has survived the tectonic shifts from the rise of the Nazis to the fall of Communism to globalization.

The first turning point for the family came in 1939, when Tom Sr. decided to flee his homeland in advance of the Nazi invasion. The company owned 1,500 acres in Canada, and he obtained permission for many members of his corporate team to immigrate. By mid-1939, the first of several hundred crates of patented Bata shoemaking equipment arrived in Canada, labelled "SHOES FOR EXPORT."

"Since I was a child I had read stories by Jack London and Zane Grey about the Arctic and stories about The Bay and the adventures of gentlemen traders. The first head of Hudson's Bay was a Czech king," said Bata in an interview with me in 1985. "I used to import Peterborough canoes to Czechoslovakia in the 1930s. I had a certain psychological affinity to Canada and, having gone to school in Britain, it looked British and was next to the U.S. To me, it was the best of both worlds, and I have not been disappointed."

He replicated a Czech company town in Ontario, called it Batawa, lived in a simple worker's cottage and landed contracts to make arms for the war effort. After the war, he rebuilt the fractured empire.

"Tom Sr.'s father was a great idealist," said Sonja over lunch in Toronto in 2007. "His view of capitalism was different. He had profit-sharing in the 1920s. In the 1930s, he provided compulsory outside education for his workers, improving their language or mechanical skills; he started a health movement at the time. He believed living accommodation was crucial, so he built the Garden City for his workers; he felt it was crucial that workers be productive and happy and make quality products. This was why there were huge glass windows in his factories—so there was daylight all the time in the plant. He believed that everyone in the company was a partner and should work together as a team."

His father was also a great innovator, the Henry Ford of cobblers who brought the assembly line to shoe manufacturing. By 1932, when Tomas Bata's life ended, his sleepy Moravian village had become one of Europe's bustling factory towns as Bata Shoes grew from 50 employees to 20,000.

But his son did even better out of Canada.

"Tom was the big expansionist, and he and his team were determined to rebuild the Czech organization," said Sonja. "They started in the developing world, where it was cheaper and less capital was required—Malaysia, Ceylon. They had to be able to market goods locally, so they did vertical integration in each country, from machine shops to tanneries."

Another motivation was a lawsuit by his uncle Jan, his father's half-brother, who sued for ownership of the company.

"There were 15 years of lawsuits in various courts, and for 14 years there was no proof that Tom was the owner," said Sonja. "His father did not stipulate ownership in his will, but had told people, 'I will give the violin to whoever plays the violin the best.' Tom won the case, but he worked hard all his life because he felt he had to prove he was the leader."

Expansion was rapid in the 1960s and 1970s, and Tom and Sonja were sought after by leaders who wanted jobs and development in a hurry.

"Tom's goal in life was to become shoemaker to the world,

like a missionary. It was exciting," she said. "We bonded with the people, and we still send cards to 25-year employees."

In 1984, Tom Sr. stepped aside as CEO and became chairman. His son took over as CEO back then, but it didn't work out, as the two disagreed about what had to happen. Subsequent CEOs did not work out either.

"So we asked Tom to come back," said Sonja.

By this time, Tom Jr. had moved with his American wife and two children to Switzerland, where he lives today.

Tom Sr. and Sonja met because her father, Georg Wettstein, was a Bata legal advisor. He had a distinguished career, helped found the Red Cross and was involved in the defence of Alfred Dreyfus, a celebrated and vindicated victim of anti-Semitism in France in the 1890s. Another forebear, Johann Wettstein, was a signator in 1648 of the Swiss peace treaty with the Hapsburgs, and his image is still found on Swiss postage stamps.

"My son is the new phase," said Sonja. "He's Harvard-educated, bottom-line-oriented, and is about adding value as the number-one priority. He reviewed the organization and realized that it needed a good cleanout of operations that would never make money. For Tom [Sr.] to close a factory was impossible—never."

Tom Jr. realized that vertical integration in each country was unnecessary and that supplies should be sourced based on logistics and price. He also shut down the Don Mills headquarters and decentralized and assigned management to local markets. Today the organization is linked by BlackBerry and e-mail. Sonja's BlackBerry goes off during our luncheon interview, her son calling from China.

"Offices don't make sense anymore, and Tom has about six people in his office in Lausanne," she said. "He calls his satellite offices MBUs, or 'meaningful business units,' that must be close to the market."

Manufacturing, retail and real estate have been pruned. Some countries were more difficult to change than others, such as India, where radical unions still represent an economic hurdle.

"The sales people in our stores in India there were limited, by union rules, as to how many pairs of shoes they could sell a week. Can you imagine?" said Sonja. A lengthy, nasty strike occurred, so her son outsourced the sales force, taking employee numbers down from 17,000 to 3,000, and began selling retail sites or turning them into shopping centres. Some manufacturing remains there.

Tom Jr.'s three sisters—Christine, Monica and Rosemarie—play small roles in the business but share ownership through Bermudian and Swiss trusts.

Meanwhile, back in Canada, Tom Sr. and Sonja are still going strong even if their remaining Bata Shoe business, Athletes World Ltd., has flagged. The 138-store chain slipped into bankruptcy protection in November 2007 after a deal to sell fell apart over a tax dispute. The money-losing chain was the last sizable Bata asset in Canada and owed creditors more than $150 million, $115 million of that to parent Bata in Switzerland.

"We've had problems here," said Sonja in an interview with the *Globe and Mail.* "Sometimes in business you might have to step back and then you step forward again. This is always a terribly sad thing to do."

Sonja Bata is a director of that company but has also created, and is CEO of, the Bata Shoe Museum on Toronto's Bloor Street, the culmination of decades of collecting shoes and related artifacts from the world's cultures in order to design better products. She now has thousands of pieces of footwear in storage, ranging from Roman Empire sandals to Elton John's platforms, and rotates her inventory in thematic displays that change often. She also serves as honorary chairwoman of the World Wildlife Federation and various other causes. Tom Sr. is chancellor of a university in the Czech Republic. The Batas also have nine grandchildren. One granddaughter, Alex, is married to Galen Weston Jr.

"We have been unusually happy," said Sonja about herself and Tom Sr. "We are 12 years apart in age, and married very early, but started working together from the beginning. If I had started my own career, we wouldn't have worked together, but I didn't. I wanted him to succeed and fight against Communism too. It was a terribly exciting period—self-satisfying—and Tom was very good about delegating," she said.

The two remain more energetic than most and are uniquely positive and optimistic about everything.

"The Aga Khan came personally to Toronto to buy our land and building. He had originally wanted to build beside the Tate museum in London, but a hospital next door wanted the land for expansion," she said. "His museum will be sensational, but that Bata building was my building. I designed the furnishings and was totally involved. It was not easy to say in public, at a city council meeting, that it should be pulled down. But everything changes. That's life. Tom and I are workaholics and need change, actually. We love it and stay busy."

THE BOMBARDIERS

In 1942, a Quebec auto mechanic named Joseph-Armand Bombardier unveiled a contraption he had invented called the B7, which was a cross between a tank and a set of snow skis. By 1959, his invention had evolved into the world's first snowmobile, a noun that became a household verb.

Six and a half decades later, Bombardier Inc. has grown into one of the world's biggest train and plane manufacturers. In 2003, it spun off its lucrative Ski-Doo and Sea-Doo division for $1.2 billion to the family and some partners.

By 2006, Bombardier Inc. had become Canada's 19th-largest corporation, with $16 billion in revenues, profits of $304 million and 56,000 employees. Its market value in mid-2007 was $8 billion, and it is the world's third-largest maker of civil aircraft, behind Boeing and Airbus; the largest regional aircraft maker, ahead of Brazil's Embraer; one of the top two business-jet makers; and the world's largest railway-equipment maker.

Bombardier Recreational Products Inc. is now a private partnership. By 2006, it had become Canada's 137th-largest corporation; in that year it sold $2.3 billion worth of Ski-Doos, Sea-Doos and other vehicles, employed 6,200 people and made $60.6 million in profit. The family owns 25%, the Caisse de dépôt et placement du Québec 25% and Bain & Company 50%.

The Bombardier fortune has grown over the years despite the firm's involvement in high-risk manufacturing businesses. The driving force has been Laurent Beaudoin, a handsome accountant who married Claire Bombardier, one of the daughters of the founder. Calls for an interview were not returned.

Beaudoin was the scion of a well-heeled family and spent his childhood in posh boarding schools. He graduated in commerce, then in 1960 set up shop as an independent chartered accountant. He married Claire and in 1963 her father convinced him to join the family business.

"Before I worked with my father-in-law, he gave me a snow-mobile," he told *Canadian Business* magazine in an interview in 2007. "A friend and I modified it to go faster by adding a carburetor. When I tested it, I was quite proud of the fact that it went faster than one driven by its inventor. Then I got stuck in deep snow. My father-in-law circled me, going putt, putt, putt on his slower snow-mobile. 'Next time,' he said, 'try three carbs.'"

Beaudoin joined the firm in 1963, but a year later Joseph-Armand died, leaving two sons and three daughters. Beaudoin and his brothers-in-law reorganized the company and, in 1966, at only 28 years of age, he became CEO. In 1967, he took the company public.

Just three years later, he started to diversify. In 1970, Bombardier acquired an Austrian snowmobile and tram-car manufacturer. It was a gutsy move that by 1979 had nearly ended in bankruptcy, but operations were turned around through cost-cutting, new techniques and increased sales.

The next diversification, into planes, came in 1986 when Bombardier took over bankrupt Crown corporation and aircraft manufacturer Canadair Ltd. Bombardier then embarked on a consolidation path in both the train and plane sectors. It has been a difficult strategy, involving upheavals due to the vicissitudes of business, economic and product cycles.

"I've made quite a few hard decisions. The hardest for me is to let people go. I've done it many times. It's not something you enjoy. But if you have to do it, you have to do it," he said in the magazine interview.

Throughout the ups and downs, the Bombardiers have kept control with only 22% of the equity because they control 60% of stock votes.

"Bombardier probably wouldn't be a Canadian company today without dual shares," Beaudoin added in the interview. "It seems Canada couldn't care less [about building global giants], but you need to keep head offices if you really want to develop industries, employ decision-makers and reap the related benefits. Think about fundraising. Don't imagine that sub-offices give like head offices give when it comes to local charities."

"Canada's problem is that it can't take sides [pick winning sectors]. It wants to treat all businesses the same. It never picks one sector to support the growth of excellence and development of an industrial base," he said.

While Canada may not adopt the "national champions" model from France that Beaudoin espoused, Quebec certainly has. So has Ottawa, to the extent that it has been run by Quebeckers who curry votes in Quebec. The result is that Bombardier has been the country's biggest government beneficiary.

For years, it has received more taxpayer subsidies, asset gifts, grants, government contracts, research financing, tax forgiveness, loan guarantees and trade initiatives or promotions than any other company. Some estimate Bombardier has received $3 billion in cash help and as much as $10 billion more in "soft" help. For instance, for most of the past decade, two-thirds of Export Development Canada's guarantees and loan deals have been earmarked for Bombardier's customers to facilitate deals.

Even so, Bombardier's growth has been a juggling act. It competes, in the airplane sector, against government-owned and subsidized entities such as Airbus and against preferred government military or commercial contractors such as Boeing and Embraer.

Survival in this business is all about consolidation and government help. For instance, Bombardier bought Short Brothers, of Northern Ireland, out of bankruptcy from the Margaret Thatcher government and got millions to shore up 2,500 jobs in Belfast. The same occurred in Canada and the United States, where Bombardier bought subsidiaries or small jet manufacturers.

"Bombardier is often in financial trouble, but the family always wins. Governments intervene to help and treat it like a baby," said Stephen Jarislowsky of Montreal money manager Jarislowsky Fraser Ltd.

Another example of favouritism occurred in the 1980s, when a $2-billion jet-fighter maintenance contract, won in a tender process by a Winnipeg company, was transferred to Bombardier by Brian Mulroney's government. It caused a political firestorm outside Quebec.

Influence at home hasn't been enough to avert external problems. Brazil's Embraer invaded Bombardier's regional-jet marketplace, and 9/11 devastated the balance sheets of all its airline customers. This led to a collapse of the stock by 50%, and a reduction in credit rating, in January 2003.

That's when Beaudoin handed the cockpit over to Paul Tellier, who had been Ottawa's highest-ranking civil servant under Mulroney. More importantly, Tellier had enjoyed great success as CEO of privatized Crown corporation Canadian National Railway Company.

Paul Tellier ended up leaving before his three-year contract was finished, but not before he had spun off the family's original snowmobile business to the Bombardiers, the Caisse and Bain. Naturally, the deal raised eyebrows because of the coziness of buyer and seller and because, a year later, profits at the division jumped eightfold and sales 15.6%. This was not supposed to be the case, according to Tellier, when he told shareholders that the division would be sold because it would be a drag on Bombardier's operations.

After Tellier left, Beaudoin and his son, Pierre Beaudoin, took over operations again. And by 2007, Bombardier was back on its feet, landing big train and plane contracts around the world. In a rare interview, Laurent discussed what he hopes will be the legacy.

"A lot of family companies are sold for profit. That's not my motivation," he said. "I want to be remembered for creating an industrial base out of a small organization that will survive the Bombardier family."

THE SAMUELS

Mark Samuel is a down-to-earth Harvard University graduate and world champion equestrian who is probably one of Canada's youngest "patriarchs."

Born in 1961, Samuel is chair of his family's private operating company, Samuel, Son & Company Limited, and also chair and CEO of its public sister company, Samuel Manu-Tech Inc. The family owns 73% of Manu-Tech's stock.

The two companies, if combined in sales, would be among Canada's 100 largest companies and are North America's third-largest steel-processing and steel-service conglomerate. They collectively buy more steel in Canada than any other entity, including automakers.

"We have a public and a private company and all in about $3.5 billion in sales," said Mark in an interview in 2007 in his Mississauga office. "Every 10 minutes of your life you are interacting with metal we've been involved in . . . in car parts, car bodies, in your house, your office, the kitchen sink or refrigerator components, your barbecue at the cottage. You name it, we cover the waterfront."

The two companies employ about 5,000 people in Canada and the U.S. and were built into giants by Mark's late father, Ernest Samuel. The Samuel family includes Mark's two sisters, Kim Samuel-Johnson and Tammy Samuel-Balaz. The three siblings have five children among them.

Mark studied English literature at Harvard and planned to do a stint at a U.S. management consulting firm. But his father had a short-term health problem, and Mark was summoned home to learn the ropes.

Mark is lean and walks with a spring, like an athlete. He still rides competitively, and following our interview in June 2007 he was going to pick up his young twin daughter and son, and other family members, to spend the weekend at an equestrian competition to be held in Bromont, Quebec.

"It's fun and we all go together and love it," he said.

Ernie Samuel loved horses and also created a large horse-breeding and -training enterprise called Sam-Son Farm.

"My dad's first horse was named Canadian Club and won the only gold medal Canada got at the 1968 Olympics," said Mark. "He loved horses. My mom did. And we all rode as kids. I still compete, as do two of the five kids in the next generation."

His sister Tammy runs Fire Racing or Sam-Son Farm, which has developed some successful horses over the years. Her two children would compete in Bromont, along with their uncle Mark.

"One of our babies won one of the Triple Crown races this year and came second in the other two races," said Mark.

Mark's older sister, Kim, is a lawyer who runs the Samuel Family Foundation and is involved globally in many organizations and causes. She was named a Young Global Leader by the World Economic Forum in Davos and attends high-powered conferences around the world. She lives in Toronto.

Tammy's husband, Rick Balaz, is an executive at Samuel Manu-Tech and serves as a director on both the Manu-Tech and the Samuel, Son & Co. board.

Mark became chair of the family holding company in 2007 after his mother, Elizabeth, decided to step down.

"She wasn't sick or anything but just wanted to spend more time doing other things, like spending time with her grandchildren," he said. "We are proud of the legacy, and of this business, which dates back to 1855. I'm the fifth generation of the family involved in management."

It all began in the 19th century when two brothers, Lewis and Mark Samuel, immigrated from Britain to Toronto and Montreal respectively to sell steel. The materials were sourced by a third brother in Liverpool.

"They went from being importers and warehousers to hardware merchandising, then stockists, processors and service centres," Mark said.

Ernie, who died in 2000, inherited a business with sales of $6 million in 1961 and grew it to sales of $1.6 billion by 1999, when he stepped down from responsibilities due to poor health.

"It was massive growth, and we've more than redoubled the business since 1999," said Mark. "In five years' time, I guess this could be a $5-billion-a-year company and still be 100% family-owned."

Samuel companies buy steel in various forms directly from the biggest mills, then sell, store, bend, shape or simply ship metal products to manufacturers. They are intermediaries and fabricators with patented technology for processing metals of all kinds.

The operations have benefited from the price hikes in all commodities since 2003 due to China's infrastructure and industrial investments. But Mark sees this development as both good and bad. Many Samuel customers or suppliers were stuck along the way with long-term contracts at fixed prices, which meant they or their customers were financially damaged as prices escalated. The Samuel companies shared the pain to help their customers get through the worst of it.

"We have core values which include building a sustainable business based on relationships and integrity," Mark said. "We had to keep our customers whole."

Other difficulties have been the increasing value of the Canadian dollar as a commodity-based currency and the slump in sales among Detroit's carmakers. The auto sector represents roughly 20% of Samuel's sales.

On top of it all, the number of steelmakers is declining due to global consolidation. In Canada, virtually all the steel mills have been bought by foreigners, and such consolidations often lead to mergers among suppliers.

"There are new managements in place, and they are not always appreciative of the relationship that's been built up over the years, so we have been busy re-establishing ourselves," he said.

The Samuel family's unique mix of a public company with a private one has some competitive advantages. They went public in 1981 for succession-planning purposes (heirs can cash in by selling stock) and to create an outlet that could tap public equity markets. But being mostly private ($2.5 billion in sales compared to $1 billion for the public company) is advantageous in the marketplace.

"We can move quickly on acquisitions as a private company," Mark said, "and yet the family cannot be taken over. This is because we are mostly a private company and also because we have no interest in selling out to anyone. This is unanimous."

This positions Samuel to become a consolidator of family-owned steel processors or those in related businesses.

"Family businesses are more likely to sell to another family business," he said. "There's a lot of equity out there buying these companies, but they are short-term in their mentality. We are not. Private equity buys a family business, then lays off people, closes down operations and flips it to someone else. Often a family sells because no one wants to run it, but they don't want it destroyed and they don't want their loyal employees adversely affected."

The increasing value of the Canadian dollar has led to Samuel's acquiring assets south of the border. Samuel has also been forced to close a factory in Ontario, and realized as well that it was wise to expand into Australia and become involved in a joint venture in China.

"We are already sourcing out of China and have to be aware of that market," he said. "Our position is that if someone's going to import from China, it might as well be us."

Going forward, Mark worries about manufacturing in Canada.

"Our public company, Manu-Tech, is manufacturing and it is retrenching operations outside of Canada because of the dollar," he said. "Manufacturing is affecting us. But it's also in free fall in southern Ontario, and that's affected our customer base."

Samuel has been well managed and has built up a "comfortable war chest" to provide flexibility in the future, he said. The family remains committed to its companies, but the next generation is always a question mark.

"I'd love to see the next generation all get involved in the company, but if that's not their desire, we have a great precedent of external executives and a strong board structure of family members and independents," he said.

ALEX SHNAIDER

One of the world's richest Canadians runs his business out of a low-rent building not far from Russian Caviar, a delicatessen run by his immigrant parents where he swept floors and made deliveries.

Now Alex Shnaider, a good-looking but stern and cautious man just shy of 40 years of age, is a billionaire several times over. He made his fortune in a handful of years after cashing in on opportunities in post-Soviet Russia and Ukraine. Our interview in 2007 lasted three hours.

Shnaider, and others like him, benefited from the fact that perestroika and glasnost left 300 million people adrift without ownership rules or business smarts. Shnaider spoke Russian and understood both the old and new systems, which were the two necessary ingredients to build a capitalist empire out of Communism's ashes.

His Toronto office is under tight security, far from downtown and housed in an industrial unit beside a gym. Signage is muted and the waiting area is utilitarian, decorated with a few models of his empire's steel and raw materials barges encased in glass.

"Building a business there was horrible, and it took years. There were no hotels, no hot water, no heat, no towels," he said.

"You had to brush your teeth with mineral water. I worked day and night. It was awful."

But it paid off and now he lives like a czar. He is chairman of the Midland Group of companies, which employs 40,000 people and owns real estate, agri-food businesses, chemical works and two of the world's biggest steel mills, one in Russia and another in Ukraine. This conglomerate, co-owned with partner Eduard Shifrin, has offices in Moscow, Kiev, Toronto and the Channel Islands.

Shnaider and his wife are raising their three daughters in Toronto but are jet-setters with homes in several countries. They own a 180-foot Benetti yacht with a crew of 12 in the Mediterranean, and until 2005 he personally owned his own Formula One racing team.

"I love it," he said about the Formula One team. "It's my hobby, but it took too much time and it was too difficult to compete with car manufacturers. There were not enough sponsors and it required obscene amounts of money," he said.

The story of Shnaider's rise to riches is about business agility, an ability to withstand hardship and risk-taking.

Shnaider's parents were able to immigrate from the Soviet Union to Israel when Shnaider and his sister were toddlers, then they immigrated to Canada in the 1970s. His parents were educated but unable to find work in their professions. His father was an engineer and his mother a dentist. So, like many newcomers, they opened a business.

Shnaider majored in economics at York University, then landed a job with another ex-Soviet, Boris Birshtein, who was buying and selling everything in Russia, from commodities to clothing. Eventually, Shnaider married Birshtein's daughter Simona, but the two men no longer speak, according to Shnaider, because they had a falling-out. Birshtein ran afoul of authorities in Russia.

Back in 1992, Birshtein sent Shnaider to Switzerland as a metals trader. Shnaider lasted a year, then he found a partner in Belgium and began building relationships at decrepit steel mills in grimy industrial towns.

"I met a guy, when working for Boris, who was a steel trader—a professional—named Lazar Fruchter, a Belgian Jew. He was managing director of a steel-trading company, and I decided to form a trading company in partnership with him," said Shnaider. "I didn't like living in Zurich. I thought it was boring and wanted to be on my own."

He moved to Antwerp and set up a company called Trans Resources.

"My role was to source the steel, and his role was to sell the steel," he said. "I would travel to the mills, sit with the managing directors of steel plants, drinking vodka with them, going out with them, asking for allocations, listening to their stories. They were all in their 60s and had no clue about markets."

They had grown up in the Communist system, which was based on five-year plans dispatched from a centralized command authority. Moscow's control ended and there was no vertical integration, nor were there any marketing/distribution systems in place. Coal mines had been told how much to produce over five years; steel mills were told the same; and end users had to wait for their allocation to arrive.

"The directives came from Moscow as to how much and when and where. They had no idea about free enterprise. They never knew the economics of a plant and prices. Their job was to hire people and produce steel and get raw materials supplied and fill an order from Moscow to specifications," he said.

Shnaider went to all the steel mills in Ukraine and Russia to order supplies for his Belgian trading company. But the task was daunting, both logistically and financially. After the Soviet Union fell apart, these operations were orphaned without capital to buy components or raw materials.

"In the beginning, allocation was about barter. These managers wanted consumer goods, microwaves or furniture or shmattes [clothing], and we would get steel in exchange," he said. "Steel was money to us, because Lazar knew what to do with the steel, who to sell it to, what prices were and what was the market demand. Steel was our cash."

Unfortunately, barter could not last, because the steel-mill managers could not buy raw materials or machinery with micro-waves.

"Paying for the raw materials was a problem, so I met with iron ore and coal mine managers too," he said. "We helped them get cash for their raw materials in order to get enough for our needs. These people had no idea about concepts like the cost of production or currency devaluation. For example, we were selling coal for US$200 a tonne and the cost was only US$20 to US$40 per tonne. So we'd give it to them for US$140 a tonne, which was good for them, but we'd still make a big margin. It was win-win. We made a fortune."

Eventually, other competitors did the same and allocations became difficult.

"We were fighting all the time to get bigger and bigger allocations from them. There were other guys, competitors. You didn't have to be a genius to see how much money there was in this trade," he said. "Boris [Birshtein] did fertilizer trading like this, and others oil, aluminum, chemicals, all commodities."

But it was a roller-coaster ride.

"The first stage was steel for barter, then it was paying cash for steel because the mills' situations became worse. There were a bunch of imbeciles running them. Then demand in 1991 made their currency go up, and so their financial situation deteriorated and they were producing below capacity. In 1992 and 1993, the situation got worse and the mills were over-promising and under-delivering," he said.

During this time, Shnaider took the Russian managers to Europe to train them about capitalism, such as how to meet customer needs, how to price and how to match innovation by rivals.

"Fortunately, many of my rivals left and got fed up. Banks wouldn't touch this business. Only those with people on the ground and in the plants watching things, like we had, could afford to advance cash to get orders," he said.

"So we took a risk by giving them upfront cash in return for big discounts in price. We also worked with them—took them to see customers so they understood the market; got them to improve their service and packaging; supplied them with waterproof paper to wrap the steel in for the voyage to reduce rusting.

"We were teaching them about free enterprise. But not too much about it," he added, smiling.

The next set of hurdles also led to opportunities. Ports were badly managed and overloaded with commodities, so Shnaider got into the shipping business to get his steel to market and now owns a fleet of dozens of carriers.

"The most important guy was the port manager," he said. "It drove you crazy. I was on the phone in the middle of the night asking whether a ship had left, hearing that another had taken its place, or that the guy was drunk or the ship didn't get in. It would cost us US$8,000 a day to have a ship sit there unloaded."

Another issue was unreliable suppliers. For instance, at one point Shnaider had to pay cash to local utilities to keep the lights on so that his coal-mine and steel-mill suppliers could operate.

"We had to make the supply chain longer, so we negotiated large purchases of power and raw materials at a discount. We then made money on the power we bought and sold, on the raw materials and the spare parts for the mills and steel. Every transaction was profitable. We had really good times in 1993 and 1994," he said.

At the same time, the steel managements were getting smarter, sometimes holding out for prices that were higher than world prices.

"But we were making money on all the transactions beneath that, so it was okay," he said.

This formula outpaced competitors, and in 1993 and 1994, Shnaider exported 15% of all steel production output in Russia and Ukraine combined.

Then, in 1994, he formed another partnership with Eduard Shifrin, a PhD in metallurgy who was selling steel around the world out of Hong Kong. They launched Midland. Then, in 1998, the ruble collapsed. What prevented disaster was that Midland made a huge profit by selling its refractory monopoly, a supplier of heat-resistant bricks that line all steel furnaces that he had acquired along the way.

The next necessity for Shnaider was to buy companies that were being privatized.

"We had to buy, or the honeymoon was over. First we paid US$70 million for shares in Ukraine's Zaporizhstal, the fourth-largest, then we bought a Russian steel mill a few years later, some iron-ore mines and steel scrap processors," he said.

(In 2006, Ukrainian courts ruled that another steel-mill privatization, to the son-in-law of the former president and others, was illegal, and unravelled the deal. Questions about Shnaider's purchase of Zaporizhstal were also raised, but he reduced his percentage of ownership and pledged to plow US$500 million into improvements.)

Shnaider and his partner also began diversifying in 2002.

"Steel was like a cash cow, so we took the cash to buy other assets. We bought 32 ships—steel and chemical tankers. We bought 100% of the power distribution in Armenia, which we turned around and sold to a Russian giant. We got into real estate development in Russia and Ukraine in residential, office and retail," he said.

The assassination of the prime minister of Serbia in 2002 convinced Shnaider to also buy in that region.

"I thought it would be a good time to buy, because Serbia would be a mess for a while, assets cheap, and then it would join the European Union," he said. "There were mass privatizations, so we opened an office and bought shares in a meat processor, copper-processing operation, hotels, real estate, a bakery chain. But we've sold a lot. We thought the economy would improve faster, but political fighting has meant the Serbs have lagged behind the others."

Meanwhile, in Canada, Midland operates its shipping business out of Shnaider's offices and plans to build Toronto's tallest condo and hotel tower, on Bay Street, in partnership with Donald Trump and others. In early 2008, he was sued by former Canadian business partners and accused of hardball tactics. Shnaider responded immediately, calling the lawsuit frivolous and vexatious.

Shnaider's meteoric rise to riches is even more remarkable because he avoided the political problems in Ukraine and Russia that felled his estranged father-in-law Birshtein, as well as the head of Yukos Oil and so many others.

"They got into trouble because they got into politics or financed political opposition. We don't do any campaign financing. We are in favour of the ruling people," he said.

Birshtein was a big political operative. I interviewed him in February 1992 in his posh Moscow headquarters, near the White House legislature. He had dozens of bodyguards and limousines and rubbed elbows with Boris Yeltsin, Mikhail Gorbachev and others. He has since disappeared from that business scene.

But being apolitical has allowed Midland to thrive.

"We have a terrific management team in Russia and Ukraine. We have a huge deal flow, and are part of the system. I couldn't live there, though, because you need bodyguards and there is not much privacy. Canada's much more pleasant, but my partner and his family live there," he said. "Real estate returns are better there—better than Asia, as long as there is political stability."

Asked to reflect on his journey, he was brief as usual.

"It was horrible. I worked for years without a social life in these places. I was just lucky: the right place, right time."

FRANK STRONACH

Frank Stronach nearly cut off a finger as an apprentice tool and die maker in Austria but did not go to the company nurse, to avoid being sidelined from playing that night in a company soccer tournament.

Ambition and sacrifice—that is what Stronach is all about, and these traits have enabled him to build auto-parts empire Magna International Inc.

"Life's been just incredible to me," he said to me over lunch in 2004. "I'm lucky at everything I touch. I think it's because everyone makes things too complicated. I do the opposite. I simplify everything."

Luck, of course, is relative. Stronach—born Franz Strohsack

in Styria, Austria, in 1932—grew up during the Depression and the Second World War. He left school at 14 to become a tool and die maker and in 1954 headed for Canada with only $200 in his pocket and a small suitcase.

He has parlayed that money into Canada's sixth-largest corporation, with revenues in 2006 of US$25 billion, profits of US$500 million and 83,300 employees working in 229 factories, 62 engineering or research facilities and 23 countries. Magna International also controls real estate company MI Developments Inc., which, in turn, controls Magna Entertainment Corp., which owns an extensive network of racetracks. Stronach owns a stable of horses that have won many important races. Horses have been his passion forever, a passion that began when he was a young lad in Austria.

"After the war the Russians invaded us. Thousands came with tanks and horses. I was only 12 and watched two of the Russians fix an abandoned car by the side of the road and get it started. When the car worked, they gave me their horse. I put it in a barn," he said. "The next day it was gone."

In 2007, Stronach decided to take another chance on the Russians. In May of that year, he sold 42% of his multiple voting control in the empire to a 39-year-old Russian oligarch with a questionable past—Oleg Deripaska. Deripaska is reportedly worth US$20 billion, is related by marriage to late Russian president Boris Yeltsin, is a close friend of current president Vladimir Putin and is alleged to have gained control over Russia's aluminum business through politics and strong-arm tactics. His U.S. visa has been revoked because of concerns about his past.

But he "is a very honourable guy," said Stronach during his announcement. Barrick Gold Corp.'s Peter Munk agrees and calls the partnership "Frank's best deal ever." Munk introduced the two at a posh party in Europe.

"Putin wants to build an auto industry in Russia and will force the Indians and Japanese to buy Russian cars in return for Russian oil," speculated Munk.

To many, that seems not only far-fetched but off-base. It may be possible in Russia for Moscow to mandate who buys what products, but oil-for-cars is a non-starter in a world with alternatives.

Even so, Magna's shareholders are used to Frank Stronach's risky ventures, which usually work out well for everyone. In August 2007, they approved the Russian partnership. The other 42% control stake will presumably be given to Stronach's two children, Belinda and Andrew, neither of whom has shown great interest in running Magna. Belinda is on the board and is vice-chair.

Belinda dropped out of university to work for her father, then spent a few years in politics, at one point switching parties. In 2007, she announced her departure from politics shortly before being diagnosed with breast cancer. She has two children by her first husband, Don Walker, now CEO of Magna. Her brother, Andrew, has been involved in competitive tennis, with horses and in various track-related projects. Stronach spoke about his son in his 2003 interview with me: "Sometimes a father's tougher on a son than a daughter. He's bright and has a good heart. I certainly hope he comes back into the business."

In 2007, Belinda came back onto Magna's board, but Andrew was still noticeably absent. For both, Frank must be a tough act to follow. He's built a crack team of executives and managers, an entrepreneurial culture and great contacts. His successful strategies, rooted in experience and technical expertise, have also helped him maintain loyalty.

"Where most people fail in business is that they don't focus enough on the human capital," he said. "You must motivate them to work hard but also to think. I tell my managers, 'Don't screw the employees and don't screw shareholders, and you can do the same thing I can do. Every factory is a profit centre.'"

Frank wrote a corporate constitution that requires that 6% of profits be set aside for bonuses: 3% for himself and 3% for the rest. It also gives him two-thirds of the voting shares of the company, despite an ownership of only 4% of the stock.

In recent years, his bonuses have been up to $50 million a

year—a staggering amount made larger considering that this is not taxed in Canada: in 1994 he moved to Switzerland for tax purposes. When challenged at a public meeting about these huge payouts, he said, "I consider myself very talented and have proven it."

To be fair, he built Magna, but he also had to rebuild it in 1989 after he became distracted by politics and other businesses. The Bank of Nova Scotia got involved directly, and during the early 1990s profits were minimal. He earned only $100,000 a year base salary, but eventually turned operations around.

"When you build a business based on entrepreneurship, you must have discipline on those entrepreneurs in the budget process," he said. "I remember a board meeting when we had 90 or 100 factories and every factory was $1 million out of budget. So we took out loans. Since then, the greatest sin in this company is if a manager goes above his budget. That's grounds for dismissal."

Changes, and Stronach's move to Europe, led to huge growth. Between 1992 and 2007, Magna grew from $2.5 billion to $25 billion in revenues. The result is that Frank Stronach lives like a Hapsburg, with a private jet and mansions on two continents. His wife, Elfriede, rarely leaves their Aurora, Ontario, compound, where Belinda and her two children live, while Frank jet-sets around North America and Europe.

Magna International's headquarters are a metaphor for Stronach's Austrian style. They are set back hundreds of feet from the roadway and sprawl for blocks like Vienna's summer palace. Inside, an employee dining area overlooks a farm, a gigantic terrace, fountains and an artificial pond that becomes an ice rink in winter for employees and their families. A golf course for workers and customers is next door, and the company also gives away $20 million a year to charities.

Frank is passionate about everything, including Canadian politics. He ran for the Liberals in the late 1980s and bankrolled Belinda's run for Tory leader in 2003. Today, however, he is clearly a globalist living in a tax haven and now hoping to conquer Russia, then Asia.

"I am loyal to Austria and Canada," he told me back in 2003. "Austria gave me my trade, and Canada gave me the chance to develop my business skills. I couldn't do that in Austria because I would've gone broke just buying permits to do business there. And I nearly took Magna out of Canada when it took three years for me to get the permits to build this head-office complex. If my kids hadn't been born here I would have said, 'To hell with you.'"

He eventually did leave, by going to Switzerland, then building a different kind of parts-maker. Magna in Europe has graduated from building factories to make parts to becoming an outsourcer, with full-scale assembly plants for Chrysler, Mercedes-Benz and BMW.

Without a doubt, Stronach is one of the most brilliant businessmen Canada has produced since the end of the Second World War. But like all entrepreneurs, he is part gambler, and his Russian partnership represents his biggest bet yet. His children and managers, living in the relative cocoon of Canada, may find themselves incapable of dealing with strong-arm tactics, or avoiding catastrophe if Russia falls apart or their partner falls out of favour with Moscow.

THE CONGLOMERATES

C anada itself began as a conglomerate called the Hudson's
Bay Company, the oldest commercial operation in North
America and one of the oldest in the world. It operated—
as did the world's first conglomerate, the East India Company—as
a de facto government unto itself. Both were owned by a variety of
partners and entities who had been awarded huge land franchises.

By the late 19th century, the Hudson's Bay Company dominated the continent's fur trade and was Canada's largest private
landowner. The company then diversified into merchandising, then
into real estate development, oil and mining. Pieces were hived off
and sold over decades.

The conglomerate business model is based on spreading risk
and involves the ownership of many differing types of businesses
and assets. Canadians have been especially good at such enterprises. This has been, in part, due to the nature of Canada itself.
The economy has been too small to reach scale in any single business, and the big banks prefer to lend to large entities.

Theoretically, conglomerates can thrive in both good and bad
times. Crises yield opportunities to buy assets at fire-sale prices,

and these large holding companies should have access to large sums of money in order to take advantage. The recent era of low interest rates, open borders and thriving businesses around the world has lent itself to conglomeration on a global scale.

Conglomerates must also demonstrate an aptitude to be flexible, to remain financially strong and to manage businesses in a variety of sectors or geographical regions. These conglomerates, and others like them, such as Warren Buffett's Berkshire Hathaway, can also create their own momentum. Their stocks increase in value along with profits, thus allowing them to sell more stock or borrow more money in order to grow even faster. Of course, this virtuous cycle can suddenly reverse if markets decline, interest rates rise, mistakes are made or operations deteriorate.

This is why conglomerates come, conglomerates go and some come back again in a different form. Difficult markets and unfortunate decisions befell Canada's biggest conglomerate in the 1970s, Argus Corporation, then Olympia & York and Brascan in the 1980s and Seagram and Bell Canada Enterprises in the 1990s. But here are some entrepreneurs who have been very successful building and running conglomerates.

THE BRONFMANS

There haven't been any "tag days" for the Bronfman family since patriarch "Mr. Sam" made a fortune selling liquor during Prohibition.

By 1986, two branches of the family—Edgar and Charles Bronfman and their cousins the late Peter and Edward Bronfman—sat atop two business conglomerates with billions in assets of various kinds. Unfortunately, within less than one generation both had lost their empires, through a series of missteps and for very different reasons.

The exception is Charles Bronfman, who has made a fortune in Israel and the United States. But the Bronfmans have mostly left

Canada; both Edgar and Charles live in New York City. Charles's son, Stephen, lives in Montreal but declined an interview.

For decades, however, the Bronfmans were Canada's biggest success story. Their road to riches all began with Samuel Bronfman ("Mr. Sam"), who was born in Russia and grew up dirt poor on a farm in Manitoba with his immigrant parents and eight siblings. The family bought a hotel and got into the booze business, and the rest is history. By the end of the Second World War, their Seagram Company Limited was a giant, and it began buying brands around the world.

In the 1950s, Mr. Sam made it a point to cut out his closest brother's two sons (Peter and Edward) by making a take-it-or-leave-it $15-million offer for their Seagram stock. The offer was below market prices and designed to pave the way for the succession of his own sons at Seagram. It was unpleasant and ruthless considering the fact that the brothers and cousins had grown up next door to one another in Montreal's expensive Westmount neighbourhood.

But $15 million in those days was still a fortune. Peter and Edward were the sons of Sam's brother, Allan, and they decided to hire business advisors to invest their inheritance. Over the next two decades, their team parlayed their inheritance into one of Canada's biggest business empires, through a holding company called Edper.

By 1986, they controlled a mix of assets, from Labatt Breweries to stakes in real estate, mining, forestry, oil and financial assets. But it was debt-leveraged and became a house of cards when interest rates rose in the late 1980s. Edward sold out his interest along the way for more than $150 million, but Peter went down with the proverbial ship and got out with only his original investment.

The Edper team, though, went on to bigger and better things. By 2007, the Edper management group, led by Bruce Flatt and South African accountant Jack Cockwell, had restructured everything. Out of the Edper ashes came Brookfield Asset Management, Canada's 47th-largest corporation. Jack Cockwell led the group and even married Peter's widow, Linda.

Ironically, a similar fate awaited Mr. Sam's own offspring. Besides Edgar and Charles, there were Phyllis and the late Aileen

Mindel ("Minda"). Edgar became CEO and moved to New York City to run the company. Charles stayed in Montreal until the early 1990s as vice-chair and his brother's confidant. By 1986, their holding company, Cemp Investments Ltd. (acronym for Charles, Edgar, Minda and Phyllis), controlled real estate giant Cadillac Fairview Corp., nearly 25% of global chemical giant E.I. du Pont de Nemours and Company, and Seagram, the world's largest distillery.

By 2007, virtually everything was gone. Trouble began in 1994 when Edgar handed over the CEO's job to his second son, Edgar Jr., an artistic and charming youngster and the apple of his grandfather's eye who became "heir" to the family crown jewels.

But the boy chose a circuitous path, dropping out of college to dabble in the movie and music businesses. In 1982, at 27 years of age, he was convinced by his father to join the family business. By 1994, he was its CEO. At the time of the handover, the family's 36% stake in Seagram and duPont was worth US$4.1 billion. By July 2002, after a series of manoeuvres and asset sales, the family's stake had become worth only US$828.8 million.

In essence, the young Bronfman sold cash cow duPont to buy Hollywood and music assets, then swapped all of that plus the distillery for shares in a French conglomerate that became virtually worthless. It was a predictable move by a young man interested in cultural industries. But it was criticized all along the way—except by his father.

One of the first red flags concerned the 1995 sale of Seagram's duPont stake. DuPont's board was thrilled that the Bronfmans wanted to sell, and borrowed $9 billion to buy them out within days. The duPont stock went on to greater success and splits while the divestiture resulted in the immediate lowering of Seagram's bond rating because duPont's dividends represented 70% of Seagram's cash flow.

Undaunted, Edgar Jr. continued his buying spree and eventually did a stock swap in 2000 with Vivendi SA in Paris. Seagram was sold off because Edgar Jr. had lost control over the assets in the merger, and the transaction fallout dragged on for months, ending in near-bankruptcy. Edgar Jr. left as Vivendi vice-chair in 2001.

His father said during the battle, "Not to pooh-pooh the money, but that's not the real disaster. The real disaster is bad judgment. [We] took something my father had built and my son converted into something which was really dynamic, and put it in with these guys to get the kind of size we needed. And suddenly, it blew up in our faces."

That put a different light on it than some would cast.

"Charles could have intervened, but it would have created a family rift again," said a cousin. "Pushing out Allan's children, by his father, had an effect on him, and he did not want to have an more fights among the family."

At the end, both Edgar Sr. and Charles took the financial hit. Their sisters had cashed in years before.

(Phyllis moved to France, married a Rothschild cousin named Lambert, then divorced. She moved to New York in 1954 as an architect, and in 1979 founded the Canadian Centre for Architecture in Montreal. Her sister, Minda, married a French aristocrat and remained in Europe.)

Since the Vivendi debacle, the brothers have gone their separate ways.

In November 2004, Edgar Jr. tried unsuccessfully to buy part of Vivendi's video assets, then fronted a successful US$2.6-billion deal with three private equity investors to buy Time Warner Inc.'s music division. He put up US$250 million, with his family, and became chair and CEO of the private company. He has also dabbled in songwriting and penned Céline Dion's hit "To Love You More" and Barbra Streisand's "If I Didn't Love You."

Meanwhile, Charles has prospered in Israel. His son, Stephen, has remained in Montreal and is a venture capitalist, a music promoter and a keen supporter of environmental activist David Suzuki. His daughter, Ellen, and her husband, film investor Andrew Hauptman, moved to Los Angeles and frequent entertainment circles. Charles, who lost his wife tragically in 2006 when she was struck by a taxi, still lives in New York City.

Charles has made a fortune in Koor Industries Ltd., Israel's biggest investment company. Between 1997 and 2002, he was its chairman; its CEO was Jonathan Kolber, son of Liberal senator Leo Kolber, who has been Cemp's business advisor for years. In 2007, Jonathan was chair of Koor.

Koor has more than 20,000 employees and is in the telecom, agrochemical, defence electronics and venture capital sectors. Charles owned 29% of the company, which had a market capitalization value in 2007 of US$4.8 billion. Its head-office address is the Azrieli Centre in Tel Aviv, built and owned by fellow Montrealer David Azrieli.

Charles has also been a substantial shareholder in Teva Pharmaceutical Industries Ltd., which bought fellow Canadian Leslie Dan's Novopharm in 2000 for a rumoured US$450 million.

Like Azrieli, who brought the shopping centre to Israel, Charles invested in Israel's first-ever supermarket, Supersol, in the 1950s. He sold out that interest but started his own investment bank, Claridge Israel Inc., which has made other successful investments there.

"It used to be that all of Israel's brains went into the army or government," he told a newspaper years ago. "Now they are going into business."

Another successful Bronfman is Edgar Jr.'s brother Matthew, a New York investment banker who sits on many prestigious boards and is an investor in Israel's third-largest bank.

By 2007, the Bronfman business magic seemed to have disappeared, apart from Charles's successes in Israel. And while the clan members are individually wealthier than most people, the fact is that Mr. Sam's worst nightmare appears to have been realized. He once said, "Shirtsleeves to shirtsleeves in three generations. I'm worried about the third generation. Empires have come and gone."

JACK COCKWELL

Jack Cockwell greeted me on a Sunday afternoon with a public relations executive in tow and one front tooth missing.

"I knocked my tooth out yesterday in the bush, cutting trails on my land up north," he said.

Cockwell has always ducked interviews, but our two-hour conversation took place in the glitzy offices of Brookfield Asset Management in Toronto's BCE Place. Its space is accessible only through a private elevator.

Cockwell is wiry and very fit. At 63, he looks 20 years younger. The "bush" he refers to is a land mass of 10,000 acres in Muskoka, 150 miles north of Toronto, where he spends Fridays and Saturdays with his brother, Ian Cockwell, blazing trails. The park is Cockwell's baby and he and his five partners, neighbouring landowners, are grooming the pristine preserve.

This is a side of Cockwell few are aware of. He is known as one of Toronto's most prominent and reclusive players who is a master at the minutiae of accounting, but he has had a lifelong love affair with land and exercise.

He is also the master of the blank stare. His answers take several seconds longer to come than normal. His questions are often disarmingly innocent, unless they deal with business.

But he's been at the centre of two of Canada's most interesting business empires in the last 20 years: Brascan Ltd., owned by the late Peter and Edward Bronfman, and its successor, Brookfield Asset Management Inc.

In 1986, Brascan was the country's largest conglomerate, with a tangle of 200 Canadian companies. Its management was all outside the Canadian establishment: South African immigrant Jack Cockwell, his team of financial engineers and the Bronfmans. Brascan had financial problems in the late 1980s, beginning with the real estate meltdown, but out of that came Brookfield. It is still headed by Cockwell and his team, and the Bronfmans are gone.

However, the two empires are structured completely differently.

Brascan was Canadian; Brookfield is global. Brascan was a leveraged-buyout artist; Brookfield is a buttoned-down asset manager.

"Back in 1976, Toronto was an old boys' club," said Cockwell. "Jews and women were not allowed into clubs. All that changed in 30 years. There was no insider reporting. No securities laws. Underwriting was done on the basis that the bankers were put on the preferred buyer list [for their personal benefit]."

"But the biggest change is access to capital. The bankers in Canada used to phone each other up and say whether somebody should get a loan or not. Now the U.S. guys are here with their suitcases. You can raise bond money or equity. They opened it right up. With one phone call," he said.

Brascan got around these constraints in the old days through its use of preferred shares and tax avoidance.

But Brookfield has been different. It is run by Cockwell's young successor, accountant Bruce Flatt, born in 1954. Cockwell and his team of 25 key managers are Brookfield's largest owners, with 17%. This company also owns 51% of Brookfield Properties. Between 2000 and 2006, Brookfield Asset went from US$10 a share to US$50, and by mid-2007 the combined market capitalization of both companies had gone from US$2 billion to US$28 billion. Between them they own US$70 billion in assets (80% in the U.S.) and employ 45,000 people.

Among assets are properties shed by the Reichmanns and others, including 17% of their Canary Wharf project in London; dozens of power plants; North America's fourth-largest timber rights position, of two million acres; and hundreds of thousands of acres of farmland in Brazil.

"In Brazil, we have power plants, a rural agribusiness, and are developing condos and shopping centres," said Cockwell. "Cattle too. We lease farmland to ethanol producers [who make ethanol from sugar cane], and give them 20-year leases with escalators in the lease based on the price of ethanol and sugar cane. It is 40% cheaper to make ethanol in Brazil than elsewhere because the soil is so rich."

Brookfield is also a joint venture partner in what will, when it's completed in 2009 or so, be the world's largest ethanol refinery, in Brazil.

Cockwell loves land and spent his summers growing up in South Africa on a relative's acreage.

"I come from a rural background," he said. "My dream was to be a farmer. My first job was to run a chicken farm."

He studied accounting, then travelled to Europe and Canada. After arriving in Montreal in 1966 with $4,000 savings, friends convinced him to stay and work for Deloitte & Touche on its Expo 67 and other high-profile accounts.

"I was happy in South Africa but decided to travel, trying to figure out why people around the world couldn't live together happily," he said. "I intended to go home but went to work at Deloitte's for a $6,000-a-year salary. I also intended to stay only one year in Canada, but got married, and then we adopted three 7-year-old girls—a set of twins and another 10 months younger. So I stayed."

One client was the du Pont family of Delaware. One weekend, he was invited to the family's scenic, expansive lake property in Quebec.

"It was just like the movie *Duddy Kravitz*, and that's what I wanted," he recalled. Mordecai Richler's fictional character goes from rags to riches by amassing a huge, beautiful land holding. Along the way, Duddy encounters problems, but Cockwell loved the scenery and space of Canada's north as represented in the film.

In Montreal, Cockwell met Neil Baker, an astute investor from Winnipeg who was financial advisor at Edper Investments Ltd., Peter and Edward Bronfman's holding company. The two brothers and their sister had been unceremoniously forced out of the Seagram distillery fortune by its founder, their uncle Sam Bronfman. But they had still received millions for their stock.

Baker ended up hiring Cockwell. (Baker eventually left to start Gordon Securities, later Gordon Capital, with Winnipegger Jimmy Connacher in Toronto and was entwined in deals with Cockwell for decades.)

In the late 1960s, Montreal had trouble with separatist terrorists. The Bronfmans and their Edper team left after 1976, when the separatists were elected and politics forced the team to abort a takeover attempt on Great-West Life.

"The [Great-West] takeover freaked everyone in Quebec out. Eventually, Neil [Baker] gave the company on a platter to [Power Corporation's Paul] Desmarais because he was French, or politically correct," said Cockwell. "We moved operations to Toronto after the separatists got elected. Peter also had his house bombed in the late 1960s by the FLQ [the terrorist organization Front de libération du Québec]. He was on a death list. It was serious."

In short order, Edper took on the Toronto business establishment, with a hostile takeover bid in 1979 for Brascan Limited. Unlike in Montreal, they won the day and overcame resistance from Toronto's bankers, brokers and large Brascan investors.

Edper, through Brascan, embarked on a spree, with borrowed funds. Cockwell's team now included hotshot Toronto lawyer Trevor Eyton, Cockwell's brother Ian, Robert J. Harding, Gordon Arnell, Tim Price, Michael Cornelissen and David Kerr. Jack was dubbed on Bay Street "the Manipulator."

By 1986, Brascan-Edper was the country's biggest conglomeration and owned Noranda Mines, the country's largest miner; MacMillan Bloedel, its largest forestry company; several huge oil and gas companies; half of the control block of Trizec, the country's largest real estate company; Labatt Brewing Company; Royal Trust, the country's largest trust company; and London Life.

The group used Neil Baker's Gordon Securities to help it sell billions in preferred shares to finance its acquisitions. Then Cockwell created a series of holding companies that bought preferred stock in one another and in underlying companies. Money flowed from the bottom up, and Cockwell's team sat on the boards of these companies to ensure that the dividends flowed even if cash flows ebbed.

This highly leveraged strategy backfired, and the real estate recession of 1989 forced a "workout." Assets were sold and the empire restructured. Royal Trust went bust. Bruce Flatt was hired to help.

Bickering added to the woes and Edward Bronfman cashed out his stake. Peter Bronfman stayed.

"Edward forced Edper to go public by cashing in, and that was one of the worst moves," said Cockwell. "We already had Brascan and another public company to look after, and for us to go from private to public with Edper was inappropriate, added to our problems and created new ones."

The Edper stock issue exposed financial problems. Noranda was put up for sale, and Calgary-based oil and gas subsidiary Canadian Hunter Exploration Ltd. was sold in 2000.

"Selling it [Canadian Hunter] for quick cash was, in hindsight, a big mistake. We sold it that spring," he said. "It was a great company, and we didn't read the world energy needs at that time accurately."

Brookfield emerged as the result of a merger of Brascan entities, and in 1993 Bruce Flatt took on its turnaround. He moved to New York City, improved operations, made acquisitions and converted the company into an asset-management operation, not just a real estate business.

"The concept was we use our own capital or manage capital for others," explained Flatt to me in an interview in 2005. "We put up 40% to 60% with partners. This is not a venture capital operation, but we are asset managers with a difference: we take a piece, manage things and put up capital too."

Flatt said he was also lucky because he tried—and failed— to buy the twin World Trade Center towers just months before they were destroyed in the 9/11 terrorist attack. Edper had already acquired, out of the Reichmann collapse, the World Financial Center and One Liberty Plaza, both next door. They were damaged in the attack, but not destroyed.

"We were amazingly lucky that we didn't get the target. We evacuated 60,000 people that day [from the World Financial Center and One Liberty Plaza], and not a single person was hurt. The collateral damage was significant but mostly cosmetic. We were back in business within two months," he said.

Flatt was a prodigy and wealthy in his own right. His father was a storied investment manager for Investors Group (part of Great-West Life and Power Corp.), and he and his brother continue to manage the family portfolio.

"Bruce never stopped working—not working until 8 p.m., but until 3 a.m.," said Cockwell. "He would finish off other people's jobs, and in time he *had* their jobs. We weeded out the natural successors, and skipped a generation, to go straight to Bruce. He has judgment and diligence."

"My job was to make sure the changeover went smoothly, that the street got to know Bruce. For two years we worked side by side. Now there has been a clean transition," he said.

Flatt has led Brookfield into bigger and better real estate deals, but also into land banking and power-generation facilities. He calls power plants "office buildings sideways" because, like offices, if price and location are correct, they generate revenue forever. Brookfield took advantage of the turmoil in utility markets in the U.S. and snapped up a few dozen, mostly in New England.

Clearly, this new team created by Cockwell will be as aggressive as the old one, only different. And in 2006, the last remaining asset of the 1986 empire, Noranda, was finally sold. The mining giant had been on the block for years, but it wasn't until the commodity boom began in 2003 that buyers began sniffing around. The most serious was China's mining giant, but "they realized it was too big for them at the time," said Cockwell.

Noranda decided to buy all of Falconbridge and to bundle the two together under the Falconbridge banner. In 2004, it offered the company for $28 a share to Canadian mining companies Inco Limited and Teck Cominco Limited.

Both declined, but Xstrata PLC of London stepped up and bought a chunk, with an option for more if control was at stake. As things turned out, Xstrata ended up paying $63.25 a share in 2006 for the rest of Falconbridge it hadn't already bought because Inco decided to buy it. Teck also got into the mix by deciding to buy Inco. In the end, Falconbridge and Inco were both gobbled up by foreigners.

"If Inco had more courage, then the largest nickel company in the world would have been Canadian. That would have happened," said Cockwell. "A number of times we begged them to be part of something. But the two Inco CEOs [Mike Sopko and Scott Hand] and Teck misread it. They are cautious people—too cautious. They missed it at $28 a share. We got out because it wasn't a business we wanted to be in."

"We didn't want to be in that business anymore. The problem with Canada's mining companies was that they had the world to themselves, then interest rates went to 20% in the 1980s and there were 10 years of lousy prices," he said. "Next, they woke up to environmental responsibilities and about 90% of our capital spending went to the environment."

"But we did not neglect Noranda. Exactly the opposite. Of the 10 major mines built in the previous 10 years, Noranda built 4 or 5 of them. These were $2-billion projects which provided enormous growth. Falconbridge [with Noranda] had $2 billion a year in cash flow, which is why Xstrata paid $27 billion for it. Because we grew it," he said.

Cockwell and his team have, like mining, weathered many business cycles. Now each one has become very wealthy. Cockwell gave $10 million to each of Toronto's Ryerson University and the Royal Ontario Museum. Others have been very generous too.

"I've been lucky. Meeting Neil Baker was an unbelievable break. After I went back to South Africa, he sent me a telegram asking me to come back because, he said, 'We need you.' Nobody ever needed me before. Now my life is perfect: I spend one-third of my time on business, one-third working up north and one-third working with charities."

MIKE DeGROOTE

Mike DeGroote left Canada in 1990 for Bermuda to retire and get out from under Canada's excessive taxation rates and government inefficiencies.

"I left for tax reasons only. Taxes are higher in Canada than almost anywhere else in the world, and you can't build businesses in that climate," he said in an interview in 2007. "I've done better since I've retired in Bermuda than I did in Canada when I was working hard. Hard work alone doesn't do it. You have to have the right government climate."

He has enjoyed living in Bermuda ever since, with his 15-room mansion on Perot's Island and 180-foot powerboat. But he found the transition difficult.

"It was tough for the first two or three years. You leave friends, clubs, family and start over again. But I see most of my friends quite often."

One constant pal is Ron Joyce, who, like DeGroote, dropped out of school in grade 9 and went on to become an enormous business success, as the creator of the Tim Hortons franchise giant. Both men operated out of the Hamilton, Ontario, region and lived in Burlington. Neither belonged to the buttoned-down, inherited-wealth establishment of Toronto.

DeGroote's success story, in Canada and outside its high-taxation regime, is quite stunning. He began by running a manure-hauling business in his teens, decades ago. He suffered a setback a few years later but bounced back to become a consolidator in service sectors: trucking, school-bus services, solid waste management, auto dealerships, security services and accounting services.

"That's my niche, service businesses," he said.

He's more European than Canadian and speaks softly, with a slight Flemish accent. He's a connoisseur of great wines and foods and travels first class on his Challenger jet. He collects art and is a student of history. I have socialized with him, and a group of us witnessed the Hong Kong handover together in 1997.

In 1988, he sold Laidlaw Transportation Ltd. to then-conglomerate Canadian Pacific Ltd. for $499 million. He turned that into billions offshore as he invested and built three U.S. corporations. In some cases, he hooked up with Florida tycoon Wayne Huizenga, Blockbuster Video honcho and owner of the Miami Dolphins.

"One of my big winners is called AutoNation, which is still a huge company. We have 200 car dealerships across the southern U.S.," he said. "Wayne was involved, and I still have a bunch of shares."

AutoNation's revenues are US$20 billion annually and its profits are relatively low-margin but total around US$500 million a year.

"I also still control Century Business Services [CBIZ, Inc.]. It has a very good CEO," said DeGroote. "Century is another roll-up of companies, 140 of them, bought over two and a half years ago, that provide accounting and other services. These were ma-and-pa operations. It's a high-margin business, and its revenues in 2006 were US$600 million and profits US$220 million."

He also owns 48% of solid waste management giant Republic Waste Industries, which he and Huizenga bought control over in 1995.

"It was small, and now it's the third-largest waste company in the U.S.," he said. "And I own another waste company I cannot name, which is six years old and does US$500 million in revenues and makes US$30 million in profits after taxes."

Unfortunately, DeGroote's good fortune in business has not been matched by good fortune in terms of his health. In 2002, he suffered a serious stroke and has been in pain ever since. He commutes between Bermuda and his estate in Naples, Florida, and also spends time in Toronto, at the Four Seasons Hotel in Yorkville, to visit friends, his four children and grandchildren.

"I work three hours a day, no more, these days," he said.

That's more than a lot of folks work after retirement, but the work ethic is part of his DNA.

DeGroote was born in Belgium to Flemish parents who immigrated to Tilsonburg, Ontario, when he was 14 years old. He never attended school in Canada and went immediately to work on the family tobacco farm.

"I didn't finish because we all had to work on the farm," he said. "My parents owned the farm and grew the tobacco. I bought a truck and began hauling manure from dairy farms to tobacco farms. It was my venture. But I left home at 18 because I was tired of going up and down the same fields every year."

DeGroote's brother still owns three tobacco farms in the region, and one of Mike's children is also in that business.

"I went from one to four trucks, then I went up to Elliot Lake during the uranium boom. We were hauling uranium ore from mines to mills. Then we were hauling from gravel pits to crushers. I also had a ready-mix company. By 21 years of age I was a millionaire, and by 26 I was bankrupt," he said. "What happened was that in 1958 the U.S. cancelled their uranium contracts with Canada. All the mines at Elliot Lake were just being built at the time."

He staved off bankruptcy by doing construction work elsewhere.

"From there we went to building sewers in Sault Ste. Marie and Sudbury. We also built highways up there. But our last big highway job outside Sudbury went bad. We weren't paid, and it did me in."

He went personally bankrupt.

"Bankruptcy was the best lesson I ever learned: not to borrow money from banks or anyone else. Always be debt-load free," he said. "I was young and cocky and still ambitious as hell. So I bought Laidlaw and built it up to being one of the largest trucking companies in Canada. In the meantime, in the early 1970s, I got into the waste business, then the school-bus business—all of which worked well. I found good people. It was a lot of work but a lot of fun. I miss the action."

Laidlaw bought control of ADT, a global home-security business run by Michael Ashcroft, now Lord Ashcroft, who lives in Belize.

"ADT did okay, but the Laidlaw people got into a fight with Michael, who was running it. They ended up selling the ADT stock for one-third the price I paid for it," DeGroote said.

Laidlaw never performed well after Canadian Pacific bought it, due to mediocre management and an environmental dispute in the U.S. courts.

"I worked 14-hour days, 6 days a week, building Laidlaw, and it was destroyed," he said.

In 1992, insult followed injury for his conglomerate. He paid $7.65 million to settle a class action lawsuit that alleged that he and his officers had "misrepresented the financial condition of Laidlaw." Then he paid $23 million to the Ontario Securities Commission to settle outstanding insider-trading allegations.

He still considers Canada home and is proud that his four children are all entrepreneurs in Ontario.

DeGroote also has been a generous philanthropist to McMaster University. He has given $13 million to its business school (named after him), and in 2003 he made the biggest donation in Canadian history—$105 million—to the university's school of medicine, also named after him. Another $6 million went to build a student centre, and he continues to finance the efforts of the DeGroote Foundation for Epilepsy Research at the school.

"I have been fortunate to be able to do these things. Not many have that chance," he said. "I believe in luck, because lots of people work hard and never do as well as I did."

PAUL DESMARAIS SR.

Paul Desmarais Sr. of Montreal possesses more "soft" power than any other businessman in Canada.

All but one Canadian prime minister since Pierre Trudeau has been on his payroll or has been related to him by marriage, as was Jean Chrétien. Through his appropriately named company, Power Corporation of Canada, he and his two sons mingle with the rich and powerful on the three continents that count.

They also, by virtue of their stranglehold on virtually all the French-language media in Quebec, wield much influence back home.

I have interviewed Desmarais twice, but only once on the record. The first time was during a delicate time in Quebec, involving a separatist government. He agreed then to talk about a specific situation but, the day before our meeting, switched the venue from his office in downtown Montreal to his home. We sat for more than an hour mid-morning, sipping tea in the solarium of his exquisite Westmount mansion overlooking the city. He's a very personable man.

By 2007, the senior Mr. Desmarais had slowed down, following a few strokes that have left him in some discomfort at age 80 years. But his two sons, co-CEOs of Power and all it possesses, have continued in the same fashion. Paul Jr. is incredibly well connected in Europe, as André is in China.

Power Corp. is Canada's fifth-largest corporation, with $30.3 billion in revenues in 2006, $132 billion in financial assets and $1.39 billion in profits. It owns 75% of Winnipeg-based Great-West Life, which employs 19,000 and includes Investors Group and Mackenzie Financial mutual funds, London Life Insurance, Canada Life Financial Corporation, Crown Life and Boston money-manager Putnam Investments.

In Europe, Power Financial controls, through a partnership, Pargesa Holding, Imerys, Groupe Bruxelles Lambert and stakes in Suez Energy, Lafarge SA and Total SA. In 2006, the Desmarais family made $1 billion in profit by selling their 13% portion of media giant Bertelsmann AG back to the German family that had founded it. As a result of their European portfolio and networking expertise, they know many of Europe's most prominent political leaders by their first names.

In China, Power Corp. owns 4.6%—and has board representation—in Hong Kong conglomerate CITIC, with stakes in Cathay Pacific, infrastructure projects and power-generation plants in China. This has gained the family entry into the highest reaches of the Chinese business and political elite.

In the U.S., Paul Sr. has sat for years on the JPMorgan Chase advisory board, along with Brian Mulroney, and on the board of the Carlyle Group, a well-connected Washington closed-end fund that includes some of the world's richest individuals.

The Desmarais approach to business and life is best described as a charm offensive. First, the Desmarais invest alongside a prestigious partner in order to develop relationships and enter the local "deal stream," or menu of opportunities. Their chosen targets are then lavished with party invitations, offered stays at beautiful destinations or to hunt and fish at the Desmarais estates in Quebec or Palm Beach, given lifts on the corporate jet and handed large-scale campaign contributions.

For instance, Paul Sr. hosts an annual Halloween party at his Quebec estate. Hundreds are invited from the worlds of business, the arts and politics. On hand is a room full of costumes with seamstresses to make alterations.

The template for all this began in 1951 when Paul Sr. dropped out of law school in Toronto to tackle a bus company in Ottawa in which his father had a minority interest. He turned it around and, while doing so, met an important mentor, Louis Lévesque. Lévesque was a dealmaker who convinced young Paul to leave Ottawa and go where the action was, which, at the time, was Montreal.

Paul was introduced around and started climbing the corporate ladder in the 1960s. Presentable, as well as politically correct because he was French, Paul was soon courted by banks, pension funds and corporations alike to do deals or serve on their boards. That's when he realized that networking trumps most barriers to entry, such as school affiliation or local roots.

"Before, a French Canadian became a doctor, a lawyer, a priest or a teacher. French Canadians were afraid of the system, of the English-language banking institutions," he said in a periodical interview later.

In no time, Power Corp. was making high-profile deals, and Paul soon outgrew the country. He tried to buy all of Quebec's television stations, Canadian Pacific Railway, Southam newspapers and Argus Corporation in Toronto (after its initial takeover by Conrad Black), but all these moves were blocked by regulators or politicians.

On the other hand, his French connection helped him capture Great-West Life and other assets. Great-West had been taken over by Peter and Edward Bronfman; their advisor Jack Cockwell said the backlash forced the brothers to abort the deal.

Despite benefits, Power went offshore in pursuit of more opportunities. Paul Sr.'s first foray was in the late 1970s in France, when he swapped a small stake in Power Corp. for 2.3% of blue-ribbon Compagnie Financière de Paribas and a board seat.

Paribas was steeped in history, but all banks came under the gun under socialist French president François Mitterrand. They had been nationalized, so Paul and another non-French director, a Belgian financier named Albert Frère, convinced the government to sell them the bank's Swiss unit, called Pargesa SA.

They eventually took control and used the bank as their investment vehicle—and a ticket into European society.

In 1991, Paul Jr. was sent to Paris by his father within days of Paul Sr.'s appointment as an officer of the French Legion of Honour for "outstanding service to the Republic." A party was held in the Canadian ambassador's home in Paris, and Prime Minister Brian Mulroney, a friend, attended with his entourage.

Paul Jr. now had the essential credentials, and lived in Paris for five years, handling the family's interests in Pargesa and working with Albert Frère and his son Gérald. These families would become an inspired partnership. Both Paul Desmarais Sr. and Albert Frère turned 80 in 2007. Both had been on the *Forbes* 500-richest list for years, and both were outsiders.

Desmarais was a French Canadian from Sudbury, Ontario, Canada's nickel belt, and Albert was a Belgian from Gerpinnes, a small town in Belgium's rust belt. Frère also left school and began consolidating companies, in his case steelmakers in the 1950s and 1960s. By 1979, he owned half of Belgium's steelworks. These were eventually nationalized, which made him very wealthy. The two met at Pargesa, trimmed its sails and invested heavily in a handful of great companies in the financial, oil, water and media sectors.

Paul Jr. inherited this portfolio but is no slouch either at networking his own generation. He's a close personal friend of France's current president, Nicolas Sarkozy, and has been appointed to Prime Minister Stephen Harper's elite advisory board on North American integration.

Likewise, his younger brother, André, learned to navigate the Ottawa maze as a young parliamentary assistant, then as son-in-law of Jean Chrétien. More recently, he took on the China dossier and is extremely plugged in, thanks in part to Mulroney and former Power executive, backroom Liberal and United Nations operative Maurice Strong.

The Desmarais family members avoid the press, even though they own Quebec's. In the past, they have had reason to remain behind the scenes because of their allegiance to Canada and the existence of sometimes violent separatists in the province.

But in March 1999, Paul Sr. let loose when I called him at his Palm Beach home to check out rumours that he had moved offshore for tax purposes. At the time, André's father-in-law was prime minister, and my query obviously hit a nerve. Brian Mulroney was in the room when I called and encouraged Paul Sr. to be candid.

"I've thought about it [leaving Canada] a thousand times," Desmarais said. "So many of my friends have done it. But I haven't, because I'm a Canadian, I've made my money here, and I've got to fight it out."

Then he added that intelligent Canadians should emigrate to the U.S. to escape "exorbitant" Canadian taxes and that he had made no secret of this opinion to Jean Chrétien privately, obviously without effect.

"Take an intelligent kid looking at his future. The U.S., with free trade, can give him a great future, more ability to do what he wants with his money because he will keep more of it. Anyone is better off in the U.S.," he said. "It's obvious. A lot of people have left and are not paying any taxes in Canada. What the hell. Can you blame them? This is a brain drain, and a drain of potential income for Canada. When the government's too greedy, people find other solutions."

"Canada is losing its most creative people because of high taxes," he continued. "Many of my friends have left Canada. Some of them have taken inherited money with them. Some are saying to themselves, 'Why pay taxes in Canada when taxes are so exorbitant?'"

These days Paul Sr. takes it easy. He still owns 64% of Power Corp.'s voting stock, and succession plans are unknown outside the family. There are two daughters, Sophie and Louise, who are not directly involved in the business but who will probably share ownership with their brothers when the time comes.

But all the elements are in place for long-term sustainability, and the brothers are certainly being rewarded along the way. Each has been getting millions in stock option profits every year and is entitled to millions more.

Today, Paul Sr. travels between his Quebec estate, his Montreal mansion and his Palm Beach property. True to form, when asked for an interview for this book, he politely declined through his assistant, who said, "Mr. Desmarais has very much enjoyed meeting with you in the past and has great respect but cannot see you in time for your deadline. He however wishes you every success."

PAUL HILL

The Hill Companies celebrated their 100th anniversary in 2003 as Saskatchewan's oldest continuing business operation. The family even sold the new province the site where Saskatchewan's legislative building was built.

Today, The Hill Companies has a single shareholder, Paul Hill, who has parlayed a small insurance business into a conglomerate. He owns interests in real estate in the U.S. and Canada, insurance, oil, manufacturing and broadcasting.

Even more interesting, he has remained headquartered in Regina, which has been afflicted by New Democrat regimes that have overtaxed, confiscated or bullied the private sector. In the 1940s and again in the 1970s, they drove out the oil industry with their excessive royalty rates. The industry began to return slowly after 2004, due to a combination of high oil prices and recognition, finally, by the government that the province had to match taxation in Alberta in order to attract economic activity.

"I never gave up on Saskatchewan, and this has been a wonderful place to raise kids," said Hill in an interview with me in 2006.

Paul Hill is an accomplished investor and entrepreneur. He is known to few outside his native province, but has slowly and steadily become a significant player in Canada. He's quiet and cautious in personality, but is a meticulous planner. I interviewed him for this book at a conference in Banff that he attends every year, taking voluminous notes during its dozen high-level business sessions.

Hill has been a soft-spoken booster for his province and is its most prominent businessman. But he is also a dual national. He was born in the United States and lived there for two years while his father attended Harvard University.

He is currently past chair of Crown Life, which he and a partner took 64% control of in 1991 for $250 million and sold in July 2007 for $850 million. He was also chair for 10 years and remains a shareholder of Boardwalk REIT, Canada's largest apartment landlord, with 33,000 units and a market value in 2007 of $2.35 billion.

But Hill mostly operates privately. His operating unit, Harvard Developments Inc., owns or manages 3.3 million square feet of real estate in Saskatchewan and 700,000 in Alberta, plus land banks such as Calgary's downtown Eau Claire area, which will be redeveloped into a massive condo-retail-entertainment-office centre.

"It's a failed piece of real estate development, but we're going to build condos, a hotel and offices in a redevelopment worth hundreds of millions," he said.

In the U.S., his Harvard Investments, Inc., based in Scottsdale, Arizona, develops planned communities. For instance, it is creating a 3,500-acre golf community with 1,600 custom-home sites in Arizona.

He also owns a recycling and packaging business that produces 55% of all the egg flats in the U.S. and Canada. The high

Canadian dollar has forced them to diversify manufacturing into the U.S. in addition to the Saskatchewan operation.

"It's a $28-million-a-year business and had made very good profits," he said.

And he got into Alberta's oil business, in the aftermath of the damaging National Energy Program. The NEP imposed huge taxes on foreign-owned companies and provided generous grants to Canadian-owned ones.

In 1981, Paul, his father, Fred, and California venture capitalist Neal Blue were able to buy, at a bargain-rate price, the subsidiary of U.S.-owned Tenneco Oil Co., which had decided to exit in a hurry. It is worth a fortune now. Blue also owns a uranium-processing company and defence contractor called General Atomic (GA Technologies) Corporation.

"That was just the right place, right time," said Hill.

But the Hills have been in the right places at the right times for a couple of centuries in the United States and Canada. They were immigrants from Northern Ireland who settled in southern Ontario. In 1899, Paul's ancestor Walter H.A. Hill moved to Saskatchewan as a teacher. He soon got into the insurance and real estate business with a partner. In those days, Saskatchewan was a bleak and remote place, but the railway had brought farmers and some prosperity.

His grandfather's cousin was James J. Hill, an American robber baron who had been involved with other Americans in the construction of the Canadian Pacific Railway. He bailed out when the fledgling Canadian government in Ottawa chose an all-Canadian route—a route that was too expensive to build. Eventually, American contractor William Cornelius Van Horne completed the project, which had to be completely subsidized by Ottawa.

The Northern Ireland immigrants in Canada—such as the Eatons and Richardsons—knew how to make money in the most difficult circumstances. And Walter Hill became the province's most successful businessman.

"I don't know how he survived," said Paul.

Walter Hill had four sons. Paul's father, Fred, was rejected by the Royal Canadian Air Force for health reasons. So he went to Harvard University for one year, then the United States got into the Second World War and he became a U.S. Army Air Force pilot. He returned to Harvard after the war and earned an MBA. Paul was born in 1945 in the U.S. and is the oldest of Fred's five children.

In 1947, Fred returned home to run the family's business interests.

"There was not much there," said Paul. "There was a small insurance agency and the building it was in. [Saskatchewan CCF Party premier] Tommy Douglas drove all the oil companies out of Saskatchewan. All the head offices had been there but went to Calgary. Imperial Oil had drilled 150 dry holes in Alberta, before its big discovery at Leduc, Alberta, because everyone thought all the oil was in Saskatchewan. Then the CCF took over our insurance company," he said.

Fred had already started a surety company, which put up bonds for construction companies, as a small joint venture. But it grew, and the Western Surety Company of Canada is now one of the country's biggest in its field.

The family had also owned, then sold, hundreds of acres around the Legislative Building. Fred Hill bought these back after the war, then developed them into a large community called Hillsdale. This became the basis for more property expansions in Regina and elsewhere.

Paul and his siblings grew up in Regina, but he opted to attend Georgetown University in Washington, DC, and the Richard Ivey School of Business in London, Ontario. After his MBA, he worked for the Burns family as an investment banker in Toronto. In 1976, he came back to Regina.

"My father and I bought TV stations from Michael Sifton, who thought they'd be forced to sell because they also owned Saskatchewan's newspapers. Then we sold them for a profit to CTV in 1987. Then we began buying radio stations, and I am still expanding this business. In 2006 and 2007, we got licences for new radio stations in Calgary, Saskatoon and Fort McMurray," he said.

Naturally, Paul was attracted in the 1970s by Calgary's oil boom. He began buying assets in 1979, then two years later along came the Tenneco opportunity. Tenneco put its US$150 million in oil assets on the block, but high interest rates, declining prices and new taxes on foreigners meant there were few buyers.

"We put up $10,000 in equity and got $150 million in loans from banks to Canadianize Tenneco," he said. "Today we own one-third of the equity [Neal Blue owns two-thirds]. This is now a significant company."

His stake is owned through Harvard Energy in Calgary, which has had revenues of up to $85 million a year and also owns small interests in 21 gas-processing facilities across the three westernmost provinces.

Paul and his wife, Carol, raised their five kids in Regina but now travel the world. These days Paul spends a great deal of time in Calgary and in Phoenix, Arizona, where he has real estate projects. But the family has homes in Regina, Lake of the Woods and Palm Springs, where he spends winters.

As Regina's leading businessman, he spearheaded the strategy during the 1990s to redevelop the city's sagging downtown by attracting head offices. In a bold move in 1991, he approached the Burns family in Toronto, whom he had once worked for, and, with a partner and with $240 million in provincial loan guarantees, bought 42% of Crown Life. One of the conditions of purchase was that the head office would relocate to Regina. Crown Life brought 1,250 high-paid jobs with it, which is why the government participated.

"This added 2% to the provincial GDP and 10% to the city's GDP overnight," Hill said. "It brought more white-collar jobs than any entity except the provincial government and was an important part of a 20-year redevelopment plan."

It was also reminiscent of past efforts by the Hills to attract people to the province.

"I guess you might say this is equivalent to my grandfather, who went down on the train and sat in the Royal York Hotel in Toronto, and made his calls and brought people to Saskatchewan,"

WHO OWNS CANADA NOW

said Hill in a newspaper interview at the time. "Well, we're bringing people to Saskatchewan again."

In 1999, Crown Life was sold to Canada Life, which, in turn, became part of Great-West Life. But the offices remain in Regina.

In 2007, Hill gave $10 million to the University of Regina business school, which is now named after him. His investment initiatives have recently been aimed mostly at Alberta's booming oil patch and at America's booming Arizona sunbelt retirement haven.

"We have 25 projects, such as residential subdivisions and planned communities, on the go down there," he said about Arizona. "In Canada, our real estate operations are in Saskatchewan and Alberta and are involved in developing residential, office and retail. Then there's our oil interests, which are significant. Go east? I don't think so. I'm a westerner and very happy doing business out here."

THE IRVINGS

New Brunswick is a company town owned by the Irving family. It was built into an empire by the late K.C. Irving and is now run by his three sons Jim, Arthur and John (Jack) Irving. But technically, ownership is held in a series of trusts in Bermuda, as stipulated by K.C., who became a resident of that tax haven in 1972. The three brothers and their two dozen children have been, since 2006, in the process of negotiating a division of assets and future incomes in order to go their own separate ways.

Kenneth Colin (K.C.) Irving was a stern, ruthless industrialist whose legacy of business practices and tax avoidance has created one of the world's richest families. In 1986, estimates were that the Irvings had about $2 billion in assets. *Forbes*, in 2006, estimated their net worth at US$5.8 billion precisely, but it's probably more like $15 billion or more, given the fact that their wealth is in oil operations and has accumulated for 20 years tax-free offshore. This wealth, when transferred, will incur no Canadian capital gains taxation either because it will consist of moving offshore ownership among offshore trusts. The heirs are also rich in their own right, and for a generation have received distributions from a series of Bermudian trusts that are untaxed in their hands under Canadian law.

The Irvings own many businesses, but the jewel in the crown has always been their ownership of the only privately owned, vertically integrated oil company in Canada. Irving Oil owns the largest gasoline station chain in eastern Canada and the northeastern U.S. in addition to wells, refineries, oil tankers and trading operations.

Their vast forestry holdings are integrated but unprofitable due to low lumber prices and the high Canadian dollar. They own dozens of mills and manufacturing operations and 6 million acres (or rights to it) in New Brunswick and Maine, an area six times the size of Prince Edward Island. They export lumber to the United States freely, without punitive tariffs or quotas, because their lands are freehold, not leased from provincial governments. Freehold properties were exempt from the softwood lumber dispute, but even though the Irving operations did not have to abide by quotas or taxes, the businesses still struggle.

The Irvings also own trucking companies, most of the province's media, a modern shipyard and the first deep-water terminal in the western hemisphere and are going to spend billions to build an LNG (liquified natural gas) operation and add more refining capacity to their site in Saint John, which already houses Canada's largest oil refinery, producing 300,000 barrels a day.

Roughly 1 out of every 12 residents of New Brunswick works for them, and the family enjoys inordinate political influence. Many fear the Irvings, and competitors have steered clear. The result is that New Brunswick does not have a vibrant, competitive economy, nor does it have a growing population. Worst of all, ownership of this empire is offshore. Essentially, the province is mostly foreign-owned.

Wallace McCain, head of that other famous New Brunswick clan, which built McCain Foods Ltd., remembers K.C. Irving fondly. He was best friends—and a fellow hellraiser—with Arthur Irving, and both Wallace and his brother, the late Harrison McCain, began their careers out of university working for the Irvings.

"We were part of the family and used to go to dinner there all the time," said Wallace in an interview with me in 2007. "K.C. was personable, a real gentleman. He was mostly a great salesman and a detail man with a great memory."

But the McCains went on their own and competed outside New Brunswick. Wallace now lives in Toronto.

The Irving empire has been divided into two main parts. The oldest son, Jim, runs the forestry, dry dock, trucking and frozen food businesses. The middle son, Arthur, runs the oil businesses. Jack ran the media and hardware businesses for years until he was sidelined with health problems, said McCain.

The three Irving sons are not as cunning or as dynamic as their father. And a new patriarch has not emerged to grow the dynasty and keep all the various relatives, and their ambitions, onside. However, there's little evidence of any dynastic decay. Despite their billions, the Irvings are still imbued with the Protestant work ethic. K.C.'s three sons live in modest homes, draw small salaries, and are listed in the Saint John telephone book. They travel mostly by commercial airline and lead low-key lives. It is a family that does not have—and would not tolerate—high-livers, playboys or layabouts.

Jim's five children work in the business, Arthur's three grown children are involved (he has a second family with a young child), and Jack's two sons are also involved. Wallace McCain said at one point that Arthur's son, Ken, a 35-year-old business whiz, would "probably take it all over." But internal power struggles between cousins have resulted in negotiations to divide the spoils.

The empire is pervasive. The Saint John headquarters open onto a graveyard, where rest the remains of hundreds of United Empire Loyalists who settled after the American Revolution. Beside the building is a familiar Maritime landmark: a red, white and blue Irving gasoline station. Across the street are the Irving newspapers and its television station. The refinery and port dominate the waterfront. This is Nation Irving.

Secrecy was sacrosanct to the family. In the mid-1970s, the Royal Commission on Corporate Concentration (the Bryce Commission) came close to suing the family for failing to provide basic financial information, saying its run-in with the Irvings was "a vivid illustration of the deficiencies in the law, which should be remedied."

The family fiercely fought politicians who wanted to bring in campaign finance limits and disclosure laws, but they eventually lost in the 1980s.

In 1982, Arthur was belligerent under subpoena to testify before the Restrictive Trade Practices Commission's inquiry into oil competition.

"No," he said to the first query, according to transcripts, when asked to confirm Irving Oil information. Asked why not, he replied, "Why should I?" and said he would not return to the inquiry. He did not.

The Irvings kept ownership of their media monopoly secret for 12 years, then, when ordered by Ottawa to divest some holdings, they fought all the way to the Supreme Court of Canada—and won.

In the 1970s, the Royal Commission on Newspapers, under Tom Kent, took another look at concentration of ownership in the media, commenting that "Irving papers are noteworthy for their obeisance to every industrial interest. They are not known for probing investigations into pollution, occupational health dangers, industrial wastes, or any of the other darker consequences of industrial power."

When asked about cross-ownership in the media, Arthur Irving responded to a royal commission, "I own 40 per cent of CHSJ [a television station, since renamed CBAT] and I intend to keep it. It is our privilege to own it, and nobody in this God-given room is going to take it away from us."

Their tough-minded attitude has not softened. In 2007 a former Irving employee launched an independent newspaper and had his home searched by police on complaints that he had taken confidential information. When asked about this heavy-handedness, Jim (J.K.) Irving told the *Globe and Mail*, in a rare interview in November 2007, "We like to get along with everybody down home. Nobody likes to be nasty."

Clearly, the Irving ethos for years has been rooted in the tough, hardscrabble background of this family of Scots. K.C. was born in 1889 in Buctouche, an Acadian village that lived on oyster fishing and rum-running during Prohibition. His father was a Scottish immigrant who made a small fortune running a general store and sawmill.

K.C. loved mechanics and became a pilot in the First World War. He then set off for Australia but got only as far as Vancouver before returning in 1923. He sold cars, opened a dealership and then opened a gasoline station for Imperial Oil. After a falling-out, he launched his own chain, with money from his father.

He built the stations on his own, then began building houses. When Imperial Oil leaned on Canadian National Railway to charge their rival K.C. more for shipping his oil, he built his own fleet of barges and trucks. From there, he got into shipbuilding and truck-parts manufacturing. Then he made a deal with Chevron Corp. to build his own refinery so that he could control supplies to his stations.

Forestry was the same story. K.C. inherited a big business and made it gigantic. In 1941, he obtained control of the New Brunswick Railway to own its million acres of timberland, then bought customers such as newspapers, hardware stores and building-supply factories. He made a fortune during the Second World War supplying wood and other material to the military effort, in part due to contracts from his friend Lord Beaverbrook, a fellow New Brunswicker who served in Winston Churchill's wartime cabinet.

In 1979, Revenue Canada took on Irving Oil and its Bermuda connection for what is known as "transfer pricing." The accusation was that for six years an Irving company offshore was charging its Canadian parent $142 million more for oil than it should have done in order to book more profit in Bermuda, tax-free. The Irvings won.

Litigious and acquisitive, the Irvings have never rested. But nobody knows the scale of their holdings. By 2007, there were dozens of members of the third and fourth and fifth generations, trust-fund kids who never have to work but who do anyway.

They still run the province as if it is their own fiefdom

and use their leverage to their advantage, just as K.C. did. For instance, when Irving Oil won huge tax concessions from Saint John's city council to create a petroleum and petrochemical cluster, the publisher of the Saint John *Telegraph-Journal* lavishly praised the deal.

The publisher was Jamie Irving, the oldest fifth-generation Irving family member. And the tax break was at the request of Kenneth Irving, president of Irving Oil and the man some see as the heir apparent of the fourth-generation Irvings. It was a fitting outcome for New Brunswick Inc. and its first family that runs just about everything that matters, including public policy.

THE JODREYS

The Jodreys are quietly rich, and that's the way they like it. Their companies are mostly private and operate in obscure B2B (business-to-business) markets.

But their wealth is huge and has been accumulated over three generations. In 2007, David Hennigar, grandson of patriarch Roy Jodrey, agreed to meet me for an interview in Toronto in 2007 at the Four Seasons Hotel. He's a likable but serious businessman with a sly sense of humour—his e-mail address begins with "codfather."

"I don't think we'll ever go public," he said when asked. "We have interests in public companies, but we prefer to operate our own companies privately, because we don't have to answer to public shareholders. We can do things quietly and efficiently and don't have to meet quarterly-earnings forecasts."

The family's interests have grown organically as well as through acquisitions. What are your "empire's" overall revenues? I asked.

"I don't have to tell you," he said, chuckling.

Your assets?

"No comment, but 'A' for effort in trying to find out," was his rejoinder.

What is more or less known, however, is that companies that the Jodreys own outright or have sizable stakes in employ 40,000 people in Canada and the U.S. and involve billions in assets.

The family holding company, Scotia Investments Limited, owns about a dozen private corporations involved in forestry, packaging, real estate development, waste collection (in eastern Canada and the southeastern U.S.) and other sectors.

It also owns portions of several public companies: more than 10% in Extendicare REIT (real estate investment trust), more than 10% in Assisted Living Concepts (nursing homes) in the U.S., 13% of Algoma Central in partnership with the Jackman family and 47.5% of the voting shares in frozen seafood processor High Liner Foods Incorporated. The family also owns 50% of a metal manufacturer in Honduras and a large real estate play in Montserrat.

Patriarch Roy Jodrey had 3 children: John, Jean and Florence. These 3 had 12 children and those 12, in turn, have had another 26 offspring, for a total of 38 Jodrey heirs and heiresses. Only 4 members of the family—Roy Jodrey's elderly son John and 3 grandsons— work in the family businesses.

"There is one representative from each [sibling] family on the board of Scotia Investments Limited," said David Hennigar.

Hennigar represents his mother, Jean Jodrey Hennigar; George Bishop represents his mother, Florence Jodrey Bishop; and Bruce Jodrey is John's son. Other directors are current patriarch John Jodrey and three outside directors, for a total of seven.

The family is a cohesive unit, thanks to the founder's philosophy.

"We have equal shares, more or less, and our philosophy is to keep the pool of capital together to enable us to do more effective management of the money," said Hennigar. "In that context, we've structured it in a way that, hopefully, will negate the need to go public."

Hennigar is an investment banker who worked for years with the Burns Investment Group. In 1994, he launched Acadian Securities Inc. with partners in Halifax. His cousin Bruce went straight from high school into the family forestry/packaging business. George is a chartered accountant who has also taught at Acadia University for many years.

The three cousins divide responsibilities and get along well. David is chairman of High Liner and of Assisted Living Centres; George is president of the family holding company, Scotia, and is on High Liner's board. Bruce is chair of the family holding company, president of CKF (a vertically integrated packaging and paper-plate maker) and on Algoma's board. Algoma is the largest Canadian shipping company in the Great Lakes and St. Lawrence Seaway.

David also sits on the board of the Sobey-controlled Crombie REIT, which contains the Halifax assets they used to share with the Sobeys, and he has been lead underwriter for Sobey stock market issues for decades.

"John Jodrey is still very much involved. He's in his early 90s now and has been an operator since the early 1930s. He ran a gas station as his first job," he said. "We get along. Some days we count the votes, and some days we weigh them."

Their Scotia empire is quite large and extensive. Extendicare is worth $1.5 billion in market capitalization, and its sister U.S. company, Assisted Living Concepts, based in Milwaukee, Wisconsin, is worth another US$525 million. The two operate 435 residences with 35,000 beds.

Scotia's website describes the company as a "private investment holding company incorporated in 1945" and "owned by the Jodrey family of Nova Scotia." It lists its business interests: "paper (linerboard, corrugated packaging and papercores), food processing and manufacturing, transportation, real estate development, environmental and waste treatment industries, medical biotechnologies, and health care."

Its Annapolis Group develops residential communities. Avon Valley operates 1.2 million square feet of greenhouse capacity, growing flowers, fruits and vegetables for canning. They own Stokely-Van Camp of Canada Inc., which makes products under the labels of Stokely, Van Camp, Gatorade and Graves, as well as Ben's bread and Moirs chocolates. In 1985, the family obtained

67% of Hardee Farms, adding four canneries to the Jodrey empire and giving it a major agricultural foothold in central Canada.

It is hard to know what the family is worth, because everything is privately held, apart from the nursing homes, Algoma and High Liner.

High Liner used to be called National Sea and was part of a four-way fishery restructuring undertaken in 1983 by Ottawa and the Bank of Nova Scotia. The Jodreys participated, and in 2007 High Liner bought a division from Newfoundland's Fishery Products International, sold to British interests.

The Jodreys also jointly controlled Halifax Developments until the early 1990s, then sold their share to the Sobeys.

"Its biggest asset was tax loss carry-forwards, and the Sobeys could use it, not us, so they bought us out for around $20 million," said Hennigar.

The patriarch was a savvy investor. Back in 1973, when Roy died, the family's fortune was estimated at $300 million, which would be worth roughly $2 billion in equivalent 2007 dollars. In 1977, just one firm, Minas Basin Lumber Co., with 40,000 acres of woodlands, had assets of $800 million and no debts.

The current patriarch, John, was born in 1911, and was an only child. He inherited his father's frugality, passion for privacy, and business smarts. A tentative talker, he belies the image of the buzz-saw businessman, whether a fast-talking used car salesman like Jimmy Pattison or a verbose financier like Conrad Black. John Jodrey is a man of few words, making every single one all the more valuable.

His father, Roy, was the son of a Gaspereau Valley cabinet-maker who left school at 13 but ultimately became a director of more companies than any other man in Canada at the time—a total of 15 corporations, according to one Canadian magazine.

Like the Sobeys in tiny Stellarton, the Jodreys built their empire out of Hantsport, a town of 1,395 residents 40 miles northwest of Halifax.

This is where, snuggled in the scenic Annapolis Valley, Roy began by growing apples. He quickly decided there was more money in farming trees than apples, so be began buying timber-lands. In the 1920s, he founded Minas Basin Lumber and Power Co., after reading a book about hydroelectricity. He bought more land with timber and powerful rivers, and built his own dam to supply cheap power for a pulp mill.

His power stations were eventually expropriated for a small fortune by the provincial utility, and those proceeds bankrolled his first stock market investments. In 1929, he was nearly wiped out in the crash, but during the Depression he continued to reinvest spare cash into land for his farming and pulp businesses.

Property he paid pennies for in the 1930s became the basis of another fortune. He signed a deal with Scott Paper in Pennsylva-nia to sell the lion's share of pulp from the Hantsport Minas mill, which generated its own cheap electricity. Whatever Scott did not buy was made into egg cartons and paper plates and cups, across the street from the pulp mill. Almost all of Canada's cardboard egg cartons are still made here, as are most of the moulded plates, the Royal Chinet line and packaging used by McDonald's Restaurants and others.

During the Second World War, Roy met Charles Burns, a Toronto investment banker stationed there while in the Royal Cana-dian Air Force. The two became pals and partners. They acquired control of Crown Life, which was eventually sold, and the nursing-home chain that is now divided into two entities with a total value of $2 billion. Burns also led him into Bay Street's back rooms and to other successes.

Roy kept notes, as did newspaper magnate Roy Thomson. Jodrey's little black book contained impressions of people as well as facts and figures. He was obviously a person who could size up people and prospects in a minute, and profit from both.

"Jodrey used to come to Montreal and Toronto to pick the brains of bankers and brokers, go into the men's room after a con-versation, and write it all down. Then he'd go back to Hantsport and make a fortune," said Robert Macintosh, head in the 1980s of the Canadian Bankers Association in an interview in 1995 with me.

Hennigar, his grandson, is also a cautious, reserved fellow with an arch sense of humour.

"My grandfather had a dictum we haven't necessarily followed," he said, "that if you are the number-one or number-two shareholder in a company, you do not have to be involved with any management problems. Nice idea, but it doesn't always work out that way."

JIMMY PATTISON

Jimmy Pattison proves that nice guys do not finish last. In little more than five decades, he has parlayed a Vancouver car dealership into a conglomerate with, in 2006, $6.3 billion in sales, 29,000 direct employees, $5 billion in assets and no debt on a net basis. The Jim Pattison Group was Canada's 60th-largest corporation and it is a 100% sole proprietorship.

He also has 25% of Canfor Corp., the world's largest lumber producer and Canada's 96th-largest corporation, with 2006 revenues of $3.8 billion, assets of $4.6 billion, profits of $471.8 million and 7,900 employees.

Pattison met me in 2007 for an interview in the posh Vancouver Club. He picked me up at my hotel in his white Cadillac and we drove around the back to a delivery driveway behind the club. The staff greeted him like a war hero, and we walked in through the kitchen and pantry to the dining room above.

There are no airs and graces about Pattison, including the fact that everybody calls him "Jimmy." He's proud of having started off as a used car salesmen. He works for fun and has a friendly, inquisitive nature. He's deeply religious but not preachy, and has earmarked most profits to charities, not to his three children and nine grandchildren, when he eventually goes to that Big Car Dealership in the Sky.

"If I'm hit by a bus, everything is all set. I don't discuss details, but nothing has to get sold. We review it all every year, of course," he said.

Pattison has always insisted that his children be financially self-reliant. Like Warren Buffett, who has given away all his billions to the Bill & Melinda Gates Foundation, Pattison is a meritocrat. Buffett has said that passing wealth along from one generation to another is as foolish as selecting the next Olympic athletes on the basis that one of their parents won a gold medal. Jimmy has yet another take on inheritances.

"I don't think it's right to take away a sense of self-accomplishment from children. Some [inheritors] in the second and third generation have done all right being given things. But not many," he said.

This attitude, along with his accomplishments and philanthropy, is what sets Jimmy apart from the rest.

"I really can't tell you what it's like to be this rich," he said. "I never have worked for money. I worked because it's fun—fun growing businesses, fun seeing people with me prosper and develop. I have some toys, the plane, the boat and Frank Sinatra's house."

The Sinatra estate is in Palm Springs, has 32 bathrooms and a theatre, and is used as a mini conference centre by the Pattison Group and its customers. Pattison also enjoys hosting five-hour dinner cruises in his gigantic powerboat for dozens of guests. The boat crawls along the scenic coast and drops anchor, and dinner is served. On the way home, Pattison sets up seats theatre-style in the ship's massive lounge, then invites guests to share four minutes on any subject.

On one of several voyages I have been invited on, he pointed out a yellow-frame beach house to me from the deck of the ship.

"That was the first house I bought when I was selling cars," he told me. "I put a tenant in the basement to help pay off the mortgage."

Today, the Jim Pattison Group sells everything from cars and groceries to billboards, packaging expertise, haunted houses, fish, coal and forest products. "I became a conglomerate because I was a car dealer and every seven years was a downturn in the forestry cycle. I couldn't control the product, its design, price or the economy, so I had to figure out how to balance my business. So I got into leasing, then radio and other things—never with any part-ners," he said.

"We had to advertise on radio, and so we went into broad-casting, then to electric signs. Electric signs got us into manufactur-ing and leasing. Then we got into billboards because we knew how to get sign permits," he said.

He entered the food business through grocery chain Over-waitea, then became involved in packaging. Magazine distribution was related to advertising and media, and his acquisition of Ripley's Believe It or Not museums led to his buying Sinatra's spread.

"The common thread is that we know about serving cus-tomers and retail from the car-dealership business," he said. "If someone offered us a nuclear power plant, we'd say no, because we don't understand that. And we looked at high-tech but didn't understand that either."

He also has declined stakes in oil, gold mines and China ("because I don't like the food"). Real estate is an interest, in a minor way, but, he says, "we're in operating businesses in the right place at the right time hopefully."

His Protestant work ethic is as legendary as is his moral backbone. Back in 1986, in the prequel to this book, he told me that he would fire the least successful car salesmen in his dealer-ship every month.

"Keeping people who are not doing well isn't about charity. I did them a favour. They weren't good at selling cars, and some of them went on to other jobs and did very well," he said.

He works 7 days a week, 12 hours a day except for week-ends, year round, and has kept his enthusiam to build new enter-prises. There's no sign of a slowdown.

"In the last 20 years, the new biz for us is the packaging biz. We make containers, polystyrene, laminated tubes. We have 21 factories in the U.S. and have a high market share there through acquisition and growth," he said over dinner in 2007. "We make cups, plates, bowls, creamers. It's highly automated, but we have 2,000 employees."

Diversity reflects Pattison's career. He cut his teeth helping his father go door to door "de-mothing" pianos for $2 per session. He later sold everything from garden seed to adhesive tape before getting into the auto business, first as a car washer and then as a salesman. His entry into the car business sped him on his way, and by 39 years of age he was a millionaire. From there, investments were progressive.

The dot-com phenomenon?

"We dodged that bullet," he said. "We're conservative and never understood any of it."

Pattison's companies are all private. He owns sizable stakes in public companies besides Canfor, but he will not say which ones.

"I prefer a private company. That way you can hide your mistakes," he said. "And I've made every one of them. I'm surprised we're even here with all the mistakes I've made. That includes strategy, operations, people, financing."

The group operates out of a building in Vancouver with a breathtaking view of West Vancouver and the harbour. Its portfolio of companies in the U.S. and Canada is monitored by 8 executives and a total of 120 employees. About 40% of the operations are in the U.S., and companies are in 23 sectors.

Pattison's inner circle consists of legal, dealmaking, banking, trading, accounting and real estate specialists, plus Maureen Chant, a talented executive who joined him decades ago as a junior employee. Now she "does everything," he said, which means handling administration, logistics, customer complaints and public events.

"We all spend a lot of time on airplanes," he said.

Canada is not as attractive economically as it should be, and Pattison has been a generous contributor to politicians he believes can make a difference.

"You do not find the anti-American tone in western Canada as you find in some other parts of the country. But this is a worry going forward," he said. "When it comes to the country's future, I would like to see our productivity improve. I would like to see a major push to improve our relationship with the U.S. I think we need to be more competitive as managers in Canada. Everyone tends to blame the unions, but improvements have to start with management. Having worked on both sides of the border, it's clear to me that American management works harder than Canadian management."

Lower taxation is also essential to economic growth, as the flight of people and capital out of BC to Alberta during the high-taxation New Democrat regime demonstrated. The current business climate in BC improved with the election of Gordon Campbell, a conservative in the provincial Liberal Party.

"We're not travelling as much since 9/11 as we were. The scandals there have been very upsetting. It's just awful when you have people putting their life savings and pension money with people who let them down," Pattison said. "I go to church and was raised in the Christian way, but look at how attitudes have changed. The world's changed. There was always change, but today the difference is its speed."

Pattison's advice has always been to quickly shift gears.

"I've had an airline and teams, hockey and baseball, but I'm not planning on owning any more," he said. "It's much cheaper to buy box seats. Heck, ownership takes the fun out of it. When I was an owner, I'd call in to see how things were but I wouldn't ask what the score was: I'd ask what the attendance was. That's no fun."

Despite his wealth and competitiveness, Pattison has never considered going offshore for tax purposes.

"This is my home. To go live some place to save taxes never crossed my mind once. All the good things happened to me here," he said. "No matter where I travel, even if it's raining in Vancouver when I arrive back, I always say this is the best part of the trip."

GERRY SCHWARTZ AND HEATHER REISMAN

Gerry Schwartz went to a technical high school in Winnipeg and became a certified auto mechanic before attending university, law school and then Harvard Business School. "My dad wanted me to have something to fall back on," said Schwartz in an interview in 2004 with me in his elegant Toronto office.

He went from Harvard to Wall Street and New York's Bear, Stearns. There, he worked under Jerome Kohlberg, along with the young Henry Kravis and George Roberts. In 1976, those three launched Kohlberg Kravis Roberts & Co. Schwartz started a similar operation in Winnipeg called CanWest Capital, with Izzy Asper.

"I wanted to come back to Canada. That was the largest motivation," he said. "Izzy was my closest friend. He saw me when I was in New York. He had finished with politics and law, and we wanted to work together. So we formed CanWest as a 50-50 venture, in 1977. The first thing we bought was a television station in Toronto called Global Television. He and I were the closest persons to each other for years. We spent 18 hours a day together and did everything except sleep together. We had adjoining offices and would shout at each other all day."

The partnership was successful but tempestuous. In 1984, Schwartz struck out on his own to Toronto and started Onex Corporation with his $2-million nest egg.

By 2006, Onex had become Canada's 15th-largest enterprise, with $25 billion in revenues, $23 billion in assets, more than $1 billion in profits and 240,000 employees. It went public in April 1987 at $20 a share and collapsed to $8 in October of that year. Since then it has split, and that $8 share would be worth $134 in September 2007.

"We had to work our way out of the market landslide," Schwartz said. "And we did then what we do now, and that is stay steady and stable, one foot in front of another."

Onex was a pioneer in Canada. It was a long-term, value investor that worked with attractive companies, as did Warren Buffett and his Berkshire Hathaway. And it has become a giant.

By 2007, Onex's eclectic portfolio of 16 subsidiaries manufactured electronic components, aircraft, plane parts and communications equipment, and were in health care, entertainment, real estate, warranty underwriting, customer-care outsourcing and personal care products; and ONCAP invests and mentors mid-sized corporations in a range of industries.

Over the years, Schwartz and his team have bought nearly 200 enterprises, sold dozens and posted annual investment returns of more than 28%, rivalling Warren Buffett's.

"We bought companies we could build, as opposed to buying companies, then doing financial engineering," he said. "We have taken half a dozen from $200 million in revenues when we bought them to $3 billion, $5 billion or $9 billion in revenues."

He has also remained steadfast to his investment model, despite fads.

"I've always been a value investor, so when the dot-com market occurred, I didn't understand it. All the precepts of value I grew up with disappeared, and I began to wonder if I should stay in business or not," he said.

What is unique about Schwartz is that he and his wife, Heather Reisman, are a super-partnership. The two run businesses, are connectors and are politically influential. Reisman is a key Onex director and partner, and a business builder in her own right. She is CEO of Indigo Books & Music, Inc., Canada's 339th-largest corporation in 2006, with 6,000 employees and sales of $849 million.

Reisman was born in Montreal and, like Schwartz, had a successful mother as a role model—she ran a chic boutique in Montreal. Schwartz's mother was the first Jewish female lawyer in western Canada.

They married in 1982 and Reisman settled into Toronto's business world as a consultant, corporate director, then CEO of Cott Corporation, a maker of private-label carbonated beverages. In 1996, she launched Indigo and began consolidating the country's booksellers. Reading and books are passions, and she has referred to herself as Indigo's "chief book lover."

Schwartz's passion is sailing, and his life has been very much an adventure based on going wherever the winds blow if the destination makes sense. From tinkering with cars and helping his father's auto-parts business, he became a lawyer who was involved in politics, as were his mother and grandmother, a pioneering female (and socialist) activist in Winnipeg. He paused to practise law for a while, then set sail for Harvard, Wall Street and home again.

"I went to law school because I didn't know what else to do. In those days you could just sign up to go. I probably wouldn't get in today," he said. "I talked my way into practising law with Izzy Asper, but then left for Harvard because law was not a portable occupation and I wanted to leave Winnipeg."

Today, Schwartz and Reisman have it all: a great lifestyle, homes in many ports of call, such as Nantucket Island and Beverly Hills, and a varied business and family life. All of their four children live in the United States. They have a collective total of seven grandchildren.

Of this, Schwartz once remarked to me, "This is very disappointing for us. We never have kids wandering in on a Friday night or Saturday afternoon. It's also disappointing to me, as a Canadian, to see four talented, educated people leave the country permanently."

Schwartz is a nationalist who left Wall Street to build Canadian-based Onex. And it is very much his creation. In the beginning, Schwartz was the captain, finding and doing the deals. He owns 67.6% of Onex's voting shares, and is now more of a mentor to his talented crew. In an interview with me in April 2004, he distilled Onex's DNA.

"Being bigger isn't the issue. We have spent 20 years building this incredible platform of human intellectual capital," he said. "The average tenure here is 12 years. Same in New York City, where the last employee left 8 years ago. And our strategy is simple. We only invest in companies headquartered in North America, where we speak the language, know the customs, understand the law and accounting and can get to it quickly. We have always bought control in the past, but not necessarily in the future."

Onex raises billions annually to cherry-pick lucrative sectors. Its team sees the global "deal stream," or what is for sale everywhere. Two-thirds of its assets are outside Canada, mostly in the United States, and both flags hang above the Onex boardroom table in Toronto.

Onex is now on every big private equity player's list of potential partners to undertake those mega-deals. In 2006 and 2007, Onex was part of consortia that made high-profile bids for Qantas Airways, Bell Canada and DaimlerChrysler.

The Onex team consists of 50 key accounting, investment, financial and top-notch legal professional partners. Turnover is minimal and the atmosphere is collegial.

Its Toronto headquarters are in a sterile bank tower, but inside, Onex is law-firm lavish, with faux French windows, ornate mouldings and fireplaces and lots of art and antiques. Both Gerry and Heather are attractive, friendly people who avoid publicity as much as possible.

Schwartz sees Onex's future as more of the same.

"There are more competitors in what we are doing because there's so much capital around, but we still look for businesses we can build," he said. "Years from now we will be doing the same thing, but the businesses we own have to adjust to changes in the world, such as today's volatile credit markets and tomorrow's Asia power," he said.

In August 2007, just after debt markets reeled from the sub-prime scandal, Onex closed a US$5.6-billion deal with the Carlyle Group to buy General Motors' Allison Transmission.

"Obviously, Asia and China are in their plans," he said.

Schwartz operates Onex much like a law firm. The flow chart is flat. Managing directors identify deals and sit on boards for Onex: Anthony Munk (investment banker), Peter Munk's son; Tim Duncanson (Harvard MBA); Ewout Heersink (CA); Mark Hilson (Harvard MBA); Robert Le Blanc (NYU MBA); Anthony Melman (a strategist and PhD in finance from South Africa); Seth Mersky (an American banker and accountant); Andrew Sheiner (Harvard MBA); and Nigel Wright (a Canadian and a Harvard-trained lawyer).

"I love the work and I love the people. It's intellectually exciting all the time," Schwartz said. "I think my strengths are good commonsense judgment. I'm a cheerleader, a natural optimist, analytically rigorous but not confrontative. I hate confrontation, which is a bad characteristic for an executive. Around here, they always say if you want to fire somebody, don't send Schwartz. He'll give the person a raise."

JACKS OF ALL TRADES

These individuals have not built conglomerates, but have personally operated and invested in many types of businesses. Sometimes they have been involved in public companies, sometimes in private ones. They hold minority positions but carry much influence with managements or other shareholders. They are often good at collaborations and partnerships and are jacks of all trades. They move easily and profitably from one asset class, sector and industry to another. They purposely place their eggs in more than one basket, and they take risks but rarely experience deleterious effects.

Each man profiled here has a very different personality and style. They are all charming and gracious but are tough negotiators. Unlike the other entrepreneurs profiled here, all were raised in relative prosperity and had successful fathers or families. In that respect, they are second-generation entrepreneurs who have parlayed whatever they were given to new, greater heights. Of the four, two inherited sizable fortunes or businesses while two did not.

These men also share other traits. They have an ability to hunt out niches and are astute observers of people and their characteristics, foibles and pluses. All four are quietly, but certainly, competitive in nature and yet low-key, unconcerned about being at the centre of attention. They prefer to operate below the radar. Most significantly, each one has mastered all facets of business, from marketing to taxation, commodity cycles, financial products, economic trends, politics, value determinants and risk evaluation. They sense opportunities. They seize them. They are artists of the balance sheet and masters of the stock, property and debt markets.

JOSEPH BURNETT

Joe Burnett made his first million at 21 but used to drive from his penthouse in Ottawa to law school in an old second-hand car.

"My father said, 'You are going to get an education no matter how much money you've got,' so I went to law school," he said in an interview in 2007 in Toronto. "I lived in the Rockcliffe Arms and drove a fabulous car. But I bought a 1938 Chevrolet junker to take to school. I didn't want to stick it in the eyes of the students that I had money."

Burnett continues to mute his wealth, which is considerable. He made fortunes in the produce business, then as a lender, money manager, retailer and developer, and now running his own hedge fund. His brother, Ted, is a partner, and Joe's children are involved in the business. Daughter Gail runs Royal de Versailles, an upscale jewellery boutique on Bloor Street in Toronto, and sons Lorne and Sheldon manage the family billions out of an unmarked low-rise office building in midtown Toronto. It's probably Canada's largest privately owned hedge-fund operation.

Headquarters for Burnac Corporation is a 10-storey red-brick building on St. Clair Avenue West. The top 5 floors are condos. Flat-screen televisions decorate the walls everywhere, and Joe Burnett's office is flanked by glass-encased wine coolers storing some of his vintage collection. He must have the only office in Canada with a granite island, crystal glassware and wet bar for tastings. Burnett's dress and deportment, like his office, are meticulous. He talks slowly, articulates every word and constructs his conversations as carefully as a contract. Swarthy and slim, he wears large horn-rimmed spectacles and bespoke tailoring.

Burnett is a controversial businessman who tangled with Revenue Canada for nine years in court but eventually won in 1991. Along the way, he was dragged through the journalistic mud and ever since has quietly gone about doing business. The Burnett name surfaces only in relationship to philanthropic gifts.

He was born in 1936 to immigrant parents.

"I'm Ukrainian and Jewish. My mother converted," he said. "There are three of us, me and Ted the youngest. Brother Jack lives in Argentina."

His father, also Jack Burnett, launched a produce business and acquired soft-drink franchises with his brother Louis. Joe and his brothers worked there as youngsters, but at 16 years of age Joe quit because he couldn't get along with his uncle Louis.

He had worked most summers in northern Ontario, and through connections there found out about an available produce business in Rouyn-Noranda in Quebec. He borrowed $10,000 from his mother, bought it, then hired a local to run the operation while he was in high school. The business grew, landing a contract to supply fruits and vegetables to northern mining and lumber camps and then to the federal government's Distant Early Warning (DEW) Line camps.

"In two years my company was twice as big as my father's was. During this time, I got a BA at the U of T [University of Toronto] and then finished law school in 1964," he said.

He joined Toronto law firm Gotfrid, Dennis.

"I was not sure I liked law, listening to everyone else's problems. It was not so interesting to me," he said.

In 1967, he also got into the mortgage-lending business with money from wealthy Jewish families in Winnipeg, Toronto and Montreal. By 1970, the fund was $80 million and he quit the law firm. At the same time, he expanded his produce business by acquiring competitors, including his father's business.

"I became the largest independent produce operator in Canada," he said.

Next came a 50-50 partnership to manage money in Canada with a huge life insurance company, Chicago's CAN Financial Corporation, which owned Paul Revere and other insurers. In 1974, the company ran into heavy weather, along with others, due to high interest rates and a recession.

Burnett entered into a workout arrangement with the First National Bank of Chicago, swapped his equity to get out from under debts, found a loophole in Canada's Income Tax Act to avoid some taxes and emerged relatively unscathed.

In 1976 he created Burnac, an acronym for Burnett North American Corp., and shifted from mortgage lending to property acquisitions.

"I was involved in real estate valuations as a lender, and during this period of time when interest rates began to soar, into the early 1980s, I realized real estate was a bargain," he said.

By 1978, he owned 74 shopping centres in Ontario and Quebec, 2 in Chicago and 2 in the state of Connecticut. Then another recession hit, and in 1981 a phone call led him to devise a new business plan, which involved merging his produce and real estate holdings. A mortgage lender called him for help. The man had loaned $14 million to a shopping-centre developer in Quebec, but there were problems after the lead tenant, Dominion Stores, backed out after being taken over by Quebec grocery chain Provigo.

"I took over the mortgage on the unfinished shopping centre, but we needed a food store as an anchor tenant to replace Dominion Stores and attract more tenants. I went back to Provigo, and they said okay but demanded $1 million in fixturing [shelving and in-store fixtures], so I said, 'I'll show you. I'll open a food store,'" he recalled.

Burnett's produce business in Ottawa had also developed into a small chain called Carousel Farms, which sold produce, cheese and meats. To this base, he recruited a team of grocery execs from Dominion Stores who were about to lose their jobs.

"I went to the bank and said, 'Put up the money for this venture. If it works, it's mine for $1. If it doesn't work, it's yours.' I also got three mortgages for other sites I owned," he said.

Burnett and his team created Quebec's first full-service discount grocery store, called it Super Carnaval and opened it along with the mall in January 1983.

"Our store was an unbelievable success," said Burnett. "We had 24 registers and within one year went from $465,000 a week to $700,000 a week in sales. We couldn't handle it all. It was only 50,000 square feet. We doubled its size, and sales, then sold the shopping centre. I was paid a commission of $6 million by the lender and got the store for $1."

Burnac then acquired two more malls in the Quebec City area and put Super Carnavals in each.

"We had three stores in Quebec City and 28% of the region's food-dollar market. This was in a city with 600,000 population and with 20% unemployment," he said. "But we had the right ingredients for success, and so I took our team to Montreal to do more stores. We eventually had 18 stores, all beautiful, clean discount stores. We had 9 to 10% margin on sales, and every time I built a store, I built a shopping centre around it."

Burnett's success attracted grocery rivals Steinberg Inc. and independent Métro-Richelieu. In May 1987, Steinberg's CEO, Irving Ludmer, approached Burnett to buy Super Carnaval, but Joe walked out of negotiations at the eleventh hour when Ludmer balked at paying for two new stores under construction.

Burnett saw Métro-Richelieu's board of directors the next morning and struck a deal in hours. He would keep the underlying real estate and hold 25-year escalator leases for the stores. That night, he paid a visit to the intractable Ludmer to tell him he'd lost out.

Burnett has been enjoying life and selling his real estate holdings. But in 2001, his oldest son, Sheldon, a Florida-based lawyer, convinced him to give him $100 million to invest and booked returns of 17% annually after three years.

"Then he brought this deal: two banks offered us an opportunity to borrow money at a fraction of the Bank of Canada or Fed Reserve rate in U.S. or LIBOR [London Interbank Offered Rate], in any currency and get nine times [the] capital," he said. "I said, 'Three times is fine, and we invest 75% of the money in triple-A bonds and make a fortune.' It's astronomical—many billions of dollars. We're a hedge fund."

In 2007, his younger son, Lorne, an experienced investment banker, launched a family equities fund.

Both sons work alongside their dad, as does their uncle Ted. But Joe will be commuting between his Toronto mansion and another on Paradise Island in Nassau. He now has five grandchildren and enjoys fine wine, fine food and excursions on his 60-foot powerboat. He is buying a new corporate jet and a new boat. And at 70, he fully appreciates his good fortune.

"It's about keeping score, not about making money anymore. We have more than enough," he said. "It's incredible to me. And it's all ours."

ALVIN LIBIN

One of the most successful individuals in Alberta is not an oil man. Alvin Libin is the son of an immigrant baker who has spent the last 50 years astutely and conservatively managing the wealth he inherited.

His offices, in a penthouse atop one of the Bow Valley Square towers in Calgary, are exquisitely decorated with sculptures, rare wood veneer and columns. He is an elegant, well-appointed man who quietly sits at the centre of Calgary's dynamic business community. He manages a wide-ranging portfolio of rental properties, ranchland, oil companies, nursing homes and hotel assets.

"We are investors and don't run businesses," he said in an interview over dinner at the Palliser Hotel. "I keep it low-key. I'm conservative and not highly levered. Why? It's because we inherited money, so we had something to lose. We are protective."

Over the years Libin has partnered with some of Canada's most successful business people, in and out of the oil patch. He is involved in nursing homes with Nova Scotia's Jodrey family, in oil and ranching with Doc Seaman, and is a close friend and partner with Canada's richest oil man, Murray Edwards, whose offices are beside Libin's. Edwards, Libin and Seaman each own a chunk of the Calgary Flames hockey team, with others such as Clay Riddell, and rarely miss games.

"I invest alongside Murray. He's very smart," Libin commented.

Libin and the Jodreys own 13% of $1.5-billion Extendicare REIT as well as 13% of its sister U.S. company, the US$525-million Assisted Living Concepts, Inc.. Libin has roughly 10% of each.

Extendicare operates 235 long-term care (nursing home) facilities in North America with more than 26,800 beds. It also offers rehabilitation services and employs 34,000 in both countries.

Assisted Living Concepts is a leader in the growing trend of providing residences that provide meals, housing, services and social/recreational activities for healthier elderly people. That company was listed in 2006 on the New York Stock Exchange and operates 200 residences for up to 8,300 people in 17 states.

Libin got into the nursing-home business years earlier.

"We were building nursing homes in the 1960s because of high depreciables, or accelerated depreciation rules for nursing homes, which were incentives. We didn't know anything about nursing homes, but we built one in Calgary like we thought they ought to be built. Some people called it a 'country club.' But it was an immediate hit. So we opened some more," he said.

"We went public in 1969 and called it Villa Centres. We had one in Calgary, Winnipeg, Montreal, Halifax and two in Toronto. In 1984 we sold nine centres to Extendicare. I'm still on the Extendicare board of directors," he said.

David Hennigar, a member of the Jodrey family, described Al as a fair, but very tough, negotiator. They were introduced to one another by the late Charles Burns, founder of investment bank Burns Fry Ltd., which was bought by the Bank of Montreal.

Hennigar recalls one scrap they had.

"Libin came in and I said to Charlie, 'I can't do a deal with him, he's really tough.' Charlie said just go back and try and we eventually did the deal," he recalled.

Libin's diversification, conservatism and caution also prevented him from succumbing to the boom-and-bust nature of the oil patch. Back in 1980, the boom ended with Ottawa's National Energy Program, high interest rates and the collapse of oil prices in 1986. Many went bankrupt.

"The National Energy Program wasn't good," said Libin. "We were in the middle of some [real estate] projects. But we never got a big hit. It was boom to bust. It was Alberta's time, but the feds decided it wasn't Alberta's time. A carbon tax could be imposed by Ottawa today, so it could happen again."

The Libins are second-generation wealth. Alvin and his two siblings, the late Leon and Muriel, inherited a booming business from their immigrant father. He escaped from somewhere in Eastern Europe (Libin thinks Russia), came to Calgary alone, then sponsored the rest of his family.

"He went to Calgary because of all the construction being done by the Canadian Pacific Railroad. They needed labourers," said Libin. "But my dad was an entrepreneur who went from a grocery-store business to a bakery and dry cleaning. His bakery was the biggest commercial bakery west of Toronto and was called Palace Bread. It was huge and eventually was sold to General Bakeries."

Libin went straight from high school into the family businesses. "I didn't like school. I was not a good student and didn't enjoy it," he said. "I went into the sales end."

In 1955, General Bakeries bought the family firm, but the Libins had already begun making real estate investments. "There was no office space in Calgary at the time. Our bakery became the head office for Shell Canada," he said.

His sister, Muriel Kovitz, married a dentist and eventually became chancellor of the University of Calgary as well as a sought-after director on Imperial Oil Ltd. and other boards. He and his brother were partners for 20 years. "My sister was a real star," he said. "My brother and I invested together until 1975, when I bought him out. He wanted to cash in to have a good time. He died in 1988. And he had a good time."

"We got involved in real estate and nursing homes and played around with hotels. We owned the Plaza 2 and the Park Plaza [Hotel] in Toronto at one time," he said. "I still own the International Hotel in Calgary."

Libin lives on a golf course beside his son Bobby, who has three teenagers, in Calgary and spends much of the winter in Palm Springs. But Al enjoys the action and he, and four professionals that work for him, make investment calls and sift through deals constantly.

"We're in the deal world and have been for a long time," he said. "But I don't do things I've done 14 times before. I'm just busy keeping what we've got. And I like the involvement. I can't imagine retiring, especially here in Calgary. It's fun to live in a vibrant part of the world."

He credits his success with the fact that he has deployed common sense and been cautious.

"My dad also taught us to be honest and truthful," he added. "That's critical to success."

Libin is a ranking as well as proud member of Calgary's establishment and counts former Alberta premier Peter Lougheed as a close friend.

"Real estate and oil are cyclical, and during the National Energy Program it was awful to watch what happened to Alberta," he said. "But now Calgary is a global investment centre. It's totally different than before. The amount of money floating around this world is unbelievable. There's so much money chasing deals that it's scary. It's a good selling opportunity, because the amount of money is driving real estate yields so low, it's hard to buy. Prices are just out to lunch."

Libin has also donated millions to medical research, along with other Flames owners, in the hopes of making Calgary a go-to medical research centre.

In 2006, he endowed $15 million for the Libin Cardiovascular Institute of Alberta, and for a decade he chaired the Alberta Heritage Foundation for Medical Research, which in 2007 reached $1 billion in endowments. He also headed the Alberta Ingenuity Fund to spawn scientific and engineering research in the province.

"Canada is a wonderful country . . . if we could run it right," he said.

ISADORE SHARP

In 2006, two of the world's richest men, Microsoft's Bill Gates and Saudi Arabia's Prince Al-Waleed bin Talal, paid $3.7 billion to buy the biggest global brand ever created by a Canadian: Four Seasons Hotels.

Founder Isadore Sharp still owns 5% of the luxury chain and remains CEO and chair.

"It was ownership for life for me," he said. "I sold because my sons were not in the business and because if something happened to me the family would have had to sell the company and it would have been like the Ritz, homogenized into a bigger chain of hotels."

Sharp is, hands down, the world's greatest hotelier, and his protectiveness toward the company and its employees is why the brand has flourished. Four Seasons is synonymous with quality and relaxed elegance. Sharp is an architect whose taste, along with that of his wife, Rosalie, who is a designer, has created stunning boutique hotels around the world that combine glamour, natural surroundings and local culture.

Sharp has come a long way. He started off building houses and factories as a young architect with his immigrant father, Max. In 1961, he tried his hand at the hotel business and was an innovator from the start. His first Four Seasons was a luxury motel near downtown in Toronto's red-light district. His second, the Inn on the Park, was an upscale hotel in the suburbs. Then in 1970, he turned the hotel world on its head by building London's Inn on the Park, a fabulous boutique hotel near the Dorchester Hotel that became the prototype for the world's largest and best luxury hotel chain.

"They called me the 'Crazy Canadian' in London, but I had a mixed bag of properties at this point and decided to build medium-sized, exceptional quality and the best in its market. We became the best hotel in London against the world's most famous hotels," he said.

Four Seasons operates 74 hotels in 30 countries, and its brand is now being extended into condominium developments beside its hotels.

The secret to Sharp's business model is not about picking prime locations and building fancy buildings. Four Seasons does not own any real estate anymore, but the company is a world-class design and management team that conceives and creates five-star hotels for developers, then recruits, trains and manages people in unique ways.

"I had worked in hotels as a busboy, and knew how hotels should work. My approach was from a customer point of view," he said in an interview over lunch with me in the Four Seasons head office in 2007. "If you make service your competitive advantage, employees have to deliver the product, so we created a work environment based on an ethical credo."

Putting the customer first is more than just lip service in his hotels. Four Seasons is the world's best hotel innovator: the first mini-bar, hotel fitness facilities, free shampoo, no-smoking floors and other innovations, such as large soaps, quiet rooms, large towels, two phones, quiet rooms, alternative cuisine, 24-hour room service, overnight laundry, pressing and dry cleaning, on/off remote TVs and the world's most comfortable mattresses.

There are imitators now, but none have replicated the corporate culture that Sharp shaped, which is, in essence, a mirror of his own personality: classy without snootiness, sensitive and civil. Issy and Rosalie are a friendly and down-to-earth couple who love to play duplicate bridge and travel. In 2006 she wrote a poignant and honest autobiography called *Rifke: An Improbable Life*, about her difficult childhood, her wonderful marriage and the loss of one of their four sons to cancer. The two started the Terry Fox Foundation and its annual run.

"She has rare talents and has been involved all along the way," Sharp said.

Sharp is also a bottom-line businessman who has imbued his workforce with his commonsense message.

"Our customers are the best promotion for us, and they appreciate the consistency and quality of our service. This can't be copied by others," he said.

If just 1% of customers are unhappy because of a bad experience during their stay, the damage is incredible, he said.

"In medicine or airplanes, a 1% failure is tragic, but it is a disaster in any business. One failure will end up being repeated at cocktail parties or wherever to 10 other people. If you do the math, in terms of the people who stay in our hotels, it could amount to millions of people knowing about a bad-service issue," he said.

This is why the level of professional development is one of the firm's greatest assets.

"It's just as important for our dishwashers to know they should throw away plates that have chips in them as it is for maids to know how to treat customers properly," he said.

Hotels are run by armies of people, and Four Seasons now employs 35,000 worldwide.

"Our industry is unskilled, so we hire personality, attitudes. Everyone goes through five interviews before they are hired," he said. "That's at any level."

In Manhattan, the Four Seasons Hotel interviewed 17,000 people to find 400 suitable employees. More significantly, the company developed the techniques to find personnel in regions where the work ethic is non-existent or people are in short supply.

"In Maui, there were no workers available—everyone had two jobs," he said. "So we talked to people who had terrible jobs, like cutting sugar cane in hot fields, which is back-breaking work. We found the right personalities and we trained them."

In the remote island of Nevis, with a population of 9,000 people, most residents had never worked, except for eking out a living as farmers and fishermen.

"These people did not know why there were two forks in a place setting or that there was more than one kind of tea," he said. "How did we train them? With patience, repeating the information over and over again without embarrassing them. I realized, after Nevis, we could go anywhere in the world. Next followed the Czech Republic, Berlin, the Middle East, China."

Good brand management is a never-ending task, and Sharp has also adamantly held to a rule that promotions should come from within. This protects the culture, or brand, and also provides an upside for staff.

"Our ethical standards are really the Golden Rule, 'Do unto others . . . ,' which is a universal concept found in all religions," he said. "It's a fundamental belief of civilization."

Sharp also required that leaders treat their colleagues as they expect hotel customers to be treated.

"When I introduced this, some of my managers laughed at me, and I had to let a lot of general managers go. These were people who thought bosses were to be bosses, not coaches," he said. "People see the way you behave toward other people, and we had to start at the top with senior leaders. It's taken us 30 years to reach it, but we have."

In 2006, the last year it was publicly listed, Four Seasons Hotels Inc. was Canada's 609th-largest corporation, earned $287.38 million in consulting and management fees, and had assets of $1.15 billion and profits of $57 million.

The company is approached by developers from all over the world who want to build and own five-star hotels. But Four Seasons selects developers and locations carefully before entering a partnership.

"We create a design brief that's two inches thick—down to how many hinges should be on doors, the scale, the concept and market research," he said. "I still enjoy this and approve everything."

Sharp's hotel concept began germinating when he and Rosalie took a trip to Europe on a tight budget.

"One night we would stay at the best hotel in a city and the next night in a fleabag to average down our costs. We stayed at the Dorchester, and George V in Paris, and that blew my mind," he said.

He found out from a contractor in Canada about a choice piece of property near the Dorchester that was targeted for a discount hotel. The scheme had problems; he approached them to get involved and waited for months. Finally, Sharp was summoned to London by legal counsel Sir Gerald Glover, who worked for the owner, the McAlpine Group.

"For three or four years I'd go over to London to have lunch with him and explain my concept. They wanted 320 rooms; I wanted to build fewer, more luxurious rooms. They owned the land and were builders; I just wanted to rent the hotel and run it," he said. "They finally made a deal. I eventually became good friends with Sir Gerald and asked him why it took so long and he said, 'My dear boy, you must develop belief and trust, which are the foundations for all business transactions.'"

"That was the most important hotel, even to this day. It took off like a rocket and became a cash cow that was so successful it paid for my other mistakes," he said.

Another turning point came in 1979, when Sharp got burned on real estate values in Vancouver. He sold the underlying real estate and concentrated on being a design and management company.

"I decided that investing in building a brand name could become more valuable than bricks," he said. "Over the years, I took four key decisions: specialize in quality and be the best hotel in a given market; provide the best service; create a culture to deliver that; and build a brand that equals quality and luxury."

Issy and Rosalie were high school sweethearts and have given millions to hospitals, the Terry Fox Run and various arts organizations, including the Ontario College of Art and Design, with its unique pencil-box addition on giant stilts.

"Rosalie is gifted and brilliant. She doesn't like me saying that, but it's true," Sharp said.

Sharp was no scholar, as Rosalie was—he told me he was a "terrible student." But he fell in love with architecture at the Ryerson Polytechnic Institute (now Ryerson University) and buckled down in his final year, winning a silver medal.

He was also a rascal and hung around with the "Italian-Jewish group" of jocks in Toronto's Forest Hill. One of his pals was billionaire lawyer-developer Rudy Bratty.

Rudy, Issy and another friend drove to California one summer. They stayed in a cheap motel along the way, then decided to keep driving, so they took one of the pillows with them. Police were called and the three were hauled before a magistrate. The friend who had registered for the room was threatened with jail until Rudy called a Toronto police chief, who vouched for them. Quipped Rudy, "Imagine the owner of the Four Seasons involved in taking a two-dollar pillow."

LARRY TANENBAUM

Larry Tanenbaum grew up in a steelmaking family but mastered the art of waging the "100-day war." That's Canadian slang for the unique ability of Canadian contractors to quickly erect buildings in record time because of the country's short warm-weather season.

"Canadians are incredibly efficient at construction because we work in difficult elements. The 100-day war starts the minute frost disappears and we have to get at it. Also, it's a war because the longer construction takes, the more capital costs go up. This means that building here is more expensive unless you work quickly. The result is, the weather and costs have made us more efficient out of sheer necessity," he said in an interview with me in his Toronto office in 2007.

Tanenbaum's success started with construction. But the Tanen-baum story begins with two brothers from Eastern Europe: Max and Joe. They got involved in steel, had a falling-out and divided the empire without any one of their 11 offspring taking control.

"I settled financially in 1984 with my six siblings," said Larry in an interview in his downtown Toronto corner office.

And did not look back. He now occupies Albert Reichmann's former office, of Olympia & York Development. "Albert moved back into First Canadian Place because his family bought the tower back, so it's good karma to have this office. They have bounced back. I know them well. I used to sell them ready-mix concrete," he said.

Tanenbaum owns 13% and is chairman of Maple Leaf Sports & Entertainment Ltd. It owns hockey's Toronto Maple Leafs, bas-ketball's Raptors and the Air Canada Centre, where both teams play. Because sports is showbiz, the job has been more of a pub-lic role for Tanenbaum than he's been used to. But it has become manageable for the private entrepreneur. He's also a jock, lean and good-looking, in a natty jacket.

"I've been a lifelong sports fan, and it's fun making people happy. The idea of having 20,000 people in an arena all cheering for the same goal is an absolute thrill," he said.

Owning a sports team was a major business departure for Tanenbaum but one that has proven to be financially beneficial.

"We have a three-legged stool: the teams, and we've got to make them winning teams; the real estate, and we own our arena; and the broadcasting. You have to control your own broadcasting to ensure quality and coverage to all the fans—you can't put more than 20,000 people in the arena. So we have a solid three-legged stool there. Without any one of these legs, it will fail. Rogers Media owns the Blue Jays and the broadcast and the stadium too."

Tanenbaum's strength is his people skills. He was born into a pugnacious family, the sixth of seven children, and stickhandled his way into a number of business partnerships that have paid off. He obtained a piece of the family business then grew that into a one-man empire that, at its peak, employed 18,000. By 2007, his payroll was down to "only" 4,000 because of divestitures.

"I love partnerships," said Tanenbaum. "In my family, which was big, you had to fight your way and also had to get along. Partners are a real strength, and I realized that at a young age."

Partners reduce risk and provide strategic information, but many entrepreneurs avoid them because they are tricky—like marriages. And the business world is littered with as many failed joint ventures as divorces.

But Tanenbaum has defied the odds. His partners in Maple Leaf Sports are the Ontario Teachers' Pension Plan, the CTV network and a unit of Toronto-Dominion Bank. Until recently, he was also partners with the world's largest cement and aggregates producer, Lafarge SA of France, as the second-largest shareholder in Lafarge North America, the continent's largest cement outfit, with US$3.5 billion in sales. His stake was acquired when he sold the country's largest aggregate, asphalt and concrete business in Canada to Lafarge. He was bought out when Lafarge North America was privatized.

Tanenbaum holds assets through his holding company, Kilmer Van Nostrand Co. Ltd., which had been involved for years in another partnership, Borealis Ltd. Borealis managed $9.5 billion in nuclear power and health care assets. He cashed out to OMERS, the Ontario Municipal Employees Retirement System. Other partners included the Canada Pension Plan and a team of managers.

"Kilmer Van Nostrand was a company my father bought in 1956, which was two families who had been building sidewalks and roads for three generations," he said. "It has morphed into my different businesses and is used as my holding company."

In 1984, he bought his siblings out of Kilmer and went on to build its construction and cement businesses. These were separately melded into Borealis and Lafarge. But along the way, Kilmer has participated in some of the world's biggest projects, from South Korea's Candu nuclear reactor to dams, bridges, part of Toronto's subway system, Calgary's LRT, subways in Atlanta and Caracas, and the elevated train system in Miami.

"We had operations in 11 countries at one time—Africa, South Korea. We just took our expertise and exported it, but I decided that there was plenty to do in North America," he said.

By 2007, Kilmer Van Nostrand had become an infrastructure investment vehicle and partner in power projects, or what he calls "brownfields" operations, which take contaminated urban properties, remediate them and then develop them.

Kilmer Capital Partners Ltd. is another entity, involved in private equity investments. It has raised two tranches of capital from investors, one of C$115 million and another of C$250 million. Both specialize in taking control of family enterprises that need expertise.

"We own McGregor Socks that make Calvin Klein and Happy [Foot] Socks worldwide and produce offshore," he said. "Another investment is a bakery that makes two-bite brownies. These are the kind of investments we like. This is because we grew up in operations. We are operations engineers, not financial engineers. We organize, acquire or restructure. I love to build companies. It turns me on."

Tanenbaum is soft-spoken and courteous. He and his wife have 3 children and 10 grandchildren, all living in Toronto.

"I say I have 6 children, not 3, because I regard my in-laws as my own kids," he said.

Over the years, he has had a similarly generous attitude toward the people who worked for him. Many were made partners too.

"I've got to say I've been lucky," he said. "But you cannot do this without excellent professional managers. In my case, there is so much diversification, no one person could run everything, so what you do is pick good professional managers."

Tanenbaum may have been born into wealth, but he said his father, Max, raised them to work hard and be frugal.

"I worked from the age of 12 years onward in the summers. I never went to camp. I went to a public school, and we had to earn every dollar he gave us," he said. "He always believed that money comes and money goes and you can never rely on money always being there. You have to work every single day. He had a good work ethic."

Tanenbaum attended Cornell University in Ithaca, NY (where he met Leafs vice-chairman and former goaltender Ken Dryden) and bought himself a car.

"My dad probably said to me, 'What do you need a car for? Take the bus back from Ithaca,'" he told me.

He graduated with an economics degree from Cornell and began work in the family firm by selling cement and aggregates.

"I enjoyed it. I enjoy everything I do," he said. "Money is not what drives you. It's the value system we grow up with: hard work, family, integrity and honesty. Your word is your bond. It's not money you pass on, it is a value system. That's the legacy that counts."

PART THREE

WHAT NEXT?

Fifty-six of Canada's 75 richest people or partnerships are self-made successes who were raised in ordinary circumstances but worked diligently to get to the top. Even those who inherited money and have remained on top have done so because they work harder than most people. There is no longer a leisure class like the Vanderbilts or Rockefellers, who sat atop money machines and travelled the world with servants and trunks full of jewels and evening gowns. The world has changed and taxes are punitive. The wealthy of old could dance through life, collecting witty companions to entertain them in their stately homes. Today's wealthy must keep their wits about them. Two world wars, incompetence and income taxes helped flatten most of the old-money aristocracy, but new perils loom. Globalization and technology threaten everyone, whether self-made or not.

Canada's new crop of capitalists are more akin to their American counterparts, such as Bill Gates or Warren Buffett, than to Britain's elite. They combine effort and business smarts with philanthropy. This is paradoxical, because their charitable impulses never extend to the business world. Bill Gates, the most generous philanthropist in the history of the world, owns a company that is a vicious contender with a decidedly mixed reputation in its marketplace. Jimmy Pattison, whose fortune has been bequeathed to charitable foundations, has a policy in his car dealerships to fire the least successful salesperson every month. These seeming contradictions really are not. These entrepreneurs are ferocious advocates of free enterprise and competition. For instance, they avoid taxes, because that's part of the game; they overtake competitors, because that's what the system is all about; and then they hand out billions to the charities of their choice, because that's what they want to do. They are like hockey players who elbow and knock out one another's teeth on the ice, then share beers together in the locker room after the game.

Sports metaphors are most appropriate when trying to understand the culture of profit. Business greats move around the ice fluidly, turning on a dime and shifting direction or tactics. This includes making major life changes. More than one-third of those profiled here were born outside Canada and immigrated, a life-wrenching decision for anyone. Others migrated within Canada because of problems or to pursue opportunities unavailable at home. Only 17 of the 75 have made their fortunes where they grew up.

These people also migrate easily within the business world. Most have been involved in many sectors, moving from one to another with alacrity and without regret. These 75 also speak many languages, understand many cultures and have lived around the world in many countries. This makes them resilient.

When Wallace McCain was fired by his brother at 65 years of age, he and his family considered buying a business and moving permanently, to the United States or New Zealand, before ending up in Toronto. Robert Friedland has lived in the United States, India, Canada and Singapore, and now in his corporate jet. Sir Terence Matthews juggles empires in Britain and Canada. The Laljis and Mangaljis were kicked out of Uganda but immigrated to Canada, from where they fanned out to live in many countries and have created huge real estate empires. Frank Stronach left Austria as a teenager for Canada, then moved to Switzerland in 1994, and now, at 75 years of age, intends to transform Russia's auto sector with a new partner, who is only 38 years old. George Cohon left the comforts of a Chicago law practice to start McDonald's in Canada and then spent a decade creating McDonald's in the former Soviet Union. And as the Soviet Union dissolved, Alex Shnaider left Toronto, to which his Russian parents had immigrated from Israel, boarded a plane for Switzerland, then lived for years in substandard conditions in Ukraine and Russia to make his fortune. Mike DeGroote came to Canada from Belgium as a teenager and left in his 60s for Bermuda, from where he built more businesses in the United States. John MacBain was born in Ontario, went to university at Oxford, then Harvard, and then moved to Montreal and then London to build a unique publishing concept globally. He now lives in Geneva, where he gives away money to worthy African causes.

Besides having an aptitude for agility, the players in this book are as smart as the slickest stickhandlers, as aggressive as hockey goons and as focused as coaches, sometimes to the point of rudeness. In meetings, as in life, they ask tough questions and, unlike most people, want honest answers, no matter how painful, which is how they have succeeded. They rely on numbers and instincts, not on wishful thinking or hope. They are brutally direct and efficient. "I'm doing this as a favour to a mutual friend. I don't like interviews, and I'm giving you an hour, so let's go," said Rai Sahi to me in his huge Mississauga office in 2006.

Those who carved out a fortune from nothing have unusual energy levels, and most would probably be diagnosed as "workaholics." Their inboxes are jammed and their schedules booked to the minute, months in advance. They multitask all the time, looking at screens while talking on the telephone. They put in as much effort, and have to take as much pain, as do linebackers. They all work more than do their employees or rivals. Even those who have cashed in or "retired" are as busy having fun or giving away money as they were making a fortune.

Ron Joyce, of Tim Hortons fame, sold out in the early 1990s and since then has created a sizable and successful charter jet service in Hamilton, Ontario, and carved out a world-class golf course and resort in Nova Scotia. Others who have "retired" juggle charitable boards, university chancellorships and corporate directorships, or manage foundations that hand out millions. Seymour Schulich joked that it requires more work to give money away properly than to make it. Robert Miller recovered from near-death illness a couple of years ago but returned to work in order to triple the size of his business so that there will be more to give away.

All these people are driven. They obsess about their businesses and make themselves as available to their team and customers as obstetricians do to theirs. Time zones and days of the week are irrelevant: half of the interviews in this book were done on weekends, at cottages, before breakfast or after restaurants closed. Daryl Katz quickly responded to e-mails from several cities while we set up our interview. Dave Sobey spoke with me on the telephone from his Florida retreat. Paul Hill returned one of many phone calls while on holiday in Rome with his wife. Sonja Bata's BlackBerry went off during our luncheon interview. It was her son, Tom Jr., calling in the middle of the night from China about a business situation. David Hennigar of Halifax lives on his e-mail and spared me time in a hotel dining room for a face-to-face meeting, in between board meetings in Toronto. Eugene Melnyk shoehorned me in for an afternoon at his family's country home on Lake Simcoe, where he was visiting his mother while she recuperated from minor surgery. He had just flown in from Ottawa and London and was on his way to Barbados, then heading back to London again.

Even when you are with these people, they are still usually multitasking—summoning information from assistants, answering phones or glancing at their BlackBerries. They are always interruptible, excusing themselves to meet with an executive or to schedule a meeting that is to be held within minutes of your departure. They log hundreds of thousands of air miles annually. Some "live" in private jets, like Jimmy Pattison, Ron Joyce, Frank Stronach, Robert Miller or Robert Friedland, who visits 45 countries a year. I once travelled with Joyce on his plane to three office parties in three cities in two separate time zones one evening in 1997. The evening started in Halifax, then on to Montreal and finally Toronto.

These people do not aspire to leisure. They do not have it in their vocabularies. And this is the way business has evolved too: it is frenetic, transactional and not relationship-oriented. Gone is the era of graceful lunches lasting for hours, where business was occasionally broached. Today, business is not conducted over meals, but on the fly.

Issy Sharp invited me during our interview to grab lunch. He took me to the Four Seasons employee cafeteria, where meals are free for workers. Fred DeGasperis invited me for a day to see his winemaking operation, but brought along his daughter and two granddaughters so we could meet and discuss business and family-management issues. Mark Muzzo, son of DeGasperis's partner, the late Marco Muzzo, said his father took only one holiday and was so restless that he woke up his children every morning to do chores around their Florida resort home.

Many—perhaps a disproportionate number—of these fabulously rich people suffered hardships in childhood. Fourteen grew up in war-torn Europe. Another fled the war just before it started. The Laljis and Mangaljis were kicked out of Uganda. Five—Ted Rogers, Ron Joyce, Barry Sherman, Michael Lee-Chin and Stephen Jarislowsky—were raised by single mothers. Eugene Melnyk's mother was widowed while he was a teenager, a seminal experience that led him to quit school to bring in money for the family. Tom Bata Sr.'s father died when he was still a teenager, leaving him with an empire to help run. Their childhoods, with the exception of Bata's, Rogers's and Jarislowsky's, were impoverished, forcing them prematurely into the role of partial breadwinner at very young ages.

Most of the others were aware, as children, of their own father's or family's financial struggles, which contributed to their driving ambition and desire for monetary security. Grandparents from both sides of Jean Coutu's family lost their fortunes as a result of the Depression, and his father struggled as a general practitioner with impoverished patients who could not afford to pay. Seymour

Schulich, Ned Goodman, Clay Riddell and Robert Miller grew up with fathers who were entrepreneurial but relatively unsuccessful. Peter Munk's father was a playboy. Ken Field's mother had to appeal to a banker to stave off his father's bankruptcy. Jimmy Pattison's family was uprooted from Saskatchewan to Vancouver, where his dad eked out a living, as did Calvin Ayre's father. As a teenager, Lino Saputo Sr. bankrolled his immigrant father, who was a trained cheesemaker, so he did not have to suffer the indignity of being an unskilled labourer in Montreal. And Norman Keevil Jr. left an academic career in the United States at the request of his mother, who wanted him to help keep afloat his father's mining company.

The fact that only 17 of the 75 founded their businesses in their hometowns is also revealing. It underscores the fact that entrepreneurship is not about social position, education, ethnicity or family background. It is an awareness of surroundings that leads to the discovery of niches or angles that can be exploited. And outsiders are always forced to be observant if they are to survive in new surroundings.

Immigrants and migrants also have advantages, because they think outside of the box, have an anxiety that drives them to find security and an aptitude for change. Joyce, who bounced around as a farm worker, steelworker, sailor and cop, told me he did not have any time to enjoy a full night's sleep for more than a year when he ran his first restaurant. Pattison worked seven days a week for years and mortgaged his little bungalow to buy his first car dealership. Michael Lee-Chin was working as a bartender, back from being an engineer in his native Jamaica, when he heard about mutual funds from a buddy and immediately joined a sales force. After a few years, he wagered his sizable savings on an investment idea that paid off and was used to start his mutual fund company.

While outsiders seem to have an edge, women decidedly do not. Expectations, both in families and in society, are lower for women than for men when it comes to business success. Women also make other choices. They still tend to gravitate toward the arts or the nurturing professions, while enrolment in engineering, finance, accounting and sciences—crucial to most businesses and to critical thinking—remains mostly male.

Those women who made it to the top in Canada have done so because they are immensely talented and hard-working, but also they have done so as the wives or daughters of entrepreneurs. Martha Billes took over Canadian Tire after fighting against her brothers over direction of the company. Nancy Southern grew up in her father's business, as did Belinda Stronach and Sue Riddell. Interestingly, Heather Reisman and Sonja Bata are partners with their husbands in business but have also built their own successful enterprises and endeavours.

Martha Billes felt that there are still barriers and that women have to establish themselves as "one of the guys." Nancy Southern, one of two daughters in her family, admitted that there was a glass ceiling in her own enterprises, despite her desire to offer more opportunities to women throughout the ranks of the company.

"Women just have it a lot tougher than men. They have husbands and children and many other relationships to look after," said her father, Ron Southern. "I just don't know how they do it all. It's really hard for them."

But the driven life is not without sacrifice even for the men and their loved ones. "What would I have done differently?" said Ted Rogers. "I would have been a better father. My son Edward is a better father. Even when I was at home I was thinking about work. I still have that problem."

Online gambling king Calvin Ayre said his constant travelling makes normal married life impossible. So he's single. Of the 75, there are three permanent bachelors and another two dozen who are divorced. The married men spoke openly about the fact they were rarely home. Eugene Melnyk said he keeps his young family intact in Barbados, despite being owner of the Ottawa Senators and of a Mississauga biotech company, by never being away for more than five days. Of course, he is always away for five days. Some others do not travel far, except to the office, but that is where they mostly live. "I was a terrible father," said Montreal developer

Marcel Adams, a widower and father of four. "I wasn't there for my kids or for my wife. There's no way around it. She did a great job. She was wonderful."

WHO FOLLOWS IN THEIR
FOOTSTEPS?

The ruthlessness of the global economy means that a business can never rest on its laurels or its market share. Long gone are the days when wealthy tycoons passed along their familial empires to their first-born sons. For starters, these first-born sons may be playboys. They may be dolts. They may choose to save the planet with their money rather than be industrialists. Sometimes offspring are really keen, fairly bright and want to participate but should not, like Edgar Bronfman Jr. or the Eaton brothers, who made catastrophic missteps. In today's Darwinian global economy, incompetence or well-meaning but inadequate owners cannot be foisted on an organization without imperilling its existence. Nepotism is not an option.

"My kids didn't want to run it," said biotech entrepreneur Leslie Dan, "and they weren't the right people. It's an exception when children continue to successfully run a company anyway. You need highly trained people."

Another who, like Dan, sold his empire declared his attitude indelicately: "My kids are just not good enough."

A third, who also did not want his name used, said that his family empire fell into the hands of large investors because the third generation could not work together. "My kids blew it," he said.

The fact is that business aptitude is not genetic and is far from predictable either. The wealthy must not only dodge the inherent dangers of a highly competitive world, but they must innovate, re-create and cull assets, then make enough money to outpace both inflation and taxation rates. The reality is that most of the children and grandchildren of the billionaires in this book will not make the cut in 2028. Half of the 32 biggest in 1986 were blown away and replaced by dozens of new players, and this churn will continue.

Owners must be preoccupied with building and keeping an effective team and partnerships. To make a fortune—or keep one—requires you to make lots of other people rich too. So wealthy individuals must surround themselves with expensive, talented and loyal people. All are involved with partners or shareholders, bond-holders, pension funds or other major investors, financial markets, the public at large, regulators, politicians, labour unions and key employees who don't hesitate to leave for more money or if there's a whiff of trouble or nepotism. Such long-standing relationships are not easily transferable to the next generation.

That is why very few of these people are training, or have trained, their children to take over the business. Only 13 have handed over the reins to one of their children as a CEO: Hal Jackman, Ned Goodman, Clay Riddell, J.R. Shaw, Jean Coutu, Laurent Beaudoin of Bombardier, Galen Weston Sr., Wallace McCain, Lino Saputo Sr., Ron Southern, the late Izzy Asper, Tom and Sonja Bata, and the late Ernie Samuel. Others may have children involved in senior capacities, but those children are not in charge. And as these families grow in size, to third- or even fourth-generation members, most will cash out or clip coupons.

Another pitfall is sibling rivalry, which can explode once the patriarch dies or as he ages. Sisters and brothers sometimes brawl to the point of estrangement, as in the case of the Steinbergs and Wolfes, who had to sell their companies following internal disagreements about which sibling, or sibling's husband, would be CEO. Family fights afflict private, first-generation businesses more than others because disaffected siblings cannot simply sell their stock to the public and do their own thing. The DeGasperis, Muzzo, Lalji and Fidani families have had to deal with dissension involving brothers, in-laws, cousins or relatives who are not pulling their weight.

Such infighting makes headlines only if it involves public or high-profile companies, as did the feud between the McCain brothers, that of the Bronfmans, or Martha Billes, who took on her brothers. Billes's battle was doubly unusual, because daughters rarely play major roles even in this day and age. Women rarely participate as directors or officers. Mostly this is by choice, but sometimes there is an imposed glass ceiling, as is the case with the Thomson family, whose founder, the first Lord Thomson of Fleet, drew up a will decades ago that reportedly stipulated that only a male heir could run the show.

The biggest impediments to creating a dynasty are that rich kids become spoiled, have little motivation to pursue money-making ventures or are disaffected by all the hard work and sacrifice they have witnessed. Besides that, the old concept of family duty or sacrifice has eroded. Brandt Louie's two sons, a lawyer and a doctor, have gone to school and settled into lives in the United States with American wives. His two siblings live fancy lifestyles and work in relatively minor roles. Louie, on the other hand, would never have dreamed of doing anything other than running his father's and grandfather's businesses. "It is different today," he said.

Similarly, Norman Keevil Jr. and Mark Samuel responded to their family's calls for help. Keevil interrupted an academic career in the States to do so, and Samuel was about to spend a few years abroad as a consultant. These two, like Hal Jackman, David Thomson and Hartley Richardson, automatically assumed the reins, becoming the "patriarchs" of their fellow heirs and heiresses. As time elapses and in-laws marry into the family, this role becomes more cumbersome. For instance, there are now dozens of family "shareholders" involved in the Thomson, Weston, McCain, Richardson, Irving, Sobey and

Jodrey empires. Even those who have assumed the family mantle these days are different. Nancy Southern, for instance, said she only did so out of a proclivity toward and interest in the business and not because she was required to or pressured. Going forward, she does not expect her children or nieces and nephews to feel the same. "My sister and I feel that our children can do what they want to do," she said. "They may not be very interested in it as we were."

If sibling rivalry among the founder's children is ducked as an issue, the third generation is usually the final straw. By the time grandchildren come along, there could be dozens of heirs involved, too many disputes to resolve, too many in-laws, too many rivalries for top positions and too many people with differing ambitions or money needs. In late 2006, the Irving empire, with two dozen heirs and their offspring, began negotiating a "divorce" amicably. The assets had been divided into a series of Bermudian trusts held in the names of the three brothers. But the task will be to divide the spoils, and for those who want to run parts of the empire to buy out those who do not want to participate. Hal Jackman was able to buy out his sister and two brothers because he could afford it and because they were not interested in running things. Some families cannot pull this off. In the case of the three Steinberg sisters, all wanted to run the company and none wanted to sell, so the entire business was put on the block. The Wolfes had disagreements, but no single heir could afford to buy all the others out.

One family that got past such obstacles was the eight members of the second-generation Greenbergs, Ottawa developers who restructured their affairs. When the last of two founders died, two of their eight children owned half the business, the other six the rest, and only four of the eight children were employed directly in the business. One eventually cashed out and two quit the family firm as officers. Ownership was then divided into seven equal parts, a task accomplished over time.

Some tycoons have avoided the succession issue by selling their enterprise or giving it away. Ron Joyce cashed in his chips, as did Mike DeGroote, Ray Chang and Leslie Dan. Frank Stronach has sold half his control block to a Russian oligarch. Toronto developer Jack Daniels financially set up his five sons and will give away the rest of his fortune to charities of his choice. Other billionaires, such as Robert Miller, Seymour Schulich, Jimmy Pattison and Barry Sherman, are doing the same. Pattison, a religious man, has established foundations to which he has already bequeathed his conglomerate when he passes on, rather than to his three children. He believes that great wealth is ruinous to children. Schulich, Canada's foremost philanthropist, explained that his wealth was created at a point in time and in places that will never be replicated again, so he has felt he owes society in general for his good fortune. So do Miller and Sherman.

THE CHALLENGES AHEAD

Since the Second World War, Canada and the United States have enjoyed economic advantages over other countries because theirs were the strongest economies left standing. They benefited from steadily increasing trade, infrastructure investments and, in the 1950s, Europe's Marshall Plan. In 1989, they benefited again, as did Western Europe, when the "Third World War," or Cold War, ended with the collapse of the Soviet Union and the economic liberalization of China, India and various Soviet client states. This sparked another economic boom and led to transformations in those countries.

One generation later, Russian and Chinese workers no longer toil in non-productive factories making useless products based on five-year plans. They no longer live on farm communes reciting the Communist catechism. Now they make widgets—or invent them—in large, modernized factories built by Westerners or local moneyed interests for export. Many Russians, and their businesses, enjoy new-found wealth thanks to resource prices. The Chinese middle class grows. So does India's as reforms are lifting people gradually out of an immutable caste system and socialism.

Elsewhere in the world millions more people are being educated and are designing software, doing medical research or making high-tech products. By 1970, for the first time in history, half the world's population was literate, and by 2007, 80% of the world's adults were literate; the United Nations predicts this will increase to 85% by 2015. These are the potential beneficiaries of the global economy as it reaches deeper into societies. The middle classes in China and India are growing by considerably more people every year than the 32 million who live in Canada. World Bank figures in 2005 reflect the fact that the rich are getting richer but that the poor are also getting "richer." The number of persons internationally living on less than US$2 a day has dropped since 1995, from 40% to 18%, and the World Bank estimates this will drop by 2015 to only 15%.

Trade has driven this growth in incomes. Between 1990 and 2005 there was as much trading undertaken by the world's nations as had occurred in total over the previous 100 years. Canada has been a huge winner in this. In 1986, 30% of the Canadian GDP, or $154 billion, was generated from exports. By 2006, exports represented 40% of the GDP, or $458 billion. Canada has also benefited from China's self-financed "Marshall Plans" and from Asia's industrialization by selling massive quantities of commodities and energy. This region's demand for materials, along with price jumps, made Canada a winner.

To contextualize the new business climate, consider the size of the expanded gene pool with whom we now do business or compete. China and India alone represent 40% of the global population, or 2.3 billion people. Their brightest 25%, in terms of intelligence, totals 600 million, or roughly the populations of North America and Europe combined. As these Asians gain even greater access to education, technology and capital, they will help grow the global economy faster, help find cures for cancers, help devise technologies, and do even more business with—or against—us. For Canada, the implications are profound.

"This is a great country, but it's a small, middle-of-the-road country," said Philip Reichmann, son of the successful real estate family. "It will never be in the dumpster, and we will always be a sidecar to the U.S., so we must take advantage of that. Competition and profit have not been [political] priorities in Canada, which is a ball around our ankles because it means taxes are too high. But the problem is that globalization is a very real threat to any economy, or company, that doesn't perform."

CANADA IN 2008

Mining billionaire Robert Friedland believes that Canadian attitudes and government policies are out of sync with new realities. Canada has performed well economically, but he believes that high commodity prices have camouflaged some underlying socio-economic and political weaknesses. "Canada has been dragged kicking and screaming into the real world," he said. "Capital and ideas are now international. Canada's benefited enormously off the rise of the United States [building businesses in Canada], and now China. China and Asia have driven up the price of wheat, oil, uranium, natural gas, farmland, gold, fish, copper, zinc, coal and everything Canada produces. It's driven up the price of real things and overcome inefficiencies. Canada wins by dumb luck."

Friedland makes a valid point that highly priced commodities have masked slippage. The 2003 OECD figure (before commodity prices began to climb) for the Canadian income per capita of GDP was 50% below that of the U.S. and other large economies. The commodity boom plumped up both GDP-per-capita figures and the Canadian dollar's value. By 2006, Canada's income per capita was up to US$34,843 per person; that of the U.S. was US$42,000, Ireland's

US$47,804, Australia's US$35,000 and Britain's US$36,533, according to the OECD (the Organisation for Economic Co-operation and Development).

Claude Lamoureux, former Ontario Teachers' Pension Plan CEO, agreed that Canadian attitudes are an obstacle to needed productivity adjustments. "We must do better on competitiveness. Take hours of work per week," he suggested. "Domtar has a mill in the U.S. and one in Quebec. The Quebec workers put in 3 to 4 hours less per week. That's a 10% difference, which is huge. Canadians have more statutory holidays, more vacation, too much maternity leave. Quebec is the worst because it is closer to Europe, in labour laws, than are the other provinces. In the end, it's an attitude. I met a German who got 6 weeks' vacation and wanted 8 weeks. He worked a 35-hour week too. This is what Canadian workers ask for, but how can a society operate this way?"

Lamoureux was upset when his pension plan's 250 unionized workers struck in 2006. "We requested that everyone work only one hour more per week, among other things. And they walked out. Can you imagine striking over that? Well, they did. We resisted and eventually we won," he said.

Canadians must also work smarter if they want to match American living standards, according to the University of Toronto's Institute for Competitiveness and Prosperity in its fourth annual report, published in spring 2007. Canadians work an average of 157 fewer hours per year than Americans because they take more vacation weeks away from work, do more part-time work and receive more paid statutory holidays.

Fewer workdays, plus cuts in education spending during the 1990s, are behind the growing divergence between Canadian and American prosperity, added Institute chair Roger Martin in a 2007 interview with the *Financial Post*. His example was that in 2004, Canadian governments invested $2,400 per capita in education, well below the U.S. level of $3,000. That continued a long-term trend by which Canada's investment in education has grown at only 0.2% per year since 1993, compared with 3.3% in the United

States, even though data show that higher educational attainment increases both wages and attachment to the labour force. "It was a truly unfortunate error. Just as we were ramping into the knowledge economy and competing on high-quality labour, we managed to head in the opposite direction," he said.

The institute is part of the Rotman School of Management at the University of Toronto, which was launched in 1972 with a bequest from Joseph Rotman, one of Canada's richest businessmen, to provide world-class master of business administration degrees and executive education programs. Rotman said Canadian parochialism and insularity are the country's biggest problems. He had pursued an academic career at Columbia University in New York City until his father summoned him back to help run the family home-heating-oil business. Rotman made his first fortune as an oil trader, then got into exploration, mining, real estate, manufacturing and merchant banking, through Clairvest Group Inc., now run by his son Ken Rotman.

In 1997, Joseph Rotman quit corporate boards and devoted himself to shifting attitudes and policies and global businesses through the school and other endeavours.

"Oil trading made me a globalist, and going to New York City was an eye-opener. I came back and realized I had to help create business education here that could train leaders who could get Canada to become global. We're not even close, which is why our companies don't grow into global giants," he said in an interview at Clairvest in Toronto in December 2007.

The takeover of four of Canada's biggest mining companies as well as of all its steel companies is a case in point. "We did not build companies with the talent they needed," he said. "The best and brightest Canadians should go out and run foreign companies. There is not enough spent training business talent here, and not enough respect given to business as in the U.S. We've got to get global. Public-sector spending in research is among the highest in the OECD, but there is no explosion of commercialization here like in San Francisco or Boston."

Rotman is co-founder of MaRS, a public/private attempt in Toronto to kick-start a cluster of biotech commercializations among the city's biggest hospitals and the University of Toronto.

"We want to build the gateway to biotech here, but politics gets involved," Rotman said. "If Saskatchewan wants to build its own little MaRS, nobody will come unless subsidized, and that will dilute what should be one national cluster of excellence."

Short-sighted governments are only part of the story. Said Quebec takeover artist Charles Sirois, "We don't have the same risk appetite that the Americans have. It's part of our culture. Canadians are more conservative. We have entrepreneurs but not enough money to back them. If we take out the oil part of our economy, we're not doing well at all. When our currency was too low for too many years, we got lazy. We need to move. We cannot sit. The oil wealth will create tensions in the country. Alberta will soon have no provincial income taxes, and head offices will continue to move there."

Sirois points out the existence of two distinct Canadas in the business world: one that is highly functional because it is competitive, sells abroad and/or competes efficiently at home, and another that is dysfunctional or may be protected by governments for political or social ends. Such cosseted companies usually lack global ambition and are often inefficient and dependent upon monopoly privileges or regulations.

THE CODDLED

Fortunately, fewer coddled Canadian corporations exist now than were around back in 1986. Many disappeared after implementation of the Free Trade Agreement in 1989 and the North American Free Trade Agreement in 1993 because the agreements began eliminating tariff protections and other barriers to entry. This was especially noticeable in retailing. Some Canadians met the new competition successfully, such as Canadian Tire. Others did not, and Eaton's, Dylex and the Hudson's Bay Company found themselves swamped by American competitors with superior technology, better marketing and, due to well-developed supply chains in Asia, lower-cost products. Two of the three disappeared, and the other struggles financially.

In 1986, more than half of Canada's 50 biggest companies were protected somewhat from competition or were government-owned. By 2007, only 15 of the 50 biggest were in this category: banks, insurance companies, telephone, cable, power utilities, media and ACE Aviation Holdings Inc. (the parent company of Air Canada). Only one of the 15 was government-owned (Hydro-Québec), but all enjoyed some form of ownership or market protection, such as monopoly rights, restricted government licensing or other barriers to entry.

Of course, protected industries are commonplace in all countries, for a variety of reasons, and are not an economic problem per se. For instance, Japan has protected some sectors over the years from foreign competition, such as the auto industry's Toyota Motor Corporation and Nissan Motor Company, both of which have become export giants. Unfortunately, most of Canada's coddled businesses have failed to expand beyond the borders or to become market leaders, innovators or global consolidators.

Canada's most disappointing protected industry, according to a number of entrepreneurs interviewed, has been its chartered banks. These have not used their market dominance and huge profitability at home as a springboard to aggressively conquer new markets around the world. It is interesting to note that, despite huge cash flows, they all missed out on the world's greatest banking consolidation opportunity right next door: the American shift in policy during the 1990s that allowed banks to buy investment banks and also to merge or be acquired across state lines. Canadian banks mostly stayed on the sidelines and instead remained preoccupied with lobbying Ottawa to allow them to merge at home. Some made relatively small acquisitions. "Our banks are a protected species. The only top-10 list they qualify for is the top-10 list for lack of initiative," said investment banker Tom Caldwell, chair of Caldwell Securities in Toronto.

Another outspoken critic is financier Hal Jackman, who believes that Canada's banking system has damaged the economy over time. "Their lobbying power in Ottawa is obscene," he says. "When they made bad loans in Latin America, Calgary or real estate, they were given permission to write down losses slowly, but trust companies were not allowed to do the same. That damaged trust companies, and the banks bought all of them off."

In 1997, Jackman sold his trust company, National Trustco, to the Bank of Nova Scotia. He was named a director but eventually quit in a huff. "I was put on the board without being asked and stayed a while. I was the only director to refuse stock options. It was pretty awful. At that time, we had an annual meeting in Mexico—all operations were in Mexico City but the annual meeting was held at a resort in Cancun. In another instance, directors held a meeting in Asia, but directors and their wives were given first-class airline tickets to go around the world, not there and back," he recalled.

Jackman believes that Canadian consumers, and many businesses alike, have been poorly served by these banks. "These guys just don't compete. ATM fees are identical, and they are protected by the federal Bank Act when it comes to securities regulations."

The banking stranglehold has led to abuses, added Ned Goodman, whose financial empire is, as of 2007, 18% owned by the Bank of Nova Scotia: "Banks have become much more powerful and are controlled by nobody. They are just coining it. You have guys that are president of a bank for five or six years and retire with $250 million in options, superannuation and other bonuses. And nobody complains."

Entrepreneur Peter Munk casts the banking situation differently: "The banks in Canada are not businesses, they are institutions. They don't create waves, they just perpetuate themselves. That's the template. Competence and decency. They are not Stronachs or Schulichs, Pattisons or the Hong Kong Shanghai Bank [HSBC] or even Credit Suisse. They are just plodding Canadian banks."

Fortunately, banking services have improved somewhat because the globalization of capital markets and change in banking functions brought about competition, said Jack Cockwell, founder and director of Brookfield Asset Management: "The competence of people in banking in Canada is far greater now. This is because they have competition from the Americans. The biggest change is access to capital now. They [Canadian bank chairmen] used to phone each other up and say whether somebody should get a loan or not. Now that the U.S. guys are here, a Canadian business or individual can raise bonds and money with one phone call to New York."

Another Canadian underachiever has been Bell Canada Enterprises. In 1986, it enjoyed a lucrative telephone monopoly and had invested profits in becoming a conglomerate in a range of businesses from financial services to real estate, pipelines, resources and high technology. The total value of its outstanding shares represented 9% of the Toronto Stock Exchange, and its operations had a collective cash flow larger than the federal government's.

But Bell has fallen back, due to mishaps and miscalculations, and to its failure to capitalize on investments outside the country. By 2007, despite huge competitive advantages in the 1980s, its market value was equivalent to only 4% of the TSX and its revenues were a fraction of Ottawa's. Along the way, it sold off Northern Telecom before that company took off in value (then subsequently collapsed) and wrote off billions of dollars worth of real estate and telecommunications mistakes. Its management was under siege for years due to underperformance, and eventually, in August 2007, shareholders approved a move by the Ontario Teachers' Pension Plan and two American private equity partners to take BCE private. Of Bell's missteps, Montreal money manager Stephen Jarislowsky glibly commented, "I guess it's been pretty boring to run a phone monopoly, so the Bell board decided to make their lives more interesting and their shareholders less prosperous."

Not all government-regulated Canadian companies have sat idle or dabbled in other sectors at home. In the life-insurance sector, where underwriting and financial products are restricted to licensed companies, three Canadian companies have gobbled up smaller competitors at home, then become global consolidators.

Manufacturers Life, Sun Life and Great-West Life have stuck to their sector and grown dramatically larger operations and revenues outside Canada than within, diversifying into related fields like money-management services, mutual funds and other financial products. Great-West and Manulife have bigger subsidiaries in the United States than in Canada. And the venerable Sun Life has been a major player in Britain for decades and remains a market force in dozens of countries throughout Europe and Asia.

NON-CODDLED WESTERN CANADA

There are many remarkable freewheeling enterprises across Canada, as the 75 profiles in this book reveal. But the most entrepreneurial region of the country is western Canada, home to the lion's share of Canada's export-oriented resource industries. The economic base of the three westernmost provinces—British Columbia, Alberta and Saskatchewan—has always been commodities, from oil to wheat to gold. And while the three have had distinct political cultures over the years, their business communities have been totally dependent upon free trade and cyclical, difficult businesses. This has forged a tougher, more globally oriented and economically conservative policy template.

Westerners are price-takers, not price-makers. The value of whatever they produce varies and is beyond their control because prices are based on speculation or on supply and demand. This means that their only key to survival is to control costs and to set aside surpluses during the good times in order to stay afloat during the bad times. This mentality of fiscal discipline was imposed on governments and the public sector in Alberta following the calamities of the 1980s.

Severe belt-tightening in the private and public sectors began after oil prices fell dramatically in 1986, from US$36 to US$18 a barrel, then tumbled to a low in 1998 of US$11.91 a barrel. The Alberta public, suffering themselves, insisted on governments sharing the pain. Taxpayers made demands to their politicians: pay down debts, lower taxes and prune costs. This discipline certainly paid off. When oil prices began turning upward in 2003, Alberta was in fine fettle and resisted the temptation to overspend. It continued to lower taxes and eventually paid off all provincial debts. By 2007, it had become the continent's only debt-free jurisdiction, a Canadian tax haven and the country's most productive and most prosperous region. Some credit oil prices, but Saskatchewan, with its socialism and high taxation until 2007, was not as productive or as prosperous, despite its oil and mining wealth.

Alberta's disciplined, pro-business policies have become contagious in the region. British Columbia elected a conservative government and in 2004 began a process of tax cuts, deregulation and lower resource royalties. Even Saskatchewan's socialist New Democrats began to slash spending and taxation while in office. Their replacement in 2007, the conservative Saskatchewan Party, ran on a platform of undercutting Alberta's taxation and royalty levels. The Yukon government has also become pro-development.

Western Canada's industries are also world-class. Engineering breakthroughs and other expertise have positioned the region for prosperity. New drilling and refinery processes have brought costs down, making Saskatchewan's heavy oil deposits and Alberta's oil sands profitable to produce even at US$40 a barrel. At those prices, for instance, there are about 174 billion barrels of recoverable oil in the Alberta oil sands region, which is bigger than New Brunswick in size. This makes that resource, along with heavy oil in Saskatchewan, second in size only to Saudi Arabia's reserves.

The oil sands area has become one of the world's biggest construction sites, with 40,000 workers on site every day. Some two dozen megaprojects worth an estimated US$200 billion and financed by companies and governments from around the world are underway or on the drawing boards. By 2010, there will be 60,000 skilled tradesmen working in the remote region and hundreds of thousands more workers supplying them with materials, equipment, goods and services. If the energy and mining wealth and potential from British Columbia and Saskatchewan are added, this three-province region is the greatest, politically safest and most promising resource play in the world.

Alberta's bonanza will make the province Canada's richest within five years. Calgary is already the country's most dynamic business centre and will become more dynamic as oil wealth leads to the elimination of all provincial personal and corporate income taxes by 2015 or so. Alberta is the country's most welcoming workplace: it is Canada's only right-to-work province, its services are new and gold-plated, and its education system has better outcomes than most. Endowments from wealthy Albertans are also attracting medical, scientific and educational expertise from around the world.

The province is unique because its history is. Prairie settlers were attracted by free land grants offered by the Canadian government and the Canadian Pacific Railway between 1890 and 1910 in a marketing campaign known as the "Last Best West." Ottawa began recruiting in Europe for Manitoba and Saskatchewan and then, when recruitment efforts there dried up, went to Nebraska and Iowa to populate Alberta's foothills and prairies. These Americans were free-enterprisers who disliked big government, a brand of populism that remains.

As the rest of the west becomes more like Alberta and pulls away from the country economically, new political challenges will arise. As Calgary's richest oil man, former Saskatchewan native Murray Edwards, noted, "It will become more and more challenging to govern this country because of the growing regional difference. The west is more entrepreneurial and financially more powerful, and the others back east are still trying to adjust to the new world."

If commodity prices remain high, the gap in wealth and attitudes will also widen. In September 2007, Canada was exporting 2.467 million barrels a day of crude oil and other petroleum liquids to the U.S. At US$70 a barrel, these exports represent, on an annualized basis, US$63 billion a year—nearly 15% of Canada's total exports in 2006. In November 2007, prices nudged US$100 a barrel.

But prices are only part of the equation. Canadian volumes are also growing dramatically, and by 2020 exports from Alberta and Saskatchewan oil fields and from the oil sands could add another four million or more barrels of production daily. If exports reach six million barrels a day, at a price of US$70 a barrel, the total will reach US$153 billion annually, equivalent to more than one-third of all of Canada's exports in 2007.

Saskatchewan also has huge tracts of arable land and the world's greatest reserves of potash and uranium. British Columbia has agriculture, metals, minerals, oil and natural gas, both onshore and offshore. For these and other reasons, the country's economic centre of gravity has been moving westward, and was doing so even in the 1990s, before oil, uranium and metals began leaping in value.

In 2005, the combined GDP of Alberta and BC was already 40% higher than Quebec's. By 2007, Albertans had the highest per capita living standards in the world, at $66,000 per person—higher than that of the U.S., double Quebec's and 40% higher than the national average, according to Statistics Canada. Naturally, people have followed the money. Between 1986 and 2006, Canada grew by 6 million people net for a total of 32 million. The populations of Atlantic Canada, Manitoba and Saskatchewan stayed level; Ontario gained 3 million people (due to immigration); Quebec added 1 million (due to immigration); Alberta added 930,000 and BC 1.23 million. In 2007, Saskatchewan started to grow again.

CANADA'S ASYMMETRY

The commodity price boom and huge future oil-production levels will continue to keep the value of the Canadian dollar around parity with the U.S. dollar. That means adjustments for manufacturers and other export industries. The currency has always been volatile, but for two generations it has traded at prices well below American levels. In 1972, the Canadian dollar hit US$1.07, then it dropped for years, dramatically, before climbing briefly to 89 cents U.S. in 1989. By 2002, the Canadian dollar had sunk back to 61.79 cents

U.S. before it began a steady climb, along with commodity prices, eventually hitting a peak in 2007 of US$1.10, in November.

The loonie's value is high because the currency has come to be considered, by foreign-exchange traders, as a petrocurrency. So its exchange rate moves in tandem with crude oil prices. At the time same, the U.S. dollar has been falling against all other currencies, including Canada's, due to low interest rates intended to cushion debt problems, war costs and trade deficits.

Such volatility makes business more difficult. Planning and capital allocation are a long-term affair, and swings that affect the bottom line often force businesses to postpone or reconsider their plans. Another danger with the loonie's lofty price is that Canada may catch a dose of what's called the "Dutch disease." This is a phenomenon that occurred in the Netherlands after its North Sea oil and gas production began. Exports of this energy brought in huge amounts of foreign reserves earnings and forced up the value of the guilder to a level that made most manufacturers and exporters uncompetitive. Many folded. Others had to spend huge amounts to retool or expand abroad. The same process is underway in Canada.

"Manufacturing is going broke due to the high dollar, unionization and Asia," said Stephen Jarislowsky. "Even the U.S. is more competitive. In just five years, wages in Canada have risen by 50% against the U.S. because of the currency increase of 61 cents U.S. to US$1 or higher. This will wipe out manufacturing and forestry in eastern Canada. Canada does well now, thanks to oil and gas, metals and minerals, but these are cyclical. Oil is less cyclical, but it doesn't employ many people. Once Fort McMurray [capital of Alberta's oil sands] has been built out, there's not a lot of job gains."

"The high dollar will destroy manufacturing, Canada will become a wilderness paradise, and then the dollar will go back into the 60-cent level again," said Jarislowsky gloomily. "Americans will have cottages up here, and we will be a wildlife refuge. Alberta and BC are fine, but Quebec faces desolation. All those billions of dollars handed out by governments to Bombardier and Alcan for nothing. Ontario's auto jobs will also go as Detroit deteriorates."

Jarislowsky is in favour of pegging the Canadian dollar to 80 cents U.S. or whatever is a fair exchange, or he would support the creation of the "amero," a new North American currency. Still another option would be for Canadians to swap their currency for the U.S. dollar at an agreed-upon ratio. Any of these options will take years to orchestrate, as was necessary in Europe to create the euro.

Another monetary option is that taken by oil-rich Norway, where the state-owned oil company and other resource exporters have kept all their foreign-exchange surpluses in U.S. dollars or euros, then invested them outside the economy. By not bringing these surpluses back into their local economy and not converting them into the Norwegian currency, Norway has been able to retain its own currency, avoid inflation and duck the Dutch disease. A similar foreign reserves model has been deployed by China, Japan and South Korea for years. Those governments keep all foreign currency reserves separate in order to keep their own local currencies lower in value for competitive purposes.

Exporters like Michael McCain, CEO of food processor Maple Leaf Foods in Toronto, believes that something has to change soon. He agrees with Jarislowsky that the best policy choice is to create a new single currency for the U.S. and Canada, like the euro: "We are a Canadian-based, export-driven manufacturer, and the move from 61 cents to 90 cents U.S. and now higher has been tough. We faced a dragon. Our calculation was that moving to 90 cents alone represented a $100 million decline off the operating profit. Our competitive advantage of a lower currency disappeared."

"Governments have to encourage the move to scale, so businesses can take advantage of technology and go global. The agrifood lobbying group in Ottawa, for instance, supports a policy for small family farms. But what does a small farm have to do with competing against American, European or Asian giants?" said McCain in an interview in 2007. "It's not tax breaks, loans or subsidies to small guys that will keep the country; it's coming up with policies to help the big guys get bigger. Canada is a subscale [small] country from a population perspective. We psychologically look at scale in the Canadian context, and that's the wrong context."

If both countries had the same currency, Maple Leaf and other exporters could expand in Canada rather than in the U.S. to attain the scale they need, he said. This would both protect existing jobs and create new ones. "I lived in Chicago for nine years, and the biggest difference is Canadians have an aversion to scale," he said. "We have a plant in Nova Scotia that processes 3,500 hogs a week and in Manitoba we do 90,000 a week, and the guys in Nova Scotia think they can be viable? There's no logic. I spend a lot of time reminding my people that we are small and some of our U.S. rivals are 10 times bigger."

Without scale, he said, technology is too expensive, and without technology a business cannot compete. "Canadians work hard, and are as smart as anybody. Our productivity gap is because we can't invest in technology because we don't have that scale," he said. "And the currency bouncing around means expansion in Canada is not a good idea."

The Institute for Competitiveness and Prosperity reinforces McCain's argument and blames the technology gap for Canada's lower living standards. North of the border, only $1,800 per worker has been spent buying new information and communications technologies, compared with $3,200 per worker invested in the United States. The same holds true for other equipment, with only $3,900 per person spent in Canada compared with $4,800 south of the border.

THE TAXATION THREAT

Taxes are the country's single biggest problem going forward. Of greatest concern is the fact that Canada's medium and large enterprises pay the highest business taxes in the world, concluded an independent study called *Survey of Canada: 2006* by the OECD. "Most countries have recognized the harmful effects of high corporate taxation and have reduced effective rates over the years," said the OECD. Its survey added that even the tax cuts announced in 2006 by Ottawa will "still leave Canada with a higher rate in 2010 than exists in most other OECD countries today."

Some tax-cut tinkering in 2007 did very little and postponed cuts for corporations to 2012. By that time, other developed countries will also have lowered their rates, resulting in no comparative gain. The failure of a pro-business Conservative government to make business tax cuts a priority is disappointing, and is rooted in the ubiquitous Canadian misunderstanding about global realities as well as in the inappropriate underlying attitudes of Canadians. The problem has been that the "business" of Canada has never been about business. The country was a British colony for generations, then for decades after that was run like a colony by a handful of wealthy industrialists, financiers and Americans. This concentration of economic power has bred resentment toward business and encouraged rampant unionization and socialist platforms.

The result is that most working Canadians are not bottom-line oriented. They are employed by a foreign multinational's branch plant or a union shop, by a large, coddled Canadian corporation protected from external competition, by a government or a public-sector entity. This means that political priorities have not been bottom-line-oriented either. The result is a workforce that does not realize, or care, if business taxes are out of step with those levied by rival nations.

Canadians, and their leaders, see high business taxes as a means of levelling the playing field rather than seeing lower taxes as a tool to keep and create economic growth, and therefore jobs.

The Canadian public is ill informed about economic matters, as are its politicians. This is why one finance minister after another, whether Conservative or Liberal, has failed to make the tax situation a priority. Worse yet, they confuse voters by favourably comparing federal tax rates with those of other nations but fail to include provincial taxes, which add up to more than double federal taxes.

The 2006 OECD survey got it right. The comprehensive independent study compared all "marginal effective" tax rates. Its figures included taxes, levies and fees imposed by all levels of government; the variation in cost to business of depreciation or write-off requirements; interest deductibility variations; research tax credits; annual taxes on enterprise value (called capital taxes); and sales taxes on services and goods that improve productivity.

The OECD figures are damning for Canada: government charges add 39% to the cost of every new investment made by Canadian businesses. This compares to 37% in the U.S., 24% in Australia, 28% in Germany and only 12.5% in Sweden. While U.S. marginal effective tax rates are nearly as high as Canada's, America's entrepreneurs enjoy other forms of tax relief on their personal incomes and investments outside their enterprises, such as interest deductibility on multiple residences or tax-free bonds. This makes

America's relative marginal effective tax rates on businesses and on owners much lower than Canada's.

"The current business tax environment [in Canada] combines together to discourage firms from growing," said the OECD report. "A dramatically smaller proportion of Canadian firms have more than 100 employees than U.S. ones. Larger firms are better placed to exploit economies of scale, especially those that come from technology."

Canadian entrepreneur and philanthropist Mike DeGroote got so fed up with overtaxation that he played the tax-dodge game by moving to tax haven Bermuda. And he did not want to do so—he said that Canada does not have to be the highest-taxed country in the world and that he resented having to leave. "Lower taxation must be the national priority. I left Canada in 1990 for tax reasons only. They are higher than anywhere else in the world, and you can't build businesses in that climate. I've done better since I've retired in Bermuda than I did in Canada when I was working hard. Hard work alone doesn't do it. You have to have the right government climate, and Canadians don't," he said in an interview with me in 2007.

He added that it took him several decades to build conglomerate Laidlaw Transport Ltd. in Canada, in part due to high taxation, while it took only a handful of years to build three conglomerates after he left.

DeGroote and others are not arguing against taxes or social support systems. They point out that corporate income taxes will likely disappear around the world within 20 years as governments chop them to create jobs. The world's smart countries must do so in order to attract increasingly mobile capital and people. The first countries to reach zero business taxation will win—a reality that is not even discussed in Canadian political or policy circles. "As the world globalizes . . . there's way more corporate tax arbitrage. I think we're in a game where [corporate taxes] are going to go away. Where companies decide to operate and make money is influenced by tax regimes. I don't want us to be the last to comply with that," said Institute for Competitiveness chair Roger Martin.

The only time a Canadian politician has dramatically taken action to slash business taxes was when former finance minister and prime minister Paul Martin Jr. looked after his own affairs by moving his shipping company offshore to Barbados in order to pay only 2.5% corporate income taxes. This was a federal government loophole he perpetuated to assist shipping companies like his. Reaction was negative when the manoeuvre became public, but nothing changed.

"Martin deeply offended me by paying 2.5% corporate taxes in Barbados," said mining magnate Rob McEwen. "Meanwhile, he did nothing about the fact that Canadian businesses have to pay the highest taxes in the world, which means we have to compete with one hand tied behind our backs."

OVERTAXATION AND THE BRAIN DRAIN

Canada's high business taxes contribute to the country's continuing brain drain. The number of people who have left, with their economic activity and capital, remains unknown. Foreign Affairs figures "estimate" that there are 1.5 million Canadians living abroad, based on outstanding passport figures. But this does not include those Canadians who permanently live abroad or who use another passport. It also does not include Canadian students or "snowbirds" who live part-time outside the country or immigrants who went back home while retaining their Canadian citizenship. My rough guess is that, if all were added, there could be as many as four million Canadians living outside Canada at any given time. This is equivalent to 13% of the population.

Their departure represents an enormous taxation and economic loss. For instance, an official with Canada's consulate general in New York City estimated in 2007 that there were as many as 300,000 Canadians working every day in Manhattan. At an average salary of US$150,000 per year apiece (and that's average in Manhattan for such expats), they would generate a collective income of US$45 billion, the size of Prince Edward Island's and Saskatchewan's GDPs combined. If Foreign Affairs' 1.5 million expats earned US$150,000 a year each, their total income would be US$225 billion, equivalent to 20% of Canada's GDP. Even at less, the drain is enormous.

The brain drain is not a problem unless it is only one-way, pointed out Joseph Rotman. "We must create global citizens and attract ours back and foreigners with brains here. Tax is a factor, but not the only determinant."

The need for a modern, strategic tax system is not unique to Canada. Most nations have antiquated systems that were devised generations ago, when businesses and individuals stayed put. "In 1917, Canada was an agrarian economy and farmers paid no taxes, so the government created income tax to get money from industries that couldn't move and from professionals who had to work there," said Alex Doulis, an offshore tax advisor and author of the bestseller *Take Your Money and Run*. "Nowadays, most industries are easily moved and people are free to leave. They simply won't pay more tax than they have to. Canada's best bet is a flat tax and high consumption taxes. This is what Estonia and Slovakia have adopted."

Another tax innovator is socialist Sweden, which charges high personal tax rates and high value-added taxes on goods and services but boasts one of the lowest marginal effective business tax takes in the OECD—some 12.5% on new investments, compared to Canada's 39%. Ireland is another leader: it devised tax policies that lifted what a generation ago was a moribund economy into one of Europe's most successful and resilient export economies. In 1988, Ireland had 17% unemployment and its biggest export was people. By 2006, it had higher per capita incomes than Canada's, or US$47,804, compared to US$34,843, according to OECD figures. The country has few natural resources and high wages, but in 2007 about 85% of its exports were manufactured goods. This was achieved, in large measure, by scrapping most business taxes and revolutionizing its educational system.

"Ireland was insular and inward-looking, protectionist, until we realized that protectionism protects no one. It destroys you. Now we are the most globalized economy in the world," said Mary Harney, Irish deputy prime minister, in an interview with me in Toronto in the 1990s. She and Ireland's other leaders realized that business was the cornerstone to prosperity, not a cash cow. They eliminated all income taxes for exporters and reduced corporate taxes to 10%. They allowed faster write-offs, eliminated taxes on capital and exempted companies from sales taxes on goods and services purchased to enhance productivity. They also targeted and enticed pharmaceutical, software, electronics and back-office companies to relocate to Ireland, then revamped the education system to train workers for those industries.

Meanwhile in tax-challenged Canada, lowering business rates remains politically incorrect. Toronto financier Ned Goodman believes high taxation, not secession by Quebec or Alberta, is the country's only threat to its sovereignty: "In 20 years, we will be part of the U.S. They'll buy everything we own by then, and Canadians will say, why not join them? They pay lower taxes. It's easier to make money in business in the U.S. It's easier to build a multinational in the U.S. or elsewhere. Our governments are run by idiots. You can't build a global company in Canada, because we don't have the lower-cost capital [which includes lower taxes] available. It's just that simple. We are losing our country because of the stupidity of our politicians."

CANADA'S GAPING TAXATION LOOPHOLES

Unable to obtain across-the-board reductions, wealthy Canadians have been stretching the tax loopholes into gaping holes, as did Paul Martin. This makes the tax problem worse, as more tax dodgers divert revenue away from governments, thus making the argument for tax cuts more difficult. The result is overcharging at home and a deeply flawed system that permits wealthy people to get away scot-free. This creates a vicious cycle of higher taxation, more departures and then the need for more of both. It saps capital away from wealth-building and drives away businesses and foreign investors.

At the same time as Canada's politicians impose uncompetitive tax rates on all the nation's job creators, they ignore loopholes that, for nearly 40 years, have allowed Canada's richest individuals to legally avoid taxes altogether. The tax-avoidance path is well trodden and quite simple. The first step is to leave Canada as a tax resident: pay a one-time departure tax of 25% on personal assets other than a principal residence, establish residency in a tax haven and then place all capital and title to assets into offshore trusts run by arm's-length, offshore trustees. The documents that govern these offshore trusts stipulate what should be done with the money, and also instruct how and to whom distributions should be made.

Revenue Canada regards any cash distributions from such offshore trusts as non-taxable even when sent back to Canadian tax residents, as long as those individuals have nothing to do with the trusts or how they are run. Canadian courts have ruled that these are distributions of capital, not of income, a technicality that has never been corrected by Canadian lawmakers.

Primers have been written about these dodges, and there is an industry of offshore lawyers and accountants in Canada.

"It's easy to get out of taxes," said offshore expert and former investment banker Alex Doulis. "A wealthy Canadian will leave and become a non-resident for tax purposes, pay a 25% departure tax [on all his or her wealth except for the value of a principal residence or of Canadian-based corporations] and never pay taxes again. They also have someone set up a trust offshore and put capital into it so that their children or grandchildren or they can be sent distributions from the non-resident trust to Canada tax-free in perpetuity."

In other words, Canada's tax loopholes actually encourage wealthy Canadians to leave: those leaving pay a one-time 25% taxation rate on their RRSP, which, if they did not leave, would be charged taxes at 46% when withdrawn. Even better, they can jurisdiction-shop and head for Ireland, where the binational tax treaty with Canada allows a departed Canadian to pay only 15% to remove RRSP savings, or to Trinidad and Tobago, where the tax treaty permits Canadians domiciled there to withdraw funds from their RRSPs without paying any taxes whatsoever. As philanthropist and billionaire Seymour Schulich said to me, "Is this insane or what? Tell me why this is allowed!"

Another loophole is for a Canadian taxpayer to ship a lump sum abroad to a third party in order to avoid paying taxes on the income derived from that capital. Explained Doulis, "Here's how it works: A Canadian resident gives a big money gift to an uncle in Pakistan or in some foreign jurisdiction. That uncle sets up a foreign trust for the Canadian resident's children and sends them money out of it back to Canada tax-free."

The American tax system, by contrast, does not allow such tax dodges. Any source of funds, whether from offshore, from a capital distribution or from a lottery win, is taxable. Passive income from abroad is taxed by the U.S. at a 35% withholding tax rate, irrespective of whom it is from.

But in Canada, some of the country's richest people—from the late K.C. Irving and his heirs to Mike DeGroote, John MacBain, Frank Stronach and others—have moved themselves offshore. Even if they leave companies behind, dividends can be transferred offshore to a tax haven and never be taxed again by the Canadian government. This means that untold billions of dollars worth of Canadian-made wealth perpetually accumulate, tax-free, somewhere else rather than in Canada. The gigantic Irving empire, for example, is owned by a series of Bermudian trusts.

Canada's laws also allow non-resident Canadians who have left for tax reasons to live here every year for up to 181 days a year. In other words, Revenue Canada lets them have their cake and eat it too: winters in the sun, summers back home and all their money and investment profits offshore tax-free. Even better, their offspring and other beneficiaries never have to move offshore but can receive offshore trust distributions and live in Canada tax-free unless they work. If they do not work, they can avoid paying taxes on trust funds, live in Canada and use all the social services such as health care or education without contributing to their cost by paying income taxes.

Canada also allows the rich people who have moved offshore to avoid taxes to reinstate their residency back home to use our health care system when they are old or sick. Diseases and age make medical insurance hugely expensive or unobtainable. So expatriates routinely return when a spouse gets cancer or has Alzheimer's—they stick Canadian taxpayers with their health care bill by coming home, living off their tax-free offshore trust distributions and getting free treatments and drugs. Canada's provinces provide health care to such returnees within three months after they have taken up residency again. Returnees can also claim pensions if they worked here for at least 10 years.

The last time a proposal was made to tax all offshore money was in 1989, and the private member's bill was promptly scrapped. "The boys in the Rideau Club and boardrooms didn't want it so it didn't happen. Same with the lawyers and accountants and trustees and money managers in Canada who make money from the offshore. This is an industry," said Doulis.

Canadian politicians have ignored these loopholes since 1972, and Canadians are unaware of them. When heiress Belinda Stronach ran to become leader of the Conservatives, the *National Post* pointed out that her family's wealth was offshore and untaxed. But the issue gained no traction and was ignored by the rest of the press.

"Fortunately, for every one of these guys like Stronach who do this, there are 10 of us who don't do this," said Seymour Schulich. "My family's here, my grandchildren are here and I made my money here. Say what you want, I think you owe allegiance to the place which gave you the opportunities. I think anybody who goes and runs off to avoid taxes is not being loyal. If you don't like the way the country is run, you have a duty to stay in order to try to work and make it better. You don't make it better by running and sitting somewhere on your pile of money offshore. I would say to these guys who leave, 'It's okay to take your money and run, but don't ever come back.'"

Other Canadian billionaires are even more blunt about these tax dodges. Toronto developer and Italian immigrant Fred DeGasperis thinks Canada should adopt the American tax laws: "Anybody successful in Canada can take their money and live six months a year plus one day and steal the money from us? No way. Americans pay taxes no matter where the profit was made, and that's the way it should be."

Quebec pharmacy giant Jean Coutu explained his disdain for the practice: "I made my money here, and I owe it to the Canadian people to spend, invest and pay taxes here."

For those who don't think this is a problem, just visit Lyford Cay in Barbados, or Bermuda, Ireland, Grand Cayman, Hong Kong, Trinidad, Turks and Caicos or any of the dozens of other tax havens that are populated by wealthy Canadians. At least 5 of these 75 success stories have gone offshore, as far as I know, but every one of them has been advised by lawyers and accountants over the years to do so. Interestingly, the majority who have not left favour an immediate and retroactive change in laws. But their children may think differently, and many have moved.

The last word on this goes to Jack Daniels, a wealthy Toronto developer who arrived in Canada in 1939 as a poor 12-year-old Polish refugee. "I would never, ever dream of doing such a thing like going offshore," he said. "It's a loophole and should be shut down and the money returned. It's just not right to do this to our country and its future. It's just wrong. It's awful, in fact."

IS CANADA FOR SALE?

B esides taxation, another perennial policy concern has been
Canada's relatively high degree of foreign ownership. On
one side are economic nationalists who believe that foreign
ownership undermines sovereignty and removes control over a
country's economic destiny. They endorse ownership restrictions.
On the other side of the debate are capitalists who say that sovereignty is about laws, not ownership, that capital has no passport
and that Canadians cannot be free to invest elsewhere unless they
offer others the opportunity to buy Canadian assets.

But ownership does matter. Head offices employ more people,
use more local suppliers and contribute more to national charities
than do branch plants. They also require more skilled employees
and put Canada first in terms of both their attention and their
investment focus. A nation's global "champions" are ambassadors
and rainmakers for their native countries. And only big, successful
entities have sufficient scale to fully take advantage of world-class
talent and technology in order to enhance productivity.

The foreign-takeover debate reached a crescendo in 2006 and
2007 after a rash of massive buyouts picked off some of Canada's

greatest and biggest corporations and resource companies. In the summer of 2007, Abu Dhabi became the straw that broke the camel's back. One of its holding companies had bought three oil companies for US$7.5 billion and announced it was on the prowl for another US$12.5 billion of energy assets in Canada.

The idea of the Arabs bidding for Canada's energy business forced the federal government to wade in. It also signalled that the gigantic petrodollar funds generated in Abu Dhabi, Saudi Arabia, Iran and Russia could lead to the takeover of Alberta's oil industry in short order. So Ottawa's industry minister cobbled together an announcement that new restrictions would become law in 2008. This imposed an immediate chill.

The new rules may beef up the "national interest" definition for Investment Canada, probably similar to what the Americans used to repel China's bid to buy Unocal Oil or to stop Dubai's bid for port operations in New York City and other cities. Then again, they may not, and a committee will study the issue in 2008.

The situation in 2006 and 2007 involved different "predators" than those in the 1970s that led to the restrictive Foreign Investment Review Agency. These were not big American multinationals but were often from developing countries, either arms of their governments or their countries' favoured, subsidized global champions. The possibility that they may harbour hidden political agendas was, and should be, worrisome to open economies like Canada's.

There was also the issue of investment reciprocity, which I pointed out in my *Financial Post* columns in 2007. Abu Dhabi companies could buy out Canadian ones, but Canadians could not invest in Abu Dhabi enterprises, nor could they even buy oil lands to drill there. Another issue that disturbed me was that these foreigners were sometimes subsidized, which meant that they had unfair advantages over their Canadian investment rivals in terms of bidding for assets.

Before Ottawa or anyone knew what hit them, every one of Canada's steelmakers had been bought by different foreign groups. The same cherry-picking happened in nickel and then aluminum mining. Falconbridge and Inco (Canada's 36th- and 70th-largest corporations respectively) were snapped up within weeks by foreigners. So were Alcan and Novelis (Canada's 7th- and 30th-largest companies).

In July 2007, the country's sixth-largest corporation, auto-parts global champion Magna Corporation, succumbed. Half of its control block was sold to a Russian oligarch who confirmed, in U.S. Securities and Exchange Commission filings, that one day his Magna stock may be owned by Moscow if the Kremlin so requests.

All these deals upset the business community more than they did the public or politicians. All had different reasons for concern. Some blamed sleepy managements for losing takeover fights. Others blamed coddled managements for not becoming global consolidators themselves, for huddling here only to be picked off by smarter, more aggressive players from abroad.

"Xstrata [the British-Swiss consolidator that bought Falconbridge] didn't exist six years ago," said Peter Munk, who built the world's largest gold-mining company. "Now look what they've got. It requires balls, it requires guts, it requires vision. And those are not qualities that come to [our] senior corporate managers in Canada."

Canadian global consolidator Dominic D'Alessandro, CEO of Manulife Financial Corp., wrote in the press and argued for restrictions: "I believe ownership matters a lot. It matters not only for economic reasons but, more importantly, for our sense of self-esteem and pride in our country."

Ned Goodman disagreed that foreign buyouts were problematic. "I don't care who owns what," he said. "We have laws in Canada, and these have to be abided [by] whether the owners are from China, South Carolina or Toronto. Canadians have the ability to change these laws and, to me, a good corporate citizen is a good corporate citizen. However, I'm against making it easy or cheap to buy a Canadian company."

Norman Keevil Jr., whose Teck Cominco tried to buy Inco, was upset at being outbid by Brazil's CVRD but added that he believed such takeovers were not disastrous for Canada or the mining industry. "Inco and Noranda have been taken over, and their head offices have disappeared, but how many new mines were they really responsible for anyway? Old names [of companies] in Australia have disappeared too, but that doesn't make Australia any less of a mining country. New players will come along, as Teck did. There may even be more room for them, particularly amongst investors, without the old names dominating the scene. The belated nationalistic musings of some populist businessmen and media types notwithstanding, Canada and Australia are going to be key players in mining, along with Brazil, China and London, for the foreseeable future," he said.

But he blamed poor managements in Canada for being eaten instead of being the eaters: "After all, Inco was run by executives who exercised their stock options at $20 a share, and just months later CVRD paid $68 a share."

As for the loss of head offices, he said, "Head offices disappearing? The same investment bankers and lawyers who negotiated these takeover deals are the major losers when head offices disappear, and that's fine with me. Investment bankers shouldn't have flogged Inco to CVRD."

Mining magnate Robert Friedland agreed: "This is not a national tragedy. There are still mines in Sudbury, and the sale of Inco and Falconbridge means that fund managers and mining-company shareholders can finance a new generation of companies that are in the $4-billion range and will eventually become worth $40 billion. But why didn't a Canadian company bid the most? The others understood the very large cycle in metals and were very aggressive. They paid more. They understood China better. They were playing in a more sophisticated market, in London, where they could raise more money. He who has the most access to capital and information wins," he added.

But some free-traders believe that Canada should somehow encourage Canadian players to become global champions. Hartley Richardson, chairman of his family's many holdings, lost a takeover bid in 2007 to Americans for a huge agribusiness in Canada. He said protectionism was not an option but that Canadian governments must do something to encourage home-grown enterprises.

"Canada has to decide what it's going to be good at. It has to look at what other countries have done to support their core businesses without shutting out or putting up walls. Governments, through tax and other policies, must encourage Canadians to truly become global. Business will always adapt, but if rules keep changing and are not favourable to growing businesses, people will take their capital and go elsewhere. I hope we'll continue to be a strong Canadian business. We have been for five generations, and I would be disappointed to think we would have to go elsewhere," he said.

CanWest Media Inc. CEO Leonard Asper, with profitable assets in Australia, the U.S., Turkey and Britain, said that foreign ownership restrictions would be a mistake, and were unnecessary except to ban purchases by state-owned or state-supported resource acquisitors: "This hollowing-out-of-Canada business is dumb, it is nonsense. Canada is creating lots of new companies, and we have a very healthy economy with a culture of entrepreneurship. But I have a concern about foreign governments owning our resources, because they may have different foreign-policy goals. Gazprom [the largest company in Russia] should not be able to buy Petro-Canada. Sometimes these government-owned enterprises are subsidized, and that is unfair too."

Former Reform Party leader and Alberta free-enterpriser Preston Manning put his concerns about resource buyouts another way in a newspaper interview: "If you don't want Osama Bin Laden fiddling with Quebec hydro lines or Beijing controlling the oil patch, there should be national-security provisions in the approval process to protect our values and objectives."

THE BEST DEFENCE IS OFFENCE

Since 1986, Canada's foreign-ownership levels have increased, but not more than in other, similar economies, such as Australia's. Between 1986 and 2006, foreign ownership among the FP 500 companies in Canada increased from 25% of the total to 30%. In

Australia, in the 10 years ending in 2006, foreign ownership doubled, to 29% of all publicly listed corporations. The main attraction in both countries has been resource companies.

Foreign-ownership incursions have also become perceptible even in the gigantic United States. Between 1994 and 2005, the foreign ownership of American stocks and bonds increased to 4.5% from 1%, treasury securities to 2.75% from 1%, and national ownership levels of all kinds (real estate and financial products) to 13% from 3%, according to figures published in 2006 by the U.S. Congress. This represents even greater foreign-buyout figures, in absolute numbers, because the U.S. is at least 12 times bigger economically than Canada and at least 15 or so times bigger than Australia.

The reason for this activity is that foreign ownership is on the rise in every economy that has opened itself up to trade and investment. And fortunately, Canadians have been more aggressive investing outside their boundaries than foreigners have been investing in Canada. Beginning in 1997, Canadian outward investment began to outstrip inbound investments by foreigners. By the end of 2006, Canadians had $523.3 billion invested abroad and foreigners had only $448.9 billion invested in Canada, according to Statistics Canada. Canadians have also been closing the investment gap with the Americans. By the end of 2006, Canadians had invested $223.6 billion in the U.S., compared with $273.7 billion invested by Americans in Canada. In 1980, by contrast, Canadians had only $17.849 billion invested in the United States while Americans had 2.5 times more that than, or $50 billion, in Canada.

"All these takeovers are due to the fact that there is a worldwide consolidation underway," said Teachers' former CEO Claude Lamoureux. "Barclays Bank wants to buy ABN AMRO, which is bigger than three of our banks. This is happening in every sector. New York City is losing head offices. So are Montreal and Vancouver and Toronto. In Canada, what we need is new people to start new businesses and for Canadians to become global consolidators."

Unfortunately, most of Canada's large foreign-owned branch plants do not have mandates to grow beyond the borders or to otherwise be entrepreneurial. (Exceptions have been companies like Canadian Occidental Petroleum, which was used by its American parent as a vehicle to invest in countries that Washington had embargoed for political reasons.)

The vast majority of foreign subs are domestic and sleepy. These operations employ 1.6 million of the 3 million persons who work for the biggest 500 companies in Canada. "Canada's tragedy is that it is mostly a branch-plant mentality. I worked for Merrill Lynch, and it was a very unhappy place to be. There was lots of paranoia. If you did a big deal, you were scared about your job and the reaction at head office, and nobody ever got moved to head office," said investment banker Tom Caldwell. "We are dribbling these head offices away. Think head offices don't matter? Ask the people in Africa. To me, the biggest failure of all time is the Hudson's Bay Company, which had oil and gas, land and hundreds of years of experience. Now it's just a few department stores with good downtown locations owned by an American speculator."

An effective, sometimes abused, means of protecting Canadian businesses from unwanted takeovers has been the use of multiple voting stock. Some markets, such as the New York Stock Exchange, frown on this two-tier ownership, but it is commonplace in Canada. Virtually all of the 50 biggest family-owned businesses in Canada are controlled with multiple voting stock. Critics believe this can lead to abuses because it allows owners, with small percentages of stock, to run corporations as though they had a majority of shares. This sometimes puts them at odds with those who own the rest. However, Canada has put in place rules and laws that protect all shareholders from such governance issues, and its biggest institutions, pension and mutual funds, exert pressure on behalf of fellow shareholders. For instance, in 2007 a majority of all shareholders had to approve Frank Stronach's sale of half his multiple voting stock block to the Russian oligarch Oleg Deripaska.

Proponents of these special voting shares also argue that these stock structures are necessary to motivate entrepreneurs and to protect Canada's relatively smaller entities from being gobbled up by American or European giants. For instance, Norman Keevil said he could never have built Teck Cominco into a mining powerhouse without multiple voting stock, or dual shares: "Dual shares have served us, and arguably the country, well. Other mining companies understand the importance of ore reserves, and we undoubtedly would have disappeared into one of the larger Canadian [or foreign] companies at some down point in the cycle when our reserves would have been attractive and cheap to them. I doubt we could have survived or could have achieved our dream without them."

Ned Goodman put their importance differently: "I wouldn't do this without multiple voting shares. It's not worth the hassle. Multiple voting shares are the best model because owners can make long-term decisions and not have to worry about short-term swings in market value. Managements like Inco's are run by bureaucrats who just suck their thumbs or are run by pension funds like the Ontario Teachers'. Their CEOs are paid to be custodians and they sit on their hands. Give them grief, then they don't do anything."

SOLUTIONS

Canada's confederation is more akin to the European Union's governance model than to the unitary state model of the United States or the United Kingdom. This means that political and policy power is as fragmented as are the cultures and economies of each of the provinces. These jurisdictions operate as silos and compete with the federal government to grab taxes, even though, in the end, there is only one taxpayer. The result is a patchwork quilt of policies, interprovincial trade barriers and varying tax rates. This guarantees that the next decade will be preoccupied with politics that pit regions against one another—mostly east versus west—in areas of tax, regulatory and monetary policy.

What Ottawa needs is to commission studies by world-class minds to examine policies as well as governance and economic models elsewhere that work and that could be adopted to repair the Canadian system. Ireland is an obvious choice. Its taxation and education model has been demonstrably successful by offering the lowest business taxes in the world, no taxes for exporters, a transformed education system that trains people for New Economy jobs, and use of the euro.

Civil-service governance models should also be examined. There is, for example, the American federal cabinet, which is comprised of private-sector experts recruited by the President to run departments and form policy. Such appointments are no guarantee of policy success but would, if adopted, at least ensure that fresh talent and ideas were brought to policymaking and public-sector management in Canada. Singapore is another model. The tiny island state recruits successful executives from its private sector to run government departments, and pays them commensurate salaries. In Canada, civil servants are hardly business A-listers, and are unionized, isolated and too often deeply politicized.

China studied outside models in Japan, South Korea and Singapore to create the template that led to its economic miracle: it honestly examined its weaknesses and strengths, then implemented change. Its success would never have been possible without its draconian one-child birth-control policy or its various economic controls on worker movements and prices. Today, the country's management board of directors is comprised of a steering committee of 12 or so brilliant, experienced Chinese technocrats who have worked in many different countries, languages, systems and cultures. This structure has been further enhanced by tapping foreign mentors and consultants, among them Singapore's patriarch and former prime minister Lee Kuan Yew. He has worked closely with China for many years.

Canada must also muster the courage to address and try to mend its "human resource" problems: the brain drain and immigration. Both are ignored despite their importance and their impact on the economy. Canadian governments are not collecting statistics as to the number of Canadians who have left or why. Figures are unavailable, which means that any analysis as to what can be done to retain these people is impossible. Some have pursued educational

WHO OWNS CANADA NOW

or occupational opportunities elsewhere that perhaps could be, and should be, made available in Canada. Others have left because of taxation, something that should be quantified too.

Likewise, there has never been a comprehensive cost-benefit analysis of current immigration policies. What is known is that despite the highest immigration levels in the developed world, immigrants are not replenishing the talent that has left, nor are they bringing with them the skills or credentials that are needed in the economy.

Canada's immigration system changed in 1986 when quotas were ratcheted up to 250,000 a year, irrespective of economic conditions. Before that, immigration worked in tandem with the Manpower Department in order to match immigrants with employment needs. Flows moved up and down based on jobs available.

Since 1986, Ottawa's bureaucracy has let in a population bigger than Atlantic Canada's, and most lack the education or language skills necessary to participate in the New Economy. They were allowed in under the "family reunification" category, not as independent economic immigrants. Many have come impoverished and have stayed that way. They have imposed enormous costs on the health, education and welfare systems. Studies by the Canadian Federation of Independent Business have quantified the skills gap and its cost to employers. Studies of child poverty have noted a huge jump in numbers, mostly in cities with large numbers of poor immigrants.

"Our type of open immigration has diluted the value of our national assets," said mining financier Rob McEwen. "These immigrants did not bring in millions or billions of dollars, or even needed skills or professions. Mostly, they have brought in costs for health care, education, welfare. Canada is a welfare state, and yet someone in Ottawa made a decision to let in a flood of people, thus diluting the asset base, without letting Canadians have a say . . . Two hundred fifty thousand new people a year. That's the size of a large Canadian city every year. This is like the personnel department telling the CEO how many people he has hired even though jobs are not there for them. It's totally wrong-headed."

THE FUTURE

B usiness realities are driven by technological advances, politics and happenstance. The future is always unknown, but increasing international interdependence and economic integration are givens. This means that countries cannot be merely internally focused, concentrating only on creating the needed growth conditions within their own economies.

Today's successful nation-state must adopt the characteristics of a business enterprise: it must regularly take inventory; hunt for niches, opportunities and winning strategies; and compete against other countries for talent, capital and innovation. In future, only those nation-states that operate along business lines will prosper. This means they must concentrate on making profits from the production of goods and services (or rack up trade surpluses); they must attract investors (or woo foreign direct investment flows); they must control costs, employ smart managers, keep debts in line, invest in research, recruit or train a productive workforce, overcome weaknesses and leverage natural advantages. The nation-state in a global economy is a gigantic holding company, in competition with other gigantic holding companies.

This mentality has been adopted by new, emerging economies more than by mature nation-states, which are often comfortable and smug. It is a form of capitalistic collectivism versus capitalistic individualism. Newly minted regimes in countries like Singapore, Dubai, Russia, Saudi Arabia and even Brazil and India are behaving more like businesses and developing a range of "sovereign instruments," from giant pools of "sovereign capital" to subsidies for "global champions" that are targeting special markets, economies and corporations.

These sovereign capital funds are growing exponentially among oil-producing entities and among super-exporters like China. They are a major financial force and are getting so large that in 2007 the Group of Seven finance ministers called upon the International Monetary Fund and the World Bank to examine their structures, transparency and accountability. The *Wall Street Journal* estimated that the sovereign capital total is between US$2 trillion and US$3 trillion, with China, Japan and oil producers each investing hundreds of billions.

Estimates are that this will grow to US$10 trillion by 2020, equivalent in size to eight or nine Canadian economies, depending on currency values. The concern is that this money does not play by any fair rules and is often buried in private equity funds or in the coffers of banks and global champions in developing countries. This is destructive to free markets, and to global prosperity, because the money's owners often have hidden political agendas that are not in the best interests of the companies, shareholders, employees, customers or societies with which they do business.

This reality is only now being perceived by members of the so-called "Anglo-Saxon Club," or the United States, Canada, Australia and Britain. Their economies have been built based on the liberalization of markets, privatization and reliance on laws and rules to perpetuate market efficiencies. But as good assets and resources become in scarce supply, they are finding that their companies are being picked off one by one or else are facing increasingly unfair foreign competition to buy assets or resources.

What all this means is that all countries must also start to think like national holding companies in order to counteract nation-states that are ruthlessly, even illegally, grabbing market share or assets through a form of economic warfare. This will be the world's next governance challenge: to try to liberalize, privatize and regulate the global economy and to monitor the behaviour of all players, both companies and nation-states.

Another reality is that the world is transforming at increasingly breakneck speeds. For millennia, knowledge and technology improved at a glacial pace, transmitted only by those few who escaped wild beasts, wars, famine or mischief. Written language and archives retained knowledge and widened its access, but today's digital storage and search engines make everything available to everyone. This has made innovation exponential, not linear.

"The first technological steps—sharp edges [tools], fire, the wheel—took tens of thousands of years," wrote futurist and technology pioneer Ray Kurzweil on his website, KurzweilAI.net. "For people living in this era, there was little noticeable technological change in even a thousand years. By 1000 AD, progress was much faster and a paradigm shift required only a century or two. In the nineteenth century, we saw more advancement in one century than in all of the nineteen centuries combined. Now, paradigm shifts occur in only a few years' time. The World Wide Web did not exist in anything like its present form until just a few years ago."

He and others have postulated that rapidly evolving technologies will bring about advances in robots and computers by 2020 that sound today just like science-fiction musings. What is known is that technology has helped bring about the propitious economic conditions we enjoy because it exerts "deflationary" pressure.

"BP Amoco's cost of finding oil is now less than $1 per barrel, down from nearly $10 in 1991," Kurzweil wrote. "Processing an Internet transaction costs a bank one penny, compared to more than $1 using a teller ten years ago." Similarly, drugs that used to cost $35,000 a year to keep HIV-positive patients alive now cost only $100 a month. In 2006, the first $100 computer was produced, using a foot pedal to generate power. In October 2008, Tata Motors will launch the world's first US$2,200 four-seater car, made out of plastic and glue, and by 2010, Google will add to its menu of free services the content of every book contained in the world's largest libraries.

TECHNOLOGY

Everything is evolving, except human nature, and within a handful of years there will be some fascinating products available as well as life-shifting technologies in place. Every product and device will become "smarter," from refrigerators that sense shortages of milk to embedded radio-frequency chips that will tell us where parcels, automobiles, bicycles, luggage, elderly parents, pets, cheating spouses or children are located at all times.

Telecommunications, already wireless, will converge with banking and media, as has already happened in Japan and South Korea. There consumers pay for groceries, clothing, subway rides, sodas and airline tickets by waving their cellphones over electronic readers. They watch live sporting events, dozens of television channels, movies and rock concerts on their cells. Eventually, cellphone users will be able to hire virtual butlers who will deliver everything from food to pantyhose, toilet rolls, medicines and cosmetics based on past shopping patterns. Customers will be billed online or via cellphone.

In two or three years, biotechnology will eliminate the need to carry around keys, remember passwords or carry credit cards. Fingerprints or retina scans will be widely used so that only appropriate people will gain access to premises, countries, lines of credit, cars and safety deposit boxes. Our gadgets will also be further miniaturized. Personal computers will be housed in cellphones with keyboards that are projectable onto screens or walls and that can sense finger pressure for touch-typing.

Video games and real warfare are converging too. The world's first robot "soldiers" will be delivered for duty in Iraq by

2008 or 2009. They will be remote-controlled by soldiers, hundreds of yards or even miles from the violence, operating Game Boy consoles and wearing virtual-reality headsets. As this technology progresses, robots will replace soldiers, police, security guards, firefighters, ambulance workers, bomb experts, fighter pilots and any others who face hazards. This will make war and policing both safer and more dangerous, because violence will be more easily executed. Isaac Asimov's *I, Robot* will come true.

Television screens will be everywhere, and all content will be on demand and available on any platform desired. Google will completely replace newspapers, and YouTube will replace broadcasters. Both entities will sign up content providers to corner the market on offerings, then monetize their investments by selling advertisements and commercials. Viewers will be able to bypass cable channels by downloading video onto their computers, then wirelessly transmitting it to their television screens. This disintermediation will force cable companies to consolidate and diversify into wireless technologies, content ownership and satellite or fibre optics to provide even richer telecom services. Canada will eventually end up with one cable outfit. My guess is that Rogers will eventually buy Shaw Communications and Groupe Vidéotron.

The car business will consolidate worldwide into a handful of players. Competitors will make parts for one another, as do aircraft manufacturers, which specialize in wings, engines, tail assemblies or fuselages. These global manufacturers will outsource most of their manufacturing to least-cost producers in developing nations and concentrate on design, marketing, financing and insurance expertise in order to sell cars. In a decade, there will likely be only a handful of global champions: one or possibly two in Detroit, one in Europe (likely a Russian-German partnership), Tata in India, Chery in China, and Toyota in conjunction with the other Japanese and Korean automakers. In aerospace, there will still be two giants—Boeing and Airbus—and Canada's entry, Bombardier, will continue to struggle against subsidized state-supported entities and will prosper only if it is more successful in Asia.

Automobiles and all other complicated products will be made to order, as Dell computers are now. Buyers will view and test-drive cars in large retail showrooms—similar to the current Apple Store concept. These outlets will also offer tutorials, accessories and servicing. Buyers will select models and options online, undergo credit checks and receive their vehicle within days. Car servicing will be done remotely by computer or, alternatively, owners will be able to bring vehicles into the showcase retail outlet and go for help or enhancements to the auto equivalent of what Apple stores now call their "Genius Bar."

Technology will continue to revolutionize financial services. In a handful of years, people will be more comfortable banking anywhere in the world via the Internet, making deposits in foreign countries and buying deposit insurance to cover any risk just as large companies do now. Canadian entrepreneurs already bypass Canada's banking and brokerage institutions and are approached by suppliers from around the world.

This means that Toronto's relative importance as a financial capital will decline and the world's most important clusters will simply grow: New York City, London, Hong Kong, Tokyo and possibly, but not necessarily, Dubai and Shanghai. Canada's bank towers, no longer owned by the banks that occupy them, will slowly empty as back-office functions move to India, Ireland or lower-cost jurisdictions. Bank branches will continue to shrink in number and so will stock, mutual fund and life insurance sales forces. People will do their own research through super-intermediaries, real and virtual, then transact themselves online. Eventually, ownership restrictions on banks in Canada may be lifted, freeing them to merge or be taken out by foreigners. But by then it will be irrelevant, and competition will be truly globalized.

RESOURCES

Canada has plenty of everything. But the winds of change are bringing about the convergence of energy, economic, environmental and foreign policies. This is because of two problems: emissions from the burning of hydrocarbons are the major cause of pollution, and dependence on high-risk, hostile regimes in the Middle East, Russia, Africa and Venezuela are a drain on the public purse as well as a financial and national-security concern.

Another issue is the concentration of oil wealth in a few countries, which means that supply chains are vast and relatively vulnerable to terrorist attacks or accidents. This increasing dependence upon a few sources will result, likely within a decade, in a major supply disruption, and will drive prices beyond US$200 a barrel. Sustained high prices will cause a temporary worldwide recession and force governments to mandate more ethanol production and use, greater conservation measures, hybrid cars and alternative energy development. But in the absence of draconian intervention, the world is still poised to consume about 50% more oil by 2015, which will also drive up oil and other energy prices. This is because of demand for transportation fuels around the world.

But technologies and fuels like ethanol promise hope of a more decentralized source of energy, one that can spread benefits and risks. The best current solution is ethanol, which greatly reduces emissions. The United States and other jurisdictions have begun to subsidize or backstop production, and growth has been, and will be, exponential. The beauty of ethanol is that traditional internal combustion engines can run better on a gallon with 85% ethanol and not require any retrofit.

Ethanol demand, plus food demand from China, is also providing a bonanza for the world's poorest nations because it is increasing farm incomes, now depressed due to massive agricultural subsidies handed out by rich countries to their farmers. Because they grow corn or sugar cane, ethanol refineries will be built around the world and also provide their nations with a home-grown replacement for expensive oil imports.

"These countries can't afford $100 a barrel for crude, and now you are starting to see huge grain crops as prices rise to make ethanol," said Ken Field, Canada's largest ethanol producer. "You will see thousands of ethanol refineries around the world in these countries, and ethanol boats coming out of Africa and South America. Ukraine, Poland, Romania are grain belts too, as is Canada, and have got to get organized."

Field and others are working on the next energy breakthrough: harnessing enzymes to break down plants or garbage into emissions-free fuels. This biotechnology may take years to devise, but many corporations and governments are spending millions to win this energy race. In the meantime, Canada's energy assets, notably its oil sands, will remain in demand and will provide the cornerstone for economic growth in the country.

Canada's mining assets will also be in more demand. Along with Russia, Canada has a huge store of metals, minerals and other building blocks needed by all economies. Since 2003, western Canada's provinces, and Canadian resource companies more generally, have capitalized on the new reality with immediate results. In 2004, BC's government created a pro-mining policy platform. Since then, tens of thousands of jobs have been created; two new mining operations have been launched, after years of hiatus; construction of five more mines was begun and 18 more were on the drawing boards. In addition, 30 discoveries were made and exploration budgets in the province jumped from $29 million in 2001 to $265 million in 2006, according to BC minister of state for mining Bill Bennett in an interview in January 2007.

In 2006, Canadian mining generated $70 billion in export income, or 17% of the country's total. Higher prices in 2007 added to this and have also sparked a resurgence of activity in other parts of the country. Abandoned mines have been reopened and exploration has been growing.

Unfortunately, the same upside does not appear to exist in the forestry sector. Consolidations, bankruptcies and rationalizations will characterize the industry, notably in eastern Canada. The industry in British Columbia and Alberta is newer and more efficient, but wood sources there are threatened by infestation by the pine beetle. Millions of acres have been decimated, and there has been little research into how to halt its spread, despite the importance of forestry to Canada's economy. Two weeks of frost in BC would kill off most of the pestilence, but that has not occurred for several years.

Another issue is competition from around the world at the same time as the lumber market in the U.S. will decline for a few years due to the subprime mortgage meltdown, and resulting lowered housing prices and construction. Canada's forestry companies face tougher competition from warm-climate countries such as Brazil and New Zealand because trees there reach maturity twice as quickly. Canadians will remain players but the industry will "Scandinavianize," or consolidate, and within five years there will likely be only a handful of forestry companies.

Ethanol's effect on the prices of food and arable farmland, along with China's effect, is also good news for Canada and other countries with large tracts of arable soil—the United States, Ukraine, Argentina, South Africa, Indonesia, Australia and Brazil. These nations will relieve their oil import bills while at the same time becoming the breadbaskets to heavily populated Asia, the factory of the world. China, for instance, has 20% of the world's population and only 10% of its arable land, a shortfall that will make food more expensive as diets improve along with wages.

Looming shortages of everything from seafood to meat will also bring about more acceptance of genetically modified seeds, irradiated foods and designer proteins grown in petri dishes. Food self-sufficiency will become a priority in China and elsewhere, in part as social policy to keep gigantic rural populations from further flooding their overcrowded cities.

Another massive asset owned by Canada is its Arctic, but this is being challenged by the Russians. In early 2008, they filed a claim with the United Nations under the Law of the Sea Treaty, claiming most of the land under the Arctic Ocean. This caused the Americans to consider signing the treaty (unsigned by them because of concerns about sovereignty). It also led Canada to announce a few token gestures, such as the construction of an arctic research station and more ships to patrol its waters. Under the Law of the Sea Treaty, the five countries bordering the ocean—Canada, Russia, the United States, Denmark/Greenland and Norway—are entitled to an area 200 miles offshore unless their continental shelves extend farther.

But in summer 2007, Russia planted a flag in Canadian waters and made its claim. At stake is title to oil, natural gas and metals in unknown quantities, and the matter will take years to resolve. Canada cannot go it alone and must rely, in any dispute, on the U.S. military for its defence, and therefore also on American diplomacy and continued good relations with Washington.

Water may also become valuable, but only if it is commoditized. In fall 2007, an official with the Chicago Commodity Exchange speculated about the launch of a water futures contract that would begin to place a market value on water. This is a necessary step in order to establish the value of water and bring about conservation. Canada has about one-third of the world's fresh water supply, but water is heavy, which makes distribution expensive. However, if shortages worldwide drive up the value of water, Canadian supplies could be easily transportable by ship to China and the Middle East from both coasts.

TEN GLOBAL BUSINESS TRENDS

As the world tumbles forward—or backward, depending upon one's viewpoint—a few overarching trends are perceptible.

1. The world of business will become more Darwinian than now as the number of moving parts to the global economy increases, along with the sheer number of players in it. No technology, monopoly or niche will be safe from competitors or substitutes. For example, in the past 20 years half of Canada's largest business empires disappeared or were sidelined. This success–failure churn will accelerate.

2. The velocity of technological change will increase too, which means that businesses and entrepreneurs will have to run hard just to stay in one place.

3. Churn and velocity will lead tò more creative disruption within business models and processes. Everything must be re-evaluated, then re-engineered.

4. The global economy will mean that more global consolidators will bundle industries or sectors into cross-border giants. This trend will be undertaken by businesses and sovereign nations alike, and size alone will not protect assets from unwanted predators. Business will have to eat or be eaten, and big won't eat small—fast will eat slow. An example has been that Canada's five steel companies and four of its biggest mining outfits took decades to create but were picked off one by one within months by foreign consolidators. No sector is safe from this trend.

5. By 2015, there will be one billion more consumers.

6. The globalization of capital markets, and enhanced access, will increase financial volatility. Prices now fluctuate wildly and rapidly in all financial markets, be they debt, equity, foreign exchange or commodity markets. This will accelerate. The Canadian dollar, for instance, jumped 20% in value in just months in 2007.

7. Continuing population and economic growth rates will aggravate scarcities in commodities, making prices remain high and increase for years. Growth will also create a talent scarcity, increasing the value of people in certain fields such as technology, science and engineering. These people will enjoy enhanced opportunities in developed countries, where luxury items and health care needs will stay in demand, and also in developing nations, where infrastructure projects will be numerous.

8. At the same time that more good jobs become available, the value of unskilled or semi-skilled labour will continue to fall as billions more workers become available. This will create a job churn in open economies. Between 1996 and 2006 in the United States, 3.3 million manufacturing jobs disappeared. Fortunately, 16 million net new jobs were created, 11.6 million

of which paid higher wages than did the 3.3 million lost manufacturing jobs.

9. Growth rates will impose huge stresses on the environment.
Air pollution, water shortages, energy outages and agricultural
degradation will bring about negative impacts. These will strain
political and financial systems but will also provide opportunities to those who devise technologies or processes that eliminate or alleviate problems.

10. Progress and change will continue to bring about more prosperity for more people, but will leave millions behind. Poverty
will dog developed nations as well as developing societies, and
will contribute to instability, terrorist threats and geopolitical
clashes. In 2007, Lloyd's of London estimated that businesses
are targets for terrorism just as much as are governments, that
150 attacks are mounted annually and that 2,000 workers have
been murdered by terrorists since 9/11. Helping the world's
"left-behinds" will dominate the geopolitical conversation.

WILL THERE BE A CANADA IN 2028?

North America in general and Canada in particular have the best
prospects of any region in the world. Others as rich today will
face severe structural or political constraints. Europe is a case in
point. Currently, the EU is the world's largest trading bloc, with
32% of the world economy, compared with North America's 27%.
(China was roughly 6% in 2007 and India half that.) The expansion of the European Union to 27 countries enhanced its prospects
by adding cheaper labour and 100 million additional consumers. Between 2000 and 2005, the European Union grew jobs and
incomes, received large foreign-investment inflows and even generated a small trade surplus as a whole.

Going forward, however, Europe faces aging and shrinking
populations, restless immigrants and growing energy dependency on
an unstable Middle East, on North Africa and on a ruthlessly ambi-

tious Russia. This means that Europe, already more energy-efficient than North America, must invest billions in alternative sources and encourage more conservation. Europe also faces the task of incorporating another six nations into its fold, countries that Russia regards as within its orbit. That, plus problems in Ukraine and Russian-supported Iran, may force Europe to pull its weight militarily or to take strong diplomatic actions in some cases in its own region. This requirement will also be necessary because of America's costly Iraq misadventure, which marks the final role of the United States as the world's principal policeman. Europe will have to spend more to defend its interests around the world in future.

Most worrisome is Europe's neighbour Russia. Now a plutocracy with superpower ambition, Moscow has been using petrodollars to buy European industries and political influence. It will boss the continent around and get away with it. There are growing alliances with German, Norwegian and Italian business interests. For instance, former German chancellor Gerhard Schroeder made 45 visits to President Vladimir Putin while he was in power and is now on the board of directors of the Kremlin's über–oil company, Gazprom. His replacement even intervened on behalf of Russian interests in a 2007 dispute involving Germany's Lufthansa Airlines.

Russian tentacles reach deeply into Europe, which is the Kremlin's strategy. Putin is a cartelist, not a free-marketer, and has been taking away assets from Russians and others inside the country, merging them into giants, putting friends in charge and mandating them to do more of the same inside and outside the country. The goal is to turn Russia into the world's most important economic empire.

Meanwhile, Asia ascends. Its fast-growing countries will collectively overtake Europe and North America in size within a generation, providing another important market for all. Fortunately, Asia's economies and politics are driven by Japan, China and India. All have proven to be pragmatic and have focused on economic, not political, conquests. The region will continue to be export-oriented, but these Asian Tigers will become increasingly competitive when it comes to acquiring needed technologies and resources. Politically, the areas of greatest concern are North Korea and Pakistan. Both are nuclear powers, and instability in either jurisdiction would be economically destructive throughout the region, if not the world.

The Middle East and Africa, with the exception of South Africa, will remain the world's problem children. Wealth there is concentrated in the hands of a small elite. In most of these countries, females are disenfranchised from education and economic participation, and their governments are run by potentates or dictators. Even those countries with resource wealth lack the soft infrastructure to create sustainable economic development: tolerance, the rule of law, decent governments, transparency and personal security. There are some improvements here and there, but in general Africa and the Middle East will lag economically in the absence of fair income distribution, more education and entrepreneurship.

South America seems destined to be dominated by populist regimes with half-baked solutions to their historical and grim social problems. The region is also plagued by concentration of economic wealth, which has kept the majority impoverished and the politicians corruptible. This cycle of dysfunction is why none of South America's nations has taken its place among the world's first nations economically. Chile is the only success story. Brazil looks promising but, as the saying goes, "Brazil is a country of the future and always will be."

But Americans and Canadians are on top and should remain that way. So will Australians and New Zealanders. This is because all four are removed geographically from immediate dangers and enemies. Both areas are prosperous, resource-rich and business-savvy. Leading this pack will be the Americans, who will continue to dominate capital markets and technological advancement globally. Americans are richer and spend more on education than any other country. This allows them to develop talent and to attract it from around the world. The country will continue to be a magnet for capital because of its beneficial business climate. American multinationals have successfully globalized, and most of the world's largest corporations are headquartered in the United States.

In North America, Mexico will be left behind. Roughly one out of every four Mexicans now lives in the United States, legally or illegally, and more will follow. Oil production declines will increase, crippling public-sector spending. And Mexico's society has failed to come to grips with corruption, concentration of economic power, mass unionization, poor leadership and inadequate education. In September 2007, Mexico's oil exports to the U.S., which used to be higher than Canada's, fell to 1.4 million barrels per day, compared with Canada's 2.467 million a day. In October, its president warned of huge production declines this decade.

Mexico is a problem child and stands in the way of the next logical step, which is to create European-style economic integration and a North American currency. Unfortunately, this cannot happen unless borders are opened to goods, services and labour. But Mexico's disparities and politics make this difficult, if not impossible. So Canadian businesses would be well advised to lobby aggressively for a bilateral process—one that would open the border between the U.S. and Canada, then, possibly down the road, open the U.S.-Mexican border. This would involve creating a customs union and using the U.S. dollar as a shared currency, and is as essential for both countries to improve economic performance as it has proven to be for Europeans.

Canada has no other option, as billionaire Ted Rogers pointed out: "Car plants are built here by the Asian producers, but they are small. People just do not realize the auto plants of the Big Three in Detroit have been hollowed out. They used to have three shifts, then two, one, and they will close completely here and we'll all wake up with a shock. The border is historically a big issue. If we don't get it fixed up with the Americans, and move to joint control in customs, immigration and transportation flows, we are going to be in big trouble."

FUTURE CANADA

Canada could become Ireland on steroids: a civilized, successful country in which to live and do business, with an educated, equipped workforce, low business taxes and the world's most enviable resource base. Canada, like Ireland, could also fully embrace the benefits of continental integration by blending rules, standardizing regulations and sharing a common currency with its neighbours. The alternative, for some Canadians, is to deny that geography is destiny and to insist that further economic integration with the U.S. is only one of several choices. There are not several choices.

Canada and the United States have been partners in the global economy since the Second World War. Canada's resources together with America's marketplace and know-how are an unbeatable combination. But in the absence of a commitment, Canada is the big loser. It is too fragmented, too small and too isolated to grow beyond the development of a few world-class companies or exploitation of its massive resource assets. It is also in danger of being lumped in with Mexico by American protectionists and border hawks.

If Canadians remain divided, or indifferent to this fundamental fork in their road, the country will drift. Concerns about independence are wrong-headed: the Irish are no less Irish, or Germans no less German, because they are in the EU and use the euro. But without a customs union and common currency, Canadian businesses will increasingly be harassed, the brain drain will accelerate, foreign investors and tourists will avoid the country due to its high taxes and currency problem, and incomes will continue to deteriorate north of the border, aggravating all the negatives.

Canada will not disappear by 2028, but it may be headed for a serious decline unless it adapts. Adjustment, both internally and externally, need not be sudden or wrenching. After all, the business climate has shifted in just 20 years from being protectionist, anti-American, inward-oriented and thoroughly parochial to that of a more diversified export powerhouse. There are pitfalls to changing direction, but even greater pitfalls in not doing so. The most worrisome possibility of all is if Canadians assume that the status quo is an option. That is not true for anyone, any business or any country any longer.

ACKNOWLEDGEMENTS

This project has been a twinkle in my eye for some time, but it took HarperCollins Canada's persuasive CEO, David Kent, to make it happen. We were both at a U.S. embassy cocktail party in 2005. I was asked to say a few words, and he came over afterward and suggested that I consider writing my next book for his firm. We bounced around a few topics, including writing a sequel to my first book, from 1986, *Controlling Interest: Who Owns Canada?*

In spring 2006, I called Linda McKnight at Westwood Creative Artists Ltd. to ask her to be my agent. After all, she had been my editor at Macmillan of Canada 20 years before and had published *Controlling Interest.* She was enthusiastic. We developed a proposal, then made a deal with HarperCollins.

I have enjoyed the project, particularly working with editor Jim Gifford, who is fun, keen and smart. All his suggestions have improved the manuscript. And reconnecting and meeting with dozens of business leaders during my research has also been invigorating. Compiling their profiles, insights and anecdotes has been a joy for a professional storyteller such as myself. Even better, the project returned me to my roots as a scoop-oriented reporter—more than three dozen of the people I spoke with had never been interviewed before.

This book is also the culmination of a charmed career. I have been lucky enough to have worked with journalistic greats such as the late Beland Honderich at the *Toronto Star* and Doug Creighton of the Toronto Sun Publishing Corp. Both had been journalists before they were publishers, loved good business tales and sent me around the world to pursue them. Another important influence was the late Alexander (Sandy) Ross, editor of *Canadian Business* magazine, who single-handedly transformed business journalism. He, along with Peter C. Newman, made Canadians enjoy business stories and understand their importance in understanding our country.

INDEX

government economic intervention, 4,
8, 254
real estate, 30
Quebec Inc., 103, 239
Quebecor Inc., 44, 273
Quinnsworth, 139

Radio Caroline, 261
Radisson Hotels, 66
Ramada Hotels, 68
Ranger Oil, 159
Ravelston Corporation, 297
RBC Dominion Securities, 99
RCMP, 303
real estate, 30–31, 47, 52–53, 74
and retail, 105, 122, 134–35
real estate investment trusts (REITs), 16
Rebanks, Wendy Weston, 138
Red Cross, 315
Red Lake Mine, 189, 191
Reed College, 179
Reeves, Keanu, 242
Reform Party, 169, 296
Regent Las Vegas, 65
Reichmann, Albert, 74, 75, 77–78, 397
Reichmann, Barry, 76, 77
Reichmann, Paul, 8, 74, 75, 77–78
Reichmann, Philip, 11, 74–77, 78,
417–18
Reichmann, Ralph, 74, 75, 77–78
Reichmann family, 11, 25, 74–78, 194,
343
ReichmannHauer Capital Partners, 76–77
Reid, Bill, 294
Reisman, Elly, 45, 50
Reisman, Heather, 378, 379, 380, 409
Reitman, Jeremy, 28
Renaud, Richard, 28
Reno, NV, 196
Rensselaer Polytechnic Institute, 285
Republic Waste Industries, 350
Research In Motion (RIM), 215, 216–18,
219, 220–21
Restivo, Kevin, 228
Restrictive Trade Practices Commission,
365
retail, 105–7, 422–23
Retirement Residences REIT, 77
Reuters Group, 266, 268
Revenue Canada, 366, 384, 439, 440
Revenue Properties, 50, 81

Rexall family of pharmacies, 125, 127,
128
Rexall Place, 128
Richardson, David, 97
Richardson, George, 97
Richardson, Hartley, 96–97, 98, 100,
413, 446–47
Richardson, James, 97
Richardson, James (19th c.), 98
Richardson, Jim, 97
Richardson, Muriel, 96
Richardson, Royden, 97–98, 99–100
Richardson Capital, 99
Richardson family, 84, 96–100, 359, 413
Richardson Financial Group, 99
Richardson Greenshields, 99
Richardson Partners Financial, 99
Richler, Mordecai, 344
Riddell, Brenda, 167, 168
Riddell, Cecil, 168
Riddell, Clay, 14, 166–70, 388, 408, 412
Riddell, Jim, 167
Riddell, Lynn, 167
Riddell, Violet, 168
Riddell Rose, Susan (Sue), 167, 409
Rider Business College, 235
Rifke: An Improbable Life (Sharp), 393
Riley, Sandy, 99, 100
Rio Alto Exploration, 159
RioCan Real Estate Investment Trust,
76, 88
Rio Tinto Group, 181–82
The Ripley Entertainment Company, 374
Ripley's Believe It or Not, 374
Ritchie, Cedric, 94
Rite Aid Corporation, 112, 113, 115
Roberts, George, 377
Robinson, Roland (Jack), Lord
Martonmere, 275
Rogers, Edward III, 275–76, 409
Rogers, Edward Jr. (Ted), 243, 244,
273–77, 281, 407, 409, 467
Rogers, Edward Sr., 273
Rogers, Loretta, 274, 275, 277
Rogers Communications, 239, 240, 273,
274, 275, 276–77, 281, 457
Rogers Media, 397
Roman, Stephen, 26, 185
Romania, 33, 460
Roosevelt, Franklin D., 58
Rose, Mike, 167
Rotman, Joseph, 28, 421–22, 437